The history of the Isle of Wight.

Richard Worsley

ECCO
PRINT EDITIONS

Eighteenth Century
Collections Online
Print Editions

Gale ECCO Print Editions

Relive history with *Eighteenth Century Collections Online*, now available in print for the independent historian and collector. This series includes the most significant English-language and foreign-language works printed in Great Britain during the eighteenth century, and is organized in seven different subject areas including literature and language; medicine, science, and technology; and religion and philosophy. The collection also includes thousands of important works from the Americas.

The eighteenth century has been called "The Age of Enlightenment." It was a period of rapid advance in print culture and publishing, in world exploration, and in the rapid growth of science and technology – all of which had a profound impact on the political and cultural landscape. At the end of the century the American Revolution, French Revolution and Industrial Revolution, perhaps three of the most significant events in modern history, set in motion developments that eventually dominated world political, economic, and social life.

In a groundbreaking effort, Gale initiated a revolution of its own: digitization of epic proportions to preserve these invaluable works in the largest online archive of its kind. Contributions from major world libraries constitute over 175,000 original printed works. Scanned images of the actual pages, rather than transcriptions, recreate the works *as they first appeared.*

Now for the first time, these high-quality digital scans of original works are available via print-on-demand, making them readily accessible to libraries, students, independent scholars, and readers of all ages.

For our initial release we have created seven robust collections to form one the world's most comprehensive catalogs of 18th century works.

Initial Gale ECCO Print Editions collections include:

History and Geography

Rich in titles on English life and social history, this collection spans the world as it was known to eighteenth-century historians and explorers. Titles include a wealth of travel accounts and diaries, histories of nations from throughout the world, and maps and charts of a world that was still being discovered. Students of the War of American Independence will find fascinating accounts from the British side of conflict.

Social Science

Delve into what it was like to live during the eighteenth century by reading the first-hand accounts of everyday people, including city dwellers and farmers, businessmen and bankers, artisans and merchants, artists and their patrons, politicians and their constituents. Original texts make the American, French, and Industrial revolutions vividly contemporary.

Medicine, Science and Technology

Medical theory and practice of the 1700s developed rapidly, as is evidenced by the extensive collection, which includes descriptions of diseases, their conditions, and treatments. Books on science and technology, agriculture, military technology, natural philosophy, even cookbooks, are all contained here.

Literature and Language

Western literary study flows out of eighteenth-century works by Alexander Pope, Daniel Defoe, Henry Fielding, Frances Burney, Denis Diderot, Johann Gottfried Herder, Johann Wolfgang von Goethe, and others. Experience the birth of the modern novel, or compare the development of language using dictionaries and grammar discourses.

Religion and Philosophy

The Age of Enlightenment profoundly enriched religious and philosophical understanding and continues to influence present-day thinking. Works collected here include masterpieces by David Hume, Immanuel Kant, and Jean-Jacques Rousseau, as well as religious sermons and moral debates on the issues of the day, such as the slave trade. The Age of Reason saw conflict between Protestantism and Catholicism transformed into one between faith and logic -- a debate that continues in the twenty-first century.

Law and Reference

This collection reveals the history of English common law and Empire law in a vastly changing world of British expansion. Dominating the legal field is the *Commentaries of the Law of England* by Sir William Blackstone, which first appeared in 1765. Reference works such as almanacs and catalogues continue to educate us by revealing the day-to-day workings of society.

Fine Arts

The eighteenth-century fascination with Greek and Roman antiquity followed the systematic excavation of the ruins at Pompeii and Herculaneum in southern Italy; and after 1750 a neoclassical style dominated all artistic fields. The titles here trace developments in mostly English-language works on painting, sculpture, architecture, music, theater, and other disciplines. Instructional works on musical instruments, catalogs of art objects, comic operas, and more are also included.

The BiblioLife Network

This project was made possible in part by the BiblioLife Network (BLN), a project aimed at addressing some of the huge challenges facing book preservationists around the world. The BLN includes libraries, library networks, archives, subject matter experts, online communities and library service providers. We believe every book ever published should be available as a high-quality print reproduction; printed on-demand anywhere in the world. This insures the ongoing accessibility of the content and helps generate sustainable revenue for the libraries and organizations that work to preserve these important materials.

The following book is in the "public domain" and represents an authentic reproduction of the text as printed by the original publisher. While we have attempted to accurately maintain the integrity of the original work, there are sometimes problems with the original work or the micro-film from which the books were digitized. This can result in minor errors in reproduction. Possible imperfections include missing and blurred pages, poor pictures, markings and other reproduction issues beyond our control. Because this work is culturally important, we have made it available as part of our commitment to protecting, preserving, and promoting the world's literature.

GUIDE TO FOLD-OUTS MAPS and OVERSIZED IMAGES

The book you are reading was digitized from microfilm captured over the past thirty to forty years. Years after the creation of the original microfilm, the book was converted to digital files and made available in an online database.

In an online database, page images do not need to conform to the size restrictions found in a printed book. When converting these images back into a printed bound book, the page sizes are standardized in ways that maintain the detail of the original. For large images, such as fold-out maps, the original page image is split into two or more pages

Guidelines used to determine how to split the page image follows:

• Some images are split vertically; large images require vertical and horizontal splits.
• For horizontal splits, the content is split left to right.
• For vertical splits, the content is split from top to bottom.
• For both vertical and horizontal splits, the image is processed from top left to bottom right.

THE

HISTORY

OF THE

ISLE OF WIGHT.

St. Catharine's Chapel

LONDON,

PRINTED BY A HAMILTON

And Sold by R DODSLEY, T CADELL, G ROBINSON, R FAULDER, and
G NICOL COLLINS and Co. Salisbury, and BURDON, at Winchester.

MDCCLXXXI.

TO

THE KING.

SIR,

THE defcription of any part of the Britifh Dominions may be offered, as a juft tribute, to the Prince, by whofe Virtues their happinefs and freedom are protected. Your Majefty's univerfal patronage of Arts and ufeful literature has encouraged a faithful Servant to folicit the permiffion of infcribing this work with the Auguft name of his Sovereign and Benefactor.

I am,

    With profound refpect,

  SIR,

    Your Majefty's

      Moft dutiful Subject, and Servant,

June 4,   *Richard Worsley.*
1781.

PREFACE.

Notwithstanding the favourable reception given by the public, to descriptive Histories of counties, and other districts of England, a History of Hampshire is yet wanting; the present publication is intended, in some degree, to supply that deficiency.

The Isle of Wight, though a portion of that county, is so detached by nature, and discriminated by peculiar circumstances, as to be pointed out for an object of separate description. This indeed appears to have been the opinion of some learned men in former times; as we find, in Bishop Nicholson's Historical Library, that there existed, in the last century, in the library of Arthur, Earl of Anglesea, a manuscript, intitled, *A General Survey of the Isle of Wight*, written by Sir Francis Knollis, Privy Counsellor to Queen Elizabeth. A History and Description of the Isle of

Wight

PREFACE.

Wight was alfo planned, early in the feventeenth century, by Doctor Richard James, of Corpus Chrifti College, Oxford, a native of the ifland, and nephew of the firft keeper of the Bodleian Library, where his manufcript, intitled, *Antiquitates Infulæ Vectæ*, is ftill preferved. It contains little more than extracts from our early hiftories, for the beginning of his work; but, from a fummary prefixed to them, it appears that his plan was very comprehenfive.

About the fame period, Sir John Oglander, a gentleman of one of the moft ancient families of the Ifland, employed himfelf in collecting *mifcellaneous obfervations* relative to it, moftly fuch as came within his own knowlege. His notes, beginning with the year one thoufand fix hundred and fifteen, and continued to the year one thoufand fix hundred and forty-nine, remain in the poffeffion of his worthy fucceffor, Sir William Oglander, Baronet. They contain a great variety of very valuable, though unmethodifed, materials.

The Hiftory now offered to the Public, owes its origin to Sir James Worfley, Baronet, of Pilewell, in

Hamp-

Hampſhire, who began to prepare materials for it early in the preſent century, and proſecuted the Work ti'l the time of his death, which happened in the year one thouſand ſeven hundred and fifty-ſeven. An unuſual length of life afforded him the means of much obſervation, and extenſive enquiry; he beſtowed no ſmall labour in ſearching and examining records; he had acceſs to Sir John Oglander's manuſcript, and made conſiderable uſe of it. Little, either of deſcription or of natural hiſtory, is found in his papers; but he had made ſome progreſs in digeſting the civil hiſtory of the Iſland, and he evidently intended it for publication. Yet, notwithſtanding all the advantages he enjoyed, he left his deſign incomplete. His manuſcript, with conſiderable additions by his ſon Sir Thomas Worſley, has deſcended to his grandſon; who conſiders this Publication as the diſcharge of a filial duty.

It would be the higheſt ingratitude to omit acknowleging the very great aſſiſtance the Editor has received from the gentlemen of the Iſland. Many of them have not only taken infinite pains to ſupply

him

P R E F A C E.

him with the beſt information concerning their neighbourhood, but have likewiſe, with the moſt liberal confidence, intruſted him with the title-deeds of their eſtates: they have alſo contributed, at a very conſiderable expence, to adorn and illuſtrate this work with engraved Views of their reſpective ſeats. To theſe gentlemen, whoſe delicacy he is apprehenſive of offending by the mention of their names, the Editor begs leave to return his grateful acknowlegements.

CONTENTS.

CHAP. I.

CHAP. II.

CHAP. III.

A   CHAP.

CONTENTS.

CHAP. IV.

CHAP. V.

CHAP. VI.

CHAP. VII.

CON-

C O N T E N T S.

C O N C L U S I O N

For the Contents of the APPENDIX, containing Copies of an-
cient Deeds, Charters, and other Records, referred to in the
Courfe of the Work, fee the Table after the Seventh
Chapter.

A MAP OF THE
ISLE OF WIGHT

Drawn & Engraved for the History of the Isle of Wight
from Surveys in the Possession of the Right Honorable
Sir Richard Worsley Baronet
by John Hayward
June 4th 1781

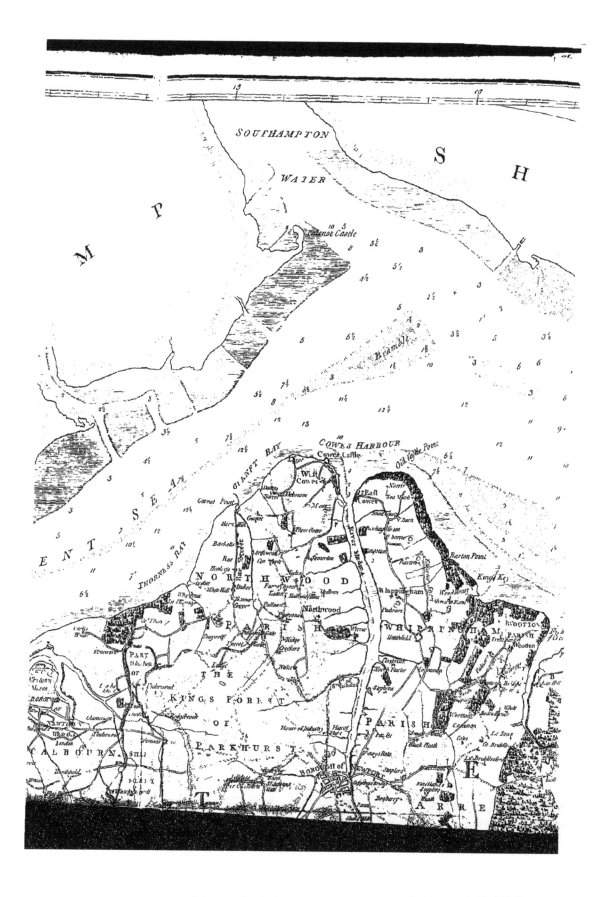

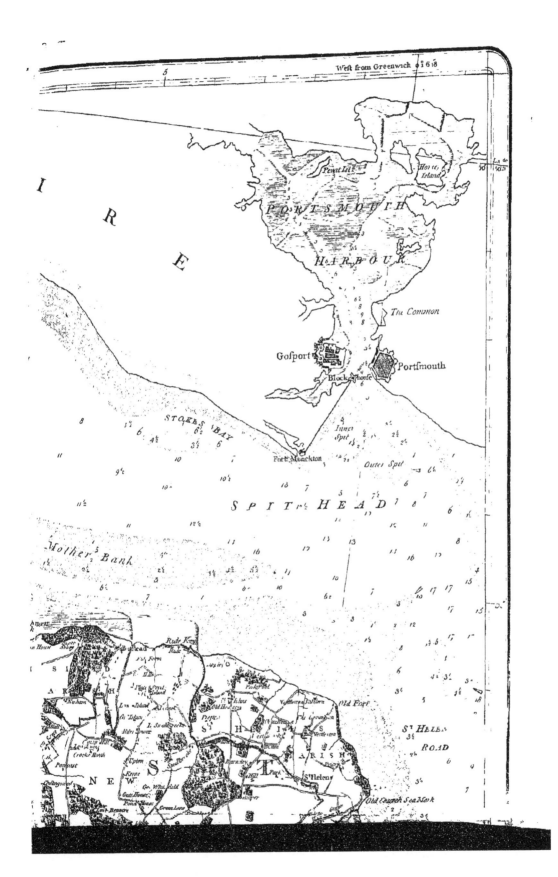

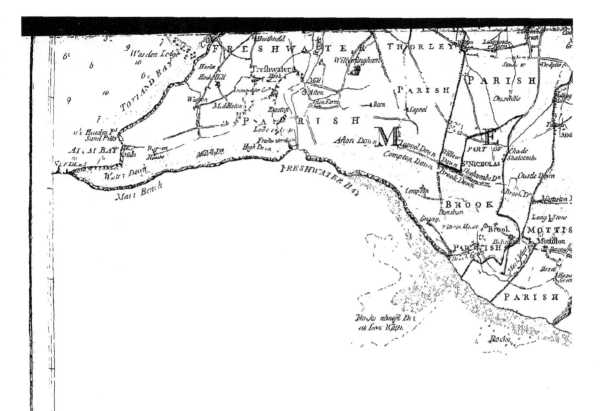

EXPLANATION

Churches .... +

Noblemens and Gentlemens Seats ....

Villages ....

Farms and Cottages ....

Hills ....

Roads ....

Cliffs ....

Sands ....

Mud or Oaze ....

The Soundings are taken at Low Water

Rocks under Water .... +

Sea Marks ....

From Cliffs End in Isle Wight to Hurst Castle is Harbour

From Rock in Isle Wight to Post Mansfton is 3 Miles

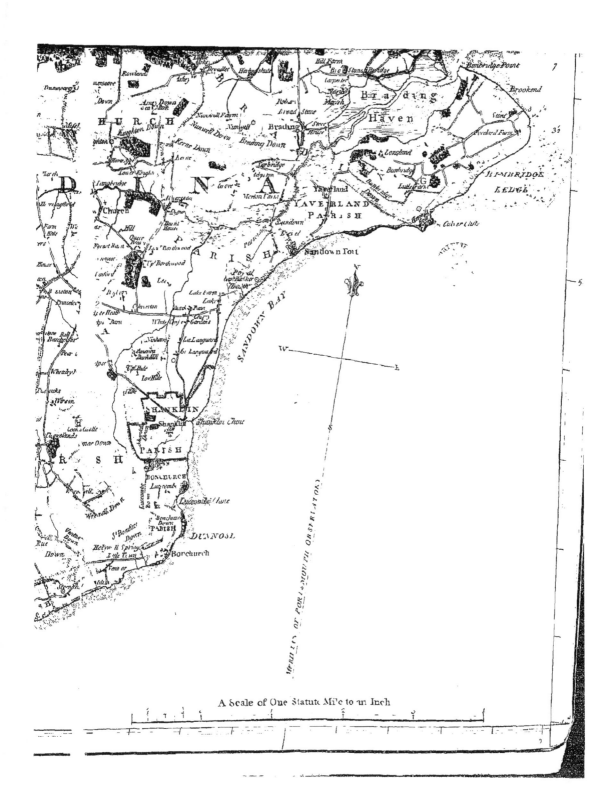

A Scale of One Statute Mile to an Inch

THE

HISTORY

OF THE

ISLE OF WIGHT.

✿✿

CHAP. I.

General Defcription of the Ifland, its Situation, Extent, Soil, Produce, Trade, Parochial Divifions, and Number of Inhabitants.

THE Ifle of Wight * is the largeft and moft valuable of the appendant Britifh iflands. It is fituated oppofite the coaft of Hampfhire, from which it is feparated by a channel, varying in breadth from two to feven miles; it is confidered as part of the county of Southampton, and is within the diocefe of Winchefter.

Situation.

The

---

* The name of this ifland has afforded great fcope for etymological conjectures, of which the mention of two or three will be fufficient Some derive the term *Wight* from the Britifh word *Guith*, a breach or divifion, alluding to the fuppofed feparation of this ifland from the main land. The variation is by them thus deduced H not being a radical letter, the rejection of it reduces *Guith* to *Guit*, G and W are convertible letters, as appears from the words *Guarantia, Warrantia, Gulielmus, Willielmus*, &c if then for G and *u* we fubftitute *W*, the word becomes *Wit* whence, perhaps, are formed the *Wuitland* of the Saxons, the *Wuight* of the ancient, and the *Wight* of the modern Englifh Others chufe to derive it from its Latin appellation of *Vectis* a word fignifying *a bar* or *bolt* perhaps from the fteep and projecting rocks with which the coaft of this ifland is in many places barred and defended, from this the tranfition is eafy to *Wit, Wiht*, or *Wight*

B

Dimensions. The figure of the island comes nearest to that of a rhombus or lozenge, but extremely irregular. Its greatest length extending from east to west, measures nearly twenty-three miles; its breadth from north to south about thirteen. The best computations make its superficial content amount to about a hundred thousand acres *.

Air and soil. The air is in general healthy, particularly the southern parts; the soil is various, affording a greater diversity than is to be found in any other part of Great Britain of the same extent †. It *Fertility.* was many years ago computed that more wheat was grown here in one year, than would be consumed by the inhabitants in eight; doubtless its present produce, under the great improvement of agriculture, and the additional quantity of land lately brought into tillage, has more than kept pace with the increase of population.

Wiet, as it is written in the oldest records, particularly Domesday Book, and Camden's Saxon Chronicle.

Bede, with some other ancient writers, have supposed this island to have received its denomination from the Vectuarii, a tribe of the Jutæ, but this conjecture falls to the ground, when it is considered that it was called *Vecta* and *Vectis* by Roman writers, long before the arrival of the Saxons and Danes on the British coast.

But, after all, these etymological disquisitions are very little to be depended on, being generally formed on the uncertain orthography of barbarous and unlettered times. Besides, allowing the doctrine of convertible letters, a man of any tolerable imagination, by displacing some and substituting others, may convert any word to what form soever he pleases, or his system requires.

‡ The first Number of the Appendix contains all that is to be found in Domesday Book respecting the Isle of Wight.

† This island affords a curious circumstance in natural history. The sea encroaching on it in some parts, whilst land is gained by its abandoning it in others. Sir John Oglander has preserved the memory of a bowling-green with a row of trees on the south-east side, near Sandown Fort, all which in his time were washed away, whereas on the north-east side the contrary has so remarkably happened, that vessels are said to have come up an arm of the sea, of which there is not at present the least trace remaining, to Nettlestone and Brunsley, now about a mile distant from the shore.

A range

A range of hills, which affords fine pasture for sheep, The Downs. extends from east to west, through the middle of the island: the wool is of a staple not inferior to that produced by the flocks fed on the South Downs in Suffex; very little is manufactured in the island, it being mostly exported in the fleece to the different clothing towns.

The hills command a most delightful prospect of the sea on Prospects. both sides; on the south, it is diversified by a variety of intermediate vales, meadows, and corn-fields; and on the north and north-east, the view extends to Spithead, and the towns of Portsmouth, Southampton, and Lymington, on the opposite shore *.

Indeed

* Michael Drayton, a bard still respected as a topographer, has the following description of this island:

" When as the pliant muse, with faire and even flight,
Betwixt her silver wings is wafted to the Wight,
That ile, which jutting out into the sea so farre,
Her offspring traineth up in exercise of warre;
Those pyrats to put backe that oft purloine her trade,
Or Spainards or the French, attempting to invade.
Of all the southern iles she holds the highest place,
And evermore hath been the great'st in Britaine's grace,
Not one of all her nymphs her soveraigne favoureth thus,
Imbraced in the arms of old Oceanus;
For none of her account, so neere her bosom stand,
'Twixt Penwith's fartheft point, and Goodwin's queachy sand,
Both for her seat and soyle, that's far before the other,
Most justlie may account Great Britaine for her mother.
A finer fleece than her's, not Lemster's self can boast,
Nor Newport for her mart, o'ermatch't by any coast.
To these the gentle south, with kisses smooth and soft,
Doth in her bosome breathe, and seems to court her oft;
Besides, her little rills, her inlands that doe feed,
Which with their lavish streames do furnish everie need;
And meades that with their fine soft grassie towels stand,
To wipe away the drops and moisture from her hand,

Indeed this island, as well from its interior parts as extremities, affords a great number of beautiful and picturesque prospects, not only in the pastoral, but also in the great and romantic style. Of these beauties the gentlemen of the island have availed themselves as well in the choice of situation of their houses as in their other improvements.

Timber.

Timber was formerly here in great plenty, but the dock at Portsmouth, and the private yards in and near the island, have left little more than is necessary for the consumption of the inhabitants.

Fish.

Besides the several species of fish common to the other parts of the Hampshire coast, this island produces the ammodytes or sand eel so called from its immediate burying itself in the sand. It is here called the sand sprat, and is in much esteem, it is taken by turning up the sand immediately upon the reflux of the tide. shell fish are also taken in great quantities, and the village of Niton has obtained the name of Crab-Niton, from the plenty of those fish found near it.

> And to the north, betwixt the foreland and the firme,
> She hath that narrow sea, which we the Solent tearme,
> Where those rough useful tides, as in their straits they meet
> With boystrous shocks and rores each other rudely greet,
> Which fiercelie when they charge, and sadlie make retreat
> Upon the bulwarkt forts of Hurst and Calsheat beat,
> Then to South-hampton runne, which by her stores supplide
> (As Portsmouth by her strength) doth villifie their pride "
>   Poly-Olbion, song the second.

The name of *solent sea*, here applied by Drayton to the channel between Hampshire and the Isle of Wight, is also used by Bede and other ancient writers But in Smith's last edition of Bede's Ecclesiastical History, it is written *solvent*, and this might be the true spelling, on the supposition of the island having heretofore been joined to the main land, and disunited by the encroachments of the sea, from the Latin verb *solvere*, to melt, loosen, or set at liberty.

Formerly

Formerly this island was plentifully stocked with game of all sorts, but of late years the quantity has been greatly diminished, though neither fox, badger, or polecat, were ever found in it.

In the month of May incredible numbers of sea-birds of different species assemble and breed in Freshwater and Bimbridge cliffs, which they leave with their new generation about the middle of August. The flesh of these birds is too rank and fishy to be eaten; their feathers are, however, purchased by the upholsterers, and their eggs, which are said to be as good as those of a duck, are taken by the country people, in a manner, and at a risque similar and equal to that of the samphire-gatherer, described by Shakspear in King Lear.

Domestic fowls and poultry are bred here in great numbers: the outward bound ships and vessels at Spithead, the Motherbank, and Cowes, commonly furnishing themselves from this island.

The water is in general extremely good, and where it issues from under the chalky hills, is little inferior in point of purity to that of Bristol. It has frequently been carried to the West Indies and brought back again perfectly sweet.

In several places the springs are found to be impregnated with minerals, though none have yet attained any degree of reputation. At a place called Pitland, in the parish of Chale, there is one, which, whilst flowing, appears pure and transparent, but on stagnating deposites a white sediment equal to half its depth, and as thick as cream. This water is supposed to abound with sulphur, but it has not yet undergone a chymical analysis; cattle drink it without any ill consequence. About half

half a mile weftward of this fpring, at a place called Black
Gang, under Chale cliff, there iffues a ftrong chalybeate water,
which, by an infufion of galls, exhibits a deeper purple than
is given to the water of Tunbridge wells by the fame experiment.

A fpring, impregnated with alum, was difcovered at Shanklin,
by Dr Frafer, phyfician to Charles the Second; it was for fome
time drank, as it is faid, with fuccefs, but as the reputation
of thefe fprings depend much on fafhion, it was gradually dif-
ufed, and at length neglected. Other chalybeate fprings are
found in divers parts of this ifland, which, added to certain appearances in the foil, fhew here are veins of iron ore; fome indeed have been found, but, on trial, proved of too coarfe a quality to anfwer the expence of working.

Minerals.

The variety of the foil has before been mentioned; the fur-
face in general is a ftrong loamy earth, but in different parts are
found marle, brick-earth, gravel, tobacco-pipe and potters clay,
fullers earth, red and yellow ochres, ftone, of good quality,
and fand of different kinds. Of the laft, a fine white fort is
found at Frefhwater, fuperior to any in Great Britain, for the
glafs and porcelaine manufactories: great quantities of it are
fhipped off for London, Briftol, and Worcefter.

A Bay, fituated on the north fide of the Needles, has obtained
the name of Alum-bay*, from the confiderable quantities of native alum found there.

* Appendix, No II is the copy of a warrant from Queen Elizabeth to Richard
Worfley, Efq Captain of the Ifle of Wight, to fearch for alum ore in the Ifle
of Wight, dated feventh day of March, 1561.

A ftra-

A stratum of coals runs through the ridge of hills before mentioned; it appears at the foot of Bimbridge cliff, a little to the northward of the point, and somewhat above low-water mark, is seen again on the side of Aireton-down, and at the west end of the island, near Warden Ledge, in the parish of Freshwater. this stratum has a vein of white sand and fullers earth lying on the north, and one of red ochre on the south side, the upper part of it is about three feet wide, and descends in an oblique direction northward, to an uncertain depth   The late Sir Robert Worsley sunk a shaft for it, on his estate at Bimbridge, but found the vein so thin, that (fearing it would not answer the expence) he desisted from the undertaking: how it lies in other parts of the island, may perhaps be some time or another worth the trial, as the coal is of a good quality.

Minerals.

There are several quarries which produce varieties of stone applicable to different uses.   Those near Quarr Abbey were once in such esteem as to furnish stone for building the cathedral at Winchester, as appears by a grant made by William Rufus to Walkelyne, bishop of that diocese, and by two precepts concerning these quarries, from Henry I to Richard de Redvers †.   This stone continued in reputation till the reign of Edward III. and in the registers of Winchester it is recorded that William of Wykeham used it in building the body of that cathedral; whence it seems as if Portland stone was not then known, since it is certainly preferable to this, both in colour and durability, and in pious works the difference of expence was at that time scarely taken into consideration.

Stone quarries.

The basis of this island appears to be a close black clay, it is often found in sinking well   and in one particular part of the

† See Appendix, III IV V

coal,

coaſt, near Mottiſton, appears at low water; the inhabitants call it plotnore, or platnore: it is ſo firm, that an oar cannot be forced into it, and after being expoſed to the air for ſome time, makes excellent whetſtones.

Coal.

The land round the coaſt is very high, eſpecially on the ſouthern ſide, being for the moſt part ſecured by the natural fortification of ſteep cliffs, and craggy rocks. One avenue only on the ſouth-eaſt has been left by nature open to the deſcent of an enemy, which is now defended by Sandown fort.

Hundreds and pariſhes.

The iſland is divided into two hundreds, ſeparated by the courſe of the river Mede, Medham, or Medine *, which, riſing near the bottom of St. Catharine's down, runs northward, and diſcharges itſelf into the channel, between Eaſt and Weſt Cowes. Theſe hundreds are diſtinguiſhed by the names of Eaſt and Weſt Medine †, according to their ſituation with reſpect to that river. They contain thirty pariſhes, ſome of which are ſo ſmall, that they have obtained the denomination of pariſhes, from having diſtinct parochial rates, according to the following liſt ‡.

---

* This river, in ancient deeds, is called the Mede, evidently from the Latin *medium*, as dividing the iſland nearly in the middle

† Formerly the Eaſt was called Hommerſwell, and the Weſt, Bowcomb hundred beſide which, mention is made in Domeſday book of a third, called Cubborn hundred, lying in Powcomb hundred; this was called a hundred on account of ſome peculiar immunities it enjoyed as belonging to the fee of Wincheſter.

‡ Strictly ſpeaking, Newport and Northwood are no more than chapels of eaſe to Carisbrooke, the church of Godſhill makes the ſame claim to Whitwell, and Brading is alſo mother church to St. Helens, Yaverland, Shanklin, and Bonchurch

Antony Devis delt.   View of the Village of S.t Lawrence

EAST MEDINE,	WEST MEDINE,
Brading,	Northwood,
St. Helens,	Newport,
Yaverland,	St. Nicholas,
Shanklin,	Carifbrooke,
Bonchurch,	Gatcombe,
Newchurch,	Kingfton,
St. Lawrence,	Chale,
Whitwell,	Shorwell,
Niton,	Brixton,
Godfhill,	Mottifton,
Arieton,	Calborne,
Binftead,	Shalfleet,
Wootton,	Brook,
Whippingham.	Thorley,
	Yarmouth,
	Frefhwater.

To gratify thofe who may wifh for more particular information refpecting the parochial arrangements of this ifland, a table is given in the Appendix *, exhibiting, at one view, the valuation of the livings, their patrons and proprietors, corrected by Ecton's *Thefaurus*, Brown Willis's *Parochiale Anglicanum*, and more recent information : together with the number of inhabitants in each parifh, tranfmitted by the refpective clergy, in the year one thoufand feven hundred and feventy-feven From the fmallnefs of thefe numbers, as well as the accuracy and knowlege of the gentlemen who procured them, they have, it is prefumed, much better pretenfions to exactnefs than is ufual in fuch eftimates. According to this table, the Ifle of Wight appears now to contain eighteen thoufand and

* Appendix, No VI.

C twenty-

twenty-four inhabitants *, exclusive of the troops quartered there.

* A curious record, still extant in his Majesty's Paper Office, serves to shew the increase of the inhabitants since the fifty-first of Edward the Third, A. D one thousand three hundred and seventy-seven, when a poll-tax of four pence per head was granted to the king from every lay person within the realm of England, as well male as female, exceeding fourteen years of age, common beggars only excepted. By the return of the collectors for the Isle of Wight, no more than seventy-eight pounds twelve shillings and eight pence was paid, as the tax for four thousand seven hundred and thirty-three persons. Supposing the persons who paid to have been about two-thirds of the people, and the other third to have been children under fourteen, and beggars, the whole would amount to seven thousand and ninety nine. It is to be observed, that at the same time a poll-tax of twelve pence per head was laid on the clergy, as well seculars as regulars, but as they are not mentioned in this return, and are known to have never been very numerous in the island, it can make no essential difference in the estimate, so that it may with safety be affirmed that the people have increased since that time in the proportion of five to two.

Although it does not immediately relate to the present subject, it may not be disagreeable to the reader to see from the same record the amount of the receipts for other places in the county of Southampton, as well as that for the kingdom in general.

Collected { In the city of Winchester 24l. for 1440 lay persons.
{ In the town of Southampton, 19l 4s for 1152 lay persons

In the whole county of Southampton, 554l 0s 4d for 19,975 lay persons.

In all England,   1,376,442 lay persons paid this tax.

Beneficed clergy, who paid }   15,380
the poll-tax of 1s.   }

Non-beneficed or regulars, ·   13,780

Total,   1,405,602.

It is to be observed that the sum paid in the Isle of Wight, does not correspond with the numbers, four thousand seven hundred and thirty-three persons, at four pence per head, come to seventy-eight pounds, seventeen shillings, and eight pence, and seventy-eight pounds, twelve shillings, and eight pence only pays for four thousand seven hundred and eighteen at that assessment. It is difficult to account for this difference, perhaps fifteen persons might have left the island between the return of the number of inhabitants and the time of collecting the taxes; or, it is probable that fifteen persons might have been paupers, who were exempted from the payment of the tax.

In

In general, such is the purity of the air, the fertility of the soil, and the beauty and variety of the landscapes, that this island has often been styled the Garden of England. The frequent visits paid to it by parties of pleasure, shew it is not undeserving of that character; though these parties too often content themselves with a sight of Carisbrooke castle, and perhaps the Needles, without visiting many delightful scenes and natural curiosities, in the southern and eastern parts.

The inhabitants cannot be supposed to differ from those *Inhabitants.* of the adjacent country; the distance is too small to cause any physical variation *, and the constant intercourse with persons from all parts of the kingdom, the metropolis in particular,

---

* A reproach cast on the natives in former days, is handed down to us by Sir John Oglander, and may at least serve to amuse the reader "It is, and hath bene a "tax layd on this island, that it never produced any extraordinary fayr handsome "woman, nor a man of any supereminent gwyftes in witt or wisdome, or a horse "excellent for goodnefs. I can answer, that no part of England in generall, the "quantitie confidered, hath produced more exquisite in eyther species than this "island."

Although this absurd notion does not deserve a serious confutation, I shall, in addition to the testimony of Sir John Oglander, in behalf of the females of this island, take the liberty of citing part of a letter from a respectable gentleman, in reference to this work. his style bespeaks him no incompetent judge in matters of love and gallantry. "I cannot (says he) dismiss my pen without expressing my wishes that "you would do proper justice to the females of your island It is a subject worthy "of historical celebration. It was my fortune many years ago to be at Newport on "a fair day, the mart for best looks and cloaths in the rural style The whole "scene was fascination! *Or ta salo*, sprung like Venus from the sea, they seemed "all of the Cyprian line; at least, there was not an individual that did not appear "a descendent of Hebe.

"For health high circling mantled in their cheeks.——

"You will think I saw, perhaps, with Ovidian eyes; I was, indeed, youthful; "but, methinks, there could not be a savage of the woods but must have learnt "the art of love among such amiable inspirers. You will perceive the soft impres- "sions are not erased, I retain them; and, possibly, may not quit them but with "life.'

C 2   has

has erafed any infular peculiarities that might have exifted formerly.

Hofpitality is faid to be more practifed in iflands than on the main land, the Ifle of Wight does not contradict that obfervation indeed no part of Great Britain can boaft a more univerfal exercife of the focial virtues.

The farmers are a fubftantial clafs of men; their fields demonftrate their induftry and knowlege in hufbandry, their teams generally confift of large and handfome horfes, each vying with his neighbour for fuperiority in point of cattle Moft of the farm-houfes are built with ftone, and even the cottages appear neat and comfortable, having each its little garden, nor is the eye offended with thofe miferable human objects fo frequently difgracing the commons and highways in many other parts of England. Here are no turnpikes; but no great inconvenience arifes from this deficiency; the common ftatute labour being fufficient to keep the roads at all times in tolerable condition.

The Ifle of Wight is, by many writers, faid to have formerly been a portion of the main land, gradually disjoined by the encroachments of the fea, a notion probably taken from Diodorus Siculus, who mentions a peninfula which he calls Vectis, as the mart to which the Cornifh merchants ufed to bring their tin in carts But the diftance, with many other circumftances, have caufed it to be doubted by fome, whether he really meant this ifland. The ingenious Mr Borlafe is of this number, and makes ufe of the following argument. " The fhort defcription which " we have of the tin trade in Diodorus Siculus * muft not be " omitted, though it is too general for us to learn many parti- " culars from it Thefe men, fays he, meaning the tinners,

* Lib iv pag 301 edit Hanov. 1664

" manu-

" manufacture their tin, by working the grounds which produce
" it with great art, for though the land is rocky, it has soft
" veins of earth running through it, in which the tinners find
" the treasure, extract, melt, and purify it; then shaping it by
" moulds into a kind of cubical figure, they carry it off to a
" certain island lying near the British shore, which they call
" Ictis. For at the recess of the tide the space betwixt the island
" and the main land being dry, the tinners embrace the oppor-
" tunity, and carry the tin in carts, as fast as may be, over to
" the Ictis or port; for it must be observed, that the islands
" which lie betwixt the continent and Britain have this singu-
" larity, that when the tide is full they are real islands, but
" when the sea retires they are all but so many peninsulas From
" this island the merchants buy the tin of the natives, and ex-
" port it into Gaul, and finally through Gaul, by a journey of
" about thirty days, they bring it down on horses to the mouth
" of the Erydanus, meaning the Rhone *. In this description
" it will naturally occur to the inquisitive reader to ask where
" this Ictis was, to which the Cornish carried their melted tin in
" carts, and there sold it to the merchants I really cannot in-
" form him, but by the Ictis here, it is plain that the historian
" could not mean the Ictis or Vectis of the antients, at present
" called the Isle of Wight : for he is speaking of the Britons of
" Cornwall, and, by the words, it should seem those of the
" most western parts, Της γαρ Βρεʃανιαης καʃα το αρμηρον το καλε-
" μενον Βελεριον οι μαʃοικευʃες, &c. Ουʃοι τοι ποσσηερον καʃασκευαζεσ'
" φιλοʃεκιας, &c. that is, those who live at the extreme end of
" Britain, called Belerium†, find, dress, melt, carry, and sell their
" tin, &c. Now it would be absurd to think these inhabitants

---

* Rhodenus, says the Latin translation , to Marseilles, says Possidonius in Strabo,
lib iii p. 147 edit Par. 1620.

† " Now called the Land's End '

" should

" fhould carry in carts their tin nearly two hundred miles, for
" fo diftant is the Ifle of Wight from them, when they had at
" leaft as good ports and harbours on their own fhores as they
" could meet with there; befides, the inhabitants are faid in
" the fame paragraph, to have been more than ordinarily civi-
" lized by converfing with ftrangers and merchants. Thofe mer-
" chants then muft have been very converfant in Cornwall;
" there trafficked for tin, that is, there bought and thence ex-
" ported the tin, or they could have no bufinefs there : their
" refidence would have been in fome of the ports of Hampfhire,
" and Cornwall would fcarce have felt the influence of their
" manners, much lefs have been improved and civilized by them
" at that diftance. Again, the Cornifh, after the tin was melted,
" carried it at low water over the Ictis in carts ; this will by no
" means fuit the fituation of the Ifle of Wight, which is at leaft
" two miles diftant from the main land; and never, fo far as we
" can learn, has been alternately an ifland and a peninfula, as
" the tide is in and out   The Ictis, therefore, here mentioned
" muft lie fomewhere near the coaft of Cornwall; and muft either
" have been a general name for any peninfula or creek (*Ik* being
" a common Cornifh word, denoting a cove, creek, or port of
" traffick), or the name of fome particular peninfula and com-
" mon emporium on the fame coaft, which has now loft its
" ifthmus, name, and perhaps wholly difappeared, by means of
" fome great alterations on the fea fhore of this country." Borlafe's Nat Hift of Cornwall, § 16, p. 16.

With great deference to fo high authority as Mr. Borlafe,
what another very ingenious author has faid upon the fubject
may be given, without undertaking to decide upon a queftion
of fo great uncertainty. Mr Whitaker, in his Hiftory of
Manchefter, after mentioning that the Phœnicians had continued the tin trade to the coafts of Scilly for near three hundred
                                                      years,

years, fays, " The Greeks of Marfeilles firft followed the track
" of the Phœnician voyagers, and before the days of Polybius,
" and about two hundred years before the age of Chrift, be-
" gan to fhare with them in the trade of tin. The Carthagi-
" nian commerce declined. The Maffylian commerce increafed
" And in the reign of Auguftus the whole current of the Britifh
" traffic had been gradually diverted into this channel. Two
" roads were laid acrofs the country, and reached from Sand-
" wich to Carnarvon on one fide, and extended from Dorfetfhire
" into Suffolk on the other. The great ftaple of the tin was
" no longer fettled in a diftant corner of the ifland. It was re-
" moved from Scilly, and was fixed in the Ifle of Wight, a
" central part of the coaft, lying equally betwixt the two roads,
" and better adapted to the new arrangement of the trade.
" Thither the tin was carried by the Belgæ, and thither the fo-
" reign merchants reforted with their wares." He adds further, " That the Ifle of Wight, which, as late as the eighth
" century, was feparated from the remainder of Hampfhire by
" a channel no lefs than three miles in breadth, was now actual-
" ly a part of the greater ifland, disjoined from it only by the
" tide, and united to it always at the ebb. And during the re-
" cefs of the waters, the Britons conftantly paffed over the low
" ifthmus of land, and carried their loaded carts of tin acrofs it "

  As Mr. Whitaker produces authorities for what he has advanced, the curious reader is referred to his work for a more
nice inveftigation of this fubject. But in fupport of the fame
opinion, I cannot omit the following remarks offered by a
gentleman of the ifland: he obferves, that, at each extremity
of the channel between the ifland and Hampfhire, the tide
rufhes in and out with fuch impetuofity as to render thefe parts
the deepeft and moft dangerous, whereas, near the midway,
where

where the tides meet, though the conflict makes a rough water, according as the wind may affift the one or the other, there is no rapidity of current to carry away the foil and deepen the bottom; accordingly we difcover a hard gravelly beach there, extending a great way acrofs the channel, a circumftance not to be found in any other part of it. Correfponding with this, on the Hampfhire fide, is a place called *Leap*, poffibly from the narrownefs of the pafs, and on the Ifle of Wight, oppofite this, is a ftrait open road, of at leaft two miles in length, called Rew-ftreet, probably from the French word Rue, to which the tranflation of it might afterwards be added: this road, after having croffed the foreft, may be traced by an obfervant eye from St. Auftin's Gate to the weft of Carifbrook caftle, over a field called North Field, by Sheat, and fo on to the fouth fide of the ifland. Many parts of this road are of little or no ufe at this time, and, unlefs it was heretofore ufed for the purpofe of conveying tin, it is not eafy to conjecture what purpofe it was to anfwer.

One more refpectable authority, that the ftaple of tin was brought into Hampfhire muft be adduced.

That learned antiquarian, Sir Robert Cotton, in a little treatife, entitled, " The Manner and Means how the Kings of " England have from Time to Time fupported and repaired " their Eftates,' printed in the year 1609, has the following anecdote.

" Henry VI. anno 2c, by advice of his council, took up, by " way of purveyance, great ftore of grain and tranfported it " into Gafcoigne, where, by reafon of the dearth, the price
" was

" was extreme In anno 3', *he arrested all tle tin in Soutl-*
" *ampton, and sold it to his own present use*."

No manufacture of any confequence is carried on in this
ifland, unlefs the making of falt may come under that denomination Even the facks, in which large quantities of grain and flour
are exported, have not hitherto been the work of the inhabitants;
but, from the laudable meafures now purfued by the governors of
the houfe of induftry, there is reafon to believe this deficiency will
foon be remedied. Timber, deals, and iron, are the chief foreign
imports to this ifland: thefe articles, not only for home confumption,
but alfo for the ufe of the adjacent counties of Suffex, and Dorfetfhire, are landed at Cowes, a port well known for its conve-
niency in loading and unfhipping of goods. The inhabitants

* King Henry VI having taken to his own ufe a certain quantity of allom foyle
of the value of eight thoufand pounds, the property of the merchants of Genoa,
being in the port of Southampton , in order to fecure the payment of the faid fum
to the faid merchants, it was ordained by the king, lords and commons, in parliament affembled, that the faid merchants fhould fhip in veffels to pafs the ftraits of
Marrok, all wools, woolfells, *tin,* and other merchandife to them belonging, in
the port of Southampton , and alfo to difcharge and put to land all merchandifes
to them belonging, coming into the faid port from parts beyond the fea, and retain
the duties and cuftoms arifing thereupon in their own hands towards the payment
of the faid fum and fhould likewife take and receive all manner of cuftoms and
fubfidies arifing and growing in the faid port, after a certain day then following,
upon all manner of wools, woolfells, hides, *tin,* and other merchandife which
after that day fhould be fhipped , until the faid fum of eight thoufand pounds
fhould be fully paid and fatisfied.

Rot Parl 29 Hen VI. 1 14.

The ftannaries were formerly held at Southampton, the houfe where the office
was kept has been lately purchafed by Dr Speed, who informed the Editor that it
was not removed from thence till the fifteenth century. There is a large cellar
near the quay at Southampton, which ftill retains the name of the tin cellar, and
was moft probably the place where the tin was depofited.

D   have

have of late years imported confiderable quantities of wines, which, with occafional cargoes of hemp, and of fruits from Spain and Portugal, make up the lift of the foreign imports; thofe from America excepted. Before the defection of the American colonies, from thirty to fifty veffels loaded with rice annually arrived at Cowes, from South Carolina and Georgia; their cargoes were from twenty-two thoufand to thirty-five thoufand barrels, or from five thoufand to eight thoufand tons of that grain; befides deer fkins, ftaves, indigo, pitch, tar, turpentine, and other articles of lefs confequence. The rice, after being landed, opened, fkreened, and re-packed, was generally re-fhipped on board the veffel in which it came, and carried to Holland, Germany, or fome of the French ports in the Channel. This was a beneficial branch of bufnefs to the port of Cowes, which it has loft by the unfortunate feparation above alluded to. Tobacco has alfo been landed in this port in the fame manner, and for the fame purpofe, as rice; and this bufinefs would, in all likelihood, have greatly increafed, had not the fame unhappy circumftances put a ftop to it.

The exports from the Ifle of Wight are, wheat, flour, barley, malt, and falt; large quantities of grain and flour are fhipped for France, Spain, Portugal, and the ports in the Mediterranean; and a confiderable inland and coafting trade to Ireland, and all the Englifh ports in the Channel, is carried on in wheat, flour, barley, and malt, which, after paying for linen and woollen goods, Indian commodities, grocery, the various articles of building, coals from Wales and Newcaftle, leaves a confiderable balance in favour of the ifland, and it being naturally fertile, well cultivated, and not over populous, even the thinnefs nest crops afford a surplus of corn for the supply of foreign and other markets. Upon the whole, prior to the stoppage of all intercourse with America in one thousand seven hundred and seventy-five, the home and foreign trade of this island was in a thriving state; and there is little reason to doubt, that if the American disputes were happily terminated, its commerce would return to its former channel [*].

The harbour of Cowes is as safe as any in the British Channel, and by far the most convenient for vessels bound to Holland and the east countries. It is, therefore, much frequented by ships, to repair damages sustained at sea, and to winter in, until the season permits them to proceed on their respective voyages. Within the present century the following ships of war were built at this port; the *Vanguard*, of seventy guns; the *Repulse*, of sixty-four; the *Salisbury*, of fifty; the *Cerberus*, and *Astrea*, of thirty two; the *Andromeda*, of twenty-eight; and two others are now building, the *Veteran*, of sixty-four, and *Experiment*, of forty-four.

In the year one thousand seven hundred and seventy, at a general meeting of the gentlemen of the island, it was proposed that an act of parliament should be obtained to consoli-

House of Industry.

---

* The exports from the island for the last two years are greatly increased. By returns from the custom house it appears that *thirty-seven thousand four hundred and ninety-nine* quarters of flour were exported in the year 1780, of which at least *ten thousand* may be said to be the produce and manufacture of the island.

The annual export of salt, upon an average of the last five years, is about *eleven hundred* tons.

The number of sheep shorn yearly, the wool of which is sent into the clothing counties, is from *thirty* to *thirty-five thousand*, about *ten thousand* lambs are also annually shorn, and *three or four thousand* sent to London and other markets.

The yearly consumption of coals about *five thousand* chaldeis.

date

date the rates made for the relief of the poor of the several
parishes within the island, and to erect one or more house or
houses of industry for the maintenance and employment of the
poor in general within the same. This proposal met with uni-
versal approbation.

The advantages proposed by such an institution are set forth in
the preamble of the act, obtained for this purpose, which passed
in the eleventh year of his present Majesty, viz. " That the
" providing a place for the general reception of the poor, would
" tend to the more effectual relief of such as by age, infirmities,
" or diseases, were rendered incapable of supporting themselves
" by their labour; to the better employment of the able and
" industrious; to the correction and punishment of the profligate
" and idle; and to the education of the children in religion and
" industry; and thereby making the poor, instead of being totally
" supported by the public, contribute to the support, assistance,
" and relief of each other, and be of some advantage to the
" community, to which they had before been only a heavy and
" grievous burthen."

Some part of his Majesty's forest of Parkhurst, near the town
of Newport, was thought the most convenient situation for the
intended building, and a clause was therefore inserted in the
act of parliament, to enable his Majesty to make a grant, under
the Exchequer seal, of such part or portion of the forest, not
exceeding eighty acres, as certain trustees therein named (of
which the governor of the island, for the time being, to be one)
should allot for the purposes of the act, for such time and term
as his Majesty should think proper, notwithstanding the limitations of the civil-list act made in the first year of queen Anne.

In

In confequence of this claufe, a memorial was prefented to the lords of the treafury, on behalf of the corporation of guardians of the poor of the Ifle of Wight, incorporated by the faid act, praying that a grant may be made to them of fuch a portion of land in the foreft, as fhould be fixed on by the truftees, for a long term of years, renewable for a fine certain, which being obtained, the truftees pointed out the eaft fide of the road, leading through the foreft, from Cowes to Newport, as the moft convenient fpot for the intended building; and a grant of eighty acres there was accordingly made to the corporation, for the term of nine hundred and ninety-nine years, at the yearly rent of eight pounds feventeen fhillings and nine pence half-penny.

Near the fouth part of this land the houfe of induftry was erected; the principal part of the building is three hundred feet in length, from eaft to weft, by twenty-feven wide in the clear, having windows on both fides, for the advantage of a thorough draught of air. At the diftance of two hundred feet from the weft end, a wing from the main building ranges fouthward, one hundred and feventy feet by twenty-four wide, from the end of which are built work-fhops for the manufacturers and mechanics, which run weftward, parallel with the principal building, and thefe, with a walk on the weft, form a fquare of two hundred feet by one hundred and feventy. On the eaft fide of the wing is a court, one hundred and feventy feet by fifty, formed by part of the principal building on the north; offices, fuch as dairy, wafh-houfe, brew-houfe, wood-houfe, ftore-rooms, &c. on the eaft, and a wall on the fouth.

In the principal building is a large ftore-room, fteward's-room, committee-room, dining-hall (one hundred and eighteen feet long by twenty-feven wide), and common fitting room for im-

potent

potent and aged poor; under the eaſt end, cellars for beer, meat, &c. which in the whole are eighty feet long by twenty-ſeven wide. over this building are the laundry, governor's and matron's lodging rooms, nurſeries, and ſick wards.

In the wing on the ground-floor are the ſchool-rooms, apothe-caries ſhop, kitchen, ſcullery, bakehouſe, bread room, governor's and matron's ſitting-room, pantry, &c. Over, are the lying-in rooms, ſick wards, and twenty ſeparate rooms, or apartments, for married men and their wives; with two common ſitting-rooms adjoining, for the old and infirm, who lodge in thoſe apartments, and are unable to go down ſtairs. In the centre of the work-ſhops before mentioned, in front of the principal building, is a large gateway, on the eaſt ſide of which is a maſter weaver's room and ſpinning room, ninety-ſix feet long by eighteen wide, with ſtore rooms over it. At the weſt ſide of this gateway is the ſhoemaker's and taylor's ſhops, with a ſpinning-room, one hundred and fifty feet long by eighteen wide, with weaving-rooms and ſtore-rooms over.

The manufactures carrying on at preſent are, ſacks for corn, flour, and biſcuit, for which there is a very great demand; and kerſeys, ſtockings, &c. for the uſe of the paupers in the houſe

The chapel is erected on the north ſide of the principal building, it is fifty feet by twenty ſeven, and over it is a ſtore room. At the diſtance of about three or four hundred yards is a peſt-houſe, with a burying-ground walled in, cloſe adjoining.

On the ſouth of the whole building is a large garden, which ſupplies the houſe with vegetables. On the eaſt, behind the offices, is a barn and ſtable, hog-ſtyes, &c.

The

The domeſtic officers are, a governor, matron, ſteward, and ſchool-maſter, who are choſen annually. A chaplain is alſo appointed, who does duty in the houſe twice a week, beſides Sundays. There are alſo two ſurgeons and apothecaries, a ſecretary and treaſurer, all of whom, except the treaſurer, have ſettled ſalaries.

The houſe is capable of containing near ſeven hundred people, the number ſupported in it are from five hundred to five hundred and fifty. It varies with the ſeaſons, and as the country in general is more or leſs healthy. The different ages and ſexes of the poor maintained in the houſe are found to be nearly as follows. Suppoſe the number to be five hundred and fifty: the proportion will be of men, ſixty-four; women, one hundred and thirty-ſix; girls, nine years old and upwards, eighty-four; ditto, under nine years, ninety-five; boys, nine years old and upwards, fifty-five; ditto, under that age, one hundred and ſixteen.

The completing the building was attended with a great expence. The act of parliament authorized the corporation to take up, on the ſecurity of the poors rates, any ſum not exceeding twelve thouſand pounds, at an intereſt of four per cent. but this was found inadequate to the undertaking. A ſecond application to parliament was therefore neceſſary, to enable the corporation to borrow any farther ſum, not exceeding eight thouſand pounds, and a ſupplemental bill was prepared, but many inconveniencies having been experienced from the defects and inſufficiencies in the former act, the whole was thought proper to be repealed, and this was done by an act of the ſixteenth of his preſent Majeſty; by which the corporation of guardians were continued, the powers of the former act confirmed, and new powers and regulations provided.

The

The perfons conftituting the corporation, and ftyled, by the act, *Guardians of the Poor*, are fuch inhabitants of the ifland as are feifed in fee, or for life, in their own or their wives right, of land rated to the poors-rate at fifty pounds per annum; heirs apparent to one hundred pounds per annum, all rectors and vicars within the ifland, and occupiers of lands rated to the poors-rates at one hundred pounds per annum.

Out of the perfons thus qualified (and returned by the refpective parifhes in a fettled proportion, according to the averaged rates paid by each parifh) are chofen yearly, by ballot, twenty-four directors, and thirty-fix acting guardians, who divide and fub divide themfelves into quarterly, monthly, and weekly committees, for the regulation and management of the houfe The weekly committee, which confifts of two directors and five acting guardians, meet every Saturday at the houfe, for the purpofe of fettling the governor's and fteward's accounts of the preceding week, and giving directions for the enfuing week, hearing complaints, granting occafional relief to perfons out of the houfe, &c &c.

All matters which come before the weekly committee, and not cognizable by them, are referred to a quarterly committee, which is to confift of not lefs than fifteen directors and acting guardians, of which five at leaft muft be directors.

The whole land granted by the crown (except the garden) lies to the north of the building, and is enclofed with a quick hedge, it is divided into fields, from five to twelve acres, the fences round which are alfo moftly quick.

The

The expence of breaking up and cultivating this land was very considerable; it is at prefent chiefly arable, but the whole is intended, under a proper courfe of hufbandry, to be laid down to pafture, and, in a few years, will amply repay the cofts, and be of great advantage to the inftitution.

The Needles 1762.

E   CHAP.

CHAP. II.

Military History of the Island; the several Descents made by the Romans, Saxons, Danes, and French; the ancient Feudal Military Force, and present State of the Militia. Of the Castles and Forts.

A. D 43. THE Isle of Wight, according to Suetonius, was first conquered by the Romans during the reign of the emperor Claudius, about the year of our Lord forty-three; when Vespasian, his general, in the course of that expedition, fought thirty pitched battles, subdued two very powerful nations, and took more than twenty towns.

These successes happened partly under the command of Aulus Plautius, a consular lieutenant, and partly under that of the emperor himself; for which services Vespasian was honoured with triumphal ornaments, and soon after with two sacerdotal dignities *.

Seneca, in the first act of his Octavia, compliments Claudius with being the first conqueror of the Britons; for although Julius Cæsar had fought successfully against them, he had not retained the least fruits of his victories. His words are as follow:

————————— Paruit liber diu
Oceanus, et recepit invitus rates.
En qui Britannis primus impofuit jugum,
Ignota, et ante claffibus texit freta.

* Sub Vita Vefpafiani

It

It seems as if the Romans were not under any great apprehensions from the islanders, or else that they staid here but a short time, and then resided chiefly in the towns, since there are not the least traces of any of their fortifications to be found in the island, which is the more wonderful, as it is well known to have been a general maxim with that people to fortify their camps, though formed but for one night.

The military history of a small and dependent island must, in a great measure, be connected with that of the country to which it belongs. The relation of its peculiar sufferings by descents and invasions, will form but a broken and uncontinued narration. These, chiefly collected from the Saxon Chronicle, are here mentioned in the order in which they happened.

In the year four hundred and ninety-five, Cerdic, a Saxon chief, with his son Henric, invaded Britain, and, after various successes, established the kingdom of West-fex. He also conquered the Isle of Wight, and slew most of its inhabitants, these he replaced with a great number of Jutes and Saxons, whom he invited over, bestowing the island on his two nephews, Stuff and Withgar *. After this revolution it probably remained undisturbed for above a century.

495

The next event recorded relative to this island, happened in the year six hundred and sixty one, when it was subdued and laid waste by Wulfer, king of Mercia, the son of Penda. He gave it to Adelwach, king of Suffex†, whom he had before conquered and made prisoner.

661.

* Chron. Sax p 18 From Cerdic, says Rapin, the kings of England are descended, in the male line, down to Edward the Confeffor, and in the female down to the present time Hift. of Engl vol 1 p 36.

† Chron. Sax p 39.

E 2

Not

686.   Not many years after it was ravaged by Ceadwalla *, the lineal defcendent from Cerdic, its firft Saxon conqueror, who refumed it as his inheritance, wrongfully feized by Wulfer.

The iflanders converted to Chriftianity

Bede relates, that the inhabitants at that time not having embraced the Chriftian faith, although it was ninety years after the miffion of Auguftine the monk, Ceadwalla had determined to root them out as idolaters, and to re-people the ifland with Chriftians; but bifhop Wilfrid prevailed on him to make ufe of lefs fanguinary meafures; and to fpare the lives of fuch as would receive baptifm. to this, it is probable, the majority fubmitted. The fame author fays, that two fons of the prince of the ifland, who had endeavoured to efcape, were taken *ad Lapidem*, which writers conjecture to have been Stoneham, near Southampton †. They were, according to the favage ufage of thefe times, doomed to death, but Ceadwalla's clemency extended fo far as to permit them to be firft baptized.

787.   The iflanders being thus converted to Chriftianity, nothing farther remarkable occurs till the year feven hundred and eighty feven, when the ifland was furprifed by Danifh pirates, with a defign to make it a place of retreat, to which they might retire with the fpoils pillaged from the Englifh coaft No appearances, however, remain of any of their entrenchments, perhaps owing to their being protected by a fleet much fuperior to that of the Saxons, who were, befides, fully occupied with their own inteftine wars.

The Saxons had for a long time neglected their navy, until, roufed by the repeated incurfions of thefe piratical freebooters,

---

* Chron Sax p 46

† It might as probably be Stone, near Fawley, lately purchafed of Mr Mitford, by Mr Drummond

king

king Alfred firſt fitted out a fleet to ſcour the Channel; and his ſucceſſors, Edgar in particular, greatly augmented their naval power. In the year eight hundred and ninety-ſeven a fleet of Daniſh pirates, conſiſting of ſix ſhips, plundered the Iſle of Wight, and ſailed from thence to the coaſt of Devonſhire with their booty. Alfred followed them with nine ſhips, took two of their veſſels, and killed many of their men; three others endeavouring to eſcape were driven on ſhore, and their crews being taken, were carried before the king at Wincheſter, where he cauſed them all to be hanged as public robbers.

Although ſuch tranſient invaſions (as they produced no extenſive nor permanent effects) cannot be expected to have been very minutely recorded; yet, from the ſilence of our chronicles on that head, it is probable, that the vigilance of Alfred procured a temporary quiet to the ſouthern coaſt; but the Danes having eſtabliſhed themſelves in various parts of England, their roving countrymen, habituated to plunder, continued to infeſt the other parts of Britain whenever an opportunity offered.

During the unfortunate reign of Ethelred, aptly ſirnamed the Unready, the Danes again appeared in the Channel, plundered the adjacent country, and carrying their booty to their veſſels, they ſailed to the Iſle of Wight, where they lived at diſcretion, no force being able to withſtand them *. Theſe outrages were ſucceeded by others ſtill greater, for, after making an excurſion to the weſt of England, and ſetting fire to ſeveral towns in Devonſhire and Somerſetſhire, they returned to the iſland, burned ſeveral villages, and a town called † Wealtham. A few years

99b

1001.

---

* Chron Sax p 131

† This Wealtham might perhaps be Newtown, or more probably Werrow, a large hamlet near Thorley, which has evident marks of being once a town foundations of very old buildings have been diſcovered in different parts of it, there is alſo a large common field, called Warrow common field, contiguous; and, in general, this is an indication of an adjoining town.

after-

afterwards, a Danifh fleet made a defcent on the coaft of Kent, plundered the town of Sandwich, and the neighbouring country; after which, they retired with their booty to their afylum, the ifle of Wight; and, about Chriftmas, making another excurfion into Berkfhire, they returned to their cuftomary retreat *.

Although this is the laft Danifh invafion mentioned in hiftory to have happened in this ifland, yet it ftill remained expofed to other occafional violence For earl Godwin having been outlawed and banifhed by Edward the Confeffor, retired to the earl of **Earl God-** Flanders, who furnifhed him with a naval force, with which he **fient on this** fteered for the Englifh coaft, and, watching a proper opportunity, **ifland.** made a defcent on the Ifle of Wight and the Peninfula of Port-**1052.** land, both which he plundered, and his fon, Harold, joining him afterwards with nine fhips from Ireland, they returned, and ftripped the miferable inhabitants of all that had efcaped their **1066.** former depredations.   Tofti, earl of Northumberland, alfo a fon of the earl Godwin, being driven out of that country for his injuftice and cruelty, was encouraged by William, duke of Normandy, to difturb Harold's government, in favour of his projected invafion, collecting, therefore, a fleet in Flanders, before he failed for Northumberland, he once more made this defencelefs ifland feel the miferies of hoftile invafion †.

French invafions. From the time of William the Conqueror to the twenty-third of Edward the Firft, the ifland feems to have enjoyed a ftate of tranquility. But at that period the coaft of England was threatened with a defcent, and a numerous fleet being fitted out by **1295.** France, King Edward, who had then purchafed the lordfhip

---

* Chron. Sax p. 135,   † Ibid. p 166.

of

of the Isle of Wight, appointed for its defence the Bishop of Winchester, Adam de Gordon, and Sir Richard de Affeton, a gentleman of the island, joining them in commission as wardens, and giving them orders and instructions for their conduct in case of an attack; no attempt, however, appears to have been made on it at that time. But when Edward the Third asserted his claim to the crown of France, it sustained several attacks; the first in the thirteenth of that king's reign, when Sir John de Langford, constable of Carisbrooke Castle, Sir Bartholomew de Lisle, and Sir Theobald Russel, were constituted wardens.

1340.

The regulations made by the inhabitants, for their security about this time, are found in an old manuscript *, to the following purport:

I. That there should be but three ports in the island, namely, La Riche, Shamblord, and Yarmouth.

II. That three persons should be appointed wardens of these ports, who were to prevent any one from retiring from the island, or exporting provisions from thence without licence.

III. That none but licensed boats should be permitted to pass, except the boat belonging to the Abbot of Quair; a boat belonging to Sir Bartholomew de Lisle, and another belonging to Robert de Pimely. And

IV. That several watches should be appointed, and persons nominated to superintend them and the beacons.

The French landed at St. Helen's Point, and marched forward, till they were met by the islanders, who drove them back

* MS penes Sim Stuart, Bart

to their ſhips   Sir Theobald Ruſſell, who Stowe calls Sir Peter, was ſlain in the action.

Although invaſions were frequently menaced, the iſland continued unmoleſted till the firſt of Richard the Second, at which time Stowe ſays, " the French took that invincible Iſle more by " craft than force" This he ſuppoſes could not have happened had the watch done their duty : from whence he formed ſo high an eſtimate of the ſtrength of the iſland, at that time, is not obvious, ſince it appears to have been expoſed to the inſults of all invaders, there being at that time no forts to obſtruct the landing of an enemy. Cariſbrooke Caſtle, ſtanding near the centre of the iſland, could only ſerve for a retreat, to which the inhabitants might fly with their moſt portable effects. This want of domeſtic ſecurity ſo diſcouraged the natives, that many families withdrew themſelves from the iſland; a circumſtance that appears from the orders iſſued to the wardens of the iſland, in the reign of Edward the Third, directing them to ſeize the lands of thoſe who, having left it, refuſed to return.

About this time the preparations of the French having given timely intimation of their hoſtile intentions, the militia, which then conſiſted of nine companies of one hundred men each, were reinforced both from the county of Southampton and London. On the landing of the enemy, the people fled for refuge to Cariſbrooke Caſtle, which was defended by Sir Hugh Tyrril, who ſlew a great number of the aſſailants. During the ſiege a party of the French, indiſcreetly coming towards the caſtle, down a narrow lane, fell into an ambuſcade, and were moſtly cut off. The lane is ſtill called Deadman's Lane, and a tumulus, where the ſlain were buried, was exultingly called Noddies Hill*. The

* Oglander's MS Memoirs.

caſe

caufe of this denomination was in danger of being loft; the hill being built upon, and forming one of the avenues to Newport, is now corrupted into *Node Hill.*

The French, unable to fubdue the caftle, withdrew; but before they reimbarked obliged the natives to redeem their houfes from being burned, by a contribution of a thoufand marks, they alfo bound them by an oath not to refift, if they fhould re-vifit the ifland within a year *.

Towards the latter end of the fifth of Henry the Fifth, a body of Frenchmen landed on the ifland, and boafted they would keep their Chriftmas there; but as near a thoufand of them were driving cattle towards their fhips, they were fuddenly attacked by the iflanders, and obliged to leave, not only all their plunder, but alfo many of their men behind.

Not † long after this, a large French fleet arrived, and demanded a fubfidy in the name of King Richard and Queen Ifabella. They were anfwered, that Richard was dead, and his Queen fent back to France, without the payment of any fubfidy being ftipulated; but if the French had any defire to try their prowefs, they fhould not only be permitted to land without mo-

---

* The expedition is thus related by Trivetus " Eodem tempore, ftatim poft
" mortem regis, Franci cum multis galeis et navibus, intrantes mare, venerunt ad
" villam de Rie, juxta monaftrium de Bello et applicuerant ad terram, ipfamque
" villam depredantes combufferunt et deftruxerunt, ufque ad folum, et fic rece-
" dentes duxerunt fecum plures utriufque fexus captivos, et reliquos quos reperire
" occiderunt. Et poftea intrarunt infulam Vectem, ubi poftquam aliqua loca pe-
" haffent et concremaffent, accipientes nille marcas pro relemptione ipfius redi-
" erunt ad mare, et continue ufque ad feftum fancti Michaelis circuerunt per
" maritima loca Angliæ, comburantes et vaftantes loca plurima, et maxime in pa-
" tibus auftralibus, interficientes quofque poterant invenire, capientefque predas
" animalium et aliorum rerum, et aliquando prifonarios, damnum modicum re-
" portarunt quia parvam refiftentiam habuerunt " *Nicolai Triveti Annales.*

' Stowe, p 379.

F   leftation,

leflation, but a'fo be allowed fix hours to refresh themfelves, after which the iflanders would meet them in the field. The French retired without accepting of this invitation.

Whilft the reft of the kingdom was alternately ravaged by the partizans of the houfes of York and Lancafter, the remote fituation of this ifland procured it an exemption from the calamities of civil war, nor was its tranquility interrupted by the French, who at that time were fufficiently employed with their inteftine troubles.

In the thirty-fixth year of the reign of Henry the Eighth, Francis the Firft equipped a fleet, confifting of more than two hundred fail, with orders to make a defcent on the Britifh coaft. The Englifh fleet, which lay at anchor at St Helens, did not confift of half that number, they therefore retreated into the Channel, hoping to decoy the enemy to follow them ; however Annebout, the French admiral, was aware of the danger to which fuch purfuit would have expofed him, from the rocks and fhallows with which he was unacquainted, and finding he could not induce the Englifh to leave their fituation, contented himfelf with making a defcent on the Ifle of Wight, where he landed about two thoufand men ; and it was propofed, in a council of war, to fortify and keep poffeffion of the ifland. but this, by the majority, being deemed impracticab'e, they began to burn and plunder the villages; they were neverthelefs fuddenly attacked by Richard Worfley, captain of the ifland *, and driven to their fhips, with the lofs of their commanding officer and many of his men.

To fecure the coaft from the like infults †, a number of forts were erected at different places, thefe, though at prefent of no

* The governor of the ifland was at that time fo called.
† Stowe, p. 58) Rapin, vol i p 841.

great.

great eftimation, were at that time deemed of confiderable importance. But the ifland was fhortly after much more fecurely guarded by the naval ftrength of England, which was augmented by Queen Elizabeth to a degree before unknown.

The ancient military force of this ifland, with the arrays, arms, beacons, watches and wards, prefcribed in time of danger, may, in fome meafure, be collected from thofe authentic records and genuine papers which have efcaped the ravages of time. By a return to an inquifition taken at Newport the feventh of Edward the Third, it appears that the land-holders were, by their tenures, obliged to defend the caftle of Carifbrooke for forty days at their own charges· and two other inquifitions taken at Shide Bridge, the eighteenth of Edward the Second *, fpecify the feveral watches and beacons, and likewife fhew that every perfon having twenty pounds per annum in lands, was obliged to find a horfeman completely armed, or more or lefs in proportion to his poffeffions, according to the ftatute of Winchefter. And by another inquifition taken at Newport the fixteenth of Edward the Third †, it is returned, that the Earls of Devon, lords of the ifland, fent feventy-fix men at arms from the county of Devon for its defence; and that after Edward the Firft obtained the ifland of the Countefs Ifabel de Fortibus, men at arms were fent for its protection by divers bifhops, abbots, and other perfons who are therein fpecified ‡ It alfo mentions that the king fent an hundred flingers and bowmen, and the city of London three hundred, for the fame fervice. The numbers of men raifed by the land-holders of the ifland are found in an

Note in right margin: Ancient military force of the ifland

* See Appendix, No VII. VIII and IX.
† Prynne on the Fourth Inftitute, p. 211.
‡ See the lift in Appendix, No X

old roll without date *; which, by the names of some of the persons charged, appears to have been made early in the reign of Edward the Third, one of them, Giles de Beauchamp, who was at that time possessed of Freshwater, attending the king in his wars abroad, received a discharge for his quota of six men †, though, in the roll referred to, he is charged with but two men at arms. probably, either the number and rank of men to be found by each land-holder, was not then positively ascertained; or the six men here mentioned might be bowmen, considered as no more than equivalent to two horsemen, or men at arms.

The authority of the warden of the island seems to have been very extensive, as appears from a commission granted the twenty-fixth of Edward the Third, to John de Gattesden, appointing him to that office ‡ · which authorised him to array the men at arms, hoblers § and bow-men, with all others, as well horse as foot; to levy new forces, if those already arrayed are found insufficient; to provide them with weapons, and to marshal them. He was empowered to take men, who were to be paid by the king, from the county of Southampton as well as from the island; and that not only within, but also without the liberties. He was likewise to summon all absentees, who were bound by their tenures to defend Carisbrooke Castle, or the island; to order them to return with their families within a limited time, under penalty of forfeiting their lands and tenements, goods and chattles, to the king's use; and, in case of

---

* See Appendix, No XI | Dugd Bar. tom i p 249
‡ Rot Franc 26 Ed. III. m 13.
§ Hoblers were soldiers lightly armed, and mounted on small horses or hobbies.

non-

non-compliance, to provide men to supply their places *. An old roll †, found by Sir John Oglander, contains the distribution of the militia into companies, with the names of their commanding officers, in the above mentioned reign. The prudence of this king is conspicuous in all his arrangements respecting this island: its exposed situation calling on him for his peculiar attention; he, therefore, granted divers privileges and immunities to the inhabitants, in order to induce persons to settle there. They were not to be charged with the aid granted to the king, which exemption was ordered to be forthwith notified to them; and no inhabitant of the island could be compelled to serve on any jury or inquest out of it. In the same parliament ‡ it was agreed, that no order should be made under the privy-seal, licensing the absence of any one during the time of war, who was bound, by his tenure, to defend the island, unless in case of the most urgent necessity, of which the council were to be apprised.

The king, at his own cost, furnished the castle of Carisbrooke with the following stores; (which the commissioners were ordered to deliver to John de Langford, then constable of the castle) ten tuns of wine; one hundred quarters of wheat; one hundred quarters of malt; fifty quarters of beans and pease; one hundred quarters of oats; with salt, coals, wood, and other munitions.

§ In time of danger he authorised the islanders to chuse a warden for themselves; the sheriff of Southampton, with the

---

* Severe as this penalty may be thought, history furnishes instances of our kings, in old times, issuing like orders to all parts of the kingdom See Rot pat 48 Hen III. m 3 dorso where the king commands the people to continue on the coast, to defend the kingdom, under pain of forfeiting all their property.
† See Appendix, No XII.
‡ Rot. Parl 13 Ed III p 2 n 28 § Idem, n. 29 See Appendix, No v.
§ Rot Parl. 13 Edw. III No 30

conftable of the caftle, were directed to call them together for this purpofe; and the warden nominated by them was to continue during the king's pleafure *: a writ was iffued to the collectors and venders of the ninth fleece, &c. in the county of Southampton, directing them to fell the ninth in the ifland; but to forbear to levy the fame until fifteen days after the enfuing Michaelmafs, when a better judgment might be formed †.

Two years after this, a commiffion was granted to John de Standford, Philip de Wefton, John de Kingfton, and Nicholas de Bokeland, fetting forth, that the king having taken it into confideration that the people of this ifla'd were frequently obliged to come before his juftices in the county of Southampton, to their great trouble and expence; and being defirous to provide for the peace and quiet of thofe people who were, in time of war, to defend the ifland, as well as to give them as little occafion for abfence as poffible; and alfo, in order that no injuftice or malfeafance of any of his officers within that ifland might pafs unpunifhed, the perfons therein named, were conftituted the king's juftices, to enquire on oath of the good men in the ifland, concerning all oppreffions, extortion, or other mifdemeanors committed by the king's officers, efcheators, collectors, and receivers of taxes, alfo of fuch as carried wool out of the kingdom without paying cuftom, to hear and determine trefpaffes, &c. and to enquire what lands, tenements, &c. had been alienated in mortmain from the reign of king Henry the Third to that time ‡.

The inhabitants, in gratitude for thefe favours, exerted themfelves to the utmoft in the defence of the ifland. Their alacrity clearly appears in the voluntary regulations already quoted, which they impofed on themfelves for their common fecurity, and they have fince, on every occafion, manifefted the fame loyalty and courage, though, as will be hereafter fhewn, they difcovered a proper fpirit of freedom whenever any encroachments on their liberties were attempted.

In proportion as civil government acquired a more regular and permanent eftablifhment, the manners of the people became foftened; this, with the increafe of commerce, and its concomitant advantages, introduced a new fet of ideas, tending to relax the rigour of feudal fubordination, and by degrees caufed moft of the perfonal fervice, required by the military tenures, to degenerate into pecuniary aids * ; and the reft, from the great alteration of circumftances, finking into difufe, were, at the Reftoration, abolifhed by ftatute; and † in its place divers laws were enacted, which, though now much altered, ferved as a foundation for the prefent regulations of our national militia. The Ifle of Wight was not, however, included in the act for fettling the militia, but, by a particular claufe, was fuffered to retain their ancient ufage‡; though what that ufage was, from a variety of alterations made from time to time, it will not be eafy to afcertain. As much as could be recovered refpecting

* The learned Judge Blackftone, in his Commentaries, makes the following obfervations refpecting this commutation. " By the degenerating of knights fervice, " or perfonal military duty, into efcuage, or pecuniary affeffments, all the ad- " vantages, either pretended or real, of the feudal conftitution were deftroyed, " and nothing but the hardfhips remained Inftead of forming a national militia, " compofed of barons, knights, and gentlemen, bound by their intereft, their ho- " nour, and their oaths, to defend their king and country, the whole of this fyftem " of tenures now tended to nothing elfe, but a wretched means of raifing money " to pay an army of occafional mercenaries " Blackftone's Comm book ii ch v.
† Stat 12 Car II. c 24.
‡ Stat 13 and 14 Car II c 3 § 30

the

the military history of the island, has been already shewn; nothing farther on that subject, worth recording, occurs till the time of Charles the First, at whose accession, according to the official state drawn up by Sir John Oglander, then one of the lieutenants of the island, under Lord Conway, the militia amounted to near two thousand men*; they were then new-modelled, and, from twelve, formed into sixteen companies. Besides this curious paper given in the Appendix, there is added Lord Conway's regulations respecting military precedence†, a list of the watches and wards kept on this island in one thousand six hundred and thirty-eight ‡, and a set of instructions drawn up for the conduct of the militia in one thousand § six hundred and fifty-one, which last, though issued under an irregular authority, may be accepted as the established discipline of the time.

Present state of the militia.

The militia of the Isle of Wight at present consists of only one company of sixty men, commanded by a captain, under the governor this small body was originally considered as belonging to the south regiment of the Hampshire militia; it was first raised in the year one thousand seven hundred and fifty-seven, but not drawn out and embodied till the year one thousand seven hundred and seventy, when it was formed into an independent company.

Parochial artillery.

The island was also possessed of a small train of artillery, every parish providing one piece of brass ordnance, which was kept in a small house built for that purpose, or in some part of the church About eighteen of these cannon still remain; they are of different calibers, from one to six pounds, and some of them appear by their dates to have been made in the time of

* See Appendix, No XIV   ‡ See Appendix, No XV.
† See Appendix, No XVI   § See Appendix, No. XVII

Edward

Edward the VI. others in that of Queen Elizabeth. The carriages and ammunition were provided at the expence of the parishes, and particular farms were charged with the duty of finding horses to draw them. They were usually brought into the field in a general muster, and the islanders, by frequently exercising themselves in firing at marks, became very expert in the use of them, as well as their small arms.

Of the fortresses on this island, the castle of Carisbrooke claims the first notice; not only from its antiquity, but because all lands were held of the lord, as of the castle of Carisbrooke, by the service of defending it against an enemy, whence it was called the Honour of Carisbrooke. It appears by Domesday-book to have been built by William Fitz-Osborne, Earl of Hereford, and the first Lord of the island, soon after the Norman conquest, and most probably at the same time that he founded the Priory. The land on which the castle stands was part of the Manor of Avington *.

Carisbrooke Castle.

This castle stands on a small hill, about a mile south-west of the town of Newport, and overlooking the village of Carisbrooke; the walls of the original fortress include about an acre and an half of ground, and are nearly in figure a rectangular parallelogram, having the angles rounded †. The greatest length is from

---

* The following translation of the survey of that manor in Domesday-book is here given to prove that the castle must have been erected soon after the Conquest

The King holds Avington Donnus held it in the time of King Edward [the Confessor] rated at two hides and a half, but now it is rated at only two hides, because the castle stands upon one virgate [or twenty acres] of land, it contains six carucates of land, wherein are eight villains, and two cottagers, with four carucates, two mills of the value of five shillings, and six acres of meadow, it is valued at three pounds per annum, but pays four pounds rent

† These angles were taken down and rebuilt by Queen Elizabeth, as appears by the date one thousand six hundred and one on the south-east angle.

G
east

east to west. The old castle is surrounded by a more modern fortification, faced with stone, of an irregular pentagonal form, defended by five bastions; these out-works, which are in circuit about three quarters of a mile, and encompassed by a deep ditch, circumscribe in the whole about twenty acres : they were added in the time of Queen Elizabeth, and are said to have been constructed on the same plan as those of Antwerp *. On a small projecting stone, on the north-east corner, is carved the date one thousand five hundred and ninety-eight. The entrance is on the west side in the curtin, between two bastions, through a small stone gate-way, on the arch of which is the date one thousand five hundred and ninety eight, with the initial letters E. R.

Castle gates.

This gate leads to a second, of much greater antiquity, machicolated and flanked by two large round towers. It is supposed to have been built by Lord Woodville, in the time of Edward the Fourth, his arms being carved on a stone at the top, and the roses of York on each side. The old gate, with its wicket of strong lattice-work, fastened with large nails at every crossing, is still remaining, and opens into the Castle-yard. Entering the area, on the right hand stands the chapel of St. Nicholas, with its enclosed coemetery, but no service is now performed in it; the present building was erected on the ruins of an ancient chapel, endowed when Domesday-book was compiled. Over the former chapel was an armory, containing breast, back, and head-pieces for two or three troops of horse; but defensive armour being out of use, they were sold by order of Lord Cadogan, when governor. Over the door is carved G. II. 1738; and by a stone tablet at the east end, we are informed that it was

St Nicholas Chapel.

* By an Italian engineer, named Genebella, who had likewise been employed in the fortifications of that city Oglander's Ms.

rebuilt

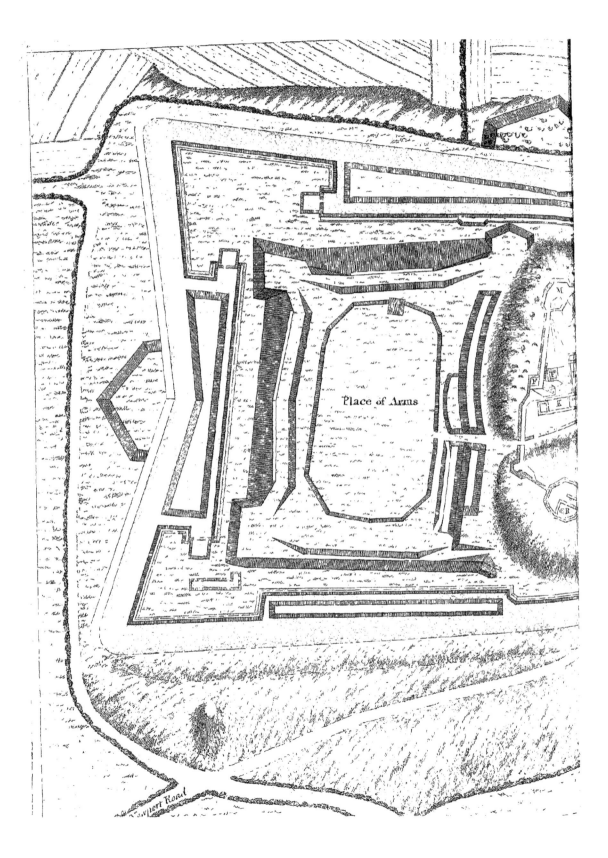

Place of Arms

rebuilt during the government of Lord Lymington. Farther towards the left hand are the ruins of some buildings, said to be those in which King Charles the Firft was confined; and a window is fhewn for that through which he attempted to efcape: beyond thefe are the barracks and governor's houfe; the latter contains feveral good rooms, with coved cielings It has, occafionally, been ufed for a military hofpital; and certainly a more proper place, with refpect to both air and fituation, could not have been found.

In the north-eaft angle of the bafe court*, on a mount raifed confiderably above the other buildings, ftands the Keep, or Dungeon; its figure is an irregular polygon, the afcent to it is by feventy-two fteps up the fide of the mount, and there are more within, each ftep is about nine inches. This multangular tower bears evident marks of great antiquity· fome of the angles are ftrengthened by walling of hewn ftone, which were probably added under Edward the Fourth, when the great gate was rebuilt. There is a well here faid to be three hundred feet deep, but it has been partly filled up as ufelefs and dangerous the Keep commands a moft extenfive and beautiful profpect, which is not con-

The Keep.

---

* The caftle of the Normans, as defcribed by Ph Strutt, in his *Horda Angel cynnan*, correfponds exactly with this of Carifbrooke He fays, " The " Norman caftle confifted of a bafe court, furrounded by lofty earthen banks, " topped with a ftrong wall of ftone, and to this they added a keep, or dungeon, " which is a high hill of earth raifed at one end of the fortification " He alfo obferves, " that the difference between the Saxon and Norman caftles is this, the ' Saxons built one regular entire fortification round, or as near fo as the fituation of " the place would admit, while the Norman caftles confifted of two feparate forti- " fications, the keep and bafe court " It is probable, therefore, that the keep or dungeon of the caftle of Carifbrooke is a Saxon fortification, and that the bafe court was added by the Normans. and what favours this conjecture is, that a part of the wall of the bafe court, which adjoined to the keep on the eaft fide of the mount, is lately fallen, and has left the place where it abutted fo very entire, as to make it probable at leaft, that the keep was originally one feparate building See Strutt, p. 89 and 92 vol 1

fined

fined to the island only, but takes in the New Forest and Portf-down, with the sea intervening at different points.

Montjoy's tower.

At the south-east angle stands the remains of another tower, called Montjoy's Tower, the walls in some places were eighteen feet thick, the view from it not so extensive as that from the Keep. The rampart between these towers is about twenty feet high, and eight feet thick, including a parapet of two feet and a half, which was carried quite round the castle

The well.

Under a small building in the castle yard is another well, more than two hundred feet deep, whence the water for the use of the garrison was drawn by means of a large wheel, turned by an ass. this duty was for forty years performed by the same animal, not long since dead, who, on account of his long services, became one of the curiosities of the place. Down this well it is usual to drop a pin, which, after a lapse of about three seconds of time, produces a greater sound than can well be conceived by those who have not heard it.

Repairs and enlargements.

The castle was probably repaired by Montacute, Earl of Salisbury, who held the lordship of this island in the ninth year of Richard the Second, the three lozenges, the arms of that family, being placed on a buttress at the corner of part of the governor's lodgings, but much the greater portion of the buildings now standing, particularly the governor's apartments, the offices and outworks, were built in the time of Queen Elizabeth, who, at the solicitation of Sir George Carey, when England was threatened with the famous Spanish Armada, gave four thousand pounds towards the expences. Sir George also procured four hundred pounds from the gentlemen of the island, and the commonalty contributed their personal labour, by digging

the

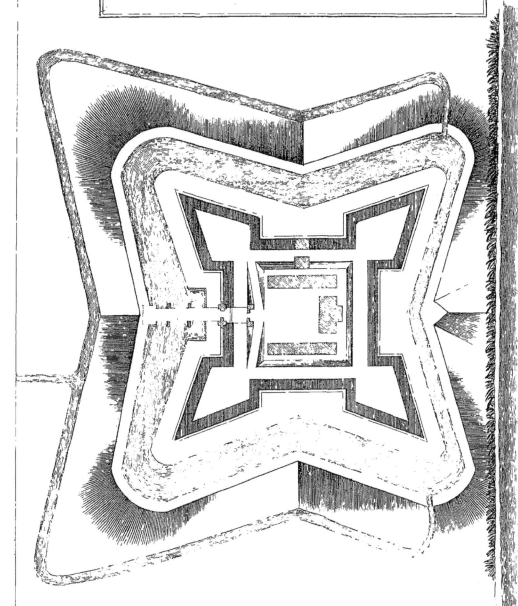

PLAN of SANDOWN FORT

in the ISLE of WIGHT

Scale of Feet

50   100   200

HIGH   WATER   MARK.

the outward ditch gratis *. The governor was affifted in the direction of thefe works by Thomas Worfley, Efq and the whole amount, including the repairs of Yarmouth caftle and Sharpnore fort, is ftill extant in a long parchment roll, figned with the acquittance of the lord treafurer Burghley. This roll contains many curious particulars of the prices of labour and materials at that time. a copy of it is given in the Appendix †. An armourer and fletcher, paid by the queen, were refident here in that reign, as appears by the appointment in Sir Richard Worfley's patent.

The lords of the ifland, and the governors fince their time, have made this caftle their place of refidence The firft charter of the Countefs Ifabella de Fortibus to the town of Newport is dated from hence; and the will of Philippa, Duchefs of York, was publifhed here the ninth year of Henry the Sixth, wherein fhe ftyles herfelf Duchefs of York, and Lady of the Ifle of Wight.

Carifbrooke caftle has been rendered remarkable by the confinement of Charles the Firft, who, taking refuge here, was detained a prifoner from November one thoufand fix hundred and forty-feven to September one thoufand fix hundred and forty-eight, when he was fuffered to remove to Newport, and to renew his treaty with the Parliament. The particulars of his treatment will be mentioned in the account given of the government of Colonel Hammond ‡. On the King's death, it was converted into a prifon for his children, wherein died the Lady Elizabeth, whom the levelling rulers of that time are faid to have intended to apprentice to a button-

---

* Oglander's MS.   † Appendix, No. XVIII.
† In Chap IV.

maker,

maker*. She was buried at Newport. It was likewise made a prison by Cromwell and Charles the Second.

There are several other forts in this island, which were all erected about the thirty-sixth year of Henry the Eighth, when many other forts and blockhouses were built in different parts of the coast of England.

Sandown fort commands a bay on the south-east side of the island, where there is a good landing-place. It is a very low square building, flanked by four bastions, and encompassed by a ditch. Being esteemed of the greatest consequence of any fort in the island, it had an establishment, consisting of a master gunner, and thirty soldiers; but this has since been reduced, and the pay of twenty two of the soldiers applied to increasing the salaries of the master gunners of the other forts It had been much neglected, but lately has been put into repair at a very considerable expence to the crown, and the apartments made fit for the reception of the captain, who resides here in the summer.

Yarmouth castle was built for the defence of the entry into Freshwater, or Yar river it is situated on the north-west part of the island, and at the west end of the town. part of it stands on the wall of the church, demolished by the French in the thirty-fifth of Henry the Eighth. It is much of the same construction with those built in that reign, and was erected under the direction of Richard Worsley, captain of the island, together with another fort, called Worsley's Tower.

Carey's Sconce, or Sharpnore fort, about a mile to the west of Yarmouth, was afterwards built by Sir George Carey, in the

*Hume's Hist of England, chap ix

room

room of Worfley's Tower, which ftood at a very fmall diftance weftward of the Sconce, oppofite Hurft caftle, but was then fallen to decay.

Weft Cowes caftle ftands on the weft fide of the river Medina: it is a fmall ftone building, with a femi-circular battery. Oppofite, on the eaft fide of the river, was another fort of the fame kind; when entire, they jointly protected the harbour. This is now fo totally demolifhed, that there is not the leaft veftige of it remaining.

Cowes Castle

CHAP.

CHAP. III.

Succession of the Lords of the Island, with their Franchises.

THE Lordship of the Isle of Wight does not appear to have been granted to any subject before the Norman conquest. The tenants of the crown, in the time of Edward the Confessor, seem to have held their estates in that island under the same conditions as the landholders in other parts of the kingdom. On the accession of William the Conqueror, that prince granted it to William Fitz Osborne, his kinsman, to be held by him as freely as he himself held the realm of England, as is recorded in the Chartulary of Carisbrooke priory [*], of which Fitz Osborne was the founder. Independent of the ties of consanguinity, he stood high in the King's favour, as being the principal adviser of his expedition to England, marshal of his army at the decisive battle of Hastings, and in other instances greatly instrumental in procuring him the crown; he therefore appears to have been much confided in, as well in council as in war, being entrusted with the castles newly built at Winchester and York, and also made the king's chief justiciary for the [†] north of England, as Odo, the king's brother, was in the south, in which capacity he acted with distinguished equity and prudence, though, with respect to his Lordship of the Isle of Wight, he seems to have assumed a more absolute authority over his dependants there, than was exercised by William over his English subjects, for that king confiscated the lands of such only as had been active in the support of Harold, whereas Fitz Osborne

William Fitz Osborne

[*] In the possession of Sir Richard Worsley, Bart.
[†] Dug. Bar. vol. i. p. 66.

ejected

ejected indifcriminately all the original poffeffors, excepting the
officers or fervants of Edward the Confeffor *, and granted their
lands to his followers He demonftrated his piety according to
the notions of thofe times, by founding two abbeys in Normandy,
one at Lyra, the other at Cormeilles, and alfo a priory at Carifbrook, which, with fix churches in the Ifle of Wight, befides
feveral others fpecified by Dugdale †, he gave to his abbey at
Lyra. it is fomewhat remarkable that among thefe donations he
omitted the church of Carifbrook.   Notwithftanding thefe foundations, it is faid he by fome means incurred the difpleafure of
the monks ‡. He furvived the Conqueft only four years, for
being fent by the Queen to the affiftance of Ernulph, Earl of
Hainhault. who pretended to the Earldom of Flanders, they
were both flain in battle, and Fitz Ofborne was buried in the
Abbey of Cormeilles. He feems to have been induced to adopt
this quarrel from having married for his fecond wife Richildis §,
mother of Ernulph, by whom he had no iffue, but by his firft,
Adeliza, daughter of Roger de Tony, ftandard-bearer to William at the battle of Haftings, he had three fons, William,
who fucceeded to his Norman poffeffions; Ralph, a Monk at
Cormeilles, and Roger, Earl of Hereford, who inherited the
Lordfhip of the Ifle of Wight, and all the other lands belonging
to his father in England.

Roger de Breteville, or de Briftolis, Earl of Hereford, fecond
Lord of the Ifle of Wight, is mentioned in Domefday-book by
the appellation of Comes Rogerus, and is there faid to have
given lands at Wilmingham, in the ifland, to Croc. The king
having, for fome unknown reafons, oppofed the marriage of this
Earl's fifter, named Emma, to Ralph de Waer, Earl of Norfolk,

* See the Survey of the Ifland, extracted from Domefday-book.
† Dug Bar. vol. 1. p. 66   ‡ See Ord. Vital. 536
§ Dug p. 67.

H   both

both Earls were fo much incenfed at it, that they refolved to
Confpires a-
gainft the
king
depofe him, and taking the advantage of his abfence in Normandy, not only accomplifhed the propofed union, but alfo, at the
nuptial entertainment, engaged many of their guefts in the undertaking. Among them was Waltheof *, Earl of Northumberland, who, either fuddenly repenting this rafh engagement,
or in hopes of great rewards for the difcovery, went over immediately to Normandy, and fubmitting himfelf to the King's
mercy, difclofed the confpiracy. This Earl had been loaded
with favours by the Conqueror, who, befides giving him his
niece in marriage, had alfo beftowed on him the Earldoms of
Huntingdon, Northampton, and Northumberland : juftly therefore provoked at his ingratitude and double treachery, the king
caufed him to be beheaded at Winchefter ; perhaps his being an
Englifhman did not weigh much in his favour. Earl Roger,
who had affembled fome forces, retired into his county of Hereford, but being taken and tried, was found guilty of treafon,
Forfeits his
lands, 1078.
and fentenced to perpetual imprifonment †, with the confifcation
of his lands   His fpirit feems to have remained unbroken by
his fufferings, for, at a folemn celebration of the feaft of Eafter,
the king fent him his robes, when he, to fhew his contempt of
what was doubtlefs meant as a compliment, caufed a fire to be
made and burned them   This being told the king, he fwore
by the glory of God, the Earl fhould fpend the remainder of
his life in prifon, which oath he ftrictly kept, as Roger was
Dies in prifon
1086.
never releafed, but died in confinement, and the Ifle of Wight,
with his other lands, efcheated to the crown. Domefday-book
was compiled in the twentieth year of William the Conqueror ;
after the reverfion of this ifland to the King therefore, in the furvey extracted from that ancient record inferted in the Appendix,
thofe lands which had been held of the Lords of the Ifland will

* Rapin, vol i p 73.   † Dugdale, p 67.

be

Plate 1.

N°1

Il anotis tip
N° 243

N°2

N°3

N°4

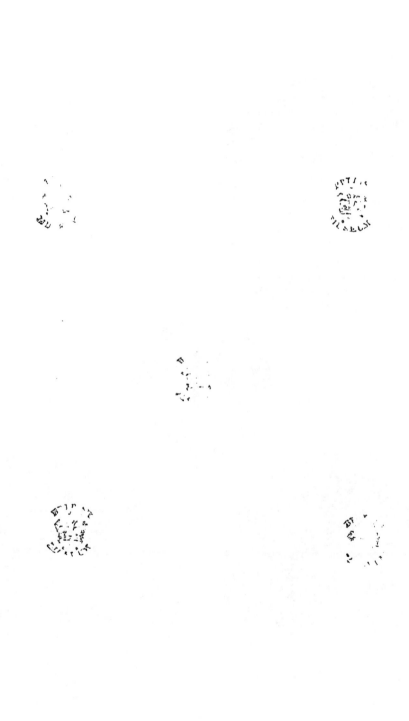

be found in the poffeffion of the crown. It is not known who Earl Roger married; but he left two fons, Renauld and Roger, who proved good foldiers in the fervice of Henry the Firft, but could never obtain the favour of that King.

The Lordfhip of the Ifle of Wight continued in the crown, until Henry I. granted it to Richard de Redvers *, Riparius, or Rivers, the fon of Baldwin de Brion, who was fon of Crifpin, Earl of Brion, the fon of Godfrey, Earl of Eu, illegitimate fon of Richard, firft Duke of Normandy; this Richard was the firft of the family who was called de Redvers†, which appellation he took from a town in Normandy of that name; and being one of the five Barons who adhered to Henry, in the conteft with his brother Robert for the crown, he was greatly in that king's favour, who, according to Camden ‡, gave him the town of Tiverton, and honour of Plimpton, created him Earl of De-vonfhire, with a grant of the third penny of the yearly revenue of that county, amounting to ten marks, and alfo conferred on him the Lordfhip of the Ifle of Wight, which was confidered fo high an honour as to be deemed an addition to his title of Earl, and he was accordingly ftyled Earl of Devonfhire, and Lord of the Ifle of Wight. This Earl enjoyed divers other marks of the royal bounty, among which were the lordfhip and hundred of Chrift-church in Hampfhire, with all the lands from thence to Beaulieu, together with many churches and chapels, namely the collegiate or conventual church of Chrift-church Twyneham, the chapel of Milford, the chapel of Boldre, the churches of Brokenhurft, Holehurft, and Sopley, thefe, with their tithes, he appropriated to Chrift-church, when, from a houfe of fecular

Richard I de Redvers.

* A genealogical table of this family down to the Lady Ifabella de Fortibus, who fold her right in the Ifle of Wight to the Crown, is given in the Appendix, No XII.
† See his feals, Plate II No 6, 7
‡ Will. Malmfb p 156.

canons, he converted it to an Auguſtine monaſtery. He gave, as prebends to the ſaid church the town of Hurne, the lands of Goſſlel, Stanput, Huboin, Strode, Dudcomb, and the two Preſhims, together with Apſe and Hamſtede in the Iſle of Wight *. At his death, which happened in the firſt year of the reign of Stephen, he was ſucceeded in his Earldom of Devon, and Lordſhip of the Iſle of Wight, by his ſon Baldwin †, who, in the conteſt for the throne, was a zealous partizan for the Empreſs Maud ‡, and fortified his caſtle and alſo the Iſle of Wight for her, both which were taken by Stephen, whereupon Baldwin fled out of the kingdom, with his wife and children; but, on the accommodation between the contending parties, was reinſtated in his honours and poſſeſſions. During the life-time of his father he founded the Abbey of Quarr, in the Iſle of Wight, for Ciſtercian Monks § from Savigny, in Normandy. According to Dugdale, the Abbot of Savigny contributed to this foundation, as Baldwin is ſaid to have given his manor of Arreton to Lot Abbot, for him to build a monaſtery.

He founded alſo the Abbey of Breamore, in Wiltſhire, and endowed it with lands granted to his father by Henry the Firſt ‖, part whereof, in the pariſh of Boldre, ſtill retains the name of Roydon ¶ Baldwin died at Quarr, the firſt year of Henry the Second, and was there buried, as were alſo Adeliza, his wife, and his ſon Henry: he left three ſons, Richard, William, and Henry.

Richard, the ſecond Earl of Devon of that name, ſucceeded to the Lordſhip of the Iſle of Wight he married Dyoniſia, daughter of Reginald, Earl of Cornwal, natural ſon of Henry

Marginal notes:
Baldwin I. de Redvers, 1135.

Quarr Abbey founded, 1132.

Abbey of Breamore.

1155.

Richard II de Redvers.

---

* Dug Mon vol , p. 790 *Le Abbat de Ford* Bar. vol. i p. 254.
† Plate I No 1 the ſeal of Baldwin, from a drawing in the poſſeſſion of Thomas Aſtle, Eſq.   ‡ Dug. Bar.   § Mon Anglic. vol 1.
‖ Ib d   ¶ Roydon, i e, King's gift.

the

Plate II

Ex Asplogia Tab 101 Brooke time de coll time

the Firft, by whom he left iffue Baldwin and Richard, fucceffively Earls of Devonfhire; he died at the city of Mante in France. This Earl not only confirmed all his father's donations to the Abbey of Quarrera, but alfo added divers lands, with the tythe of his falt at Lymington, on condition that they fhould pray for the fouls of his father and mother.

Baldwin de Redvers fucceeded his father, and was, like him, the fecond of his name; he married Alice, daughter of Ralph de Dole, in Berry, and died without iffue.

Richard fucceeded his brother in his honours and eftates · he married Margaret †, daughter and co-heirefs of John, Lord Biffet. He gave lands to the Abbey of Breamore ‡, that prayers might be offered up by the monks for the foul of Earl Richard his father, his own health, and that of the Countefs Margaret, his wife. He died without iffue, and was buried at Montzbourg, in Normandy.

William, furnamed de Vernon, from the place of his birth in Normandy, was the fecond fon of the firft Earl of Devon of the name of Baldwin, and fucceeded his nephew §. He was one of the four nobles who fupported the filken canopy over Richard the Firft, at his fecond coronation at Winchefter, after his return from captivity in Germany. He was there ftyled Earl of the Ifle of Wight ‖ He married Mabel, daughter of Robert Earl of Mellent ¶. He gave lands to the Abbey of Quarrera, for the benefit of the fouls of Henry the Second, Baldwin his father, Adeliza his mother, Earl Richard his brother, and Mabel his

---

* Mon Ang vol. i   † See her feal, Plate III No 12

‡ Clau 47 Hen. III m 7.   § Plate I No 2, 3

‖ Rog. Hoveden.   ¶ Dug Bar. vol p 256

wife.

Is oppreffed
by King
John

wife. He, among the other Barons, experienced the tyranny and extortion of King John, who obliged him to pay five hundred marks to be reinftated in his caftle at Plympton and other eftates, with permiffion to govern his tenants and others in the Ifle of Wight by military fervice, and according to the laws of the land, by judgement in his court, and that he might do with his lands as he ought. Although thefe conceffions amounted to very little more, than a permiffion quietly to enjoy his right, they were favours not to be obtained gratis in thofe times. Juftice in the king's courts being often fold by the crown, till at length the Barons, made defperate by immoderate and repeated extortions, fought redrefs by the fword, and obtained a ratification of that bulwark of liberty, juftly ftyled the Great Charter.

Its death,
1216.

King John, fearful of the Earl's refentment for this extortion, obliged him to deliver his grandfon as a hoftage for his fidelity. William refided moftly at his caftle of Carefbrooke, he expended three hundred pounds in erecting a monument for his father and himfelf in Quarr Abbey, where he died, and was buried, in the firft year of Henry the Third.

His iffue,
1209

Thus far Sir William Dugdale's account of this family has been followed, but in the fucceffions form this period there are feeming contradictions and difficulties not eafily reconciled, but from the moft careful examination, it is collected that William de Vernon had iffue Baldwin, who married the daughter of Waryn Fitz Gerald, Chamberlain, to King John, and died before his father, leaving a fon of his own name, William had alfo two daughters, Mary, the eldeft, who married Sir Robert Courtney, fon of Reginald, from which marriage proceeded the Earls of Devon of that family; the fecond, named Joan, efpoufed William Bruer the Younger, Lord of Torbay; after

whofe

Plate III

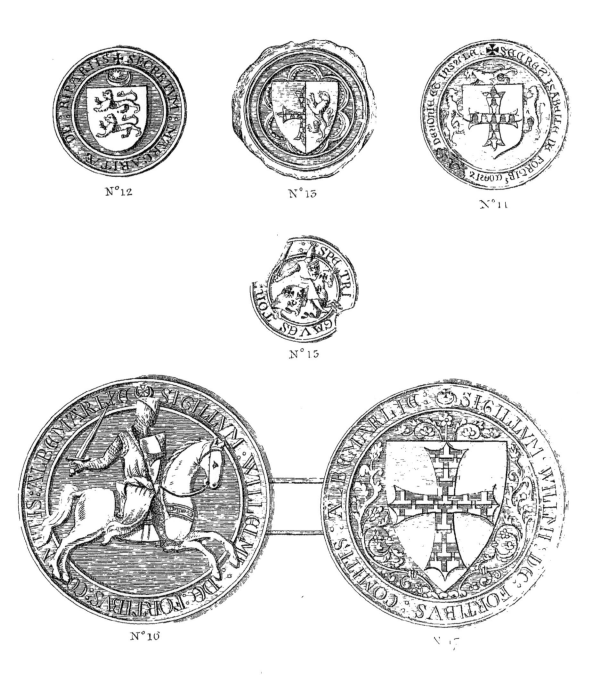

Nº 12

Nº 13

Nº 11

Nº 15

Nº 16

Nº 17

whose death she married the famous Hubert de Burgh, Earl of Kent*, and had for part of her portion the Lordship of the Isle of Wight; she dying without issue, the island reverted to the male heir of her father.

Baldwin, the third Earl of Devon, and Lord of the Isle of Wight, was the grandson of Earl William: he died soon after his grandfather.

Baldwin III. 1227

Baldwin the fourth succeeded his father. being a minor, his wardship was granted to Richard, Earl of Cornwal, but this grant was shortly after recalled; and, for a fine of two thousand marks, paid by Gilbert de Clare, Earl of Gloucester, the marriage of this Baldwin was granted to him, through the mediation of the Earl of Cornwal; he also obtained the investiture of the Isle of Wight†, and married Amicia‡, daughter of the Earl of Gloucester, by whom he had issue a son named Baldwin, and a daughter called Isabella: he died five years after his marriage, and was interred in Quarr Abbey.

Baldwin IV

1240.

Baldwin, the fifth of that name, Earl of Devon, and Lord of the Isle of Wight, married the lady Avicia, of the house of

Baldwin V.
1251.

---

* This fact is ascertained by the following record

Sciant præsentes et futuri quod ita conven inter Willhmum de Vernon comitem Devon & Hubertum de Burgo domini Regis camerarium super maritagio Johannæ filiæ ipsius comitis junioris, quam idem comes dedit in uxorem prædicto Huberto, ad petitionem et voluntatem et assensum domini Regis, quod idem comes assignavit filiæ suæ priori natu, caput honoris sui in Devon cum castello de Plimpton cum esneseya et cum rationabili parte quam cum contingit de hæreditate sua, Johannæ vero filiæ suæ juniori assignavit totam insulam de Wicht. et Christchurche cum rationabili parte, &c. &c. Cart. 1 Johis, pt. 11 No. 41.

See his Seal, Plate I. No 4 and 5.

† Matt Paris

‡ See Plate II No. 8 and 9, the seals of Baldwin and Amicia his wife.

Savoy, coufin to Queen Eleanor. He received the honour of knighthood at the nuptials of the Duke of Britanny with Beatrix the King's daughter. The firft charter of franchifes to the town of Yarmouth was given by this Earl, who alfo obtained the grant of a market and fair to be held at Carifbrooke. He is faid to have died of poifon, given him at the table of his kinfman, Peter de Savoy. He had only one fon, named John, who died at ten years of age.

Grants a charter to Yarmouth.

The fucceffion then devolved on Ifabella *, who, though heir to all the honours and eftates of her brother, did not obtain poffeffion of the Lordfhip of the Ifle of Wight, Chrift-church, and other lands of her inheritance, till the twelfth of Edward the Firft, on the death of her mother Amicia, who enjoyed them as her dower. The Countefs Ifabel married William de Fortibus, Earl of Albemarle, and furviving him, was ftyled Countefs of Albemarle and Devon, and Lady of the Ifle of Wight. Her chief refidence was at the caftle of Carifbrooke, where fhe maintained great ftate and dignity; fhe alfo gave many inftances of her piety, by very confiderable benefactions to different religious houfes, both confirming the grants of her anceftors, and adding frefh ones of her own. In particular, fhe gave to her mother Amicia the inheritance of the manor of Buckland, in Devonfhire, Brickeley, Woolhampton, and Celliton, with the hundred advowfons of churches and appurtenances, with which that Lady endowed the Abbey of Buckland †. She moreover confirmed her mother's gift of the manor of Shorwell to the nuns of Laycock, in Wiltfhire; as alfo the donations of her predeceffors, and thofe who held under her in the Ifle of Wight, to the monks of Quarr. And gave to the canons of Bolton the Lordfhip of Wiggedon

Ifabella de Fortibus, 1283.

Her grants.

* See her Seal, Plate II No 13, 14
† Monaft. Anglic vol I p 790 b n.

Plate IV

Nº 18

Nº 19

Nº 20

Nº 21

Nº 22

Nº 23

and Brandone, with other lands *. To the Abbey of Mont-burg in Normandy, she confirmed the manor of Lodres, in Dor-setshire, with the Lordships of Armue, Wolveley, Appuldur-combe, and Wyke, which had been granted to that Abbey by her ancestors †.

Notwithstanding her regard for monastic institutions, she was a strenuous defender of her rights against the encroachments of the monks, with whom she had several controversies, claiming and exercising the authority of patron over such religious houses as had been founded by her ancestors. Among these were the Abbey of Quarr, with the priories of Carisbrooke, Christ-church, and Breamore. The Rolls of Parliament ‡ record a complaint made by the Abbot of Quair against the Countess Isabella, for with-holding lands belonging to that Abbey; where-upon the King issued his precept to William de Braybeuf, Sheriff of Hampshire, directing him to take the Abbey and lands into the royal protection, until the differences should be determined §. What was the cause of contest with the Abbey of Breamore does not appear, but Edward the First desired the Bishop of Winchester to give the church of Brading to the Convent of Breamore, in con-sideration of their great losses, sustained chiefly by the Lady Isa-bel de Fortibus. On the vacancy of a Prior of Christ-church, she assumed the power of holding the lands of the Convent in her hands; and a Prior of Carisbrooke being elected, without her approbation, she summoned him to answer in her court. Powers of this nature were sometimes asserted, even in those times, by patrons of religious houses, and that even to the Pope himself, as may be seen in a letter from Pope Alexander the Fourth to the nobility of England, cited by Mr. Selden.

* Monast. Anglic vol. ii p 103. a n. 10 20 30
† Idem 992. a n. 60.   ‡ Rol Parl 7 Edw. I.
§ See this precept in the Appendix, No. XX.

I   The

The Counteſs Iſabella, by a charter of franchiſes, formed a new borough, ſince called Newport *. To authenticate her public deeds ſhe made uſe of two different ſeals, the one with her own paternal coat, including her huſband's arms, with which ſhe ſealed her charter to Richard de Affeton †, the other her huſband's arms only ‡. It appears by the records in the Exchequer §, that Robert Ragolf, ſervant to the Counteſs of Albemarle, came before the Treaſury and Barons of the Exchequer, where he declared that he had loſt the great ſeal of that Counteſs, in Weſt Cheap, proclamation was therefore made in the courts of Exchequer, Chancery, and the Great Hall, that any deed ſealed with it, either by Chriſtian or Jew, ſhould be void. It ſeems as if this ſeal was never found, or at leaſt not reſtored to the owner, as Biſhop Nicholſon informs us ‖ he had ſeen a grant, dated in twelve hundred and forty-ſeven, concluding with theſe words, " in teſtimony whereof I have ſealed this writing with my new ſeal, my former one being loſt." This ſerves to ſhew the great authority carried by the ſeal in ancient days; the learned Biſhop cites Glanville ¶, to ſhew that the ſeal was not only the eſſence of the deed, but that when the ſeal was well proved it was concluſive evidence againſt the grantor. And being of ſuch force, in thoſe times, it was frequent, among ſuch inferior people as bore

* See Appendix, No XXI

† Releaſing a rent of thirteen ſhillings, payable for his water-mill in Affeton.

‡ The coat of argent, a chief, gules was the paternal arms of the Earl of Albemarle, named de Fortibus, the croſs vaire was borne by the family of Le Groſſe; but on the marriage of William de Fortibus with Hawiſe, the heireſs of William le Groſſe, Earl of Albemarle, in conſideration of her being ſo rich an heireſs, he, as was formerly uſual, aſſumed her arms; as may be obſerved by the ſeals of Iſabella de Redvers, and William, Earl of Albemarle, her huſband. See Plate III. No 13, 14, 16, and 17.

§ Inter recogniciones de term. Sanct. Trin. 1 Edw I.

‖ Hiſtor. Library, p. 111 chap. 6. " In cujus rei teſtamonium huic ſcripto ſigillum meum innovatum appoſui, quia ſigillum quod prius habui amiſi."

¶ Glanvil lib. x. cap. 12

Plate V

N° 24

N° 20

N° 27

no arms, to have their deeds fealed with the common feal of fome public office or corporation, affigning for reafon, that their feal was altogether unknown *.

The Countefs Ifabella had by her hufband, William de Forti-bus, three fons, John, Thomas, and William; with two daugh-ters, Avice and Aveline: who, furviving her brothers † and fifter, became the fole heir of thofe vaft poffeffions; her ward-fhip was granted to Richard, Earl of Glocefter, for the term of her minority, being fifteen years. This grant was fhortly after furrendered, and transferred to Edmund, furnamed Crouch Back, fecond fon of King Henry the Third, to whom fhe was afterwards married.

King Edward the Firft, in the fourth year of his reign, en-tered into a treaty with Edmund and Aveline for the fale of the Ifle of Wight, on certain conditions, that they fhould affure it, with other lands, to him; but fhe dying foon after, without iffue, and before the purchafe could be concluded, the propofal did not take effect. The King, perfifting in his defire to obtain this ifland, prevailed, as it feems by repeated follicitations, on Ifabella to dif-pofe of it to him, and fhe fealed the conveyance on her death-bed, its validity was however questioned in parliament after her deceafe.

Ifabella de Fortibus enjoyed the office of Chamberlain of the Exchequer, which fhe executed by a deputy, named William de Cotton, as had formerly been done by Margaret de Redvers, a precept having been iffued to the Barons, to admit fuch deputy, notwithftanding he was not a knight.

* Nicholfon ut fupra, " Quia figillum meum penitus eft ignotum, figillum offi-cialis de N apponi procuravi."

† Dug. Bar. vol. 1, p 65.

Ifabella

Isabella built Powderham castle, in Devonshire, which devolved, with other lands in that county, to Hugh Courtney, her heir, afterwards Earl of Devon. She died at her manor of Stockwell, near Lambeth, in Surry, a few hours after signing the above mentioned instrument, and was interred in the Priory of Breamore, in Wiltshire.

Hugh de Courtney, as heir to the Countess Isabel, claimed the Isle of Wight *, the manor of Christ-church, with divers other possessions in the county of Southampton, of which he alleged she died seised, disputing the authenticity of the conveyance to the crown · an examination into that transaction was brought before the Parliament, when the following allegations were made by the contending parties.

On the part of Courtney it was urged, that the conveyance was suspected to be either forged, or fraudulently obtained, as the deceased Countess had constantly refused to part with the Isle of Wight, not only when applied to by the King's agents, but also when sollicited by himself in person. Sir William Dugdale appears to be of this opinion.

On the contrary, it was deposed by Sir Richard Afton, Steward of the Houshold to that Countess, that she had been negociating with the King for the sale of the Isle of Wight, upwards of ten years, at the price of *four thousand pounds*. That in a journey to Canterbury she made London in her way, purposely to conclude the bargain, but that the King told her, it would be time enough at her return And that he had often heard the Countess, in her life-time, declare her resolution to sell the island, assigning for reason, the remote degree of relationship between her and her

* See Appendix, No XXII.

heir,

heir, declaring that fhe might, if fo difpofed, marry one nearer allied to her, without trefpaffing on the prefcribed degrees of confanguinity.

Gilbert de Knouill, another fervant of the late Countefs, teftified that the Bifhops of Durham and Coventry were deputed by the King, to treat with that Lady for the fale of the ifland, that they agreed, in behalf of the King, to pay *fix thoufand marks* for the purchafe, and that the deed in the King's poffeffion was executed at Stockwell, and the money paid the day following, at the houfe of the Bifhop of Durham, to the merchants of Spina †, for the ufe of her executors.

---

* *A mark is thirteen fhillings and four pence; fix thoufand marks are equal to four thoufand pounds fterling.* When the value of money and land, at the time of the purchafe (which took place on the death of Ifabella de Fortibus, in the year 1293, are compared with their prefent eftimation, the confideration money here paid will be found much greater than it at firft appears. According to feveral inquifitions taken at different periods, it appears that lands, on an average, have increafed in value fince that time in the proportion of eighteen to one, or, in other words, were, about the year 1293, worth only one eighteenth of the prefent value. It is alfo agreed that the value of money has decreafed fince that year in the proportion of *fifteen to one*, that is, fifteen fhillings will now purchafe no more of any commodity than could be bought for one. From thefe data it may be concluded that the *four thoufand pounds* paid for the Ifle of Wight, was in value equal to *fixty thoufand pounds* at this prefent time, and farther, if the land at one eighteenth of its prefent value coft a fum equal to *fixty thoufand pounds*, a proportional purchafe in its improved ftate would amount to *eighteen times fixty thoufand pounds*, or one million and eighty thoufand pounds, the ifland containing about a hundred thoufand acres, this fum amounts to about ten pounds fixteen fhillings and three-pence the acre. Nor is it to be fuppofed that four thoufand pounds was the value of the whole ifland in 1293, for before that time the religious houfes had confiderable property in the ifland, befides which there were other freeholds, for which Ifabela de Fortibus could not receive any confideration, the encreafe the of defending the ifland muft have leffened the confideration money paid by Edward the Firft.

† Spina, or Spene, was formerly a town of note, now a village, about a mile from Newbury, in Berkfhire, in which a great woollen manufactory was at that time carried on by a company of merchants, called in the record, merce town de Spina. It feems, from the money being paid to them, as if they alfo acted as brokers.

Brother

Brother William de Gainsborough, Confessor to the Countess, deposed, that the Bishop of Durham asked her, if she continued in the same mind with respect to selling the island to the King; that she replied, she did: that the Bishop then asked her, if he should draw up a deed for that purpose; and, on her, answering in the affirmative, he immediately caused the deed to be prepared, and brought it to the Countess, when it was read to her in the presence of Gilbert de Knouill, Geoffry, her Chaplain, her waiting women, and himself, with many others of the family: that she made her woman fetch her seal, when she sealed the deed, and delivered seisin of the island, and other lands conveyed to the King, by delivering the Bishop's gloves, which she held in her hand. That the Bishop then left her, and she reposed herself. and about nine o'clock he asked her, if she would not make her will; she answered, she was so much fatigued, that she feared speaking much would weaken her, but, on a second sollicitation she complied, and signified by her fingers that her executors should be, the Abbot of Quarr, the Priors of Breamore and Christ church, and Gilbert de Knouill: that she then lay down to rest, and, after some time, was shrived by him, the said brother William; and died between midnight and morning.

Walter, Bishop of Litchfield and Coventry, testified that, pursuant to an order from the Bishop of Durham, he met him at the Countess's house at Stockwell, at one o'clock; and that in the garden there he drew up the deed, by direction of the said Bishop, who took it from him and carried it to the Countess to be executed, and afterwards brought it back to him sealed with her seal [*].

[*] The whole process of this transaction, taken from the Rolls of Parliament, is referred to in the Appendix.

The

The contents of her will are not known; but as she died without issue, and as three of her executors were ecclesiastics, and superiors of monasteries, founded by her ancestors, and also considering it was made on her death-bed, it is probable that great part of her property was appropriated to pious uses. Five years after her decease, in the twenty-sixth year of Edward the First, Hugh Courtney, her heir, on his proving himself entitled to the third penny of the county of Devon, was admitted to the Earldom, without a new creation.

King Edward having thus obtained the Lordship of this island, retained it in his own hands during his life, appointing keepers or wardens over it, styled Custodes: these he frequently changed, as will appear in the next chapter. On the accession of Edward the Second, that prince, in the first year of his reign, granted it to his favourite Piers Gaveston *, his wife, and the heirs of his body; commanding Nicholas de Bosco †, then warden, to give him possession; but, on the remonstrances of his nobility, Edward resumed the grant the ensuing year, and conferred both the Lordship of the Island, and the castle of Carisbrooke, on his eldest son, Edward ‡, then styled Earl of Chester, afterwards King Edward the Third §. That prince kept them in his possession as long as he lived, governing them by wardens, as had before been practised by his grandfather; these he generally chose out of the chief gentlemen of the island, judging them the fittest to defend their own lands. An instance is recorded in the Rolls of Parliament, where he even permitted the inhabitants to elect their warden. That monarch's pretensions to the crown of France gave the islanders frequent occasions to exert their courage in

1307

Piers Gaveston.

1308
Prince Edward

* See Plate V. No. 24 and 25.   † Lisle of Wootton.
‡ Rot. Parl. 11 Edw. II.   § See his seal, Plate III No 15.

then

their own defence, feveral attacks having been made on them in this and the fucceeding reign.

Richard the Second, in the ninth year of his reign, granted the Lordfhip of this ifland, and caftle of Carifbrooke, to William Montacute, Earl of Salifbury *, for life: he was the fon of Sir William Montacute, who, for his fervice in apprehending Roger Mortimer in the Queen's apartment, in the fourth year of Edward the Third, was created Earl of Salifbury †. Nor was his fon lefs remarkable for his military exploits, being deemed one of the greateft foldiers of the age, and had been employed by King Edward in moft of his expeditions againft the French and Scots, in which he acquired much honour. He firft married Joan, daughter of Edmund, Earl of Kent, the fon of Edward the Firft, but fhe having been before married to Sir Thomas Holland who was then living, the marriage was declared void. This lady, who by the death of her brother became Countefs of Kent, after the deceafe of Sir Thomas Holland, and whilft the Earl of Salifbury was alive, married Edward the Black Prince, by whom fhe was the mother of Richard the Second. The Earl of Salifbury afterwards efpoufed Elizabeth, daughter of John, Lord Mohun of Dunfter Caftle, by whom he had only one fon, named William, who was unhappily flain at a tournament at Windfor, in the fixth year of Richard the Second. By his teftament, executed at Chrift-church Twyneham, in the twentieth year of Richard the Second, wherein he ftyles himfelf Earl of Salifbury, and Lord of the ifles of Wight and Man, he directed that his body fhould be interred in the conventual church of Buftlefham, founded by his father, and that every day until his corpfe fhould arrive at that place, feventy-five fhillings fhould be diftributed

* See his feal, Plate II No 10, and No 11, that of the Countefs of Salifbury.
† Dugdales Bar. vol 1 p 647.

in

In alms to three hundred poor perſons · that twenty-four poor perſons, each dreſſed in a gown of black cloth, with a red hood, ſhould bear torches of eight pounds weight on the day of his funeral: as alſo, that there ſhould be nine wax lights, and three mortars of wax about his body, and banners of his arms placed on every pillar of the church Moreover, that thirty pounds ſhould be given to the religious to ſing trentals, and pray for his ſoul; and laſtly, that his executors ſhould expend five hundred marks in finiſhing the ſtructure at Burſtleſham, and on erecting a tomb there for his father and mother, as alſo another for himſelf and ſon. He died the ſame year *, without iſſue, his large poſſeſſions † were inherited by Sir John de Montacute, his nephew.

1397.

Edward, Earl of Rutland ‡, ſon of Edmund de Langley §, the fifth ſon of Edward the Third, created Duke of Albemarle, obtained a grant of the Iſle of Wight, and caſtle of Cariſbrooke, in tail male; he had alſo a grant of the Iſles of Guernſey and Jerſey for life, and was at the ſame time conſtituted Warden of the New Foreſt, in Hampſhire, Chief Juſtice of all the foreſts ſouth of Trent, Conſtable of Dover caſtle, and Warden of the Cinque Ports, and afterwards Conſtable of England. From all theſe appointments, it is evident he was much loved and truſted by the King. He heſitated at nothing to gratify his mother's licentious humour, and was not only privy and conſenting to the murder of his uncle, the Duke of Glouceſter, but alſo ſent his cook to aſſiſt in it: for which he was rewarded with a grant in

Edward, Earl of Rutland, afterwards Duke of York.

---

* On the death of William, Earl of Saliſbury, Thomas Holland, Earl of Kent, afterwards Duke of Surrey, had a grant of the cuſtody of Cariſbrooke caſtle, with its fees for his life: he was beheaded in the firſt year of Henry the Fourth.

† Dugd Bar vol 1 p 648, 649

‡ See his ſeal, Plate V No 27.

§ Edmund of Langley was the firſt Duke of York of the blood of the Plantagenets.

K   tail

tail fpecial, of feveral manors, lands, &c. belonging to the Duke, together with other manors of Richard, Earl of Arundel, and Thomas Earl of Warwick, who were attainted in parliament. But he did not long enjoy thefe large poffeffions: for Richard the Second being fhortly after depofed, Henry the Fourth degraded him from the Dukedom of Albemarle. He

1399. then entered into a confpiracy with the Dukes of Surrey and Exeter, and John, Earl of Salifbury, to kill the King at Windfor, on the Twelfth Night, but, on difclofing this plot to the King, he was both pardoned and reinftated in his lands; he fhortly after fo far gained the King's confidence as to be appointed his Lieutenant in the Duchy of Acquitaine. His father dying, Auguft the firft, one thoufand four hundred and one, in the third year of Henry the Fourth, he had livery of all his lands, and in the parliament, held in the feventh of that King, was reftored to his hereditary title of Duke of York. In the fecond year of Henry the Fifth, he was conftituted Juftice of South Wales, and Warden of the Eaft Marches towards Scotland. The next year, attending the King to France, he obtained leave to lead the van at the battle of Agincourt; but, being a fat and unweildy man, was thrown down and fmothered in the throng*. His body was brought to Fotheringay †, and interred in the choir, under a flat flab of marble, with his effigy on a plate of brafs: his obfequies were celebrated with great pomp, at the King's expence, on his return to England. This Earl, though perhaps too obfequious a courtier, was neverthelefs a gallant foldier: he married Philippa, the third daughter and coheir of John, Lord de Mohun, Baron of Dunfter, by whom he left no iffue.

* October the twenty-fifth, one thoufand four hundred and fifteenth

† He built the collegiate church of Fotheringay, vefting feveral eftates and churches in the hands of truftees for finifhing and endowing it, but it was not completed till the twenty-fixth of Henry the Sixth.

On

On his death the Duchefs of York obtained a grant, in the third year of Henry the Fifth, of the Lordfhip of the Ifle of Wight, for her life, the caftle and manor of Carifbrooke, with the manor of Bowcombe, and the church of Frefhwater: fhe died in the year one thoufand four hundred and thirty, feifed alfo of the manors of Niton, Whitfield, Pann, and Thorney, with the foreft of Bordwood, in the fame ifland, which fhe enjoyed in fatisfaction of dower.

Philippa, Duchefs of York. 1415.

In the feventeenth year of Henry the Sixth, Humphrey, Duke of Gloucefter, fon of Henry the Fourth, fucceeded to the Lordfhip of this ifland, by virtue of a grant of the reverfion thereof, after the deceafe of the Duchefs of York; this deed bears date only fome few days fubfequent to the grant made to that Duchefs. Although Humphrey was not only brave, but alfo a zealous promoter of learning, his character is varioufly delineated; and the propriety of the diftinguifhed appellation of the *Good Duke,* fo commonly beftowed on him, is far from univerfally allowed He died in the twenty-fifth year of Henry the Sixth, and is fuppofed to have held the ifland to the time of his death *. Although, two years before that event, Henry Beauchamp, Duke of Warwick, fon of Richard, Earl of Warwick, late Regent of France, was crowned King † of the Ifle of Wight ‡; King Henry, in perfon, affifting at the ceremonial,

and

Humphrey, Duke of Gloucefter, 1439.

---

* Henry Trenchard had the office of Conftable of Carifbrooke caftle, by a grant from the King, commencing from the death of Duke Humphrey

A copy of a grant from Henry the Fifth of the Lordfhip of the Ifle of Wight to the Duchefs of York is given in the Appendix, No XXIII. it recites the form of grant to her hufband; the office of Conftable of the caftle of Carifbrooke is particularly excepted

† By Pat twenty-fourth Henry Sixth

‡ Leland Itiner. vol vi fol 91 " Henricus Comes de Warwike ob Henric " VI. cui chariffimus erat, coronatus in regem de Wighte, et poftea nominatus

K 2

" primus

Henry, Duke
of Warwick,
crowned
King of this
island.

and placing the crown on his head. This, though a very honourable mark of the royal favour, conveyed no regal authority [*], the King having no power to transfer the sovereignty of any part of his dominions, as is observed by my Lord Coke, in his Institutes, where this transaction is discussed; and there is reason to conclude, that though titular King, he did not even possess the Lordship of the island, no surrender appearing from Duke Humphrey, who was then living, and had, as before observed, a grant for the term of his life. Henry died soon

1415

after these honours had been conferred on him by the King, at his castle of Hanley, in Worcestershire, on the eleventh of June, one thousand four hundred and forty-five, in the twenty-second year of his age: leaving no issue male, the regal title expired with him, and the Lordship of the island, at the death of the Duke of Gloucester, reverted to the crown.

Among the records in the Tower of London are found two petitions from the inhabitants of the island, dated the twenty-eighth of Henry the Sixth [†], one to the King, and the other to the Parliament, complaining of the bad government, and de-

"primus comes totius Angliæ Henricus VI rex Angl post 2 annos dedit in ti-
"tulum Ducis Worwicensis Dedit etiam in castrum Pristolliæ, &c et insulas
"de Garnacy et Gersey, &c" Leland takes this ex Libello de Antiquitate Theol si-
burensis Monasterii, in the church of which house this Duke of Warwick was
buried very little notice has been taken of this singular event by our historians,
and was it not for some other collateral evidence, the authenticity of it might be
doubted, especially as the monks were apt to magnify in setting forth the grandeur
and antiquity of the families of their Patrons, but the representation of this Duke
with an imperial crown on his head, and a scepter before him, in an ancient window of the college church at Warwick, leaves little room to doubt that such an
event did take place See the Plate copied from an accurate drawing.

† Mr Selden, treating of the title of King of Man, observes, that it was like
that of King of the isle of Wight, in the great Beauchamp, Duke of Warwick,
who was crowned King, under Henry the Sixth Titles of Honour, p. 29.

‡ See Appendix, No. XXIV.

fence-

Henr, Duke of Warwick and King of the
Isle of wight

Elianor Dutchess of Somerset sister to Henry
D. of Warwick King of the Isl. Wight

fencelefs ftate of the ifland at that time; and, though the particulars are not clearly ftated, nor, perhaps from the confufion of affairs, illuftrated by any contemporary records, yet they neverthelefs afford fufficient evidence to rank Richard Plantagenet, Duke of York*, father of King Edward the Fourth among the Lords of the ifland. He is not indeed expresfly fo termed, but is mentioned in the fecond petition as exercifing fuch acts of government there, as could only be performed by one vefted with that authority. for he had appointed one John Newport his Lieutenant, and Steward of the ifland; and, on his mifbehaviour, difplaced him, and conferred that employment on Henry Brune. Newport, after his difmiffion, although negotiating with the King for his re eftablifhment, took advantage of the relaxed ftate of government, and committed great outrages on the inhabitants, both by land and fea, which are pathetically fet forth in the petition; but the King and Parliament, as well as the Duke of York, were then too much engaged to afford them relief.

1449
Richard,
Duke of
York.

The hiftory of this Duke is well known, the King's conftitutional imbecility increafing, he was invefted with the adminiftration of government, under the title of Protector. his birth, influence, and connexions infpired him with the hopes of afcending the throne, but his conduct in the attempt was too mild and cautious for the turbulence of thofe times, though fufficiently explicit to drive him into meafures that terminated in his deftruction. He loft his life at the battle of Wakefield, leaving his more daring fon to reap the fruit of his pretenfions.

1455

In the thirty-firft year of Henry the Sixth, Edmund, Duke of Somerfet, who married the fifter and coheir of Henry, Duke of Warwick, before mentioned as King of the ifland, having

Edmund,
Duke of
Somerfet,

---

* See Plate IV. No 18 and 19, No 20 his wife.

fome

some time before supplanted the Duke of York in the Regency of France, obtained a grant of this island, and the castle of Carisbrooke, to him and the heirs male of his body, in satisfaction, as it was alleged, for certain sums of money due to him from the King's Exchequer, and for the duties of petty customs in the port of London, which were part of his inheritance *. This Duke was slain at the first battle of St. Alban's, in the thirty-third year of Henry the Sixth †.

Henry, Duke of Somerset.

Henry, Duke of Somerset, his son, succeeded him in the Lordship of this island on some disgust he quitted the royal party, and went over to that of the Duke of York, but afterwards returning to the King's service, he was taken prisoner by the Yorkists, at the battle of Hexham, and by them beheaded.

1461 Anthony, Earl Rivers.

In the sixth year of Edward the Fourth, Anthony de Wydeville, or Woodville, Lord Schales †, and after his father's demise, Earl Rivers, had a grant of this island, with the castle of

1466.

Carisbrooke, and all other rights appertaining to the Lordship, to him and his heirs male; after the decease of that King, he, standing in the way of the ambitious views of Richard, Duke of

1483.

Gloucester, was seized, and, without any legal process, beheaded in Pontefract castle §.

Sir Edward Wydeville.

Sir Edward Wydeville, brother of the aforementioned Anthony, Earl Rivers, was, in the first year of Henry the Seventh, made Captain of the Island. Sir William Dugdale ‖ supposes him to have been the brother of the first Earl Rivers; but in that

* In Officio Remembr Thes.
† See his seal, Plate V No 28
‡ Lord Schales was uncle to Edward the Fifth.
§ See his seal, Plate IV. No 23
‖ Dugd. Bar. vol II. p 231.

he

he is miftaken, as well as in terming him Governor of the Ifle of Wight, a title not affumed till many years after, by the Captain of the ifland. This Sir Edward Wydeville, in the fourth year of Henry the Seventh, undertook, with a force raif- ed in this ifland, to affift the Duke of Brittany, againft the King of France, conceiving it would be pleafing to his mafter, who was fuppofed fecretly to favour the Duke's intereft, though then acting as a mediator between the contending parties Sir Ed- ward, therefore, firft afked permiffion to engage in that caufe, and receiving a denial, imagined it was only given to fave ap- pearances, and that the King would not be difpleafed with a private attempt in the Duke's favour; he therefore repaired to the Ifle of Wight, and, convening the inhabitants by a ge- neral mufter, he then propofed the bufinefs to the Gentlemen, telling them how acceptable it would be to the King, how ho- nourable to themfelves, and how greatly demonftrative of their regard to him, which he fhould ever gratefully retain in his me- mory; and that to requite them, he would not only employ his whole fortune, but alfo all his intereft with his Sovereign. He farther expatiated on the juftice of the caufe, informing them that the King of France was not only endeavouring to poffefs himfelf of the Dukedom of Brittany, but alfo of the Duke's daughter, the lawful wife of Maximilian, King of the Romans, and that if thefe defigns were fuffered to fucceed, they would have a very difagreeable neighbour, inftead of their ancient and good allies the Dukes of Brittany. This harangue had but too good fuccefs, great numbers flocking to his ftandard, out of thefe he felected about forty Gentlemen, and four hundred of the ftouteft from the commonalty, who embarked at St. Helen's in four vef- fels; they were clothed in white coats, with red croffes, and were joined by fifteen hundred of the Duke's forces, dreffed in the fame uniform, to make the auxiliaries appear the more nu- merous. Unfortunately, at the battle of St. Aubin's, in Brittany,

His unhappy expedition to Britany 1488

He and all his men slain.

tany, the Duke was defeated, and Sir Edward, with all the English slain *, except one boy, who brought home the melancholy tidings, particularly so to this island, as there was scarce a family but what lost a relation in this expedition. Sir Edward died unmarried.

It was this tragical event that occasioned an act of Parliament to be passed, intended to promote the population of the island, by prohibiting any of its inhabitants from holding farms, lands, or tithes, exceeding the annual rent of ten marks †. A regulation that could not, from the constant decrease of the value of money, remain long in force: to make a law of this nature permanent, the quantity of land, and not of rent, should be ascertained, but political writers are by no means agreed as to the effects of such restrictions. —

No grant of the land made after this time.

It is not certain whither Sir Edward was Lord of the island, or, as his title imported, only Captain thereof ‡, though, from the great influence he appears to have had over the inhabitants, influenced in their engaging in his ill-fated expedition, the former seems most probable. After his decease, Henry the Seventh, intent upon lessening the power of the Barons, never granted away the Lordship of this island, which has ever since remained in the crown thus its government was changed into a more military appointment; and though the Captain, or Governor, might hold some lands, that remained to the castle, they are annexed to the charge of it, and were enjoyed, *jure officii* only. An account of the crown lands in the island, in the twenty-third year of this

* Bacon's Life of Henry the Seventh, p 48—62.
† Stat fourth of Henry the Seventh, cap 16
‡ To enable our readers to judge of the difference of those offices, in the Appendix, No XXIII is given a grant of the Lordship, and in No. XXXIX that of the Captain, or Governor

prince,

prince, and also their present state, is given in the Appendix [*].

When King Henry the First granted, not only his lands in the Isle of Wight, but also the dominion over the whole, to Richard de Redvers, to be held in escuage [†], *at fifteen Knights fees and a half*; the Crown had from that time no demand on the landholders of the island. The King received escuage from the Lord of the island only, whose tenants were chargeable only in aid to him; they held their lands as of the castle of Carisbrooke, from whence, in the *Liber Feodorum*, and in many Escheat Rolls, it is styled the Honour of Carisbrooke. They were chargeable towards making the eldest son of the Lord a Knight, and to the marrying of his daughter. All heirs under age were in the wardship of the Lord of the island. The tenants were bound to defend the castle of Carisbrooke for forty days, at their own charges, when ever it should be attacked, and were also to attend the Lord at his coming into, and at his leaving the Island. The Lord [‡] had the return of the King's writs, he nominated his own Bailiffs and his Constable, was Coroner with-

Rights and franchises included in the Lordship of the island.

---

[*] See Appendix, No XXV, XXVI

[†] Escuage, or scutage, was a pecuniary satisfaction or composition anciently paid by landholders in lieu of personal military service, and named from scutum, a shield or buckler.

[‡] In Antiq Rot 5 Stephen, which Madox, in his History of the Exchequer, has curiously examined in a particular discourse, there is found under *Isura de Wi h*,

" Paganus Trencaidus debit iiij*l* de preteritis Danegeldis insulae v annorum de " tempore Hugonis de Vernon. Et idem Paganus reddit compotum de novo Da- " negeldo insulae in thesui xj*l* & viij*s* Et in perdonis per breve regis Willelmo " de Vernon xxxij*s* Rudulfo de Bellinghurst vis & quietus est "

The Danegeld remaining due for five years past, may be presumed to have been changed from the time when Baldwin de Redvers had forfeited the Lordship for opposing King Stephen, for the island is not found to have been charged with this tax but when it was in the hands of the Crown.

in the island; he had a chace, now called the Foreſt of Park-hurſt; and a fence month, not only there, but in certain moors, with a free warren on the eaſt ſide of the river Medina. He had alſo wrecks, waifs, and ſtrays, with fairs and markets at Newport and Yarmouth.

Notwithſtanding theſe immunities were duly proved and al-lowed, two fines are recorded to have been exacted by King John, for the livery of lands in the iſland; Margery Vernon, heir of John Aiſie, was fined forty marks and one palfrey, for livery of the manor of Freſhwater; and John Argenton was fined forty marks and two palfreys, for his lands in Cariſ-brooke *. The Crown is not found to have at any time in-terfered in the cuſtody of the iſland until Henry the Third, in the firſt year of his reign, immediately after the death of William de Vernun, ordered the caſtle of Cariſbrooke to be delivered to the Sheriff of Southampton, and by him to Wal-leran, Warden of the iſland; but this, from the unſettled ſtate of the kingdom, ſeems to have been a neceſſary precaution, in order to ſecure the iſland from Lewis, the Dauphin of France, then in England, where, in the diſtractions of the pre-ceding year, he had been crowned King. William de Ver-nun, the late Lord, was a known favourer of his cauſe †, in-ſomuch that he had been obliged by King John to deliver up his grandſon as a hoſtage; and, after his deceaſe, it is pro-bable the iſland was left in the cuſtody of perſons of the ſame party: there was, beſides, a degree of propriety in the King's taking it into his hands; Baldwin, the heir, being

* P. +. 6 Joh.

† An evidence of his adhering to the party of the Barons is extant in the win-dows of the church of Boldre, in Hampſhire, then under his patronage, where are the arms of Lewis, the Dauphin, with thoſe of the Lords of his party

then

then a minor, and, according to Dugdale, a ward of the Crown.

The fame King, in the thirteenth year of his reign, committed the charge of the island to Savary de Malo Leone, and about the fame time granted the Wardship of Baldwin, the young Earl of Devon, to Gilbert de Clare, Earl of Gloucester. This circumstance requires fome explanation, becaufe Prynne, in his Animadverfions on Coke's fourth Inftitute, has afferted, fpeaking of the Ifle of Wight, that our Kings, in former ages, appointed from time to time efpecial guardians of the island, erected and repaired caftles and forts, and, in time of war and danger, were very careful to fend forces, and to array the inhabitants, &c. To prove thefe inftances, he cites a record in the thirteenth year of Henry the Third, which he terms the return of an inquifition, though it is in fact no more than a precept to the Sheriff of Southampton, reciting *, ' That whereas, in the times of ' " Henry, our grandfather, Richard, our uncle, and John, our " father, the Sheriff of Southampton never diftrained black cat-" tle in the Ifle of Wight for the ufe of the King, but for the " ufe of the Lord of that island; and that there were no Coroners " in that island in the times of the aforefaid Kings; therefore we " command you, that if you have diftrained any cattle in that " island, you deliver them without delay to our beloved and " faithful S de Malo Leone, to whom we have entrufted the

---

* " Quod temporibus H regis avi noftri, & R regis avunculi noftri & Dom J
" regis patris noftri, nunquam vicec Southampton boves ceperunt pro defenfinis
" in Infula Weet in itinere juftic ad opus iplorum regum, fed ad opus com ad
" eft cuftodis de infula femper capi confueverunt, & quod nunquam temporibus
" prædictorum regum in prædicta infula coronatores coftiterunt & ideo tibi præ-
" cipimus, quod fi quos boves cepifti pro defenfinis in prædicta infula ees dilecto &
' fideli S de Malo Leon cui cuftodiam ejufdem infula commifimus, fine dilatione
" reddi facias & coronatores .ibidem effe non permittes " T rege apud Weftm
12 die Feb. Prynne on the fourth Inft p 208

" cuftody

" cuftody of the ifland, and that you permit no coroners to be
" there, &c " Nothing injurious to the rights of the Lord of
the ifland is contained in this precept, nor was there any injuftice in committing the care of the ifland to S de Malo Leone,
as the young Earl of Devon, Lord thereof, was then a ward to
the King. Prynne is under a grofs miftake in his comment on
the word Comes, not knowing that the Lords of the ifland were
frequently ftyled *Comites Infulæ*. for in a marginal note on the
expreffion, " ad opus Comites," id eft, fays he Cuftodis. he
might have obferved the fines and forfeitures accrued to the
Earl, and therefore were to be delivered to him who had the
cuftody of the ifland during his minority. This is the firft
inftance on record of the King having appointed a Warden of
the ifland.

No Warden
appointed by
the Crown
when the
ifland was un-
der its proper
Lords Another inftance occurs, in the twenty third year of Edward
the Firft, when that King had purchafed the ifland of Ifabella de
Fortibus, nor are any other to be found, except when the Lordfhip
of the ifland was in the Crown; it may therefore be concluded
that this ifland was entirely under the government of its
Lord which is corroborated by the return of an inquifition in
the feventh year of Edward the Second, wherein it is declared,
that whilft the ifland was under the Earls of Devon, they conftantly fupplied feventy-fix men from their county for its defence, but that when it became the property of Edward the Firft,
the King furnifhed the men for its protection: nor does the fha-
dow of a proof appear, that the Crown took any precautions for
its fecurity, until it became part of the royal poffeffions.

Prynne cites a record from the White Tower, wherein is
ftated, that the iflanders claimed an exemption from contribut-
ing to an aid for marrying the King's eldeft daughter *, but it

* See Appendix, No XXVII

does

does not appear that this claim was founded in the plea of their services and great expences in warding and defending the island, as is asserted by Prynne *, no such plea being even hinted in the record The islanders defended themselves by ancient custom, and the plain reason of such exemption was, that they discharged all such services to the Lord of the island; the Lord paid the King scutage for the island, which in the grant from Henry the First was rated at *fifteen Knight's fees and a half*; and the land-holders, who held under him, contributed their proportions, whenever that tax was imposed. Indeed the turbulent reigns of King John, Henry the Third, and Edward the First, afford divers instances of exactions on the people. one in particular was complained of in the eighth year of the last mentioned King, when it was alleged, that in the thirty-eighth and thirty ninth of the preceding reign, James de Norton, and Richard de Porhunt, Collectors of the King's Scutage, had unjustly distrained on Ralph de Gorges, and Peter D'Evercy, the Council, to whom this complaint was addressed, ordered that the Treasurer and Barons of the Exchequer should call the Collectors before them, and if the allegations in the petition were found true, to do the complainants full justice †

---

* Arimadv. on the fourth Inst p 214.

† " Ad petitionem Radulfi de Gorges et Petri de Ve ccy pro se et tota com-
" munitate insula Vectæ sugerrentem, quod cum teneant terras suas in dicta insula
" de domino dictæ insulæ, pro insula illa custodienda, absque aliquo alio servitio foren-
" seco alicui faciendo, Jacobus de Norton et Ricardus de Borhunt collectores scu-
" tagii regis ibidem de annis Hen reg 38 & 39, prædictos Radulfum Perram, et
" communitatem distringunt p scutagio illo solvendo unde petunt remedium sibi
" fieri.

" Responsum per Concilium

' Mandetur thesaurario et baron de scaccario, quod vocatis coram eis collectori-
" bus infra scriptis, et inquisita super contentis in petitione, si necesse fuerit plenius
" veritate faciant, inde conquerentibus justiciam " Rot Parl 8 Edw. I

It

It is true alfo, that after Edward the Firft had obtained the Lordfhip of the ifland, he ordered the Knights to be fummoned to his wars *, among thofe commanded to attend him to Berwick were Peter D'Evercy, John Trenchard, Jorden de Kingfton, Robert de Glamorgan, Roger de Langford, Henry de Oglander, and Adam de Compton, all of the Ifle of Wight; but no evidence is found that any of them obeyed this fummons: poffibly it might have been fuppofed, that the King having purchafed the ifland, the nature of the tenures of the landholders were therefore altered, for the King's efcheators having frequently taken inquifitions on the deaths of the inhabitants, and the parties refufing to fubmit to their decifions, were vexed with actions at the King's fuit. To fettle this point, a bill was prepared for Parliament, in the year one thoufand fix hundred and forty-one †: but the diftractions then fubfifting in the kingdom prevented its taking effect.

With regard to the franchife of foreft enjoyed by the Lords of the ifland, it has been doubted whether the foreft of Parkhurft, confifting of about three thoufand acres, is with ftrict propriety entitled to that denomination. It appears by a warrant of the Duke of Suffolk, Chief Juftice of the King's Foreft in the reign of Henry the Eighth, directed to the Warden of Carifbrooke Foreft, that a court of fwainmote was formerly held there ‡, and alfo that a ranger and two forefters were appointed. And among the liberties claimed by Ifabella de Fortibus, and allowed her by the Itinerant Juftices, in the eighth year of Edward the Firft, is that of a free chace in the foreft §. When the ifland
was

Parkh. ?, or Carifbrooke foreft.

* Twenty ninth year of Edward the Firft
† For the draught of this bill, fee Appendix, No XXVIII
‡ See Appendix, No XXIX
§ See Appendix, No XXX In the next reign, in the fecond year of Edward the Second Parkhurft was granted to Piers Gavefton as a free chace —"Ex grari "querela dilecti & fidelis noftri Petri de Gavefton, accepimus qd quidem male- "factores

was in the Crown, Edward the Third imposed on John Maltravers, for certain lands held by him in the county of Dorset, the following service. that he should, in the season for buck-hunting, attend the King at the castle of Carisbrooke, in the Isle of Wight, for one day, at his own charge both for himself and horse, and afterwards to remain during the King's pleasure, but both himself and horse to be maintained at the expence of the Crown. The whole of the Forest, was anciently called the Park, and was probably emparked in or before the reign of William the Conqueror, being so styled in Domesday-book, under Watchingwood, which is lowered in the rate, *because part of the land formerly belonging to Watchingwood, was then taken into the King's park* *. It has been denominated a forest for three hundred years past, as appears by a

---

" factores, &c liberam chaceam ipsius Petri apud Parkhurst in insula Vecta, et
" liberam warrenam suam ibidem et apud Thorle, Westrugge, et Bordwood, in
" eadem insula, vi et armis intraverunt & in iisdem chacea et warrena, sine licen
" tia et voluntati ipsius Petri fugaverunt, &c. ac arbores in boscis suis ibidem nu-
" per crescentes succiderunt, et arbores illas, nec non feras, lepores, et cuniculos
" in chacea & warrena prædict ceperunt et asportaverunt, & alia enorm ei intu-
" lerunt ad damnum ipsius Petri viginta librarum, & contra pacem nostram, &c "
Rymer, vol iii p. 125 We have, moreover, the evidence of another grant, in
the sixth year of Edward the Second, " Rex Roberto le Sauser custodi chacea de
" Parkhurst in Insula Vecta sal cum 2do die Decemor. an regni nostri 6to p char-
" tam nostram dederimus & concessimus Edwardo filio nostro charissimo, castium
" & manerium de Karesbrook ac omnia alia manein, terr & ten in insula Vecta,
" cum eorum membris & omnibus aliis pertinen suis, habend & tenend eidem
" filio nostro & hæred. suis regibus Angliæ, una cum omnibus libertat consuet
" homagiis, &c vobis mandamus, &c " See a Treatise concerning the Dignities,
Titles, Offices, &c granted by the Kings of England since the Conquest, to their
Eldest Sons, Princes of Wales 4to 1737

At the beginning of the oldest court book of the corporation of Newport is an inquisition into the right of common belonging to Reginald de St Martin, Lord of the manor of Avington, in which the limits of the Forest are ascertained See Appendix, No XXXI

* Coker's Dorset, p. 48.

grant

giant in the twentieth year of Henry the Sixth, to Henry Trenchard, of the office of Conftable of Carifbrooke caftle, and that of Keeper of the King's foreft in the ifland, with a ftipend of ten pounds per annum. In an account alfo of rents, iffues and difburfements of this ifland, in the twenty-third year of Henry the Seventh, mention is made of a falary paid to an officer, ftyled Ranger of the Foreft, and to two others as Underkeepers.

Bordwood foreft.

Bordwood, on the eaft fide of the Ifland, is alfo called a foreft; but as no appointment of a Keeper or Ranger appears on record, it probably obtained its name from being a large extent of wafte land belonging to the Lord, overgrown with wood, and ferving as a harbour for red deer. In the third year of Henry the Fifth it was granted to Philippa, Duchefs of York, by the name of the Foreft of Bordwood; and there is a fmall building, called the Queen's Bower, on the top of an eminence, from whence, perhaps, fhe ufed to view the chace.

Wrecks of the fea.

The Lords alfo claimed wrecks of the fea throughout the ifland, which franchife was tried by *quo warranto*, before the itinerant Juftices, and allowed to the Countefs Ifabella · counter claims were preferred by John de Infula, Thomas de Evercy, Robert de Glamorgan, Thomas de la Haule, and the Abbot of Quarr, each claiming for himfelf half of whatever fhould be wrecked on their refpective lands, as a compenfation, or falvage, for preferving the other half for the ufe of the Lord; but thefe claims not being fupported by fufficient evidence were difallowed †

† Record of pleas before the Juftitum. at Winton in Octabs Martini, 8 Edw. I.

But

But the chief privilege enjoyed by the Lord was that of ho'ding a judicial tribunal, called the Knighten Court, properly the *Knight's Court**. The ftyle of this court is *Curia Militum*, becaufe the Judges were fuch as held a Knight's fee, or part of a fee in capite, from the Lord of the ifland, who gave judgment, as courts of equity, without a jury. This court differed in jurifdiction and procefs from a court leet, and it may be obferved, that a *curia militum* was granted to Ifabella de Fortibus, befides the *vifus franci plegii*, &c. From the peculiar conftitution of this court it may be prefumed to have been inftituted by William Fitz-Ofborne, who had the firft grant of the ifland from William the Conqueror, to be held as freely as he himfelf held the kingdom of England; Fitz Ofborne might not, perhaps, in the formation of this tribunal, think himfelf bound to obferve the national cuftom of trials by jury. The nature of this court † will be beft explained by the following reprefentation, tranfmitted to Lord Conway, Governor of the ifland, Auguft twenty-firft, one thoufand fix hundred and twenty-fix, with a view to the improvement of its jurifdiction.

KNIGHTEN COURT.

I. It hath been always kept by the Captain's Steward of the ifland, or his fubftitute, by virtue of the Captain's patent, and by no other particular patent, for ought we know.

---

* A Knight's court is alfo held twice a year, under the Bifhop of Hereford, at his palace there, wherein the Lords of manors and their tenants, holding by Knight's fervice, are fuitors which court is mentioned in Butterfield's Survey, p 244 If the fuitor fails in his appearance, he pays two fhillings fuit fervice, for refpite of homage. Cowel and Jacob.

† See the office feal at the end of the chapter.

M

II. It.

II. It hath been always kept in the town-hall of Newport, on the Monday every three weeks, unlefs that day happen upon a feftival day, and then it is adjourned for fix weeks.

III. It hath jurifdiction throughout the whole ifland, the Corporation of Newport excepted.

IV. It holdeth plea of all actions of debt and trefpafs, under the value of 40 s. and upon replevins granted by the Steward or his fubftitute that keeps the court.

V. The procefs in actions of debt and trefpafs, are fummons, attachments, and diftringas, to bring the defendant to appear, which if he do in perfon, he muft confefs the action, or elfe he is condemned by default: if by an Attorney, he is admitted one effoine; if he prays it, and the next court muft appear, or be condemned by default. And in actions upon replevins, if the defendant appear not in the three firft courts, he is condemned by default: and in thefe actions upon replevins, no effoine is admitted.

VI. The pleadings are Englifh bills and anfwers; and, if the cafe require, replications and rejoinders.

VII. All the actions are entered, profecuted, and pleaded, by certain Attorneys, allowed in that court.

VIII. The actions of debt are tried by proof of plaintiff or defendant, or the defendants wager of law with two hands, if he pray it; and in trefpafs by proof only.

IX. All the actions are adjudged by the court, without jury; which it is conceived will be better with jury, as in other courts of record, if the value of actions be increafed.

X. The

X. The Judges are freeholders, which hold of his Majesty's castle of Carisbrooke, whereof there are known to the Steward, not above eighteen *. The which freeholders, for their better ease, have been appointed by the Captain of the isle to sit by four or five at a court by turns: but some being aged and impotent, one under age, some live out of the isle, and some of the rest being negligent of that service, there hath been much defect in their attendance; which is to the great prejudice of the court, and hindrance of the people, by delay of trials.

Therefore, under favour, we conceive, that a certain form of election of a certain number of judges, of other sufficient men of the country, be added, and a strict order taken for their due attendance will be very necessary, especially if the value of actions be raised: and that if there be not an especial restraint of removing actions in that court triable from thence into higher courts, that court will do little more good than it doth already.

---

* In the first page of a Court-book in the reign of Elizabeth, their names are,

Tho. Worsley, Ar.	Rob Dillington, Gen.
Anth Lisle, Ar	David Urry, Gen.
John Erlisman, Gen	Tho Dennis, Ar
Ed Richards, Ar.	John Mewes, Ar.
Jo. Heron, Gen.	John Rice, Gen.
Will. Oglander, Ar	Tho. Levybond, Gen.
Tho Urry.	Tho. Cheeke, Gen.
	Mich. Kite.

And in another Court-book, 1 Charles I. the list consists of the following Gentlemen,

Sir Jo. Mews, Knt	Sir Hen Worsley, Bart
Sir Jo. Richards, Knt.	Sir Jo Oglander, Knt.
Wm Bourman, Esq.	Sir Jo Leigh, Knt.
Jo. Harvey, Esq	Jo Worsley, Esq
Sir Wm Lisle, Knt.	Sir Fd Dennis, Knt.
Sir Rob. Dillington, Bart.	Sir Hen Knowles,
Capt Mann,	Tho Newnham,
Wm. Stephens, Esq	Rich Gard.
Tho Knight, Gen.	
Will. Nutt,	

In

In confequence of thefe reprefentations, inftructions were given by the Lord Treafurer, Vifcount Grandifon, to the King's Attorney-geneial, to prepare a grant for enlarging the jurifdiction of this court " *to all cafes whatfoever, civil or criminal, under the* " *value of* 20*l provided that the fame extend not to the life, mem-* " *ber, or freehold of any of the inhabitants:*" but nothing was effected; for the court ftill remains in the fame ftate.

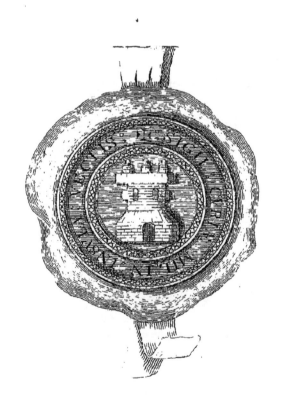

C H A P.   IV.

Of the Wardens, Captains, and Governors of the Island, with the principal Events under their Administration.

THE perfons honoured with this charge were generally felected from among the principal Gentlemen of the ifland, and commonly commiffioned by the crown, though fometimes appointed by the Lord of the ifland, or, with efpecial permiffion, elected by the inhabitants.

The firft inftitution of this office was during the minority of Baldwin the Third, grandfon of William de Vernun, Earl of Devon, in the firft of Henry the Third, when the cuftody of this ifland was entrufted to Walleran de Ties *, famous for his defence of the caftle of Berkhemftead againft Lewis, the eldeft fon of Philip, King of France   He was high in King Henry's favour, who beftowed on him fome lands, which formerly had belonged to the Earldom of Cornwal, and were claimed foon after by the King's brother Richard, in confequence of his being created Earl of Cornwal, but the King fupporting the grant he had made, the Earl entered into an affociation with the Earls of Pembroke, Chefter, Warenne, Gloucefter, Warwick, and Ferrars, and taking up arms, obliged the King to give him fatisfaction by grants of much greater importance.   The only evidence that proves this Walleran to have been Warden of the ifland, is his appearing a fubfcribing witnefs to a grant made to the Abbey of Quarr, which is thus figned, *Tefte Wallerano Teutonico cuftode infulæ* †; he lived

1216.

Walleran.

---

* Matt Paris.   It is doubtful whether Teutonic was a furname, or an addition, denoting him to have been a German   Hume ftyles him Walcran de Ties.
† See Appendix, No XXXII.

till

till the reign of Edward the Firſt, when dying without iſſue, his manor of Ringwood, in Hampſhire, eſcheated to that King *.

1229 Savery de Mauleon.
In the thirteenth of Henry the Third, Savery de Mauleon, or, de Malo Leone, was made Warden of the iſland, probably at the death of Baldwin the Third, his ſon, Baldwin the Fourth, being then a minor; he was a Poictevin, and had been very ſerviceable to the King during the war with France; but afterwards, on ſome diſcontent, changing ſides, he became extremely troubleſome. Prynne produces this man as an inſtance, that the appointment of a Warden was always in the Crown; but what he alleges on that ſubject has already been ſufficiently conſidered.

1293 John Fitz Thomas
Soon after Edward the Firſt had purchaſed the Lordſhip of this iſland, he conſtituted John Fitz-Thomas Warden thereof; nothing farther is known concerning him, but that he was alſo ſteward of the New Foreſt.

1294 Richard de Affeton
By two commiſſions in the White Tower, cited by Prynne †, Richard de Affeton appears to have been made Warden of the iſland in the twenty-ſecond of Edward the Firſt, which he was to guard with the aſſiſtance of Humphrey de Doneſterre, Conſtable of the caſtle of Cariſbrooke. Sir Richard de Affeton had been commiſſioned in the preceding year, during the war with France, to ſeize on all the lands and goods of the alien Priories for the King's uſe, leaving the Monks as much as he ſhould deem ſufficient for their maintenance ‡. In the twenty-third of the ſame reign he was joined in a commiſſion with the Biſhop of Wincheſter, and Adam de Gourdon §, whom he was ordered to meet at Portſmouth,

---

* Lib Feod Edw I.
Dated 2do die Aug anno regni 22.

† Records, vol iii p 627, &c.
§ E Regiſt Winton.

to confult with them for the defence of the ifland Adam de Gourdon had appeared in arms againft Henry the Third, and, maintained himfelf fome time in the forefts of Hampfhire, where he had committed great depredations Being defeated by Prince Edward in fingle combat, he was not only pardoned, at the Prince's requeft, in confequence of his courage, but alfo received into favour [*]. The commiffion, laft mentioned, appears to have been occafionally iffued for the defence of the ifland, which at that time was threatened by the French, a record of the fame year fhews that William Ruffel was Warden at the fame time [†].

William Ruffel

In the thirtieth of Edward the Firft, Sir John Lifle [of Wootton, ftyled de Bofco, to diftinguifh that family from the Lifles of Gatecombe] was conftituted Warden of this ifland, and Captain of the caftle of Carifbrooke; he ferved in feven parliaments during the latter part of this reign, and in the third, fourth, and fifth years of that fucceeding, he was fuperfeded by his brother, Nicholas Lifle, on the acceffion of Edward the Second, when that Prince ordered him to put Piers Gavefton, Earl of Cornwall, in poffeffion of the ifland [‡]: Nicholas was murdered by Robert Urry, who was tried, and imprifoned at Rochefter.

1302 Sir John Lifle

1307 Nicholas Lifle

Sir John Lifle, was reinftated in the Wardenfhip of the ifland, in the third of Edward the Second, and no other Warden appears till the fourteenth of the fame reign. When the Lordfhip was in Prince Edward, Sir Henry Tyes was appointed Warden under him, a petition was exhibited againft him to the

Sir John Lifle again

1321 Sir Henry Tyes.

---

* Rapin, vol 1 p 342

† This record is cited in Ryley's Placita Parl p. 441 being a petition from the Prior and Convent of Chrift-church, complaining that William Ruffel, Warden of the Ifland, had refufed them the tithe of the conies of Thorley, which had been granted to them.

‡ Rot Parl. 1 Edw. II. See chap. iii. Plate IV. of feals No. 22.

Par-

Parliament[*], by Ralph de Gorges, complaining that he had defrauded the Lord of part of the falvage of a wreck; and, moreover, protected one Henry Trenchard, at that time an outlaw. Sir Henry Tyes was probably the perfon who loft his head the following year, for being concerned in open rebellion with Thomas, Earl of Lancafter, who alfo fhared the fame fate foon after.

1325
John de la Hufe and John Lifle.

Nicholas de la Felde.

John de la Hufe and John Lifle were Wardens of the ifland, in the eighteenth of Edward the Second; the inquifitions of the watches and beacons, mentioned in the account of the ancient military force of the ifland, were taken before them. Nicholas de la Felde occurs under the title of Cuftos in the fame year [†].

1336
John de Langford

1338
Theobald Ruffel

In the ninth of Edward the Third, John de Langford, of Chale, was Warden of the ifland, and Captain of Carifbrooke caftle [‡]. In the eleventh year of the fame reign, Theobald Ruffel is named as Captain general of the ifland [§].

1340
Abbot of Quarr

The office of Warden appears not to have been incompatible with the monaftic profeffion, as in the thirteenth of Edward the Third, it appears to have been held by the Abbot of Quarr, who received inftructions to array all the able men, and to fupply them with arms, and alfo to caufe beacons and other fignals to be erected on the hills, to convey fpeedy notice of the approach of an enemy.

The office was alfo occafionally elective, as is inftanced in an order entered on the Rolls of Parliament, in the fourteenth of Edward the Third, when an invafion being apprehended, the Sheriff of Hampfhire, together with the Conftable of Carif-

---

[*] Rot. Parl. 14 Edw. II
[†] Put in Turri p. 2. m. 24.
[‡] Rymer, vol. ii. p. 97.
[§] Rymer, vol. iv. p. 781.

brooke

brooke caftle, were directed to convene the inhabitants of the ifland to elect a Warden, who fhould take charge of the defence of the ifland during the King's pleafure, inftead of one, three were elected, Sir Bartholomew Lifle *, John de Langford, Lord of Chale, Sir Theobald Ruffel, Lord of Yaverland, thefe, with the concurrence of the inhabitants, iffued, for the fecurity of the ifland, thofe ftrict orders and regulations already alluded to, and inferted in the Appendix.

1311. Sir Bartholo- mew Lifle, John de Langford, and Sir Theo- bald Ruffel.

Three other Wardens are found in the fixteenth year of the fame King, when a precept was directed to Bartholomew Lifle, John de Kingfton, and Henry Romyn, Cuftodes of the ifland †, commanding them to make inquifition what fervices were due from the inhabitants in time of war, of what nature, and from what lands and tenements. The refult of this inquiry is mentioned in the account of the ancient military force of the country.

1343.

John de Gatefden was Warden of the ifland in the twenty-fixth of Edward the Third, when he received a commiffion to array the inhabitants; a precept is alfo found, dated the fame year, and directed to the Abbot of Quarr, as Warden of the ifland; probably the fervice to be performed being of a mi-

1353. John de Gatefden.

* See Chap. iii Plate V of feals, No 26.

† " Edwardus Dei gratia rex Angl & Franc. & dominus Hibern dilectis et " fidelibus fuis Bartholomeo de Infula, Johanni de Kyngefton, & Henr. Romyr, " cuftodibus infulæ Vectæ, falutem. Mandamus vobis, quod per facramentorum " proborum & legalium hominum de infula prædicta, per quos rei veritas melius " fciri poterit, diligenter inquiratis, quæ et cujus modi fervicia infulæ predictæ " tempore guerræ debentur? et per quos? et de quibus terris et ten et qualiter, " et quo modo? Et inquificionem inde diftincte et apertam factam, nobis fub fi- " gillo veftro ac figillis eorum per quos facta fuerit fine dilatione mittatis, & hoc " breve. T. meipfo apud Weftm 13 die Maii, anno regni noftri, Angl fexto de- " cimo regni vero noftri Franciæ tertio "

N   litary

litary nature, the King thought it better placed in the hands of a soldier than an ecclesiastic.

Abbot of
Quar
Theobald de
Gorges, and
William
Dale

In the thirty-third year of Edward the Third, the Abbot of Quarr, Theobald de Gorges, and William Dale were appointed Wardens. Theobald de Gorges was son of Sir Theobald Ruffel, flain in the defence of the ifland a few years before; the name of Gorges he affumed from his mother.

Sir Hugh
Tyrril.

In the firft of Richard the Second Sir Hugh Tyrril was Conftable of Carifbrooke caftle, which he defended with great fkill and bravery againft the French, who burned the towns of *Newtown* and *Yarmouth*, but at length the enemy agreed to retire on the payment of *one thoufand marks*, and a folemn engagement from the people, not to refift them, fhould they return within twelve months. Sir Hugh died foon after, poffeffed of the manor of Langley, in Hampfhire [*].

On the death of Humphrey, Duke of Gloucefter, Lord of this ifland, in the twenty-fifth year of Henry the Sixth, that King appointed Henry Trenchard to the office of Conftable of the caftle of Carifbrooke, with a falary of *twenty pounds per annum*, alfo *ten pounds per annum*, as Keeper of the Foreft of Parkhurft, and *four pence* per day for the pay of the porter of the caftle.

In the reign of Henry the Sixth [†], John Newport was Lieutenant and Steward to Richard, Duke of York, Lord of the Ifland, who, for mifconduct, removed him from his office, and appointed Henry Bruin in his place. When Newport was

[*] Efch 4 R II

[†] In the Appendix, No XXXIII is a lift of the landholders of certain eftates in the feventeenth year of this reign.

dismissed

dismissed from his employment, he committed several piratical depredations on the Islanders, notwithstanding that he was at the same time soliciting the King to be reinstated. The inhabitants, on their part, petitioned the King and Parliament that Bruin might remain in his trust, and Henry Trenchard, Constable and Porter of the castle of Carisbrooke, might have orders to reside in the island during the continuance of the then war.

In the first of Edward the Fourth, the Captainship of this island was conferred on Sir Geoffrey Gate, for life, but he surrendered it in the sixth year of the same reign, thereby enabling the King to bestow the Lordship on his uncle, Anthony. Lord Schales, in compensation for this surrender, he was made Captain, or Marshal of Calais *.

1461. Sir Geoffrey Gate.

1467

Sir William Berkeley was made Lieutenant, or Captain of the island, in the first of Richard the Third, by a patent dated the twenty-seventh of July, whereby he was also constituted Captain of Carisbrooke castle, Receiver of the King's rents, and Keeper of the Forest, or Chace; no stipend is assigned for either of these offices, but he was allowed the Advowson of the church of Freshwater, wrecks of the sea, with all fines and forfeitures. He did not long hold these appointments, for in the same year Sir John Savile was nominated to them by a similar patent

*1 S.
Sir William Berkeley*

Sir John Savile

On the accession of Henry the Seventh, the command of the island was entrusted to Sir Edward Woodville.

*1485
Sir Edward Woodville.*

* On the tomb of his relict, at High Eastham, in Essex, is the following inscription, " Here lyeth dame Agnes Gate, the wife of Sir Geoffrey Gate, " Knight, the which Sir Geoffrey was six years Captain of the Isle of Wight, " and after Marshal of Calais, and he kept with the P. lords, worshipful ways, " and ever entendyd, as a good Knight, to please the King in the parts of Normandy, " with all his might, &c." Weaver's Fun Mon p 610

In the tenth of the same reign the King granted unto Sir Reginald Bray, a lease of the island, with the castle or Honour of Carisbrooke, and its appurtenances, the Crown lands in the island, and the manors of Swainston, Brixton, Thorley, and Wellow, late in the possession of George, Duke of Clarence, subject to the annual rent of *three hundred and seven marks*, reserved to the Crown: he had been a servant to the Countess of Richmond, and was extremely useful to the King in his negociations, as well before as after his accession to the Crown; he was a Knight of the Garter, Justice of all the Forests south of Trent, and had divers valuable grants of land. He died,

without issue, and was succeeded by Sir Nicholas Wadham, grandson of Sir John Wadham, of an ancient family in Devonshire, who marrying one of the coheirs of Stephen Popham, Esq. became possessed of the manors of Avington, Shide, and Northwood, with other estates in this island, which descended to Sir Nicholas, who married two wives: the first was daughter of Robert Hill, Esq. of Antony, by whom he had issue: Nicholas Wadham, founder of Wadham College, in Oxford, was his grandson from this marriage. His second wife was Margaret, daughter of John Seymour, of Wolf-hall, in Wiltshire, sister of Jane Seymour, afterwards married to King Henry the Eighth. She was buried in Carisbrooke church, where, on the north wall, is a handsome monument, whereon is the figure of a Lady kneeling, but without inscription. The family coat is dimidiated, with that of Wadham, who quartered the arms of Popham.

Sir Nicholas Wadham dying, in the beginning of the third year of Henry the Eighth, was succeeded by Sir James Worsley [*],

---

* Sir James Worsley had lately married the daughter and heiress of Sir John Leigh. In the Appendix, No XXXIV is given the copy of a curious dispensation granted to Sir John Leigh, to hold the manor of Appuldurcombe, the Priory of Carisbrooke, &c. which was contrary to an act of Parliament then in force.

Keeper of the King's Wardrobe *, and Mafter of the Robes:
he was the younger brother of a very ancient family of that
name in Lancafhire, and had been many years page to Henry
the Seventh; he was conftituted Captain of the ifland for life,
with a falary of fix fhillings and nine pence per diem for
himfelf, two fhillings for his deputy, and fix pence each for
thirteen fervants; he had befides a reverfionary grant of the
office of Conftable of Carifbrooke caftle, when it fhould become
vacant, and was by the fame commiffion made Captain of all
the forts in the ifland †. He was Steward, Surveyor, Receiver,
and Bailiff of all the Crown lands; and was either to retain
his falary and allowances out of the moneys he received, or to
take the fame from the King's Receiver in the county of
Southampton He was likewife conftituted Keeper of Carifbrooke Foreft and Park, with a fee of two fhillings per diem;
and Warden and Mafter of the Duckcoy of Wild Fowl, as well
within the faid Park and Foreft there, as within and throughout the whole Ifland. He was empowered to leafe any of the
King's houfes, demefne lands, and farms, either by leafe of
years, or by copy of court roll for lives, where the lands have
ufually been paffed in that manner: the old rent being referved
by fuch leafe or copy. He had the return of all writs, the
execution of procefs, and the office of Sheriff within the faid
ifland, the Sheriff the county, or his officer, being excluded
from acting there, unlefs in default of the Captain; he was alfo
Clerk of the Market, and Coroner in the ifland.

Richard Worfley, Efq. on the death of Sir James his father †,
in the twenty-ninth of Henry the Eighth, fucceeded him in the
office

* See Appendix, No XXXV.
† See Appendix, No XXXVI.
‡ By his will, dated fifth of October, 1538, after many pious and charitable
bequefts, he gave to the King his beft gold-chain, to the Lord Cromwell, then
for t

office of Captain, and soon after had the honour of entertaining the King at his seat at Appuldurcombe *. The King was attended by his favourite the Lord Cromwell, then Constable of Carisbrooke castle, which office was, on his Lordship's attainder and execution, conferred on Mr. Worsley.

Five years after, the French, having failed in an attempt against our fleet, notwithstanding their superiority at sea, made a descent on the island, which they intended to take possession of; but were, by the bravery of the islanders, and good conduct of their Captain, soon driven back to their ships, with the loss of their general, and a great many of their men. It was on this occasion that new forts were ordered to be erected for the protection of the island, which were executed under the direction of the Captain; one of them was called Worsley's Tower; by his representations the inhabitants were prevailed on to provide a train of artillery for the defence of the island, at their own charges. He continued in office till the death of Edward the sixth, but being zealous in promoting the Reformation, as appears by his acting as a Commissioner for the sale of church plate † on the suppression of religious houses, at the accession of Queen Mary he resigned his offices, and Mr. Gilling, a man of low extraction, succeeded him; of whom, although no particulars are recorded, yet it is to be presumed, that he was no ways unfavourable to a restoration of the Romish religion. On

Lord Privy Seal, his largest standing cup, and to eight others of his friends, to each a lesser cup.

The King probably made this feast to amuse himself with hawking, or some other species of chace, as it appears by a certain letter, copied in the Appendix, that he had, some time before given directions for the preservation of the game in the Island, &c. See Appendix, No XXXVII

† No XXXVIII is the answer of accounts made out of the ordnance, church plate, &c. in the Island, a receipt dated fourteenth, 1557

the

the Queen's death, Richard Worsley was again reinstated. He was previously sent with Lord Chidiock Paulet, son of the Marquis of Winchester, and Governor of Portsmouth, with a commission to survey and repair the fortifications there, and was joined with a gentleman of the name of Smith, in a like commission to put the forts in the Isle of Wight in a state of defence, as a French invasion was then apprehended, four months after this he received his commission as Captain of the island, and among other instructions was ordered to introduce the use of harquebusses among the people. He was also to signify to the Queen and Council, wherein his legal authority proved deficient, that it might be taken into consideration but this was unnecessary, he conducting himself with such affability and prudence that the people readily complied with his directions, in whatever appeared to him necessary to guard them against an enemy; as is instanced by their providing the field pieces before mentioned, which were supplied by several of the parishes. He was likewise employed by the Queen in fortifying the sea-coasts, being afterwards sent with Sir Hugh Paulet, Captain of the Isle of Jersey, and others, to survey and order forts for the protection of Jersey and Guernsey. In conformity with his instructions, he introduced the use of fire-arms in the Isle of Wight, and an Armourer was settled in Carisbrooke castle, to make harquebusses, and to keep them in order.

On the death of Richard Worsley, the command of the island was bestowed on Edward Horsey, Esq who was soon after knighted. He was of an ancient family at Melcombe-Horsey, in Dorsetshire, and had performed good service as a naval commander, by clearing the Channel of the enemy's

* No XXXIX is a copy of the patent to Richard Worsley, Esq with the Queen's instructions

ships, with which it had been much infested.   He needed however no better recommendation than the favour of the Earl of
Leicester, who reposed the greatest confidence in him.   It was
from the hand of Sir Edward Horsey that Earl received the Lady
Douglas Sheffield, which marriage was so secretly performed
that the crafty Earl was able to elude it, when under the tempta-
tion of a fresh amour.   This circumstance is only mentioned to
shew in what intimacy Sir Edward was with that great favourite
of Elizabeth; though he was a much better man than his patron.
He not only kept the island in a proper state of defence, but lived in perfect harmony with the Gentlemen there.   The great
plenty of hares and other game, with which the island is stored,
is owing to his care: he is reported to have given a lamb for every
hare that was brought to him from the neighbouring countries.
He was buried in the chancel of the church at Newport, where
his virtues are celebrated on his monument.

Sir Edward Horsey was succeeded by Sir George Carey,
afterwards Lord Hunsdon, nearly related to Queen Elizabeth,
Henry, Lord Hunsdon, his father, being nephew of Queen
Anne Boleyn.   He was Lord Chamberlain of the Household,
one of the Privy-Council, and a Knight of the Garter.   In the
beginning of his government the castles and forts received a
thorough repair, under the direction of Thomas Worsley, Esq.
but much disagreement arose afterwards between the Gentlemen
of the island and Sir George, on account of some undue stretches
of authority over them.   Sir John Oglander informs us, that the
Gentlemen took great offence, when a fawning minister at Newport, in the prayer before his sermon, gave the Captain the title of
Governor, which Sir George Carey afterwards assumed, though
not expressed in his patent.   It was suspected from this alteration in his style, and from his assuming conduct, that his

intention

intention was to fubject them to the military power, but this con-
tention happening at a time of public danger, had not that attention paid to it at the Council Board that the cafe deferved.

When Philip the Second of Spain menaced England with
his Invincible Armada, Sir George Carey, availed himfelf of
the general alarm fpread over the nation, by attempting an
undue exertion of his authority, he might doubtlefs, with a
little management, have prevailed on the inhabitants to fubmit to all things required for their fecurity. His rank and
affinity to the Queen gave him a hauteur difagreeable to the
Gentlemen of the ifland, and his confcioufnefs of fupport
from Government made him adopt the prudent orders given
for the defence of the ifland in the reign of Edward the Third,
not confidering that thofe orders were iffued with the confent of
the inhabitants.

This caufed the following reprefentations to be laid before the
Lords of the Council : they may be confidered as a little Bill of
Rights of the ifland.

Demaunds by the Gentelmene of the Ifle of Wight for Reformation of a certein abfolute Government lately e affumede by the
Captayne there, tendinge to the Subvertione of the Lawe, and
to the takinge awaye of the naturall fiedome of the Inhabitants there.

" Firfte, we demand the benefitte, protection, due courfe, and
common good of her Majefties lawes, frelie to be had and enjoyed, withoute any private licenfe of the Captayne for the fame
to be firfte obteyned and gotte. that is to faye, ferving of common proceffe, execution of writs after judgement, as well in
actions reall as perfonall, and all other benefitte and protections

1588.

Remonft
rance again'ft
the conduct
of Sir George
Carey.

O   of of the lawe, the which we are boin inheritable unto, and heretofore have enjoyede within this iflande, and all other hir Majeftie's fubjects within his realme nowe do ufe and enjoye. Foi by meanes of the ftop of the due courfe of the common lawe, and by reafon of the protection of fuch as itt fhall pleafe the faid Captayne to favore in that behalffe, there enfueth, not onelye the common difciedit of the countrie, as with whom no othere of hir Majeftie's fubjects will willinglie meddle or trade, in buyinge, fellinge, or lendinge, to the generall ftaye of all our commodities, and to the utter wekeninge and impoverifhmente of the faid ifland, but alfo the abolifhinge of the ufual trade of bargaininge of eftates in land, and all other chattels and goods, where payment in parte oi in whole, is for any tyme to be forboine, and the neyghbourlie courtefey of lendinge betwene man and man in the faid iiland: feeing the meanes of having and recoveiie agaynft ech man's due and righte, is tyed to the pleafuie of the faid Captayne, and therefoie we demand herein iedreffe.

" Item, whereas of late tyme, againfte all right, there hathe byn caufeleffe ieftraynte made by the faide Captayne of fellinge, utteringe, or carryinge into the mayn land of all other commodities, viz. fateware, lambes, corne, buttere, cheefe, woode, and fuche lick provifion, to the common decaye of the countrie, bieache of the ufuall trade betwene us and others, in the fayd mayne land hade, and pryvate gayne of fuch particulai perfons as it hathe pleafed the faid Captayne to licenfe agaynfte the reftiaynte aforefaid · now we demand that we maye, withoute anye fuch licenfes of the faid Captayne fieelie tranfporte all our faid commodities into the faid mayne land, as in tymes pafte of iighte we have done.

" Item, we demande that we may have our maikets frelie to be ufede, for all hir Majefties good fubjects to reforte unto, to buye, fell, and cailie awaye fuch commodities as aie there to be hade,

withoute

withoute the faid Captayne's licenfe . unlefs hit be uppon fome fpeciall and apparent knowen caufe to the contrarie.

" Item, we demand our free paffage over the water into the mayne land at all times to be hade, without the faid Captaynes licenfe, as in tymes pafte we have always hade, unleffe it be reftrayned upon fome fpeciall caufe for hir Majefties fervice

" Item, whereas of late the countrie hath byn in fome forte commanded by authoritie to carrie with there carts unto the caftell of Carefbrooke greate ftoore of woode for the faid Captaynes provifion, leavinge their owne bufynes undone, to the greate hyndrance of the meanere forte of men ; we demaunde that we maye nott be compelled thereunto by commandement agaynfte the good will and fredome of the people.

" Item, we demand that there maye not be anye impofition or othere confideration taken or demanded by the faid Captayne, or anye of his fervants or deputies, for the tranfporting of corne, but that the commoditie thereof may come and redounde wholie unto the fellers, unto whome of righte it dothe appartayne, and as heretofore it hathe byn ufed · and that licence for the fame maye be had at fuche tymes as the provifion of this countrie will fuffer hitt, and the generall trade between hir Majeftie's fubjects and forreners unto whome it fhalbe tranfported, fhalbe open and permytt the fame.

" Item, we demand the goode and honefte intreatie of all trew merchants, beinge hir Majefties friends, that fhall happen to come unto anye roade, porte, or cryke, within this ifland for that greate benefytt unto the contrie heretofore hathe enfewed therebye , and we demand that pyracie, robberie, and fuche licke, tendinge to the uttere difkreditt of the contrie, and the difpleafure of Almightie God, maybe abolifhed.

" Item, we demand that there maye nott be anye unlawfull and unjuriouffe prohibitions, or denyall made by the faid Captayne to ympeache anye perſon of this countrie to ſell or buye anye land, which tendithe to the overthrowe of the free eſtate of the inhabitants of this iſland

" Item, we ſynde ourſelves muche grieved with the gready and inſatiable deſire of ſome perſons to gett our lands and rightfull poſſeſſions, under pretence and colour of concealed lands, which by the purchaſeinge of the late commiſſion of conccalements, and the indiſcrete dealinge therein, is apparenthe maryfeſted where-as there is noo doubte nor colour of anye unjuſte withholdinge of anye lands within this iſland from hir Majeſtie to oure knowledge

THOMAS WORSELEY,	THOMAS BOORFMAN,	WILLIAM OGLANDER,
ANTHONE LISLE,	JOHN LYGHE,	EDWARD RICHARDS,
THOMAS HOBSON,	JOHN BASKETT,	GEORGE BASKETT,
JOHN MEWYS,	JOHN RYCE,	JOHN EARLLSMAN,
THOMAS DENNYS,	THOMAS MEUILS,	EDWARD SCOTTE.
ROBERT DYLLINGTON,		

Although theſe claims were perhaps no more than what the parties might have been entitled to, yet the making them at a time, when the terrors of the Spaniſh Armada ſtill occupied the minds of the people, was unſeaſonable and injudicious, and afforded Sir George Carey an opportunity of repreſenting them as diſaffected perſons, which he accordingly did, accuſing Mr Dyllington in particular, of a combination with the Papiſts to diſturb the Government, of ſtirring up the Gentlemen of the iſland againſt him, and farther, of uſing menaces, by declaring that he neither could nor would brook Sir George Carey's Government, and that, if the abuſes complained of were not redreſſed, he would ſeek a remedy with his poniard, at the ſame time ſhouting out in a ſeditious manner, liberty ! liberty !

In

In confequence of thefe charges Mr. Dyllington was fummor-
ed to appear before the Privy Council, where he acknowleged
that he was very uneafy under the arbitrary proceedings of the
Captain, as were all the reft of the Gentlemen who had figned
the demand of right; but denied ever having threatened a re-
courfe to his poniard, or having in a feditious manner fhouted
out liberty, liberty. The Council, after having heard his
defence, ordered him to be committed to the Fleet-prifon.
on which the following letter was addreffed to the Lord Chancellor.

" With all humble ductie fubmytting ourfelves unto your honour; whereas we underftand by Mr Robert Dyllington, that
att his appearance before yowe, and others of his Majefties moft
honorable Privie Counfayle, he was commytted to the Fleete,
and thinketh the caufe thereof to be for that he was chaged to
have follicited the articulatinge for the libertie of the ifle in a
dangerous tyme, as alfo that he was fo defperatelie mynded that
he was redie to ufe force therein. Thefe are to refolve your honour that the tyme was taken when the greateft foare amongft
others (which was the impeachment of the fale and byenge of
our lande) was greene, being certaynlie perfuaded that our
neighbour, Mr Dyllington, wold not fo much as thinke any
thinge agaynft our moft happie and bleffed publicke eftate of this
realme, and mofte affured that he fhould offer us great wronge,
which fhould conjecture that we were to be labored to any fuch
difcontentment. And for any force mente agaynfte our Cap-
tayn, although it pleafeth him to objecte it, he hath byn fuffi-
cientlie refolved by us to the contrarie, and he'd himfelf there-
with fatisfied For any untrewth conteyned in the articles where-
with we are charged, the proffe thereof doth att your honours
pleafure reft upon the creditt of thefe that have fubfcribed their
names thereunto. Wherefore we humblie defire your honours,

Letter to the Lord Chan-cellor

as well for the difcharge of our neighbour his imprifonment, as alfo for that good regard of our fmall and poore countrie to be hadd, that it may enjoye fuch freedome and lawfull benefytt, as all other hir Majefties domnions doth. By which your moft godlie and charitable care, yowe fhall bynd the inhabitants thereof daylie to playe God that he will beautifie your moft noble mynd with fuch graces and vertues, as fhall caufe encreafe to greater honour, and thus commything the trewth and equitie of our caufe unto God and your honourable judgement, we leave any further to troble your honour, this xviij of November, 1588. Your honours moft humble att

commandment.

THOMAS WORSELLY,	WILLIAM MEAUSE,
ANTHONIE LYSLE,	THOMAS MEWILS,
EDWARD RICHARDS,	JOHN RICE,
JOHN LIGH,	WILLIAM OGLANDER.
EDWARD SCOTT,	

The Gentlemen at the fame time wrote the following letter to Sir George Carey:

" Sir George, our dutie remembred, whereas we underftand by Mr Robert Dylington, he was commytted to the Fleete at his appearance before hir Majefties Counfell, for that yowe have enforced ageynft him that he principallie follicited the articulating for the liberties of the iflad, and caufed mutenie in a dangerous tyme, wherein we fund ourfelves grieved to be thought men to be labored to fuch difcontentment, and whereof we knowe yowe were refolved otherwyfe. Nowe, notwithftanding thefe trobels, contrarie to your promife, upon him fallen; as in the begynnynge we offered yowe to be judge of our griefs, we contynew the like curtefie to graunt yowe the determination of the

caufe,

caufe, fo that yowe releafe our neighbour his imprifonment, and contynew the grauntinge not to impeach our liberties heretofore enjoyed, which good order of dealing if yow refufe, as we hope yowe will not, yowe fhall enforce us to that courfe, that it fhall ftand upon our creditt nether to confeffe ourfelves fo fimple as to fubfcribe to untrewthes, nor for any miflike to be fo blinded as to demaund that which we were never denyed, wherefore we defire fuch end as may content yowe, and warrant our liberties, and commytt yowe to God's protection. The xxiij of November, 1588.

Yours to command.

THOMAS WORSFLEY,	JOHN LEIGH,
ANTHONY LYSLE,	EDWARD SCOTT,
THOMAS DENNYS,	JOHN ERLESMAN,
EDWARD RICHARDS,	WILLIAM MEUX,
WILLIAM OGLANDER,	

Sir George Carey returned this Anfwer.

" Your letter of the xxiij, I receyved the xxvi of this inftant, the which being myngled with a curtefie carienge an inclofed conftrainte, and charginge of furmifes withowte profes, contryved by the cunyng of fome of you, and confented unto by the carelefs regard of others, in briefe I thus anfwere

" To that yowe charge me that before the Lords I enforced agaynft Dyllington that he principallie follicited the articulating, and caufed a mutenie in a daungerous tyme, wherein yowe fynd yourfelves greved to be thought men to be labored to fuch difcontentment, if he have wrytten fo, and yowe fo credulus to

beleve

Sir George Carey's reply.

beleve him, the Lords her counfell is able to difpiove you bothe. But that he piincipallie follicited the aiticulating, and fought what in him laye to bieede a mutenie betwixte fondrie gentle-men of the ifland and me, befides flaunderous untrewthes made in his repoits to my difcredit to the Lords, I did affirm, and will juftifie the faid affiimation trewe, to his fhame that fhall dare to faie the contraiie. Wherein what fmall caufe any of yowe hadd to be agreeved, and what great caufe I have to dif-dayn your taking parte with him, I wifh their Lordfhips may be judges. In another paite of your letter yowe dephe charge me, that contiarie to my promife, theis tiobles are fallen upon him, which is no leffe untrewe then you fo wryting undifcreet and to be difproved. for I knowe yowe cannot forgett that I wold nevei accept him into the reconcilement made betwixt yowe and me; as knowing his fundrie private injuries offeied me, unleffe his fubmiffion fhould be fuch as fixe of yowe fhould think fytt foi me to ieceyve, which none of yowe can faie to have byn fithence peifoimed, and theiefoie your affeition veiie injurious to laie breach of piomife wheie none hath byn made. Thiid-lie yowe offer that as at the begynnyne yowe offeied myfelf to be the judge of youi gieeves, that yowe will contynewe the like curtefie to giaunt me the deteimination of the caufe, fo that I re-lcafe youi neighboui of his impiifonment, and ccntynewe the giaunting not to impeach your libeities. If the fiift paite of youi offer hadd not been yoked with a condition of conftrainte, yowe had offered me a mattei worth thanks, and but what in reafon I have deferved at all your hands, but for the conditions of youi obligation, I thus anfweie them, Dyllington, upon the full hearing and debating of his piivate and all your geneiall caufes at laige, being heaid what he could allege befoie the Lords of hii Majefties Counfell, was by them commytted to the Fleete, and eajoyned to what they thought fytt for him to be

performed

performed, in whofe good pleafures his libertie or conftreinte lyeth. But if it laye in me to difcharge him, affure yourfelves he
fhould there remayne untill the moft gallant amongft you fhould
dare to come upp to trye whether he were not fytt and likelye
to kepe him companie. To contynewe my graunt not to impeach your liberties, is but what I have ever performed, and
therefore determyn not to denye what I never thought fytt to
refufe yowe. Hir Majeftie and the world may wyttenes the care
and love that I have borne to the countrie and people; protefting
that I hadd never intent to extorte or injurie the meaneft of
them, defyeing his mallice and chalinging him to the tryall that
thinketh I have done eyther more than I might, more than was
fytt for me, or what I did not avow to be lawfull : and if anye
of yowe fhall dare to charge me with the contrarie, let him come
up to fpitt his venome here in the place of indifference, and I
doubt not but to retorne the poyfon thereof to himfelf, and
prove him eyther a papift or a mifliker of the prefent ftate And
becaufe yowe fhall knowe howe clere I know myfelf from touch
of reproof, in Dillington's prefence before the Lords, I recyted
the articles of your pretended grieffs, whofe cenfure and viewe
of my patent approved all my actions, as himfelf can wytnes
unto yowe. But if any of yowe fhall infift in the demaunds of
thefe fryvolous fuppofed wrongs, I fhalbe moft gladd that he
will come upp to open the fmothered furmifes thercof, where, if
I have injured yowe, yowe may fone be releved, and if yowe
have injuied me yowe may be reformed. Your favours to forbeare me in any refpecte as I defire not, fo what any of your private mallice can do againft me, I feare not· and whereas not
anfweting your demaunds yowe threten to take that courfe that
fhall ftand upon your creditt not to confeffe yourfelves fo fimple
as to fubfcribe untrewthes, I wifh your fimplicities hadd not byn
fuch as it hath appeared, or that the lewde perfwafions of fome

P   fewe

fewe could not have drawen fo manie of yowe to buyld your opinions upon their conceits and malice. To conclude, that yowe may knowe what to expeĉt during my government in that place, think and believe that what hath byn gyven me in charge by hir Majeftie, what is warranted by my patent, and what I fhall fynd to be good for the benyfytt or ftrength of the countrie during my tyme, I will not forbear to execute withowte refpeĉte of anye. And fo I commytt yowe to God. This xxvjth of November, 1588.

Your frynde, if fryndlie ufed,

GEORGE CAREY."

To Thomas Worfeley, Anthonie Lyfle, Thomas
   Dennys, Edward Richards, William Oglander, John Leigh, Edward Scott, John Erlefman, and William Mewes, Gentlemen, and
   to any of them gyve this

This appears to have been the firft inftance of any complaint exhibited by the inhabitants of the ifland againft their Captain, for exerting his authority to provide for their fecurity; they having hæetofore readily concurred in every meafurè, and, as it were, anticipated every requifition for that purpofe; of which the train of artillery, then recently provided at their own charge, affords an inftance. It is probable that the manner of Sir George Carey's behaviour to them might be more offenfive than the matters infifted on; and when diftruft and diflike have once taken place, every word, every aĉtion becomes fufpeĉted and alarming   The foregoing remonftrance, however, procured the defired effeĉt; for the powers therein objeĉted to, were never afterwards claimed, either by Sir George Carey, or his fucceffors.

Sir

Sir George succeeded his father, not only in his title of Lord Hunsdon, but in the office of Lord Chamberlain, and was also a Knight of the Garter. He married Elizabeth, daughter of Sir John Spenser, of Althorp, in Northamptonshire, and died in the year one thousand six hundred and three *.

---

* Sir John Oglander, in his Memoirs, commends Sir George Carey for residing in the castle of Carisbrooke, and for his great hospitality there, and speaks of the time of his government as the period when the island was in its most flourishing state: from which the following extract may not be unpleasing, as it exhibits a very striking portrait of the manners of the times " I have heard, says " Sir John, and partly know it to be true, that not only heretofore there was " no lawyer nor attorney in owre island, but in Sir George Carey's time, an " attorney coming in to settle in the island, was, by his command, with a pound " of candles hanging att his breech lighted, with bells about his legs, hunted " owte of the island insomuch as oure ancestors lived here so quietly and secure- " ly, being neither troubled to London nor Winchester, so they seldom or never " went owte of the island, insomuch as when they went to London (thinking " it an East India voyage), they always made their wills, supposing no trouble " like to travaile "

Sir John, in another part of his Memoirs, observes, that

" The Isle of Wight, since my memory, is infinitely decayed, for either it is " by reason of so many attorneys that hath of late made this their habitation, and " so by sutes undone the country, (for I have known an attorney bring down after " a tearm *three hundred writts*, I have also known *twenty nisi prius* of our country " tried at our assizes, when as in the Queen's time we had not *six writts* in a " yeare, nor *one nisi prius* in six yeares) or else, wanting the good bargains they " were wont to buy from men of war, who also vented our commoditys at very " high prices, and readie money was easie to be had for all things Now peace " and law hath beggered us all, so that within my memorie many of the gentlereen, " and almost all the yeomanry are undone "

" Be advised by me, have no sutes at lawe, if it be possible agree with thine " adversary although it be with thy losse, for the expence of one tearm will be " more than thy losse. Besides the neglect of thy time at home, thy absence from ' thy wife and children, so manie inconveniences hangeth upon a suite in lawe, " that I advise thee, although thou has the better of it, let it be reconciled with- " out law at last twelve men or one must end it, let two honest ones do it at " firste This country was undone with it in King James his reign Hazard " death and all quarrels rather than let thy tongue make his master a slave "
MSS Memoirs.

He

1603.   He was fucceeded in his office of Captain of the Ifle of Wight,
in the firft year of James the Firft, by Henry, Earl of Southampton; who had been attainted for taking arms with the Earl
of Effex, and was a prifoner in the Tower when Queen Elizabeth died   But, on the acceffion of King James, he was reftored in blood by an act of Parliament, obtained a new patent
for his title of Earl of Southampton, and was made a Knight of
the Garter; he was Governor and Captain of all the Ifle of
Wight, Captain of the caftle of Carifbrooke, and all other caftles
and fortreffes in the faid Ifle; alfo Conftable of the caftle of Carifbrooke, Warden of the Foreft of Parkhurft, likewife Steward,
Surveyor, Receiver, and Bailiff of all the lands, woods, revenues, &c. of the Crown, within the ifland.   His juft, affable,
and obliging deportment gained him the univerfal efteem of all
ranks of people, and raifed the ifland to a moft flourifhing ftate;
many Gentlemen refiding there in great affluence and hofpitality.   Sir John Oglander * relates, in his Memoirs, that he had
                                                           feen

* The following lift of the freeholders is indorfed as follows, by Sir John Oglander:
" This is my father Sir William Oglander's hand, when he was Hygh Sheryfe;
" he, by command, prefented a copy hereof to King James, then at Bewlye."

A Noate of the Freeholders in the Ifle of Wight, 3 Februarij, anno 1606.

John Leigh, knight.	Alexander Weight, gent.	John Kyngfwell, jure ux-
John Mewes, knight	Richard Champion, gent	or.s.
Richard White, knight.	William Shambler, gent.	John White, of Bockham.
William Lyfley, knight	Emanuel Bad, gent	William Meadmore.
William Oglander, knight.	Stephen March, gent.	Edward Hayles.
Richard Worfley, efq.	Edward Loveing, gent.	John Cole.
Thomas Bowreman, efq	Michell Knight	Edward Medmore.
William Mewes, eq	John Fitchett	John Dagwell.
Barnabie Leigh, efq	Henry Knotte.	Thomas Dore, of Wellow.
Thomas Cheike, efq.	James Byfhop.	William Urry.
Thomas Hobfon, efq	William Rive.	Robert Goodale.
Edward Richards, gent.	Henry White.	John Goodale.
Edward Dennys, gent.	William Facey.	David Urrey
John Dingley, gent.	Henry Joones, jure uroris.	John Dore, of Frefhwater.
Bowyer Worfley, gent	William Elemen.	John Godfrey.
		Edwa-

feen thirty or forty Knights and Gentlemen at bowls with Lord
Southampton on St. George's Down, where they had an ordinary twice every week, on Tuesday and Thursday.

On the death of the Earl of Southampton, in December, one
thousand six hundred and twenty-five, John, Lord Conway,
was made Captain of the Isle of Wight; and, in the May following, Secretary of State, and afterwards President of the
Council. Lord Conway never resided in the island, but governed it by his Lieutenants, Sir Edward Dennis, and Sir John
Oglander. He died in the sixth of King Charles the First,
and was succeeded by Richard, Lord Weston, who was two
years after created Earl of Portland, and died in one thousand
six hundred and thirty-four.

1625.
John, Lord
Conway.

1631.
Richard,
Lord Weston.

Edward Cheike, gent.	Edward Harbard	Richard Godfrey
Robert Dillington, gent.	Alexander Harvy, gent.	John Hancock
Richard Basket, gent.	Edward Harvy, gent.	William Broade.
Barnabie Colnett, gent.	Peter Garde	John Collens
John Harvy, gent	Michaell Holbrooke	Henry Godfrey.
George Fashion, gent.	John Serle, of Sanham.	Richard Galpin
John Rice, gent.	William Colman.	William Temple.
Thomas Erlisman, gent.	Richard Colman.	David Lacey.
Thomas Erlisman, jun gent.	William Howe.	William Lacey.
Thomas Budden, gent.	William Peare	William Boye
John Serle, of Coshin, gent	William Nutte.	Thomas Younge.
George Serle, gent	Thomas Legge.	Richard Arnold.
Thomas Urrey, gent.	Nicholas Newman.	Thomas Urrey, } of Comp-
Thomas Worsley, gent.	William Newman.	John Urrey, } ton.
John Somers, gent jure	Stephen Blake.	Thomas Bull
uxoris	John More	William Salter.
John Serle of Witcombe,	Peter Wadford.	David Wavell
gent	John Leach	Thomas Wavell.
William St. Crosse, gent.	Thomas Bruse	William Jackman.
Thomas Lovibond, gent.	Andrew Legge, jure uxoris.	William Bynches.
Edward Eaden, gent.	John Rydge.	Edmund Puckford

Jerom

Jerom, Earl of Portland, succeeded his father Richard, Earl of Portland, and continued Captain and Governor of the Island, until he was displaced by Parliament, during the civil war. Clarendon says that " the Parliament threatened the Earl of Port-
" land, who, with extraordinary vivacity, crossed their expecta-
" tions, that they would remove him from his charge and govern-
" ment of the Isle of Wight (which last they did *de facto*, by com-
" mitting him to prison without assigning a cause), and to that
" purpose objected all the acts of good fellowship, all the waste
" of powder, and all the waste of wine, in the drinking of healths,
" and other acts of jollity, which ever he had been at in his go-
" vernment, from the first hour of his entering upon it *."

* Clarendon's Hist. book vi. p 531. The estimation the Earl of Portland was held in by the inhabitants in the year one thousand six hundred and forty-two, is clearly manifested by the following petition

" To the Honourable the Knights, Citizens, and Burgesses, of the House of
    " Commons assembled in Parliament

" The humble Petition of the Deputy Lieutenants and Justices of the Peace,
" the Mayors and Corporations of Newport, Newtown, and Yarmouth, and of
" the rest of the inhabitants of the Isle of Wight

" Presenting to your gracious consideration our generall griefe for the question-
" ing of Jerom, Earl of Portland, our noble and much honoured and beloved
" Captayne and Governor.

" The principal imputation, as we are given to understand, being a jealousy of
" his Lordship's inclination to popery

" For ourselves, we have a pregnant testimony amongst us of his pious affection
" and love to the reformed religion, by a constant weekly lecture at Newport, to
" which his Lordship is a principal benefactor. So are there on the other side, so
" small effects to be seen of his Lordship's discourse or practice that way tending,
" that amongst all the inhabitants of this isle, we have not one professed papist,
" or, to our knowledge, popishly affected, so rare a blessing, in these times, as
" we suppose cannot be boasted in any tract of ground of this extent in all the
" kingdom of England

" Some other weake aspersions uppon his Lordship, we thought not worthy of
" our owne regard, much lesse dare wee presume to remember them to so grave
" and wise a senate, wee do therefore, at once, with this petition present our
" humble and grateful acknowledgement to this greate and good assembly, of
" the care that is taken of our weale and safety, which we conceive can no waye
" be better advanced and continued uppon us, than by your just approbation of
" the vigilance and fidelity of our prudent and able Governor "

The

1642
Philip, Earl
of Pembroke.

The Parliament, having removed the Earl of Portland, they appointed in his place Philip, Earl of Pembroke, a man more conformable to their views and interest; upon his appointment he applied to Sir John Dingley, who had been Deputy-governor, for the state and condition of the island, in answer to which, the following letter was written by that Gentleman.

" March, 31st. An Do. 1642.

Sir John
Dingley's
account of
the state of
the island at
this time.

" According to your Lordship's command, I have thought of
" the state and present condition of the Isle of Wight, most
" part of which is of my own knowledge, the rest from good
" hands. The King hath the disposing of the castles follow-
" ing, and consequently hee that is chosen Captaine hath the
" ordering and disposing of the same. A land Castle, or Fort,
" called Cafe-brook Castle, which stands near the middle of the
" island, belonging to it is a porter, and diverse gunners and
" waiters, to what number I doe not well know; and withall
" there is an armory for diverse hundreds of men, but the true
" number I know not, and in that Fort is the Islands magazine
" of Powder, both for itself and all other Castles, for all services
" and accomodations his Majesty shall appoint it; and by
" the way I thought good to lett your Lordship know, that since
" Sir Henry Knowles, of the Green-cloth, got the fee farme of
" the mannor of Bucham, and what other thinges I doe not
" well know, hee then gott away the stables, meadows, and
" lands, worth 40 if not 50 pound p. ann. that alwayes apper-
" tained to the Captaine of that Castle, which stables, land, &c.
" were called by the name of Frognoll, since which time there
" hath bin, a poore homly stable built up with a few boards in
" the midst of the Castle, adjoyning to the garden wall, which
" must needs be very noysome and unfitt to bee in that place
" There is a Park alsoe belonging to the Captaine, which is 3
" miles about; and there is alsoe a common for the whole
" country

" country to putt in horfe or beafts without ftint, which is called
" by the name of Parkhurft Chace; the King and confequently
" the Captaine hath fallow deere in it, and doth keepe a Keeper
" and a Rainger to keepe them and to looke unto them, that
" they do not ly in mens inn-grounds, which hath bin very
" much abufd, by fuffering the deere to ly out and foe they are
" allmoft quite deftroyd, and in my time the country hath quite
" deftroy'd the woods and bufhes, and alfoe fome have made en-
" croachment and have taken in fome of the common for pri-
" vate ufe. Another fort there is, called Sandam Caftle or Fort,
" to which belongs a Captaine *, and a Livetenant, and Gun-
" neis, and Waiters, but to what number I know not, and fince
" the Kinge new built it, he hath added more Waiters, how
" many I cannot fay, but I believe, if it be well lookt into, it
" is but poorly man'd ftill; confideiing this Fort is of gieater
" confequence than any other, for that it lies open uppon the
" maine fea between Fiance and us, tis iequifite there bee a
" fpeciall and fpeedy care taken of it. Theie is an other Fort,
" called Cowes Caftle † ovei againft which lies a Caftle, called
" Caylfhott Caftle ‡. Thefe Caftles lie for the fafe coming to and
" fio between the Ifland and the mayne land, and feive to keepe
" the enemy fiom landing within the Ifland; but they are not
" of fo gieate confequence as the foiementioned Fort; to thefe
" Caftles belong Gunneis and Waiters, but I believe 'tis very
" weakly man'd Theie is anothei Caftle, called Yarmouth
" Caftle §, which ferves for the fame purpofe as Cowes Caftle
" doth, and to it belongs Gunners and Waiteis, but I believe 'tis
" not much better man'd than Cowes Theie was alfo a Sconce
" built in K Haiiy the 8th's time, called Woifley's Sconce, which
" was oppofite to Hurft Caftle, which Sconce, when my Lord

* " Piomii is one Buck"
‡ " Cab Tuiiey"
| " Con Tames."
§ " Cip Baikay"

                                                 " Conway

" Conway was Captaine of the Island, and my old Lord Port-
" land Treasurer, was, by order from him, taken down. foe
" by it, the Island is much weakened · and I heare that Hurst
" Castle * is in a weak condition, I wish your Lordship would
" take care of it.

" My Lord, as for the Traine Bands, which (next to the
" Castles) is the strength of the Island, it is much weakened and
" decayed, and if there bee not a speedy courfe taken, will be
" dayly worfe and worfe, by reafon the Lords of the mannors
" take in theyr tenaments or copy-holds, and alfo farmers lay
" together as many farmes as they can gett, foe by this meanes
" the Island is much depopulated and weakened, and the most
" part of thofe men that are in the country lives in cotages or
" empty farm-houfes, and live either upon keeping dame, or
" elfe by dayly work, foe that they are very poore, that if an
" enemy should invade the country, tis to be fear'd they would
" foon run away, and there are good laws if they were putt in
" in execution to remedy all this. Since the coming of K.
" James, there is a town in the island (called Newport) made a
" Mare-town, which heretofore was only a Bayly-town, and
" then the Livetenants and Juftices had the fame power the e
" they had in the reft of the country; but now they have got-
" ten a Charter to be a Mare-town and have Juftices, a Recorder,
" Aldermen, &c which the other two Mare-towns have not,
" as Yarmouth and Newton, they will not be governed as thofe
" two Mare-towns, and the reft of the Island are, which
" is very prejudiciall to the country, and I wish it might be re-
" gulated And in that town of Newport the Captaine of the
" Island is Clark of the Markett, and hath the ordering of the
" country; this town notwithftanding will take the power to
" themfelves, and hinder men from buying and felling at theyr

" pleafure, I hope your lordfhip will look into it. My Lord
" the Clergy of the Ifland, for the moft part, are loofe and idle
" livers, and neglect their charge, I wifh your Lordfhip would
" take it into your ferious confideration.

" My Lord, there hath bin of late yeares diverfe goodly man-
" nors of the King's fold (which I have heard is Crown land)
" and greateft part of them is very well wooded, which wood
" did ferve for the mending, repayring, or the building of his
" caftles there, or any ufe his Majefty hath of wood, and now
" they are fold, there is fcarce a ftick for any fuch ufe, unlefs
" very little in the park: his Majefty and the country fuffer
" much by this fale And as for the men of quality, I think it
" fitter to acquaint your Lordfhip of them by word of mouth,
" and for the prefent leave you to your worthy employments
" and reft.

Your humble fervant to command,

JOHN DINGLEY."

To the Right Honourable the Earl of Pembroke,
    Captain of the Ifle of Wight

The peace of this Ifland was greatly difturbed by the rupture
between the King and his Parliament, which now began to
break out into acts of open violence. Happily its fituation was
too much detached from the fcenes of hoftility to be expofed to
the occafional depredations of the troops of either fide; but fo
important a conteft could not take place without interefting all
men in the event, and exciting great inteftine animofity The
people had petitioned warmly in favour of the Earl of Portland,
and many of the Gentlemen figned a declaration, that they
would, with their lives and fortunes, fupport the Proteftant religion, protect the peace of the Ifland, and " admit no forreyn
" power, or forces, or new government, except his Majefty,

" by

" by advife of his Parliament, uppon occafione that may arife,
" fhale think itt neceffary to alter it in any particulars, for the
" good and fafety of the kingdom *."

Notwithflanding this declaration, and the former petition in
behalf of the Earl of Portland, the fickle populace in an inftant
changed fides, and Mofes Read, the Mayor of Newport, reprefented to the Parliament, that the town could not be deemed fafe,
fo long as Colonel Brett, and the Countefs of Portland remained
in Carifbrooke Caftle.   On the Earl of Portland's being difplaced,
the King had by his commiffion given the cuftody of the caftle
to Brett; and the Countefs, depending on the affection expreffed
by the inhabitants for her hufband in the petition, had taken refuge in the caftle with her five children, accompanied by her
hufband's brother and fifter, hoping by her prefence to preferve
that fortrefs for the King.   The Parliament, in confequence of
Read s reprefentation, directed the Captains of the fhips in the
river to affift him in any meafures he fhould think neceffary for
fecuring the ifland.   Read accordingly marched the Newport militia, with four hundred naval auxiliaries againft the caftle, where
Brett had not above twenty men, many well-wifhers to him and the
Countefs being deterred from affifting them by the menaces of the
populace, who now threw off all kind of refpect for their fuperiors.
Harby, the Curate of Newport, a man under peculiar obligations
to the Earl of Portland, diftinguifhed himfelf in fpiriting up the

' Subfcribed, Auguft 8, 1642, by

John Oglander,	Edward Leigh,	Hugh Leigh,
William Hopkins,	Jeromie Brett,	Robert Dillington,
John Leygh,	Robert Dillington,	John Meux,
William Oglander,	John Richards,	Henry Knowles,
William Booreman,	Brutus Bucke,	Nicholas Weflon,
Stephen March,	Edward Worfley,	Edward Denys,
Thomas Leygh,	Humphrey Fourney,	Edward Checke,
Bar Burley,	Bar. Leign,	John Burlvgh.

Q 2   befiegers

befiegers againft his lady and children, affigning for reafon her being a Papift, and exhorting them, in the canting phrafeology of the times, to be valiant, as they were about to fight the battle of the Lord.

The Caftle had not at that time three days provifions for its flender garrifon, yet this Lady, with the magnanimity of a Roman mation, went to the platform with a match in her hand, vowing fhe would fire the firft cannon herfelf, and defend the caftle to the utmoft extremity, unlefs honourable terms were granted. After fome negotiations, the articles of capitulation were agreed on, and the caftle furrendered. thefe were, that Colonel Brett, the Gentlemen with him, and their fervants, who compofed the garrifon, fhould be allowed the freedom of the Ifland; but were reftricted from going to Portfmouth, then held for the King by Goring. The Countefs was to enjoy her lodgings in the Caftle, until the contrary fhould be ordered by the Parliament An order arrived foon after prefcribing her removal from the ifland within two days after notice given her, and fhe was then indebted to the humanity of the feamen for the veffel which conveyed her and her family *.

The other forts on the Ifland were alfo feized, and, on the arrival of the Earl of Pembroke, he was refpectfully received by the Gentlemen and principal farmers, who affembled at Cowes, and tendered him their beft fervices. The inhabitants having thus taken a decifive ftep in clofing with the prevailing power, they remained afterwards undifturbed fpectators of the enfuing commotions, until the King injudicioufly fought here an afylum.

October. 51

---

* Oglander's MSS. Memoirs

The

The Earl of Pembroke conformed fo thoroughly to the temper of the times, that, after the death of the King and the fuppreffion of the Houfe of Lords, he was returned, with all his titles, Knight of the Shire for the county of Berks, and was admitted into the Houfe of Commons, with peculiar marks of refpect *.

Colonel Robert Hammond was Governor of the Ifland when King Charles the Firft took refuge there; and had the cuftody of that unfortunate Prince, who was induced to hope for protection from him on account of his being nephew to his Chaplain, Doctor Henry Hammond, but his connections with, and expectations from the other party, gave him an infuperable biafs in their favour he was entirely dependent on Cromwell, through whofe intereft he had married the daughter of the famous Hambden, and alfo lately obtained the Government of the Ifle of Wight The unconditional manner in which King Charles refigned himfelf into the hands of Colonel Hammond, at Titchfield houfe, is fully related by Lord Clarendon and other hiftorians, but the circumftances of his treatment, and perfonal tranfactions in the ifland, are not fo generally known.

1647
Col Hammond

It may be collected from Sir Thomas Herbert, that on the firft arrival of the King in the ifland, Colonel Hammond lodged him in Carifbrooke caftle; not as a prifoner, but as a gueft there was not the leaft appearance of reftraint on any of his actions; he rode out for his recreation when, and where he pleafed, his faithful fervants were permitted to repair to him, and all who defired it, were admitted into his prefence without diftinction.

Nov 1
Arrival of Charles I in the ifland.

* Rapin, vol. 11. p 574, note.   † Rapin, vol. 11 p. 540.

Is deprived of his servants.

The first restraint on this freedom was respecting his Chaplains, Dr Sheldon and Dr Hammond, who were not long permitted to exercise their functions, a loss the King supplied by his private devotions, and, on the Lord's day by reading the Scriptures, and other pious books, not being disposed to hear those preachers who used the directory then adopted

The enjoyment of this degree of liberty was however of no long duration; for about the middle of February Hammond, one afternoon, informed the King, that he had received orders not to permit the attendance of Mr. Ashburnham, Mr. Legg, or any other of his servants who were with him at Oxford, their continuance about his person being judged improper. The King, with a countenance that betrayed both surprize and trouble, communicated this order to Ashburnham and the rest of the persons concerned, as a circumstance he did not expect, and which was by no means consistent with the promises made him by some considerable persons   The next day, after the King had dined, these Gentlemen came all together, and prostrating themselves at his Majesty's feet, offered up their prayers to God for his preservation, and, kissing his hands, departed.

Is confined.

The day following, his imprisonment became no longer equivocal, he being denied the liberty of going about the country. Still, though he was limited by the walls of the castle, they included a sufficient space for the exercise of walking, and afforded good air, and a delightful prospect both by sea and land, and, for the King's recreation, Colonel Hammond converted the Barbican, a spacious area used as a parade, into a bowling-green, and at one side erected an agreeable summer-house for his amusement, where the King passed his vacant hours, the castle having no gallery, room of state, nor even a garden; so that

that his Majesty constantly exercised himself in the morning by walking on the ramparts, and in the afternoon in the bowling-green, at the same time carefully observing stated hours for reading and devotion. Mr. Harrington and Mr. Herbert constantly waiting on him in his bed-chamber, to the latter he gave the charge of his books, of which he himself kept a catalogue. The books he most usually read were the sacred Scriptures, Bishop Andrews's sermons, Hooker's Ecclesiastical Polity, Doctor Hammond's works, Villalpandus upon Ezekiel, &c. Sandys's Paraphrase upon David's Psalms, Herbert's Divine Poems, Tasso's Jerusalem, in Italian, with Fairfax's English translation, Ariosto, and Spencer's Fairie Queen. At this time he is supposed to have written his *Suspiria Regalia*, the manuscript of which Mr. Herbert found among the books the King gave him, in his own hand-writing.

Notwithstanding the strictness with which the King was guarded, many persons found means to present themselves to him at his usual times of walking within the lines, in order to be touched for the disease called the King's-evil. The Governor's Chaplain, a young man, named Troughton, seldom failed attending in the presence-chamber when the King dined, he possessed all the arguments in favour of his sect, in opposition to episcopacy: the King used frequently to walk about with him an hour after meals, and engage in familiar conversation on those subjects. Troughton maintained his arguments with great earnestness, and the King never discouraged him, but being a better logician, and deeper read in history and polemics, always obtained the advantage. Once, whilst they were in the heat of argument, Charles took a sword from the side of one of his attendants, and drawing it suddenly, frightened the young Chaplain, but another gentleman present, who

later

better underftood the King's intentions, foon quieted Troughton's apprehenfions, by kneeling down and receiving the honour of Knighthood *. This was Mr. John Duncomb, who came into the ifland to concert meafures with the King for his efcape, when the King told him he had not at that time any better means of acknowleging his fervices. After the Reftoration Sir John Duncomb was made Chancellor of the Exchequer.

Dec 29th. Soon after the arrival of the King at Carifbrooke caftle, an attempt was made for his refcue by Captain Burley, mentioned in Sir John Dingley's letter as Captain of Yarmouth caftle · the particulars of this tranfaction are not handed down, but it appears that the plan was fo ill laid and conducted, that he was himfelf apprehended and executed. This attempt, in the prefent fituation of affairs, was extremely prejudicial to the King the Army and Parliament were contending for the fuperiority they had jointly gained, and as the poffeffion of the King's perfon was a matter of great moment to each party, fo a prevention of his efcape was a point in which they were both interefted. This therefore will account for the fubfequent rigour of his confinement.

Mr Henry Firebrace relates, that, having the honour to be known to the King by feveral fervices rendered him during the treaty of Uxbridge, and elfewhere, he received a private letter from him, commanding him to haften to the Ifle of Wight, with what intelligence he cou'd procure from the moft faithful of his friends about London. He accordingly applied to the Speaker of the Houfe of Commons, and other Commiffioners, for permiffion to attend his Majefty, as one of the Pages of his Bed-chamber, which precaution he made ufe of, that he might ferve him with more freedom and lefs fufpicion. His firft object

* Sir T. Herbert's Memoirs   ⊦ Rapin, vol ii p. 545

after

after his arrival, was how fafely to deliver into the King's hands
the letters he was charged with. having found a convenient and
private place in his chamber for depofiting his difpatches, he
flipt a note into the King's hand, as he was retiring to reft, informing him where they were hidden: the next morning Mr.
Firebrace found a letter in the fame place, by which his Majefty
expreffed his approbation of what he had done, and directing a
continuation of the fame mode of correfpondence, which they
accordingly made ufe of for feveral weeks. Firebrace had, pre-
vious to his leaving London, fettled a good channel of communication with the King's friends there, by means of two trufty and
unfufpected men, always coming and going, fo that his Majefty
never wanted intelligence from the Queen, the Prince, and many
of his friends, even at the time when the vote againft any more
addreffes to him took place. Mr Firebrace alfo infinuated himfelf into favour with the perfons appointed by Colonel Hammond to watch the King, by turns, at the two doors of his bed-
chamber by day, and at night to fleep in beds fet fo clofe againft
thefe doors, which opened outwards, fo that they were kept faft
till the beds were removed. The King conftantly retired to his
bed-chamber as foon as he had fupped. Firebrace, one night,
pretending he had no appetite, offered his fervice to one of thefe
guards, promifing to fupply his place at the door opening to the
back-ftairs, whilft he eat his fupper, this offer being accepted,
he enjoyed an uninterrupted freedom of converfing with the
King; who defired him to renew the like opportunity as often
as he could Firebrace, fearing he might be furprifed with the
door open by any one coming fuddenly into the bed chamber,
cut a flit through the wall or partition behind the hangings,
which, on the leaft noife, he could inftantly let fall: in thefe
converfations they frequently deliberated on fome means for the
King's efcape, his imprifonment being by this time grown in-
tolerable. Among other fchemes, Firebrace propofed his getting

R

out of the chamber-window, but fearing the bars might render the paffage too narrow, he propofed cutting them with a faw; but the King objecting the danger of a difcovery, commanded him to prepare all things elfe for his departure, being confident he could get through the window, having tried with his head, and judging that where the head could pafs, the body would eafily follow. Firebrace imparted the defign to fome trufty friends, and with them concerted the plan of operation *. Thefe

* Two letters from the King to Mr Worfley are ftill extant; they are written in a fmall neat hand, and are here exactly copied from the originals.

" 16 May, 1648.

" Z I finde fo good fruits in the paines that you take for me, that againe I muft " put you to a little more troble (affeuring you that you fhall finde me thankefull " to you for altogether and that not in a meane way) it is that you would goe to " Southampton to one Mrs Pit's houfe, where you will finde W and deliver to " him the inclofed w ch you will find directed to him, and alfo advife with him, " where I fhall take the boat and where land and the watch word as foone as you " can the other is to 395 w ch I defyre you fend fafely and fpeedely to him but " I would not have any bodie know that I have written to him So I reft,

your moft affeured frend,

" Leaft you fhould not underftand J

" The Cypher, the thin letter is 101 him, for whom I fent you one, upon the fifth " of this month to w ch (I thanke you for your care) I have had an Anfwer and " now this is a reply to that If I knew certainely that you had the Cypher out of " w ch I have written this name, I would wryte more freely than I now care."

Mr Worfley muft have been in poffeffion of a key when he received the following letter

" 22 May, 1648

" Z I am verie well fatisfied with the difcreete and carefull account that you " have given me of my Bufines and particularly that you did 208 · 343 : 294 " 74 9 45 86 18 96 1 40 82 395 380 2 20 3 230 388 45 " 36 4 11 7 43 31 62 270 248 now it will be 36 · 19 : 5 32 39 · " 12 37 8 97 I defyre you to enquire whether or not 396 . 213 355 204 " 28 21 363 257 64 36 46 9 32 395 42 35 14 53 38 23 : " 18 50 88 but for this 236 308 267 · 356 . 282 96 62 : 86 · 205 17 . " 356 62 50 97 206 231 248 38 1 20 2 230 388 46 . 36 . 257 " 208 86 25 268 8 3 · 50 240 6 51 248 416 · 303 78 9 68 . " 45 . in the meane tyme lett me know 379 4 28 5 348 : 354 · the ... .. " 206 18 So I reft

your affeured frend,

J "

were

THE ISLE OF WIGHT.

were Mr. Edward Worfley, a Gentleman of the ifland much efteemed, afterwards knighted for his fervices on this occafion; Mr. Richard Ofborn, a Gentleman appointed by the Parliament to attend the King; and Mr John Newland, of Newport, who all proved themfelves worthy of the confidence repofed in them. The plan agreed upon was as follows: at the time appointed Firebrace was to throw fomething up againft the window of the King's chamber, as a fignal that all was clear, on which the King was to come out and let himfelf down by a cord provided for that purpofe, being defcended, Firebrace, under favour of the darknefs, was to conduct him crofs the court to the main wall of the caftle, from which he was again to defcend into the ditch, by means of another cord with a ftick faftened crofs it, ferving as a feat, beyond this wall was the counterfcarp, which being low, might be eafily afcended, near this place Mr Worfley and Mr Ofborne were to be ready mounted, having a fpare horfe, with piftols and boots for the King, while Mr. Newland remained at the fea-fide with a large boat, ready to have conveyed his Majefty wherever he fhould have thought fit to direct. At the appointed time, when all things were in readinefs, and every one inftructed in his part, Firebrace gave the expected fignal, on which the King attempted to get out of the window, but found, when it was too late, that he had been fatally miftaken, for although he found an eafy paffage for his head, he ftuck faft between the breaft and fhoulders, without the power of advancing or returning; but having the inftant before miftrufted fomething of this nature, he had tied a piece of cord to the bar of the window, by the means of which he might force himfelf back again. Firebrace heard him groan, without being able to afford him the leaft affiftance; however, the King at length, with much difficulty, having releafed himfelf from the window, placed a candle in it, as an intimation that his attempt was fruftrated.

Had not this unfortunate impediment happened, there is the greatest reason to believe he might have effected his escape; every part of the plan being so judiciously arranged   It now became necessary to give notice of the disappointment to those who waited without, which Firebrace could find no better means of doing, then by throwing stones from the top of the wall, from whence the King was to have been let down, to the place where they were in waiting: this so well answered his intention, that they went quietly away, without having caused any alarm.

After this disappointment, files and aqua fortis were sent for from London, to corrode or cut through the bars of the window; but in the interim, Hammond received a letter from Derby-house, directing him to keep a watchful eye over those about the King, as there were some among them who gave him intelligence. This, though a general hint of suspicion, was not pointed at any particular person; Hammond therefore employed his emissaries to make discoveries, who gave him so much light, that he entertained some suspicion of Firebrace, and examined him; but not being able to come at any material discovery, he told him the reasons by which he was actuated.   Some time after, Firebrace was again sent for by Hammond, who informed him he had received more letters of intelligence, which would oblige him to dismiss several of the King's attendants, himself among the rest; but that he might, if he pleased, remain three or four days longer   Firebrace plainly saw this permission was an intended snare, he nevertheless determined to accept of it, and guide himself accordingly; informing the King of his suspicions, and settling with him such a mode of correspondence, that his Majesty received intelligence from his friends, and had his dispatches forwarded with the same success as before [*].

* Firebrace's Narrative, in Herbert's Memoirs.

Another

Another ineffectual attempt for the King's escape was made after the departure of Mr. Fire's ace, by his remaining associates the particulars are thus related by Lord Clarendon, and also by a private account drawn up by Sir Edward Worsley. The King remembering his former miscarriage, owing to the bar of his window, now took care to have that impediment removed, either by aqua fortis, or a saw, but when he was coming through the window, he perceived more persons under it than he expected. This made him suspect, what was but too true, that his intention was discovered: he therefore shut his window, and returned to his bed. soon after which the Governor came into his chamber, and examining the window perceived the bar had been eaten away. It appears that Major Rolfe, an officer of the castle had so far insinuated himself into the confidence of Mr. Osborne, that he was deceived into an opinion that Rolfe would heartily join in any attempt for the King's deliverance, whereas his real design was to kill him as he came through the window. Hammond was privy to this intention, and also posted musqueteers near where the Gentlemen were of necessity to pass, and in riding off, they luckily received the fire unhurt, getting safely to the vessel that lay in readiness to carry off the King, but as they came without him, the master refused to take them on board, so that, leaving their horses on the shore, they were obliged to conceal themselves for several days in the woods, finding means in the night, by the assistance of a kinsman of Mr. Worsley's, to procure sustenance, and a vessel to take them off from the south side of the island.

Another attempt to escape

These unsuccessful attempts afforded pretences to increase the rigour of the King's confinement, who, from the time his servants were removed, had laid aside all care of his person, suffering his hair and beard, grown to an extraordinary length, to hang dishevelled and neglected; a decrepid old man, employed to kindle his fire, whom he afterwards fhewed to Sir Philip Warwick, was, as he affirmed, the beft company he enjoyed for feveral months.

The Army, who now in fact held the fword over the heads of their nominal mafters, were engaged in the fuppreffion of the remaining Royalifts; an opportunity the Houfe of Commons made ufe of to revive their negociations with the captive Monarch The refolution, ftyled the Vote of Non Addreffes, was repealed, and a new treaty fet on foot, the appointed place was Newport, in the Ifle of Wight, where the King was to enjoy the fame ftate of freedom as when laft at Hampton-Court, and to be attended by fervants of his own appointment.   On his part to ftand bound by his royal word not to go out of the ifland during the treaty, nor for twenty days after, without the advice of both Houfes of Parliament *.

Thus was the King fo far releafed as to be a prifoner at large on his parole.   The treaty now opened, but by the artifices of the Independents, it was fpun out to fuch a length, that the infurrections being every where fuppreffed, the Army were at liberty to put an end to thefe negociations, which they effected, by once more feizing the perfon of the King.   Fairfax was returned to Windfor, when he fent Colonel Ewer to take the King into his cuftody, with orders to Hammond to attend him at head-quarters.   The particulars of this tranfaction are related by Colonel Cooke, to the following effect.

On the evening of the twenty-ninth, between the hours of feven and eight, the King fent for the Duke of Richmond, the Earl of Lindfay, and Colonel Cooke, defiring their immediate

* Rapin, vol ii p 559.

attend-

attendance; they were then altogether at the Duke of Richmond's lodgings, and immediately waited on him, the Lords entering into the inner chamber, whilst the Colonel remained without for orders. The King then acquainted them, that one of his servants had been sent for by a person in disguise, who, having informed him that the Army would that night seize the King, left him abruptly. Colonel Cooke was then called in, and asked by his Majesty, whether he had heard any rumour that the Army intended to seize him that night. He answered, he had not heard any thing so much as tending towards it, adding, that if he had he would surely have informed the King thereof. Charles acquainting the Colonel with his reasons for this question, ordered him to find out Major Rolfe *, who was then left as Deputy-governor by Colonel Hammond, and to enquire whether he knew of any such design. Cooke opportunely found Major Rolfe in his chamber, and communicated the King's message. Rolfe denied all knowlege of any such thing, saying, you may assure the King from me, that he may rest quietly this night, for on my life he shall have no disturbance this night The Colonel observing he laid so much emphasis on the words, this night, urged him farther to declare if there was any such design at all? After some pause, he answered, it was impossible for him to know the purposes of the Army, at so great a distance, but that as yet he had received no such orders If you should hereafter, rejoined the Colonel, shall I be so timely acquainted with them, as that the King may not be surprised with their execution? To which request he seemingly consented; answering, that was but a respect due to the King. Colonel Cooke returned with a punctual account of all these circumstances, but the King, having in the mean time been informed that a considerable number of the army had that evening landed on the island, remanded

* The same man who betrayed the King's intention to escape

him

him back to Major Rolfe, to learn the truth of that report. Rolfe faid, he knew frefh troops would e'er long come over to relieve thofe then on duty there; but was not yet certain of their arrival.

During the fhort interval of Cooke's fecond abfence, the King received intelligence that two thoufand foot were drawn up round Carifbrooke caftle; at this he feemed greatly agitated, exclaiming, furely there muft be fome very extraordinary bufinefs in hand, that could caufe fuch a body of men to be fo fecretly landed, and in fo bitter a night as this, expofed to the extremity of the weather; the wind then blowing very high, and the rain falling very faft. As the King expreffed an anxious defire of certain information, doubting he might be deceived by Major Rolfe, Colonel Cooke once more offered his fervice for that purpofe; but the King, reflecting on the feverity of the weather, refufed to expofe him to it any more. the Colonel, however, knowing no other expedient for his Majefty's prefent fatisfaction, at length obtained permiffion to go; the King adding his hopes that the Colonel, being young and healthy, would not receive any prejudice thereby.

The Colonel having mounted his horfe, with great difficulty found the way to the caftle, the night being extremely dark: having rode round it, without meeting any troops, he took fhelter under the gate-way, to cover himfelf from the violence of the rain; and recollecting that Captain Bowreman, a Gentleman of the 'fland, with whom he was well acquainted, commanded a company of militia there, he fent in a meffage, defiring to fpeak with him, difcourfing, in the mean time, with the foldiers, to try what he could learn from them, thefe he found altogether ignorant, being of a company newly marched in, the two army companies that formerly were in garrifon here having

been

been drawn out into the town of Newport, probably to ftrengthen the guards doing duty at that place. After a long ftay, the meffenger returned to Colonel Cooke with an excufe, that the Captain could not conveniently come out to him, but defired he would walk in: Cooke accepting the invitation, was, on entering the parlour, furprifed with the fight of above a dozen officers of the army, moft of whom he knew: after mutual falutations, he addreffed himfelf to the Governor, defiring to fpeak to him in private, when he obferved him to afk leave of thofe officers; on enquiring of Captain Bowreman the meaning of that application, he plainly told him that he was no better than their prifoner in his own garrifon, being threatened with immediate death if he fo much as whifpered to any of his fervants, the Colonel then afked him if he could imagine the caufe of all this, he anfwered, he fuppofed there was fomething extraordinary going forward, but he knew not what it was, only he underftood the Captain of the horfe in the ifland was in the fame fituation with himfelf, and that his Lieutenant had the command of the troop, he added, he knew no caufe for this treatment of either of them, unlefs they were fufpected of being too much attached to the King, this gave Cooke an opportunity of enquiring particularly whether he knew of any intention to feize the King that night; Captain Bowreman anfwered, poffibly fome fuch thing might be defigned, although he knew nothing of it.

Colonel Cooke, on his return to Newport, found a great alteration in circumftances there, guards were not only placed round the King's lodgings, and at every window, but even within, at his very chamber-door, almoft fuffocating him with the fmoke of their matches; this haftened the Colonel back to complain to Major Rolfe of the rudenefs of the foldiers: he found the Major in bed, it being then near twelve o'clock, and received for anfwer, that he was far from intending to inconmode the King, but the two companies having been drawn out of the caftle fo late, that quarters could not be provided for them that night, he had therefore thought of the expedient of having the guards all doubled, in order to difpofe of them for the prefent, never forefeeing the confequence complained of, but that in the morning he would redrefs all things himfelf, and in the mean time was confident, if the Colonel would fpeak to the Captain of the guard, he would remove thofe men who proved offenfive; adding, that if he found it neceffary, he might make ufe of his name for that purpofe. Cooke applied accordingly, and fo far prevailed, that the centinels, whofe matches annoyed the King, were removed to a more tolerable diftance.

Upon Colonel Cooke's return to the King, his Majefty made him repeat the feveral events and circumftances which had occurred that night; thefe, when weighed and compared together, caufed all prefent unanimoufly to conclude, that the army defigned fuddenly to feize on the King's perfon: this being taken for granted, the next queftion was, what was moft advifeable to be done in fo defperate a cafe.

The Duke of Richmond and the Earl of Lindfay ftrongly recommended it to the King immediately to attempt an efcape, as the readieft way to procure that perfonal treaty with his Parliament which he fo earneftly defired, as well as to fecure his perfon from danger; but, before they could proceed to confider on the method of efcape, the King cut them fhort, by objecting againft the efcape itfelf. He urged the great difficulty, if not impoffibility of accomplifhing it, and the confequence, fhould he mifcarry in the attempt; that it would exafperate the army, and difhearten his own friends; and befides, that fuppofing the army fhould feize him, they muft preferve him, even for their own fakes, for he was convinced no party could fecure their own intereft, without joining his with

it,

it, his son being out of their reach. The Earl of Lindsay replied, Take heed, Sir, lest you fall into hands that will not steer by such rules of policy; remember Hampton Court, where your Majesty's escape was your best security. The Duke of Richmond added, that he thought an escape feasable enough, and turning about to Colonel Cooke, asked him how he passed to and fro? The Colonel replying he had the word; the Duke asked him whether he believed he could pass him also; to which he answered, he made no question but he could On this the Duke put on a cloak without a star, and, in company with the Colonel, passed through all the guards, and returned again, to encourage the King, and shew the possibility of the measure. But on a sudden, his Majesty turning from the Duke of Richmond and the Earl of Lindsay, who were in discourse with him at the window, to the Colonel, who was drying himself before the fire, said, Ned Cooke, what do you advise in this case? The Colonel answered, he suspected his own judgment too much to offer any advice, considering the greatness both of the danger, and the person concerned in it, but his Majesty had his Privy Counsellors with him, to whom he humbly begged he would listen. The Lords then resumed their persuasions; but the King, turning about again, said, Ned Cooke, I command you to give me your advice. Whereupon the Colonel craved leave that, after he had premised some particulars, his Majesty would permit him to propose a question, which being granted, Suppose, said Cooke, I should not only tell your Majesty that the army mean suddenly to seize upon your person, but, by concurring circumstances, should fully convince you of it; supposing also, that beside the word, I have horses ready at hand, a vessel attending, and hourly expecting me at Cowes, myself both ready and desirous of attending your Majesty, and the darkness of the night as it were suited to the purpose, so that I can forsee no visible difficulty in the thing: the only remaining question is, what will your Majesty resolve to do? After a short

S 2 pause,

paufe, the King delivered this pofitive anfwer: They have promifed me, and I have promifed them; I will not break firft.

Colonel Cooke begged leave to argue the point with the King,
who replied, with all his heart. I prefume, Sir, faid he, by thofe
words *they* and *them*, your Majefty intends the Parliament to
whom you have made that promife, if fo, the fcene is now quite
changed; the prefent apprehenfion arifing from the army, who
have already fo far violated the votes and promifes of the Parliament as to invade your Majefty's freedom and fafety, by changing the fingle centinel of ftate at the outward door, contrary to
their declared promife, into guards on your very bed-chamber;
which in itfelf is no better than confinement, and in all probabi-
lity the fore-runner of fomething worfe. The King replied,
that however he would not do any thing that fhould look like
breaking his word, and fo bid him and the Earl of Lindfay good
night, for the Duke of Richmond was then in waiting, faying
he would go and take his reft too as long as he could: Which,
Sir, faid Cooke, I fear will not be long: the King rejoined, As
it pleafes God: but perceiving Cooke to be very uneafy, he
added, Ned, what troubles you, tell me? He faid, To confider
the greatnefs of your Majefty's danger, and your unwillingnefs
to obviate it. Never let that trouble you, anfwered the King, for
were it greater, I will not break my word to prevent it. Cooke
begged him to fufpend his refolution, and give him leave to ftep
and fetch the Earl of Southampton, but he told him there was
no need, for, pointing to the Duke of Richmond and the Earl
of Lindfay, he faid they were his true friends. Be pleafed to confult them, replied Cooke. I have refolved already, faid the King;
go ye both to bed, and if I have need I will fend for you. on
which Lord Lindfay and Cooke took leave and departed.

The

The Duke of Richmond stepped after Colonel Cooke, to consult with him whither he had better go to bed that night, or lie in his cloaths; Cooke said, as for himself, wet as he was, he would not pull off his; for, notwithstanding Major Rolfe's promises, he feared it would not be long before the King would be disturbed, unless the face of affairs deceived him. The Duke asked him whether it would not be best for him to repeat this opinion to the King? Cooke said, with all his heart, and he would stay in the outward room to wait the result: but the Duke then returned with information, that the King was determined to go to bed. It was then about one o'clock, and though Colonel Cooke, wet as he was, did not undress all night, yet every thing was conducted so quietly and secretly, that not the least noise was heard, nor any cause of suspicion given.

Just at the break of day, the King, hearing a great knocking at his outer door, sent the Duke of Richmond to learn the cause, he found there a person who said his name was Mildmay [*], and the Duke requiring his business, he answered that there were several Gentlemen from the army very desirous to speak with the King: the Duke carried in this message, but the knocking still increasing, the King gave orders for their admission. The door was no sooner opened, than those officers rushed into the bed chamber, before the King could rise from his bed, and abruptly told him, they had orders for his removal. From whom? said the King; they replied, From the Army. The King asked, To what place? They answered, To the castle. The King demanded, To what castle? They again answered, To the castle. The castle, said the King, is no castle, but added, he was well enough prepared for any castle, and therefore required them to name it: after a short whisper together, they said, Hurst castle. Indeed,

[*] The brother of Sir Henry Mildmay, and one of the servants placed by the Parliament about the King

replied

replied the King, you cou'd not well have named a worfe. He
then defired the Duke of Richmond to fend for the Earl of Lindfay and Colonel Cooke: at firft they objected to Lindfay's coming; but the King faying, Why not both, fince they lodge together? they, after a whifper, promifed to fend for both, though
in fact they fent for neither. The Duke of Richmond ordered
the King's breakfaft to be haftened, prefuming there was little
provifion made in that defolate fortrefs; but before his Majefty
was well ready, the horfes being come, they hurried him away,
only permitting the Duke to attend him for about two miles
only, and then telling him he muft go no farther. He therefore took a fad farewel of the King, being fcarcely permitted to
kifs his hand: his laft words to the Duke were, Remember me
to my Lord Lindfay and Colonel Cooke; and command Colonel
Cooke from me, never to forget the paffages of this night *.

The Duke of Richmond returned directly to the Earl of Lindfay's lodgings, on which a guard had been ftationed all night,
to prevent his ftirring out during this dark tranfaction: and the
Duke furprifed both him and Colonel Cooke with the firft intelligence of the King's removal; delivering alfo to both his Majefty's gracious remembrance, as well as his particular injunction
to the Colonel They then all left the ifland, embarking, with the
Earl of Southampton and his Countefs, on board a veffel that attended Colonel Cooke, and landed near Titchfield, the feat of the
Earl of Southampton Juft at their landing they were feized by
a party of Colonel Okey's regiment, but, upon Colonel Cooke's
engagement for their appearance, they were permitted to go to
the Earl's houfe The next morning, whilft all the paffages
were frefh in their memories, in conformity to the King's com-

---

* The King happening to fee Mr Edward Worfley in this journey, gave him
the watch out of his pocket, as a token of his remembrance. This watch is now
in the poffeffion of James Worfley, Efq of Stenbury.

mand,

mand, they met and drew up a narrative, materially as here
stated [*].

The final cataſtrophe of this affair is too well known to require a recital here : to ſay that the unhappy Monarch was entirely blameleſs, might perhaps be deemed too bold an aſſertion,
on the other hand, to judge of his character by revolution prin-
ciples, would be both unjuſt and abſurd ; poſſibly, when the
prerogative and powers claimed and exerciſed by his predeceſſors
are taken into conſideration, his tragical end may be thought
more than an expiation of his errors. With regard to his enemies, although liberty and religion were their pretended motives,
power and emolument were their real incentives, and that tribunal, which doomed their ſovereign to death for a breach of
the laws, were themſelves aſſembled, and acted contrary to, and
in defiance of thoſe very laws.

Colonel Hammond was ſucceeded in the command of the Iſland
by Colonel William Sydenham, ſon of William Sydenham, Eſq.
of Winford-Eagle, in Dorſetſhire, and brother of the celebrated
phyſician of that name. He was an active man againſt the
King, had been Governor, for the Parliament, of Weymouth and
Melcomb, and afterwards Commander in Chief in Dorſetſhire,
Oliver Cromwell made him one of his Council, a Commiſſioner
of the Treaſury, one of the Committee of Safety, a Member of
his *other* Houſe of Parliament, ſubſtituted for a Houſe of Lords,
Governor and Commander in Chief of all the Forts and Forces in
the Iſle of Wight [†].

1649
Colonel Sy-
denham

---

[*] Colonel Cooke's Narrative was printed ſoon after the Reſtoration, but being
now ſcarcely to be met with, the above circumſtances are taken from the original
MSS in the Harleian Collection, Brit Muſ vol 7705 p. 93
[†] Myſtery of the Good Old Cauſe, printed in 1660.

During

During the civil war, the Iſle of Wight enjoyed a much happier ſtate than other parts of the kingdom, being early ſeized by the Parliament, and forces ſtationed in different parts, the inhabitants were kept in ſubjection: the quiet they enjoyed invited many from the neighbouring counties to retire hither, which raiſed the rents of the farms in the proportion of twenty pounds in the hundred. That the riſe originated from this cauſe only, appeared by their ſinking again ſoon after the Reſtoration.

1660.
Thomas,
Lord Cul-
peper.

Upon the re-eſtabliſhment of regal government, Thomas, Lord Culpeper, was appointed Governor of the Iſland, who, by ſeveral unpopular and arbitrary acts, excited ſo much diſcontent, that the Gentlemen of the Iſland preferred the following petition to the King and Council againſt him.

Petition a-
gainſt Lord
Culpeper.

" To the King's moſt excellent Majeſty, the humble Petition
" of your Majeſty's Subjects, Inhabitants of the Iſle of
" Wight,

   " In all humility ſheweth,

   " That they conceive it to be their duty at this time humbly
" to repreſent to your moſt excellent Majeſty, that the Right
" Honourable Lord Culpeper, who, by your Majeſty's letters
" patent, hath the grant of the office of Captain of the ſaid Iſle dur-
" ing his life, hath incloſed a great part of a certain foreſt there,
" called Parkhurſt, in which, during the reigns of your Majeſty's
" predeceſſors, there hath been, time out of mind, enjoyed
" common paſture for their cattle, by the inhabitants of the ſaid
          " Iſle,

" Ifle, to the great damage and impoverifhment of many poor
" people, who have a great part of their livelihood thereby, and
" to the great grief and difcouragement of your Majefty's good
" fubjects of the faid Ifle.

" That the faid Lord Culpeper, your Majefty's Captain of
" the faid Ifle, affuming to himfelf, in his commiffions to the
" officers of his Majefty's militia there, the additional title of
" Governor of the faid Ifle (which they humbly conceive
" doth no more of right belong to his Lordfhip, than it doth
" to your Majefty's Lieutenants of the feveral counties within
" this your kingdom), doth exercife an arbitrary power in
" the faid ifland, frequently intermeddling in the civil go-
" vernment thereof, by giving a difturbance to the proceed-
" ing and due execution of your Majefty's laws, to the great
" vexation and trouble of the inhabitants thereof · and hath
" fometimes proceeded fo far, as, by his fole arbitrary power,
" to imprifon the perfons of fome of your Majefty's good fub-
" jects in a noifome dungeon in Carifbrooke caftle, to their
" great grief and difcouragement, and contrary to your Ma-
" jefty's good laws.

" That fince it hath always been thought fit by your royal pro-
" genitors, in all times of war and danger, to put the faid ifle,
" being a confiderable frontier of the kingdom, into fome good
" pofture of defence; they humbly prefent it to your moft excel-
" lent Majefty, as a danger more immediately threatening them-
" felves, but of manifeft confequence to the whole kingdom,
" that the ancient magazines and ftores of the faid ifle, are nei-
" ther fo full, nor in fo good repair as in former times ; nor the
" militia of the faid ifle in fo good a condition and pofture of
" defence, as they humbly conceive it ought to be for your Ma-
" jefty's fervice, and the defence and fafety of this your king-
" dom.

T   " The

" The premifes confidered, they do humbly befeech your moft
" gracious Majefty, that the faid ftores and magazines may be
" viewed and replenifhed, that your Majefty's faid ifle may be put
" in fome better pofture of defence than it is at prefent; and that,
" by order from your Majefty, the inclofures of the faid foreft may
" be laid open, and the other grievances of the poor ifle fome
" way redreffed, as to your Majefty's great wifdom fhall feem
" meet,

" And your petitioners, as in duty bound,

" Shall ever pray."

Lord Claren-
don's anfwer. To this petition Lord Clarendon, the Lord Chancellor, returned the following anfwer.

" As to yourfelves, you have acquitted yourfelves very hand-
" fomely in the bufinefs, both in the fubmiffive tender of it to
" the King, and in the managing of it for the country; and I
" can fay you have proceeded with great refpect and civility to
" the Lord Culpeper. but as to the bufinefs, the King neither
" likes the manner nor the matter of the petition The man-
" ner, in your having fo many hands to it, contrary to the laft
" act, confidering the late times when fo ill ufe has been made
" of petitions; and that you have prefented it at this time, being
" fo unfeafonable, that were not fome of you known to the
" contrary, you might be fufpected to be difaffected. The matter,
" my Lord being the King's officer, and the particulars moft of
" them trivial, do favour of anger and malice to the Lord Cul-
" peper.
" As to the foreft, I wifh you have not awaked a fleeping
" lion, by acquainting the King with his right, but the King is
" a gra-

" a gracious Prince, and the Lord Treafurer, the Lord Afhley,
" and I myfelf, we are friends to the country, fo there is hope
" you will be in no danger of lofing your foreft.

" As to the imprifonment, there is nothing of weight in it;
" though in the matter that concerns Anthony Dowding, my
" Lord may probably have been a little rafh, and have pro-
" ceeded too far; and as to the caufe of the firft imprifonment
" of the mayor, poffibly my Lord may not be wholly jufti-
" fied in it, though there might be good caufe for the detaining
" him

" As to the militia, my Lord Culpeper will be appointed to
" go down to put it in order. My Lord Culpeper, had not this
" petition been prefented, would before this time have been re-
" moved, and another put in his place, for as much as the King,
" being in the ifland, took notice that he was not refpect-
" ed by the gentry as became his government: and truly my
" Lord is not to blame to be willing to leave the command of a
" place where he is not refpected; but now he fhall go down to
" fhew you he is not out of favour with the King, although his
" Majefty is unwilling to put perfons to employments not fuit-
" able to their capacities. As for inftance, he would not com-
" mand me to ride poft. And finding this a place not fo proper
" for his command, he intended to remove him to fome employ-
" ment fitter for him But I believe, though you may poffibly
" have one that fhall live more fociably among you, you may
" never have one that will ufe his power lefs than my Lord
" Culpeper."

The Lord Culpeper however refigned the government of the
Ifle of Wight foon after, and was fucceeded by Admiral Sir
Robert Holmes, who had diftinguifhed himfelf in the hoftilities

1667.
Sir Robert
Holmes

com-

commenced by Charles againſt the Dutch, having been ſecretly
diſpatched to Africa before any declaration of war, with a
ſquadron of twenty-two ſhips; where he not only expelled
the Dutch from Cape Corſe, to which the Engliſh had ſome
pretenſions, but alſo ſeized their ſettlements at Cape Verd,
and the iſland of Goree, taking alſo ſeveral veſſels trading
on that coaſt, and ſtretching over to America, he likewiſe
poſſeſſed himſelf of Nova Belgia, ſince called New York.
The States complaining of theſe depredations, Charles, unwilling to avow what he could not well juſtify, pretended total ignorance of Sir Robert Holmes's enterprize, and to amuſe them,
committed him to the Tower [*]: but releaſing him ſome time
after, gratified him with the Government of the Iſle of Wight.
Sir Robert Holmes appears to have been in great favour at court;

Sir Robert
Holmes viſit-
ed by King
Charles II
1671.

the King making an excurſion, in the ſummer, paid the Governor a viſit at Yarmouth, where he had built a handſome
houſe, on lands granted by the Crown. Yarmouth was at that
time a garriſoned town, ſtrongly fortified, having a draw-bridge
at the eaſt entrance. The King landed at Gurnard-bay, in
the pariſh of Northwood, and paſſed through the foreſt of Park-
hurſt, to the Park, now the Park-farm, belonging to the Governors of the iſland, by a road made by Sir Robert, ſome
traces of which ſtill remain The foreſt is ſaid to have then
been ſo full of wood, that ſquirrels leaped from one tree to another. This timber has long ſince been cleared, and nothing
but under-wood remains

Is ſtyled Go-
vernor in his
commiſſion.

He was, in his patent, ſtyled Governor, and Captain of the
Iſland, and of the caſtles and forts therein. He ſupported the
dignity of his office with great propriety, and by conſtantly reſid-

* Rapin and Hume.

ing

ing in the ifland, acquired great popularity. He died in the year one thoufand fix hundred and ninety two, and was buried in a vault in the church at Yarmouth; where an elegant monument of fine marble, with his ftatue as large as the life, is erected to his memory.

Soon after the death of Sir Robert Holmes, the Government of the Ifland was conferred on John, Lord Cutts, of the kingdom of Ireland; he was of an ancient family in Cambridgefhire: his Lordfhip had made a confiderable progrefs in polite learning, but was much more remarkable for his daring courage, of which he gave many inftances both in Ireland and Flanders, when he ferved under King William, whofe favour he fo highly obtained by his gallant behaviour, that he was promoted to the command of the Coldftream Regiment of Foot Guards, with the rank of Lieutenant-general, he alfo reprefented the County of Cambridge in feveral Parliaments. On the firft acceffion to his Government he was extremely unpopular, interfering improperly with the Corporations, disfranchifing feveral Burgeffes of Newtown, and imprifoning a Clergyman for feveral weeks in Cowes Caftle. The Gentlemen of the Ifland prepared a petition to the Houfe of Commons, complaining of the arbitrary exertions of authority in their Governor, but at length his Lordfhip, finding he had gone too far, thought it prudent to recede from his pretenfions, and by articles reciprocally figned between them, agreed to rectify whatever had been done amifs, particularly to reftore the Burgeffes of Newtown. after this accommodation, they continued to live in a friendly manner. His Lordfhip procured the habitable part of Carifbrooke Caftle to be repaired, where he often gave handfome entertainments. He died in Ireland, where he was one of the Lords Juftices, and General of the Forces.

To

1693
John, Lord
Cutts

1706

1707.
Charles,
Marquis of
Winchester.

To Lord Cutts succeeded Charles, Marquis of Winchester, afterwards Duke of Bolton, Warden of the New Forest, Lord Lieutenant of the Counties of Southampton and Dorset, and was one of the Commissioners to treat of the Union between England and Scotland   This nobleman residing very little in the island,

A Lieuten-
ant-governor
appointed by
commission.

it was thought necessary to appoint a Lieutenant-governor, under him, by Royal Commission, with a salary of twenty shillings per diem; which office was conferred on Colonel Morgan. It had before been customary for the Governor to nominate one of the Gentlemen of the Island to act as his Deputy during his absence, but without any pecuniary gratification, till the government of Sir Robert Holmes, who in a manner prepared the way for this establishment, by obtaining a salary of four shillings a day for his Deputy, Sir Edward Worsley.

1710.

General
Webb.

Among the many alterations that attended the great change of Queen Anne's Ministry, the Duke of Bolton was removed, and the Government conferred on General John Richmond Webb, who had been bred a soldier, and for his services under King William, was first made a Colonel of Foot, and in the reign of Queen Anne attained the rank of Lieutenant-general   He was a gallant officer, and his conduct appeared in that memorable action at Wynendale, where, with seven thousand men, he defeated the French General La Motte, who, with more than three times that number, attempted to cut off a convoy with ammunition sent to the siege of Lisle.

1711.
William,
Lord Cado-
gan.

General Webb was succeeded by William, Lord Cadogan, afterwards created an Earl for his eminent services, he was educated in the army, and so well recommended himself to the

Duke

Duke of Marlborough, that he was appointed Colonel of the Cold-
stream Regiment of Foot Guards, Quarter-master General to the
Army, and afterwards became a Lieutenant general: the Duke
reposed the greatest confidence in him, employed him in negociating with the confederate Princes and States, and was
afterwards, by his Grace's influence, sent Ambassador Extraordinary and Plenipotentiary to the United Provinces. On the
death of the Duke of Marlborough, in June, one thousand seven
hundred and twenty-two, his Lordship was appointed General
and Commander in Chief of his Majesty's Forces, Master General of the Ordnance, and Colonel of the First Regiment of Foot
Guards, and also declared one of the Lords Justices of Great
Britain during his Majesty's absence at Hanover. On the death
of the Earl of Cadogan, in August,

Charles, Duke of Bolton, Lieutenant of the Counties of Southampton and Dorset, Warden of the New Forest, and a Knight
of the Garter, was appointed Governor and Vice-admiral: he
was dismissed from all his offices in the year one thousand seven
hundred and thirty-three, and was succeeded by

*1726.
Charles,
Duke of
Bolton.*

John, Duke of Montagu; who resigned the Government of
the Isle of Wight, and the Lieutenancy of the County of
Southampton, in July, one thousand seven hundred and thirty-
four; when

*1733.
John, Duke
of Montagu.*

John, Lord Viscount Lymington, had a grant of the Government of the Island, and office of Vice-admiral, which he surrendered in July, one thousand seven hundred and forty-two, and
was soon after created Earl of Portsmouth.

*1734
John, Lord
Lymington*

Charles,

Charles, Duke of Bolton, was reinstated; but his Grace soon after resigned his appointments.

John, Earl of Portsmouth, on the twenty second of February, was again made Governor, Vice-admiral, &c. of the Isle of Wight his Lordship remained Governor till his death, which happened on the twenty-third of November, one thousand seven hundred and sixty-two.

Thomas, Lord Holmes, who had been lately created Baron Holmes, of Killmalloch, in Ireland, succeeded the Earl of Portsmouth, in April, one thousand seven hundred and sixty-three, but died in July, one thousand seven hundred and sixty-four, when

Hans Stanley, Esq. one of the Lords Commissioners of the Admiralty, was appointed Governor, Vice-admiral, &c of the Island; but when the changes in Administration took place, two years afterwards, he was removed, and the Government was given, on the twenty-third of December, one thousand seven hundred and sixty-six, to

Harry, Duke of Bolton, Vice-admiral of the Counties of Southampton and Dorset: his Grace was removed in the year one thousand seven hundred and seventy, and

The Right Honourable Hans Stanley, Cofferer of his Majesty's Household, and a Privy Counsellor, was again appointed. In the year one thousand seven hundred and seventy-four, it was, by a new grant, confirmed to him.

He

He was succeeded in the offices of Governor, Vice-admiral, &c. of the Isle of Wight, on his death, in the month of January, one thousand seven hundred and eighty, by the present Governor,

The Right Honourable Sir Richard Worsley, Baronet, Comptroller of his Majesty's Household, and one of his Majesty's most Honourable Privy Council *.

* See Appendix, No XL the present Military Establishment of the Island.

The Land Mark on Ashey Down

U   CHAP

CHAP. V.

Of the Broughs of Newport, Newtown, and Yarmouth .

ALTHOUGH many eminent writers† have treated of the origin and constitution of Boroughs, the time when their representatives were first admitted into the National Council is by no means positively ascertained ‡ It is however certain that Cities and Boroughs did send Members to Parliament as early as the twenty-third of Edward the First §.

THE

The first e-presentation of Boroughs in Parliament. 1295

* A list of the Members returned to Parliament by the three Boroughs is given in the Appendix, No XLI

† These subjects are fully treated of in Brady's Account of English Boroughs, Prynne's *Brevia Parliamentaria* and Madox's *Firma Burgi* from these it may be collected, that in the Saxon times, Boroughs being either the property of the Crown, or of the principal Lords, were under their immediate protection, and by them they were invested with municipal and commercial privileges, for which they paid in return tolls, stallage, and other reserved dues, collected by a Bailiff, or *Præpositus Burgi* sometimes a Borough obtained grants of lands pertaining to it, and of the duties imposed on it, as toll, stallage of market, pontage, paage money, customs on goods imported, with other payments under various denominations Others were exempted from hundred courts, and obtained the liberty of holding pleas, in cases under limited values, arising within the town; with the power of collecting tolls and customs by a bailiff chosen by themselves, and these are the considerations for which fee farm rents are due from cities and incorporated towns

‡ This matter has been much agitated, and different opinions have been maintained with great plausibility, some carry it back to the Saxon æra. Rymer, vol 1 p 802, places it in the 49th Hen III anno 1265, which is answered by Prynne, though he does not pretend to have found any writs of summons of that antiquity

§ Dr Brady produces authorities to shew that cities and boroughs did not send members till the 23d Edward I This difference between Prynne and Brady may be accommodated, if, as Hume observes, the first precedent of representatives from the boroughs, occasioned by the Earl of Leicester, was regarded as the act of a violent usurpation, and had been followed in all the subsequent Parliaments.

He

THE BOROUGH OF NEWPORT.

The first charter of immunities granted to this town was from Richard de Redvers, Earl of Devon, the son of Earl Richard. Its exact date is not known, but it must have been in the time of Henry the Second, as this Earl died in the thirtieth year of that reign. This charter, like most of those of that early period, is very concise, being no more than a grant of liberties in general terms. the names of the witnesses are given in the note below.

First charter of Newport

A second charter was granted to this town by Isabella de Fortibus, Countess of Devon, which is in the customary terms, it is, inserted in the Appendix, with explanatory notes.

Charter of the Countess Isabella

When the Isle of Wight was purchased by King Edward the First, the Borough of Newport sent representatives to the Parliament

When first represented in Parliament

He therefore considers the 23d of Edward I as the real and true epoch of the House of Commons. The same historian adds, that the clergy scrupled to meet on the King's writ, lest, by such obedience, they should seem to acknowledge the authority of the temporal power; but that at length a compromise was found out, which was, that the King should issue his writ to the Archbishop, he, in consequence thereof, was to summon his clergy, who, as they appeared to obey their spiritual superior, no longer hesitated to meet in Convocation. This expedient was the cause why the Ecclesiastics met in two Houses of Convocation, under their Archbishops, and formed not one estate, as in other countries of Europe, which was the King's first intention. The summons directed to the Archbishop of Canterbury for convening his clergy, is inserted in the Appendix, No XLII. Brady, in his Treatise on Boroughs, p. 27, cites records to shew, that the King's tenants in demesne deliberated separately from the Knights and Burgesses, and generally taxed themselves, in a proportion higher by one-third than the rest of the laity.

Will Fil Ellis, Rob de Affeton, P de Estey,
Walter de Insula, Adam de Compton, Richard de Glare ge
Roger de Aula, Rob Fil Brien, ... de Insula,
Will Mykan ..., Rob de Sniwell, Homan Trenchard,
Rob ..., Will d ...

U 2

affembled in the twenty-third year of that King; fuppofed to be the firft wherein the reprefentatives of the Commons were legally convened But whether they reprefented this Borough only, or the Ifland at large, feems uncertain.

In the fecond year of Edward the Second, Prynne finds that writs were directed to the Bailiffs of the liberties of the Bifhop of Winton, of the Prior of Winton, of the town of Southampton, of the town of Portfmouth, of the *Ifle of Wight*, Chrift church, Andover, Bafingftoke, Odiam, and Alton, but that thofe Bailiffs made no return to the Sheriff. In the fourth year of Edward the Second, other writs were directed to the Bailiffs of the Ifle of Wight, and feveral of the towns above named, but no returns were made of them [*].

The charter of Ifabella de Fortibus received feveral royal confirmations [†]; that of Edward the Fourth included a grant of the forfeitures of outlaws, felons, fugitives, and of *felo de fe* within the borough. and to the confirmations by Henry the Seventh and Edward the Sixth are added the petty cuftoms within any port or creek of the ifland.

---

[*] Prynne's Brev. Parl. p. 205

[†] The preamble to the confirmation of Queen Elizabeth, in the records of the town, enumerates the feveral following Princes who had ratified the charter of the borough of Newport.

"Elizabeth, by the grace of God Queene of England, France, and Ireland,
" defender of the faith, &c beheld the charter of her brother Edward the vith.
" Edward vith beheld the charter of his father Henrie the viiith Henry viiith
" beheld the charter of Henry viith Henry viith beheld the charter of Edward the
" iiiith Edward the iiiith beholde the charter of Richard the iiid Richard the iiid
" beheld the charter of his parent father Edward the iiid Edward the iiid be-
" holde the charter of the good Ladye Ifabell de Fortibus, who, in her pure wi-
" dowhood gave, granted, and confirmed the charter of Medyne, now concerning
" old Newport, to the bailives and communs burgeffes of the fame, as in her faid
" charter here under full and more at large appeare."

The

The town of Newport was probably of very little importance till the reign of Henry the Second, as it seems to have been without a church till that time, this supposition is grounded on its church being dedicated to St. Thomas Becket, the popular Saint of that period; who was not canonised till the year one thousand one hundred and seventy-two. It appears by the cartulary of the Priory of Carisbrooke, that it was covenanted between William de Vernun and the Monks of that house, that two of their body should perform divine service in the church of Newport, and this being about fifty years before the town enjoyed the privilege of a market, which, as being prejudicial to the market of Carisbrooke, could not have been obtained without the permission of the Monks, to whom it belonged, was perhaps the reason of the reservation of two marks to be paid annually by the town of Newport to the Monks of Carisbrooke, mentioned in the charter granted by the Countess Isabella Hence arose the vulgar tradition, that the town of Carisbrooke sold its market to Newport.

There is a customary, entered in the old books of the corporation, enumerating the duties paid for the several kinds of goods sold there, among them a claim of four pence per ton from the shipping which pass the coast · but whether this was ever legally enjoyed by the borough of Newport is doubtful, possibly the duty still imposed on all vessels anchoring in Cowes Road, at the mouth of Newport River, may have originated from that claim.

By a charter of incorporation, granted to this borough in the first year of James the First, the Bailiff and Burgesses were constituted a body politic, to consist of a Mayor, twenty four Burgesses, and a Recorder, with power to chuse a Town Clerk. the Mayor to be sworn into his office before the Captain of the Island,

The church built

Obtains a market.

Newport incorporate by James I.

Island, or his Steward The Mayor, Recorder, or his deputy, with two Burgesses, are impowered to hold a court every Friday, for the trial of all causes of debts, trespass, &c arising within the Borough, according to the laws of England they take recognizances of debts according to the statutes of merchants and staple, and have a goal, with power to hold such persons as they commit for debts, felonies, &c.

By another charter, granted at the suit of the Mayor and Burgesses, in the thirteenth year of Charles the Second, they are incorporated by the names of Mayor, Aldermen, and Burgesses, viz a Mayor to be chosen from among the Aldermen, who are to be twelve in number; the Aldermen are to be chosen, by the Mayor, and Aldermen, out of the chief Burgesses the Mayor to be sworn into his office before the Governor of the Island, or his Steward. By this last charter, the petty customs within all ports and creeks of the island, are granted to be held, as hath been, or ought to have been aforetime held and enjoyed: and the Mayor, Aldermen, and chief Burgesses, are exempted from serving on juries at the Assizes or General Quarter Sessions.

The Borough of Newport does not appear to have sent any members to Parliament, from the twenty-third year of Edward the First until the twenty seventh year of Elizabeth, when many other Boroughs, particularly all the Boroughs in Hampshire, Southampton and Portsmouth excepted, received precepts to send two Burgesses each, to the Parliament called in that year.

The great alteration then made in the House of Commons was not in consequence of any act of the Legislature, but only of the discretionary instructions given to the Sheriffs by the general terms of the writ, which ran, " to send *duos burgenses* " *et quoslibet burgo*, two Burgesses from whatever Borough " they thought proper." Prynne is of opinion that this autho-

ity given to the Sheriffs was the original caufe of the privilege
of reprefentation being fo unequally diftributed *. Exemptions
from parliamentary duty had been frequently granted, as well
to individuals † as Boroughs, upon petition: and Prynne has
preferved a patent of this kind, granted in the forty-fecond year
of Edward the Third, excufing Sir Robert Lifle from all attendance on Parliaments and Juries during his life. Many ancient
Boroughs were exempted from fending Burgeffes, on their plea
of poverty, without any patent, but folely on the following return being made by the Sheriff to the writ of fummons "Non
funt aliqui cives feu burgenfes in . . . . qui ad parliamentum
in brevi content. venire poffunt, debent, aut folent, propter
eorum debilitatem et paupertatem ‡." "There are no citizens or Burgeffes of . . . . able to attend this Parliament, they
are neither ufed nor ought to be required to come on account
of their poverty." It may be obferved, that almoft all the
Boroughs which had this revived, or newly conferred privi-

* Prynne's Brev. Parl p 231. † Prynne on the Fourth Inft p 37

‡ Sir Henry Worfley, Baronet, one of the Burgeffes for Newport, in the year
one thoufand fix hundred and forty two, prefented a petition to the Houfe of Commons, defiring leave to be difcharged from his duty in Parliament, but no notice
feems to have been taken of this petition, as he continued a Member of the Houfe

To the Honourable the Knights, Citizens, and Burgeffes of the Houfe of Commons, the
humble Petition of Henry Worfley, Baront, a Member of that Houfe, 1642
humbly fheweth,

That your Petitioner, by reafon of fome fcruples that he hath in his confcience in thefe
late Publiques, is much indifpofed at prefent and unfitted for doing his fervice in the Parlia-
ment

That he hath bene at great difpute with himfelfe whither he fhould adventure on this re-
fentation of his cafe, with his following requeft unto this Honourable Houfe, fearing
why to incurre your difpleafure, but being confcious unto himfelfe of his own condition,
and well knowing that his place in Parliament may foon be fuppled by another, that any
the King home, and particularly the Ifle of Wight, and that Borough from which
him thither, better fervice, he hath refigned to the favour of this Honourable Houfe,
humbly to defire that, in regard of the premiffes, he may be enlarged from his fervice at
prefent, and that this his Petition may receive fo favourable conftruction,

And your Petitioner fhall ever pray, &c.

HENRY WORSLEY

lege,

lege of reprefentation, in the twenty feventh year of Elizabeth, were either in the Crown, or in the hands of men of influence and power dependant on the Court: and the perfons elected appear, for the moft part, to have been Gentlemen of family and fortune, who were able to bear their own expences in attending the Parliament. This year may, however, be confidered as the epocha from whence the Houfe of Commons began to acquire that weight and power it has fince fo amply poffeffed.

About this time the Members may be fuppofed to have begun to ferve their conftituents without requiring or receiving the regulated wages for their attendance *, otherwife the Boroughs would not have accepted the privilege of reprefentation as a favour; and that it was fo efteemed appears by the following entry in the town books of Newport.

Remarkable entry in the town records

“ Memorandum, That at the fpecial inftance and procurement
“ of Sir George Carey, Knt. Marfhall of her Majefties moft
“ Honourable Houfehold, and Captain of the Ifle of Wight,
“ two Burgeffes were admitted into the high court of Parlia-
“ ment, holden at Wefminfter, the 23d day of November, in
“ the 27th year of the reign of our moft gracious and fou-
“ veraigne Lady Elizabeth, by the grace of God Queen of Eng-
“ land, France, and Ireland, defender of the faith, &c. for our
“ town of Newport, that is to fay, Sir Arthur Boucher, Knt.
“ and Edmund Carey, Efq. whereas there were never Bur-
“ geffes admitted in any Court of Parliament before that time,

* The famous Andrew Marvel Member for Kingfton upon Hull, who died in 1678, appears to have been the laft Member of the Houfe of Commons paid by his Conftituents for his attendance in Parliament. As early as the 3d of Edward IV. John Strange, Efq. of Bromton, entered into an agreement with the Bailiffs of the town of Dunwich in Suffolk, to take no more for his wages in Parliament than a cade and half a barrel of herrings, whatever might be the duration of the faid Parliament. The original deed is in the poffeffion of Thomas Aftle, Efq.

“ during

" during the memory of man for the said town, and for a me-
" morial that we the said Bailiff and Burgesses of the same, doe
" account ourselves greatly bounden to Sir George Carey, have,
" with our assent and consent, given full power and authority
" unto the said Sir George Carey, to nominate one of the Bur-
" gesses for us, and in our names, during the natural life of
" the said Sir George Carey, whose life God long preserve *."

Newport has given title to four Earls · the first, Lord Mount-
joy Blount, natural son of the Earl of Devonshire, created by
Charles the First, in the fourth year of his reign, Baron of
Thurlston, and Earl of Newport; he died in the year one thousand six hundred and sixty-five, and was succeeded by George
Blount, his son and heir : he dying unmarried, in the year one
thousand six hundred and seventy-six, the title devolved to his
brother Charles, who did not survive him above a year, and was
succeeded by his brother Henry, who dying unmarried, in the
year one thousand six hundred and seventy-nine, the title became extinct. Lord Windsor, was also Baron Newport, in the
reign of Queen Anne.

Newport give title to four Earls, and one Baron.

The town of Newport stands nearly in the center of the island,
of which it may be considered as the capital The river Medina empties itself into the Channel, at Cowes harbour, distant
about five miles, and being navigable up to the quay, renders it
commodious for trade. This river affords plenty of flat fish,
and great quantities of excellent oysters. The air is clear and
wholesome, and the cold is seldom felt with that degree of
severity, common to more inland places, partly owing to the
effect of the surrounding sea, and partly from its being shelter-

Description of the town

---

* The Sheriffs precept to the Bailiff and Burgesses of the Borough of Newport is dated
Oct 18, 1584.

X c·i

ed by circumjacent hills, which encompass it at about the distance of a mile.

The three principal streets extend from east to west, and are crossed at right angles by three others; all these are spacious and clean, and have been lately paved according to the modern fashion, with footways on each side. The buildings are in general regular and neat. There are several good houses in the

town, and two elegant assembly-rooms.

Over the largest of the market-houses is the town-hall, where the Mayor and Corporation hold their meetings, the Knighten-court, already mentioned, is also held here by the Steward of the Governor of the island

The free-school, which is a plain stone building, was erected by public subscription, during the government of the Earl of Southampton; in this building are convenient apartments for the master. The school-room is fifty feet long the treaty be-

tween King Charles the First, and the Parliamentary Commissioners, was held in this room. The maintenance for the master arises from lands adjoining to the forest, granted to the Bailiffs and Burgesses of Newport, in the reign of Henry the fifth, by Agnes Attelode and John Erlesman *. These lands are described as lying on Hunny-Hill, on the north side of the stream called Lukely, and consisting of about thirty-four acres. The Earl of Southampton, after taking the advice of counsel, allowed them to be inclosed, and appropriated to the support of the free-school †.

The endowment of the school appears therefore to have been owing to the Corporation of Newport, and not to any encroach-

* See Appendix, No XLIII for the Deed of Conveyance
† Entered in the books of the Corporation of Newport, Aug 30, 1619

men.

ment on the foreft, as has been improperly fuppofed The fchool-
mafter is appointed by the Corporation, under the common feal [*].

Here are two markets held every week, one on Wednefday, Market.
the other on Saturday, but that on Saturday is the principal;
two hundred waggons loaded with different grain are frequently
brought thither for fale, amounting to fourteen or fifteen hundred quarters; great part of this produce is manufactured in
the ifland, into flour, malt, and bifcuit for the ufe of the navy;
and the remainder is bought up by factors and merchants
for exportation.   Various other articles of provifion are brought
to this market, efpecially poultry and butter; large quantities of
both are bought up for the ufe of the outward bound fhips, and
much of the latter barrelled up for foreign confumption.

A confiderable manufactory of ftarch is carried on here, the Starch manu-
duty for which annually amounts to at leaft one thoufand factory.
pounds.

T H E   B O R O U G H   O F   N E W T O W N.

Newtown, or as it was anciently called, Francheville, is a
Borough *by prefcription*, and firft fent Members to Parliament
in the twenty-feventh year of Elizabeth.   Several immunities
were conferred on this town by the firft charter from Aymer, Charters.
Bifhop of Winchefter, then Lord of the Borough, who granted
to his town of Francheville, all fuch liberties and franchifes as
were enjoyed by the Burgeffes of Taunton, Alisford, and Farn-

---

[*] The feal is given in the plate of feals in this chapter, but Newport hath not
any armorial enfign

The rate made by the inhabitants for the maintenance of their minifter is feen
Appendix, No. XLIV.

ham.

ham. This deed is dated at Swainston, and was confirmed by Edward the Second, Edward the Fourth, and Queen Elizabeth. It appears by ancient deeds that this Borough bought and fold lands as a body corporate, under a common town feal * There is a grant exifting of the freedom of the Borough, by the Mayor and Burgeffes, in the thirtieth year of Edward the Third, another dated in the fourth year of Richard the Second, fhews a grant to the Mayor and Burgeffes of Newtown, of forty acres of land in Calbourn ; and by other old deeds, they are found to have granted many burgages at feveral times, to fome in fee, and to others for life. In their charter of the eleventh of Edward the Second, the King grants to his fon, Edward, Earl of Chefter,

afterwards King Edward the Third, a market, to be held at his town of Francheville, every Wednefday, and a fair for three days annually, on the feaft of St Mary Magdalene, on the eve preceding, and on the day following. Since that time the Borough has obtained the name of Newtown, probably from its having been rebuilt, after it was deftroyed by the French, in the reign of Richard the Second. Circumftances point it out to have been

formerly a large town, though, at prefent, it has no pretenfions to that name. Some ancient deeds of lands defcribe it to have extended from the High-ftreet on the fouth to Gold-ftreet, and many fmall burgage lands lie on each fide of the old ftreets. Two long ftreets, extending from eaft to weft, were connected by other ftreets, lying from north to fouth · it is not therefore improbable, that this might have been the town mentioned in the Saxon Chronicles to have been burned by the Danes, in the year one thoufand and one.

* The feal of this Borough, given in the plate of Seals of the Corporations, is very ancient, it reprefents an antique fhip on the fea, with one maft fails furled, and pennon flying, on the fhip a lion paffant gardant, in chief, on the dexter a mullet, on the finifter fide, a crowchean of St George

The

The haven of Newtown affords the beſt ſecurity for ſhipping of any about the iſland; and is, at high water, able to receive veſſels of five hundred tons burthen: the water and fiſhery is claimed by the Mayor and Burgeſſes; they hold a court leet, and appoint conſtables, but pay a rent to the Lord of the Manor of Swainſton, which is collected from the holders of borough lands.

The qualification for voting at the election of repreſentatives in this Borough, having been often conteſted, and varied, was at laſt ſettled by Parliament. The oldeſt books ſhew the qualification of a burgeſs, to have been the holding *a borough land*, paying rent to the Mayor and chief Burgeſſes; but in the reign of Charles the Second, an order was made, reſtricting the number of Burgeſſes to twelve. In the reign of William the Third, the Mayor and Burgeſſes pronounced this limitation illegal, and declared that the poſſeſſion of a freehold in a Borough land, included the right of being a Burgeſs * Some few years after,

1698

on

* Newtown als Francheville 1698} At an Aſſembly had in the ſaid Burrough, on Tueſday the 20th day of Sept. 1698, appear the Chief Burgeſſes then that are marked thus (—),

— John, Lord Cutts, Mayor

—| Joſeph Dudley, Eſq } Deputy Mayor
—| Hen Dore.
—| Coll David Urry.
—| Mr John Chiverton
—| Maj Henry Holmes
—| Mr John Philips
—| Mr. David Urry

—| John Leigh, Eſq.
—| James Worſley, Eſq
—| Coll. Richard Holms
—| Mr Edward Hayles
—| Sir Robert Worſley, Bart
—| William Stephens, Eſq
—| William Bowerman, Eſq.

Twentieth day of Sept 1698, Order of Mayor and Chief Burgeſſes to admit thoſe poſſeſſed of Burgage Tenures to vote

At this aſſembly, upon examining the ancient records of the ſaid Corporation, and taking the depoſitions on oath of James Overy, as alſo upon the averment of ſome of the chief Burgeſſes there then preſent, it is reſolved, that the reſtraint of the chief Burgeſſes of this Corporation to the number of twelve, or any leſs number than are Freeholders of Burrough Lands is againſt law, and contrary to the ancient uſage of this Corporation.

Alſo

on infpecting the old books of the Borough, the laft mentioned declaratory order was found to be contrary to the ancient ufage of *the borough*, it was therefore erafed out of this book, and the Borough reftored to the right of electing Burgeffes out of thofe who enjoyed a freehold in a borough land.

Ap 22, 1729

On a petition being brought before the Houfe of Commons, complaining of an undue election, the Houfe refolved, with great juftice, that the right of electing Members to ferve in Parliament for the Borough of Newtown, in the county of Southampton, *is in the Mayor and Burgeffes, having Borough lands*, which refolution of the Houfe was made final.

THE BOROUGH OF YARMOUTH.

In it charter

This Borough has regularly fent Members to Parliament, from the twenty-feventh of Elizabeth. It obtained a charter of franchifes from Baldwin, Earl of Devon, brother of the Countefs Ifabella de Fortibus. It was re-incorporated by King James the Firft, in the feventh year of his reign, its charter is in fubftance as follows.

Recital of the charter of James .

Whereas the Borough of Eremuth, alias Yarmouth, in the Ifle of Wight, is an ancient Borough, and the Mayor and Burgeffes have prefcribed to have and ufe diverfe liberties and privileges, which they claim alfo under colour of charters of confirmation from feveral Kings and Queens of this realm, con-

Alfo 'tis ordered and agreed, that whofoever fhall prove himfelf to be a Freeholder of any Borough land in fee, either by the rent-roll now produced in this affembly, bearing date and beginning in the year of our Lord 1685, (whereof a true copy fhall be kept by the Mayor for the time being), or otherwife effectual'y in law, fhall upon demand, be fworn a Chief Burgefs

In confequence of thefe difputes, an agreement was entered into between Lord Cutts, the Governor, and the Gentlemen of the Ifland, which is copied in the Appendix, No XLV

firming

firm'ng an ancient grant made to this Borough, by Baldwin de Redvers, some time Lord of this Isle; viz. the charter of confirmation under the great seal, in the eighth year of the reign of King Edward the First; a like charter, granted in the eighteenth of Henry the Sixth, another charter of the sixth of Edward the Fourth, and another charter of the second of Elizabeth; and whereas the said Mayor and Burgesses, and their predecessors, have always paid to the King and his predecessors, for the said privileges, immunities, and liberties, the fee-farm of *twenty shillings* yearly; and whereas it appears by the records, in the Remembrancer's office in the Exchequer, in the second year of Richard the Second, that the town of Yarmouth was entirely burned by the enemy, and its inhabitants greatly impoverished; and whereas the said town lies near to a good harbour for shipping, and for that reason King Henry the Eighth caused a castle to be built, since which the town is better inhabited than before, and it is to be hoped that it will be yet more filled with people, for increasing the strength of the island, and guarding the said castle, if his Majesty would vouchsafe to re-grant them their liberties and immunities · that the said Mayor and Burgesses, esteeming the charters before mentioned insufficient to authorise them in the using and enjoying the said liberties and immunities, have petitioned the King to make, confirm, and new create them a body politic and corporate, with such franchises as shall be by the King thought expedient. that the King therefore being willing to settle the rules for the government of the said Borough, and the people there, declares it to be a free Borough, and that they shall be a body politic and corporate, by the name of Mayor and Burgesses of Yarmouth, in the Isle of Wight, with capacity to purchase, &c. to grant, &c. to plead, or to be impleaded, and to have a common seal *; that there shall be twelve

* The seal of Yarmouth represents an antique ship, with three masts, on a — in base.

chief

chief Burgeffes to be the Common Council of the Borough; that out of thefe, one fhall be chofen Mayor of the Borough; that they fhall have power to make laws, ftatutes, and orders for the government of the Borough and its officers, that the Burgeffes of the faid Borough fhall continue for life, excepting any of them fhall be removed for reafonable caufe; and on the death or removal of a Chief Burgefs, the Mayor and major part of the Burgeffes then living, fhall elect another in his place, who fhall be fworn before the Mayor, and major part of the chief Burgeffes that the Mayor and Steward of the Borough fhall hold the courts of the faid Borough; that they fhall hold a view of frank-pledge of all inhabiting and refident in the faid Borough, and to redrefs abufes in the fame: the Mayor and Burgeffes are empowered to elect and conftitute a Steward †, a common Clerk, and a Serjeant at Mace, to continue during the pleafure of the Mayor and Burgeffes: that the Mayor and Burgeffes fhall have all the fines, forfeitures, and profits of the courts, which they fhall have power to levy, by their own officers by diftrefs; they have alfo a grant of ftrays, and the goods of felons, within the limits of the borough; a market is granted to the town, to be kept every Wednefday, and a fair to be held yearly, viz. on St. James's day, the eve before, and the day after, together with a court of pie powder, &c. with all the profits and emoluments belonging to fuch markets, fairs, and courts: a fpecial licence and authority are given to the Mayor and Burgeffes, to purchafe and hold to them and their fucceffors for ever, any manors, lands, &c. not holden of the King *in capite*, or by Knight's fervice, not exceeding the value of twenty pounds per annum, the ftatute of mortmain notwithftanding, and licence is alfo given for any perfon, &c to grant

† Thomas Cheke, Efq was, by the charter, appointed the firft Steward, and Barnaby Legh, Efq Mayor.

and

and alien to the faid Mayor and Burgeffes *, under the like reftric-
tion, all liberties, privileges, franchifes, and immunities, which
the Borough has held and enjoyed, by reafon or colour of grants
by the King or any of his predeceffors, or by any other perfons

* The following petition, complaining of the arbitrary conduct of the Governor, was prefented to the Houfe of Commons by the Gentlemen of the Ifland, in the year one thoufand fix hundred and eighty three.

To the Honourable the Knights, Citizens, and Burgeffes in Parliament affembled,

The humble Petition of the Gentlemen of the Ifle of Wight, and the Mayor, Burgeffes of Yarmouth, and feverall of the Burgeffes of Newtown, in the faid Ifland,
Sheweth,

That the Lord Cutts, Governor of the faid Ifland, in order to fubvert the freedom of election of Members to ferve in Parliament, and fubject the free votes of
your Petitioners to his arbitrary pleafure, hath abufed the power intrufted in him,
to the great grievance of his Majefty's good fubjects under his Government in the
faid ifland, and endangering the free liberties of England, viz

1ft. By threatning thofe who have votes in Elections, that if they do not ferve his
intereft, he will ufe his power over them as enemies to the Government.

2dly. By quartering fouldiers arbitrarily, in order to over awe the Corporations

3dly By imprifoning a Clergyman for the fpace of two months for voteing againft
his the faid Governor's intereft

4thly. By putting the Officers of the Militia out of their Commiffions for voteing
againft his intereft, fince which the Militia have wanted great part of their Officers,
whereby the faid Ifland has been expofed to danger during the war.

5thly. By encouraging the late Mayor of Newtown to expell Sir Wm Stephens
and Mr Williams, on pretence of their being rend'red uncapable to act as Burgeffes,
for not having figned the Affociation, notwithftanding their Burgefsfhipp is in right
of Burrough lands, and no office within the act of Parliament.

6thly By difpofing the truft of the forts belonging to the faid Ifland as rewards to
fuch as ferve his intereft in Elections, and who are unfkillfull and unable to difcharge their offices, by which means he has now a third tyme made himfelf Mayor
of Newtown, tho' not rightfully a Burgefs there

7thly. And by feveral other arbitrary and illegal practifes, of all which your Petitioners humbly pray the confideration of this Honourable Houfe, and to do for their
relief as to your great wifdome fhall feem meet

And your Petitioners fhall ever pray, &c

Rob. Worfley,	Tho Urry,	Thomas Barrett,	William Urry,
John Dillington,	David Urry,	Wm. Combes,	Robert Dodd,
Will Stephens,	John Richards,	Ed Guyer,	Tho Goodman,
Cha Worfley,	Jo. Crouch,	Timothey Heath,	John Warder,
Ja Leigh,	Tho. Newnham,	John Combes, Dep Mayor,	Jonathan Combes.
Will Bowerman,			

Y made

made heretofore, are confirmed, faving and referving out of this grant, the caftle of Yarmouth, its ditches, trenches, and limits, wherein the faid Mayor and Burgeffes have no power or authority to enter. They are to pay the fee-farm of twenty fhillings yearly, at the feaft of St. Michael; a claufe is added to indemnify them from all profecutions for any liberties or franchifes ufed, had, or ufurped by them, before the date of this charter, and no fine is to be paid to the Hanaper office for it. Dated the firft day of September, in the feventh year of James.

Yarmouth Jaile

C H A P.

CHAP. VI.

The Religious Houses, their Foundations, and Endowments.

THE Isle of Wight received the Christian faith later than any other part of Britain   There is no account of the state of the churches till the compilation of Domesday-book, wherein it is recorded that the Island then contained ten churches, six of which were given by William Fitz-Osborne to the Abbey of Lyra, in Normandy, whereof he was founder, and these were under the direction of the Priory of Carisbrook, founded also by him   The names of the churches are not specified in Domesday-book, but are mentioned, with the tithes enjoyed by them at that time, in a general charter of confirmation granted from William de Vernun, Earl of Devon, in the reign of King John, to the Abbey of Lyra : they are the churches of Arreton, Whippingham, New Church, Godshill, Niton, and Freshwater, together with that of Carisbrook, and several chapels [*]; probably erected between the time of the foundation and this grant. The other churches found in Domesday are Brading, Calbourn, and Shalfleet. the Abbot and Monks of Lyra had assigned the profits of the churches of Godshill, Arreton, and Freshwater, to be applied as a provision for the poor, and to hospitality; which assignment was confirmed by Popes Celestine the Third, and Innocent the Third, at the request of the Abbot and Monks, with a prohibition against converting those revenues to any other use.

686.

1086.
Carisbrook
Priory.

[*] Cartul de Carisbrook, penes Ric Worsley, bar. cart 3

The charters, grants, and confirmations of the Priory of Carisbrooke are registered in the Chartulary; they consist of between two and three hundred, of which very few are of consequence, being chiefly grants of inconsiderable parcels of land, the most important are

Charters of confirmation.

The Charter of Earl Baldwin, in the Reign of King Stephen.

Baldwin, Earl of Devon, and Lord of the Island, confirms to the Abbot and Convent of Lyra, all tithes, lands, rents, and benefices, which they hold in the Isle of Wight; to hold as freely as they held the same in the time of William Fitz Osborne, or Richard de Redvers, father of the said Baldwin. But under this condition, that Geoffrey, the Clerk, shall enjoy one moiety, and Stephen, the Clerk, the other moiety, during their lives, paying thirty shillings each yearly to the Abbey of Lyra, in acknowledgement of its being the mother church; and after their deaths the church of Carisbrook shall remain to the Abbot and Convent of Lyra, to be freely by them enjoyed, either as demesne, or they may send Monks to the said church. *Testibus Pagano vice comite, Brieno de Insula, Gervasia Abbate de Quadraria, et aliis.*

The Charter of William de Vernun, in the Reign of King John.

He grants and confirms to the church of Carisbrook, *two marks per annum*, devised by his nephew, Richard de Redvers, Earl of Devon, to be received out of the toll of the island, by the Bayliff of his New Borough (Newport). and the Monks of Carisbrook, delivered into the hands of the said Earl, in the presence of his Barons, the charter of the said Richard: by the terms of this grant, the Monks of Carisbrook are bound to perform

form daily fervice in the chapel of Newport; yet the Burgeffes, both men and women, are to go to the mother church of Carifbrook on the great feftivals, according to cuftom. *Teftibus Mabilia Comitiffa, Waltero Abbate, Willo. fil. Stuy, Roberto fil. Brieni, cum multis aliis.*

General Charter of Confirmation by William de Vernun.

This Charter confirms to the Abbot and Convent of Lyra all former grants; namely the church of Carifbrook, with the chapels of Northwood, Shorwell, the chapel of the Infirm, and of the New Borough; the churches of Arreton, Whippingham, Newchurch, Godfhill, Niton, and Frefhwater, alfo the tithes of all his demefne lands in the ifland, viz. the tithes of Frefhwater, Affeton, Compton, Brook, of Ningewood, held by the Prior of Chrift-church, and two parts of the tithes of Shalfleet, and Chefsle, the tithes of the demefnes of Robert of Shorwell, there and at Ulwarton; of the demefnes of Niton, Stenbury, Week, and Appuldurcombe, and other the demefne lands of Montfburg, and Apfe, belonging to the Canons of Chrift-church; the tithes of the demefnes of Ralph de Glamorgan, at Yaverland, alfo of Nunwell, and Whippingham: the tithes of the demefnes of Herbert Fitz-Turbert, and Hugh de Clerken-hull, and from Shide, of the demefnes of William de Argenton, and the moiety of the church of Chale, with forty fhillings annual rent, paid by the Monks of Quarr to the Monks of Lyra, for the tithes of Arreton, Hafely, Boucombe, and Shalcombe, twenty fhillings rent paid out of Boucombe, one yardland in Boucombe, and another in Wroxall, four fhillings from Week, and three fhillings from the two Nitons; in Frefhwater, two men with a yardland; and in Compton and Brook, two men and two yardlands; and in Witcombe, one free tenement with its land; in the hamlet of Caldlands in the New Foreft, one man

with

with his lands; two marks from the New Borough, of the toll of the island, according to the will of Richard de Redvers; with lands near Carisbrook, given by Paverell de Argenton, and his brother William, and the lands exchanged with Robert Cross.

From the charter of Earl Baldwin it appears that he asserts a right of nominating the Monks to the Priory of Carisbrook, probably as heir to the founder; and many years afterwards, Isabella de Fortibus claimed a right of approbation of the Prior. It being entered in the Chartulary, that Richard de Perans, appointed Prior of Carisbrook, by the Abbot and Convent of Lyra, complained that Isabella pretended that the house was in her hands on the vacancy of the Prior, and that the Advowson of the Priory belonged to her, that she took occasion on these pleas to disturb and vex the Prior, had cited him to appear and answer in her courts, and had amerced him · on which the Prior obtained an injunction, the seventh year of Edward the First. This dispute seems to have been afterwards accommodated, as there are releases between the Countess and the Prior, wherein she reserves to herself the right of advowson and lordship over the Priory; these releases bear date the ninth year of Edward the First

The claim of a right in the patron, or representative of the founder, to the temporalities of a religious house, in case of a vacancy, is by no means unprecedented, and in some instances seems allowed in the decrees of the synod convened by Ottoboni, in the fourth year of Henry the Third, where patrons were forbid, by the sixth canon, to retain the profits of vacant benefices, excepting they are entitled to them by ancient usage   It is to be observed, that at this time the nobility of England, who were heirs to the founders of religious houses, and to those who

had

had given the Advowfons of churches to Monafteries, had generally taken great offence at the Monks; who, by procuring
the appropriation of their churches, and taking the profits to
themfelves, had, as they conceived, abufed the truft repofed in
them. the churches being conferred on them, not as finecures,
but under the fuppofition of their being the beft judges what
perfons were moft fit to be prefented to the livings; whereas by
thefe appropriations, the churches were neglected, and the intention of the donors defeated   The Englifh nobility prefented
a remonftrance on this fubject to Pope Alexander the Fourth,
ftating, " That they and their predeceffors, out of refpect to the

1259.

" appearing fanctity of the religious focieties in England, had
" liberally conferred on them their right of patronage; that by
" fuch means they might have the opportunity of chufing fit
" perfons, and prefenting them to the Bifhops, as a moft effec-
" tual provifion for the cure of fouls, and relief of the poor:
" whereas they found this pious intention fruftrated, not only
" by Papal provifions, that interrupted the right courfe of pre-
" fentation, but chiefly becaufe the religious, by clandeftine and
" indirect ways, with the neglect, or contempt of their own
" Bifhops, had obtained thofe churches to their properties, by
" conceffions from the Apoftolic fee: on which account they
" thought themfelves obliged to refume the patronage of fuch
" converted churches, and reunite the Advowfons to their own
" demefnes; becaufe they faw the good intentions of them-
" felves and their predeceffors intirely defeated."   All this his
Holinefs excufed in his anfwer, by protefting " a pure and fin-
" cere defign in fo appropriating fome churches to religious
" places, with the affectionate bowels of piety and mercy;
" firmly hoping and believing, that fuch conceffions of charity
" might relieve the wants of the religious, and promote the
" worfhip of God within the refpective churches: and there-
" fore, if their complaints were true, he was forry the Apofto-
" lical

" lical judgment fhould be deceived, and the facred intention of
" the fee of Rome be fo perverfely difappointed : but far be it
" from them, obedient fons, for this caufe of appropriations
" and provifions, to revoke and take into their hands the right
" of patronage, beftowed·on fuch religious houfes, fince they
" had no authority to difpofe of ecclefiaftical affairs, and muft
" not prefume to touch any facred thing. However, with the
" affiftance of the Bifhops, he would fo effectually labour to
" redrefs all abufes, as to leave no juft matter of complaint or
" fcandal."

The fame Pope, in an epiftle, two years afterwards, complained, " that the covetous defire of the religious, had by falfe
" pretences obtained from the fee of Rome, the appropriation
" of many parochial churches within the kingdom of England,
" and had by that poifon infected the whole nation. while, by
" thefe means, the worfhip of God was loft, hofpitality was
" intermitted, epifcopal rights were detained, the doors of cha-
" rity were fhut againft the poor, the encouragement of
" ftudious fcholars was abated, with many other fcandals and
" offences "

This practice of Convents procuring the appropriations of
churches became fo fcandalous, that even the Monks were
afhamed of it Bifhop Kennet, in his Parochial Antiquities,
mentions an inftance, when Hugh de Levon *, Abbot of Meaux,
in Yorkfhire, would have beftowed the appropriation of the
church of Effington on that Abbey : the Monks themfelves ob-
ftructed his intention for the fpace of five years, protefting
againft the enormous injuries which would arife, to be lamented
by perfons yet unborn. Nor was the difcontent on this fubject
confined to the Laity, but even the Bifhops fought to have the

* Hift. Abb de Meaux, p 455

evil

evil redreffed, and many canons were enacted in the fynods for that purpofe, to which the Monks refufed obedience, and much violence was ufed by them in oppofition to the canons; nor did they fubmit till they were reduced by force. The Monafteries, poffeffed of churches, not only appropriated the rents to their own ufe, but frequently farmed them out, by which means the good intentions of the donors were fruftrated.

In the Synod affembled at Oxford by Archbifhop Langton, the thirteenth canon forbids the vicarage of any church to be given to a Vicar who fhall not ferve the church: the fourteenth obliges thofe who have benefices to refide: the fifteenth appoints a fufficient portion of the benefice to be allowed for the maintenance of the Vicar: and the fortieth forbids the letting to farm, excepting it be done for fome caufe, which fhall be approved by the Bifhop. *1222.*

Thefe canons were alfo ordained by the fynod convened at London, by Otho, the Pope's Legate; and again by another fynod held by Ottoboni, both of which require churches to be fupplied by a refident Vicar. *1237.* *1268.*

A neglect in the obfervation of thefe canons, occafioned the Bifhop to collate to thofe churches which fell to him by lapfe: as fully appears by the regifter of William of Wykeham, who collated to the Vicarage of Carifbrook, void, as he exprefsly fays, through neglect of the conftitutions of Otho and Ottoboni. There had been great commotions in the ifland on this occafion, and to what a height they rofe at Godfhill, are feen in Bifhop *130.*

Z Wood-

Woodlock's Register, wherein the Monks, with their friends, are recorded to have held the church by force. the Bishop's letter to the King on that occasion, with another on a subsequent one, are inserted in the Appendix *. The Bishop also ordered the Dean of the island, to put the Clerk, collated by him, in possession of the church of Godshill, devolved to him, by virtue of the canon of the General Council |

1308   In the year following, the same opposition arose at the church of Areton, when the Bishop directed the Dean of the island to induct the Clerk by him collated, *contra omnes et singulos contradictores et rebelles* ‡, "against all opposers." After which the Bishop excommunicated nine persons for obstructing his Clerk, with all those officiating in the said church, commanding the Dean of the island to denounce this excommunication in all the churches of his Deanery, at the time of high mass, in which ceremony the cross was to be elevated, the bell rung, the candles first lighted and then extinguished, with every other circumstance that could give solemnity to the act This was followed by a sequestration of the churches of Freshwater and Godshill, for contempt of the canons, and the bishop excommunicated those who had violated the sequestration.

When King Edward the Third asserted his pretensions to the crown of France, Carisbrook, as an alien Priory, was, with all its churches, seized by the crown, the King then presenting to them, and the Priory § was granted to the Abbey of Mont

---

* See Appendix, No XLVII.   † Regist Winton.
| Regist Winton.
§ See a curious grant to the Monks, Append, No XLVIII

Grace,

Grace, in Yorkshire, founded by Thomas Holland, Duke of Surry; but Henry the Fourth, in the first year of his reign, probably to remove all causes of discontent between the Courts of England and France, restored it, with others which had also been seized *.

In the reign of Henry the Fifth it was again resumed, and given to the Monastery of Shene, in Surry, founded by the King, where it continued till the time of its dissolution. In the reign of Henry the Eighth, that Abbey leased it, together with the tithes of Godshill and Freshwater, to Sir James Worsley, at the annual rent of two hundred marks, which lease† was renewed by his son Richard, whose widow marrying Sir Francis Walsingham, Secretary of State to Queen Elizabeth, it came into his possession. It was afterwards purchased by Sir Thomas Fleming, from whose family it came to the present possessors; the Vicarage remained in the Crown, until Charles the First gave it to Queen's College Oxford. To the church of Carisbrook belongs the chapels of Northwood, West Cowes, and Newport. At the time of Cardinal Beaufort's taxation, this church was valued at twenty marks per annum, the Vicarage at sixteen marks, and the Procuracy of Lyra at forty marks‡. This Priory, having been founded when there were not more than nine or ten churches in the island, the Monks enjoyed a larger jurisdiction than those of later institution, when most Lords of great possessions, having built new churches, had appropriated the tithes of their lands to them

The Abbey of Quarr, called in some of the oldest grants Quarraria, probably obtained its name from the neighbouring

* Reg. Winton.
‡ Appendix, No XLIX. contains an account of the tithes of the Priory, A D 1565, when in the possession of George Worsley, Esq.
‗ Reg Winton

Z 2

stone

ftone quarries. It was among the firft monafteries of the Cifter-
cian order founded in England *, and was begun by Baldwin, Earl of Devon, who, in the thirty-fecond year of
Henry the Firft, gave the manor of Arreton to Geoffrey,
Abbot of Savigny, in Normandy, for the building of
this Monaftery, which was dedicated to St. Mary. The
earlieft charter to this Monaftery now remaining, is that of
Engler de Bohun, who gave them Hafely, probably foon after
the donation of Baldwin, above mentioned: the deed appears to
have been executed in Normandy, from the circumftance of its
being witneffed by Serlo, Abbot of Savigny †, fucceffor to Geoffrey, and divers other Norman Bifhops and Abbots. This,
with many other benefactions to Quarr Abbey, is confirmed by
Richard, the fon of Baldwin ‡; whofe deed, though without
date, muft have been in the reign of Henry the Second; and
from this may be collected, that the chapel of St. Nicholas,
with its endowments, had been given to Quarr by the chief
men of the ifland, who are there ftyled his Barons. moft
of the lands, with which the Abbey was then endowed,
appear to have been given in the reign of Stephen, when
the order was in high eftimation. There is likewife a
grant from Henry, Duke of Normandy, afterwards the fecond
of that name King of England, of a place called Locwelle,
in that province, for the Monks of Quarr to build an Abbey there §: and a grant of confirmation from the fame Henry, as King of England, to the Abbey ‖. This liberality
was perhaps an act of gratitude in Henry to Earl Baldwin then
founder, who had been exiled and deprived of his lands for ef-
poufing the caufe of his mother, the Emprefs Maud. Several
other grants and inftruments relating to this Abbey are copied

---

* Dugdale's Mon vol 1 p. 750　　　† See Appendix, No I.
‡ See Appendix, No II　　　§ See Appendix, No LII.
‖ See Appendix, No LIII.

The Remains of Quarr Abbey

the Property of

in the Appendix, or referred to; thefe, though moftly without dates, are ranged as nearly as poffible in the order of time
in which they were made, *viz.*

A grant of a mill at Shalfleet, from Geoffrey de Infula *.

Atteftation of a devife to Quarr, by Richard, Earl of Devon †.

Grant of eleven acres of land in Whippingham, by Henry
Clavill ‡.

Grant of a rent, by Robert de Giros §.

Two grants from Geoffrey de Infula ‖.

Grant of land and a mill in Sway, in the parifh of Boldre, by
Hugh de Witteville, attefted by Warin de Aula ¶.

Archbifhop, Thomas Beckett's, confirmation of the grant of
the manor of Whitfield ⊥.

Petition of the Abbot of Quarr, in relation to the before
mentioned manor **.

Grant from Hawife de Rivers, of the church of Fleet, in the
diocefe of Sarum, in which the Monks of Montefburg are
charged with a fraud ††.

Grant from Walter Motte, of twelve acres of land to Quarr
Abbey §§.

Grant from Walter de Infula, of land lying on the fide of St.
Boniface Down ‖‖.

Grant from William de Vernun, Earl of Devon, of two hundred acres of land in Wellow, to the Monks of Quarr ¶¶.

Grant of William de Vernun, of two fmall iflands near Chrift-
church ⊥⊥.

Grant from Alwarie de Newton, or Niton, of lands in Niton [k].

Agreement of releafe from Thomas de Newnham to the Monks of Quair †.

Exchange of Blackland for Combley, between the Monks of Quair and Simon Fitz-Hubert ‡.

Compofition with the Convent of Lyra for the tithes of feveral lands belonging to Quarr §.

Exchange of lands between the Abbey of Quarr, and the Rector of Arreton ||

Grant from the Priory of Chrift-church, of a rent charged on their manors of Ningewood and Mitford, in lieu of lands tranffered from Quarr to that Priory ¶.

Grant of lands in Sway, from Ralph Fulcher, for which the Convent were to admit his fon into the houfe ⊥.

Grant from William de Oglander, of lands in Pann to Quarr Abbey ┼*.

Grant from William de Calbourn, of his water at Marefleth, and part of the river Medina ††.

Grant from Matilda de Eftur, of a rent out of Gatcombe to Quarr ‡†.

Charter of confirmation from Ifabella, Countefs of Albemarle and Devon, to Quarr Abbey §§.

Grant of a penfion, by the Abbot and Convent of Quair, to Cardinal Beaufort, Bifhop of Winchefter, for appropriating the church of Arreton to the faid Abbey, by his Apoftolical autho-rity ¶¶.

⁎ Append No LXVII.		Append No LXVIII.	‡ Append. No. LXIX
‖ Append No LXX	‖ Append No. LXXI.	¶ Append No LXXII.
⊥ Append No LXIII	⁎⁎ Append No LXXIV	|| Append No LXXV.
‡‡ Append No LXXVI	§§ Append No. LXXVII.	¶¶ Ap No LXXVIII.

A com-

The King's precept to William de Braybœuf, Sheriff of Southampton, to take the Abbot and Convent of Quarr, with their lands, &c. into his protection against the Countess Isabella de Fortibus.

A grant of lands at Briddlesford to Quarr Abbey, by Thomas de Aula *

A composition between the Monks of Quarr, and the Rector of Godshill, concerning the tithes of Rew Farm †.

A grant of lands from Elias de Thalaife ‡.

A grant or charter of free warren from Edward III. in the lands of Quarr Abbey, to the Abbot and his successors ||

Licence for the Abbot of Quarr and his successors to fortify their lands at Fishhouse, and on the coast, with stone walls and towers §

These deeds shew, as well from whom the Monastery derived their lands, as the first origin of several compositions and *modus decimandi*, and are of use in tracing the descents of families of those times, the sons, and sometimes the wife of the grantor, being made subscribing witnesses, and their concurrence signified in the deed.

Sir William Dugdale calls this Abbey, filia Savignianæ, " the " daughter of Savigny," for which he cites the annals of St Werburg; but it is not to be inferred from this expression, that the Abbey of Quarr had any dependence on that of Savigny. The grants to that Abbey make no mention of any such relation between them, and yet there was no impropriety in terming Quarr the daughter of Savigny, not only because its co-founder was Abbot of that house, but also from the first Monks of Quarr being brought from Savigny to introduce the discipline of the Cistertian order, then new in this country.

* These two deeds have been referred to in a former part of the Appendix.
† Vide Madox Firm. Burg. p. 50.   ‡ Vide Madox
|| Pat. Edw. fil. in Turr. Lond.   § Pat. Edw. III. in Turr. Lond.

In

In a valuation of the fpiritualities in the diocefe of Winchefter, in the time of Cardinal Beaufort, the lands of this Abbey were taxed in the following manner *.

" De redditu affis. taxat ad	viij *marks.*
" Apud Newnham, ad	xv *m.*
" Apud Sambele, (Combley) ad	xvj *m.*
" Apud Arreton, ad	xviij *m.*
" Virga de Bykeburie, (Bugbury) ad	lx. *s.*
" Apud Haffeley, ad	xviij *m.*
" Apud Lovecomb, ad	xij *m.*
" Apud Staplehurft & Claybrook	xl *s.*
" Apud Roweburgh	l *s.*
" Apud Schete	vij *m.*
" Apud Shalcomb & Compton	x *m.*
" Apud Beneftede	xl *s.*
' Apud Foxoie	lviij *s.*
" Apud Schiob & Goy, ad	xlij *s.*
" De duobus molendinis apud Xti ecclefiam	xij *s.*
" De 4 molendinis in Inf. Vecta	xv *s.*
" De proventu tannaiia,	xl *s.*

" Sm ͯͯiiij xvj *l.* iij *s.* iiij *d* Inde decima ix *l.* xij *s.* iiij *d*†."

There is a Bull of Pope Gregoiy the Ninth ‖, giving licence to the Abbot and Convent of Quari ‡, in the Ifle of Wight, to

* Ex Regift. Winton.

† Some eirors are to be apprehended in the tranfcript of the particular fums, which do not amount to the given total which is however juftified by the amount of the tithe

‖ Vide Aftle's Bullarium, No I

‡ Lambaid, in his Account of the Ifle of Wight, concludes with the following remark, " Finally, faith he, although Paulus Jovius wrote that th'inhabitants of " this ifland be wont to boaft merely, that they neyther had amongeft them, monks, " lawiers, wolfes, nor foxes, yet find I them al fave one, in one monafterie, called ' Quarie, valued at 134 poundes of yearly revennue, and founded in the yeare " 1132, after thorder of Savignac, in Fraunce, as the Chronicles of Chefter have ' mention " *Topogr & Hift Dict of England*, art Wight.

chufe

chufe a Confeffor from their own body, this Bull is dated, 6 Kal. Feb. Pont. 10. A D. 1238.

This Abbey was purchafed, after its diffolution, by Mr. George Mills, a merchant of Southampton, when it was deftroyed for the fake of the materials, without refpect to the fepulchres of the many illuftrious perfons buried in its chapel *. It was fold by his fon to the Lord Chief Juftice, Sir Thomas Fleming, in whofe defcendants it ftill remains.

The fite of this magnificent Abbey contained upwards of thirty acres of ground within the walls. The buildings are almoft demolifhed, yet the fituation of many of the offices may be traced.

The refectory, or common hall, is the only building remaining entire, it is now a barn to the eaft of it ftood the church or chapel of the Monaftery, and on the weft end are the veftiges of fome ftone vaulted cellars. The gate towards the fea has been armed with a port cullis, and juft above high water mark appear the ruins of a fort, built in the reign of Edward the Third, by virtue of a licence obtained from the crown

The Convent, or Oratory of Burton, or Barton, having been diffolved long before the general fuppreffion of monaftic foundations, efcaped the notice of Dugdale, Speed, Tanner, and other writers on religious houfes, fo that its exiftence had nearly funk

The Oratory of Burton

---

* Among the perfons of confequence known to have been buried here, are Earl Baldwin, the founder, Adeliza, his Countefs, and their fon Henry, Willm de Vernun, bequeathed three hundred pounds for the erecting a tomb here for himfelf and his father. the chapel alfo contained a monument to the Lady Cicel, fecond daughter of King Edward the Fourth

into total oblivion. Sir John Oglander indeed mentions it in his manuscript Memoirs, but his information appears to have been merely traditional: its history is however preserved in the register of John de Pontissera, bishop of Winchester, wherein the statutes of the house are confirmed by an instrument, in which the Bishop affirms he had seen the charters of John de Insula, Rector of Shalfleet, and of Thomas de Winton, Rector of Godshill, founders of the Oratory of the Holy Trinity of Burton, for the ordering and governing the said Oratory made, and in full force, under the seals of the founders, as follows:

Founded about the year 1282.

Constitutions of the Oratory

I. That there shall be six Chaplains and one Clerk to officiate both for the living and dead, under the rules of St. Augustin.

II. That one of these shall be presented to the Bishop of Winchester, to be the Archpriest; to whom the rest shall take an oath of obedience.

III. That the Archpriest shall be chosen by the Chaplains there residing, who shall present him to the Bishop within twenty days after any vacancy shall happen.

IV. They shall be subject to the immediate authority of the Bishop.

V. When any Chaplain shall die, his goods shall remain to the Oratory.

VI. They shall have only one mess, with a pittance, at a meal, excepting on the greater festivals, when they may have three messes.

VII. They shall be diligent in reading and praying.

VIII. They

J. Brettell sc.

A View from the East Front of the
in the Possession of

VIII. They fhall not go beyond the bounds of the Oratory, without licence from the Archpriest.

IX. Their habit fhall be of one colour, either black or blue; they fhall be clothed *pallio Hiberniensi*, de *nigra boneta cum pileo*.

X. The Archpriest fhall fit at the head of the table, next to him thofe who have celebrated *magnam miffam*; then the Prieft of St. Mary; next the Prieft of the Holy Trinity; and then the Prieft who fays mafs for the dead.

XI. The Clerk fhall read fomething edifying to them while they dine.

XII. They fhall fleep in one room.

XIII. They fhall ufe a fpecial prayer for their benefactors.

XIV. They fhall in all their ceremonies, and in tinkling the bell, follow the ufe of Sarum.

XV. The Archpriest alone fhall have charge of the bufinefs of the houfe.

XVI. They fhall, all of them, at their admiffion into the houfe, fwear to the obfervance of thefe ftatutes.

Thomas de Winton, and John de Infula, Clerks, grant to John, Bifhop of Winchefter, and his fucceffors, the patronage of their Oratory at Burton, in the parifh of Whippingham, that he might become a protector and a defender of them, the Archpriest, and his fellow chaplains.

The

The Bifhop, at the inftance of John de Infula, the furviving founder, Thomas, being then dead, orders that, after a year and a day from their entering into this Oratory, no one fhall accept of any other benefice, or fhall depart the houfe. *Actum et datum in dicto Oratorio de Burton. a.* 1289. *Jordano de King-fton et aliis teftibus.*

1386.

The Archprieft being fufpended by the Bifhop, the Dean of the Ifland was ordered to take charge of his Oratory in the houfe at Burton: foon after, the Archprieft being a captive in France,

1390.

and the houfe of Burton in a ruinous condition, the Bifhop gave orders for the houfe to be repaired, and other neceffary things to be done [*].

1439

The Oratory was, in the eighteenth year of Henry the Sixth, furrendered into the hands of the Bifhop, and, together with its lands, by the procurement of Bifhop Wainfleet, granted to the College of Winchefter [†]. it was endowed with the manor of Whippingham, the demefne lands of Burton, or Barton, and fome lands at Chale. The fite and demefnes of the Oratory are ftill held under a leafe from the Warden and Fellows of Winchefter College; and part of the old building is yet ftanding.

Priory of St. Helen..

There was a Priory at St. Helen's, which belonged to fome Abbey in France, of the Cluniac order. The founder is un-

---

* Ex Regift Winton

† Walterus Trengoff, *Archiprefbiter Oratorii S Trinitatis in Infula Victa,* infra *parochian de Whippingham, conceffit Colugio S Mariæ juxta Winton per Willul-mum de Wickham, &c. fundato, manorium de Barton, in dicta Infula.* Clauf. 18 Hen VI m 35

Walter Trengoff was afterwards made a Doctor of Divinity, and Archdeacon of Cornwall.

known;

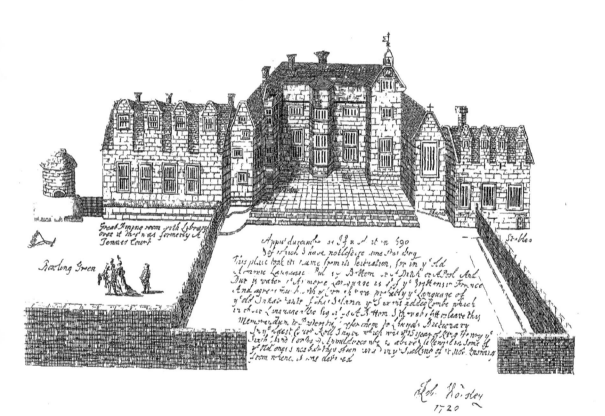

Great dyning room with Library
once it this was formerly A
Tennes Court

Bowling Green

Stables

Apputdurcombe as I found it in 390
Of which I have notlessegre some that Seing
This place took its name from its seituration, for in ye Ald
Armenic Language Put is Bottom or A Ditch or A Pool And
Due ys water is A moore Language as is of ye Brittons in France
And agrees neer with ye torn theere probably ye Language of
ye old Inhab anto of his Ielana ye Saxns added Combe which
in theer Language the signes A Bottom Ith web btt releave this
Memorandum to posterity, reference to Lluyd Dictionary
In ye oldest Court Roll I have which was of 35 year of King Henry ye
Sixth And Combs As Provildences nte as above is templ in some of
ye old ones nos but they sheen wee my Dwelling oc ye said Learning
from whence it was derived

Rob. Horsley
1720

known; but it may be fuppofed to have been founded foon after the Conqueft, before the introduction of the Ciftertian order. This was one of the alien Priories given by Henry the Sixth to his College at Eton, to which it ftill belongs.

The Priory of Appuldurcombe was a cell to the Abbey of Montfburg, in Normandy; and was given to them by Richard de Redvers, founder of that Abbey, as appears by a charter of confirmation, in which thefe lands are defcribed as given to the Abbey of Montfburg by that family[a]. That Convent had a Prior and two Monks here, in charge of the profits of their lands; which were Appuldurcombe, Sandford, and Week. King Henry the Fourth, during the war with France, gave it to the Nuns without Aldgate, London[†], who afterwards obtained a grant from the Abbey of all their right and title to thofe lands. Ifabella de Fortibus fhewed fo much regard to the Convent of her anceftors foundation, that in her charter to the town of Newport, fhe exempted the Prior of Appuldurcombe from the toll and petty cuftoms granted to that Borough. Edward the Third, apprehending a defcent of the French on this ifland, ordered the Bifhop of Winchefter to remove the Priors and Monks belonging to the French Monafteries from thence to Hide Abbey, near Winchefter, and it appears that a Prior and two Monks were fent from Appuldurcombe[‡].

The Priory of St. Crofs, near Newport, appears to have belonged to Tirone, in France. Its founder is unknown. It feems

[a] Monaft Anglic. vol. ii p 892
[†] Ex Cart. Antiq penes Richard. Worfley, Bart.
[‡] See Appendix, No. LXXIX.

to have been an hospital, for in Pat. 6 Ric. II. p. 1. m. *Rex dedit Johanni de Coweshall custodiam hospitalis Sancti Crucis in Insula Vecta ad totam vitam.* They obtained a licence from the Bishop for burying their own dead, for which an acknowledgement was paid to the Priory of Carisbrook; but being an alien priory, it was given to the College of Winchester, before the general dissolution of religious houses.

Church-house.

Besides the Monasteries already specified, there was in the parish of Northwood, near the church, a religious house, consisting of *fratres et sorores fraternitatis Sancti Johannis Baptistæ, in ecclesiâ de Northwode*; " Brothers and sisters of the fraternity " of St. John Baptist:" as appears from a conveyance in Latin, still extant, of a tenement and two or three strips of land, to the Stewards *(Seneschales)* of that fraternity, by John Wynnyatt. The deed is dated the fourth of Henry the Eighth, wherein the fraternity is said to have been lately established: hence it could not have subsisted but a very short time, all these establishments being suppressed in that reign [*]. The building, known by the name of the Church-house, is said to have been standing about a century ago.

1534.

1553

King Edward the Sixth, in his last illness, signed an order for a general visitation of churches, to examine their plate, jewels, vestments, and other furniture, and to compare the account with inventories made in former visitations. The visitors were to leave in every church one or two chalices of silver, with linnen for the communion table, and for surplices; and to bring in all superfluous articles of value to the Treasurer of the King's Household, to sell the rest of the linen, copes [†], and altar

---

[*] The small Monasteries were granted to the King, by stat 27 Hen. VIII. cap 28

[†] Rapin, vol ii. p 25.

clothes,

clothes, and give the money to the poor. An account of what was taken out of the churches in the Isle of Wight, found among the Harleian Manuscripts, in the British Museum, is seen in the thirty-eighth number of the Appendix before alluded to.

The Church of St. Lawrence

C H A P.

CHAP. VII.

The Parish Churches and Chapels; their Founders and Endowments; the moſt conſiderable Manors and Seats, their ancient Lords and preſent Proprietors *.

1280.

THE Regiſters of the Biſhops of Wincheſter reach no higher than John de Pontiſſeia, who filled that ſee in the reign of Edward the Firſt. no mention is there made of the churches in the Iſle of Wight, founded and endowed before

1305

that time; but in an ancient manuſcript, containing a return made by the Dean of the Iſland † to Biſhop Woodlock, is ſpecified what tithes the different churches and chapels were endowed with, as well as the proprietors of the Lordſhips from which they were paid: from this manuſcript it may be collected, that ſeveral churches endowed with tithes of lands long held by one family, and therein ſtyled chapels, have ſince become pariſh churches, whilſt others, with more ample endowments, are only chantries ‡.

The other churches in the iſland are alſo named in this return, but as they were Rectories, which enjoyed their tithes and oblations entire and independent of any claims from religious houſes, it will be ſufficient to remark them as they occur in the

---

* An abſtract of the moſt conſiderable manors, with their ancient and preſent Lords, is given in the Appendix, No LXXX

† There was anciently a Dean of this Iſland, to ſuperintend eccleſiaſtical affairs we find alſo, by the Epiſcopal Regiſters of Wincheſter, that William of Wykeham ſubſtituted a Suffragan Biſhop here, as was afterwards done by King Henry VII

‡ See Appendix, No LXXXI the deed is much defaced by time

review of the parishes. The following chapels are not included in the Dean's return, either because they were not built, or, not being endowed, were esteemed private chapels, and others, as belonging to Abbeys, were exempt from episcopal jurisdiction. Many of them are now so totally ruined, that their very situation is scarcely to be ascertained *.

I. A chapel dedicated to St. Austin, belonging to the Priory of Carisbrook, called in the ledger-book of that house, *Capella Sancti Augustini pro leprosis*, "For lepers."

II. A chapel, *pro infirmis*, "For the infirm," licensed by the Bishop, who vested the appointment of the Chaplain in the Abbot of Lyra.

III. At Knighton, in the parish of Newchurch, was a chapel built by Sir Ralph de Gorges, Lord of Knighton, in the year one thousand three hundred and one. It probably was not endowed when the Dean made his return, and was therefore unnoticed; but in the register of the diocese, it appears to have often been presented to by that family.

IV At Appleford, in the parish of Godshill, was a chapel built by the family of Lisle, who were Lords of Appleford: in the same register, Sir John Lisle appears to have presented to it in the year one thousand three hundred and thirty-one; and Sir Bartholomew Lisle, in the year one thousand three hundred and forty-four.

---

* Sir John Oglander, in his manuscript, observes, that he had heard there were above a hundred churches, chapels, abbeys, priories, nunneries, and oratories in the island, in the tenth year of the reign of Edward III

V. St. Catharine's, on Chale Down, was a chapel founded by Walter de Godyton, in the year one thousand three hundred and twenty-three.

VI. The Chantry of Gatcombe was a chapel in the church at Whitwell, dedicated to St Radigund; but it is uncertain whether this chantry was founded by the family of de Estur, or Lisle.

VII. Brennew was a small chapel in the parish of Freshwater; it is rated at one mark *per annum*, in Cardinal Beaufort's book for taxing the spiritualities.

VIII. Woolverton,⎫ These three chapels were situated in
IX. Middleton, ⎬ Bimbridge, and belonged to a Lordship
X. La Wode,   ⎭ of the same name; which, with the advowson of the chapels, are granted away by a deed in the forty-sixth year of Edward the Third, and are described as lying in the parish of Woolverton. No presentation to these chapels appears in the register, so that it may be presumed they were not endowed.

XI. A Chantry at Newport, dedicated to the Blessed Virgin, founded by John Garston, of that town.

XII. A chapel, *de Sancto Licio*, mentioned in Cardinal Beaufort's valuation, but exempted as insignificant.

Most of the old parishes in the island are extensive and dispersed; the tithes of particular estates were, in some instances, paid to a distant church, and the tithes of others to the impropriators *. When the Lord of a manor founded a church for
the

* The origin of these irregularities is accounted for by Selden, in the following manner. " The first express mention, says he, of a limitation of profits to be
" given

the ufe of himfelf and his tenants, he appropriated the tithes of
his lands to his own church, and the parifh was large or fmall
in proportion to the extent of his poffeffions.   In many places
where the Monafteries had been founded before the parifh church,
the Monks had obtained a giant of the tithes of the adjoining
lands, which confequently could not go to the parifh chuich.
Neverthelefs, with the confent of the Bifhop, tithes appropriated to an ancient church might be transferred to one of a later
foundation; of which this ifland affords the following inftances.
Hugh Vernun, in the fifteenth year of Henry the Fuft, built
the chuich at Chale *, then part of the parifh of Carifbrook.
Walter de Infula built the church at Wootton, in the parifh

" given to a particular chuich, is in King Fdgar's laws, ann 970, where is a
" threefold divifion of churches: the firft is *the ecclefia fenioi*, or the cathedral;
" the fecond, was fuch a church as had a place for burial, the third, is that church
" which hath no place for burial   By this law it is ordered that every man who
" hath not erected a church of his own, fhall pay his tithes to the ancienteft
" church, or to the Monaftery where he hears divine fervice.   In the Synod of
" London, held by Anfelm, Archbifhop of Canterbury, 1102, it was ordered,
" *ut decimæ non nifi ecclefiis dentur*   whereby it is plain that the tithes were before
" paid at liberty   Nay, fuch had been the ufe to pay tithes where they pleafed,
" that Pope Innocent III *a* 1199, writes to the Archbifhops of Canterbury, *t*
" *ecclefiis paiochialibus juftæ decimæ perfol antur*   It is moft certain, that before
" that time, it was moft commonly practifed by the laity, to make arbitrary con-
" fecrations of the tithes of their poffeffions to what Monaftery or church they
" would, fometimes giving half, fometimes a third part, and at their pleafure, in
" perpetuity, or otherwife, according to the nature of confecrations in other coun-
" ties   In the national Synod, held at Weftminfter, ann 1124, by John d
" Crema, the Pope's Legate, it was conftituted, *quod nullus abbas, nullus prior,*
" *nullus omnino monachus, vel clericus, Ecclefiam vel decimam, feu quod bet beneficia*
" *ecclefiaftica, ex dono laici, fine propria epifcopi authoritate et affenfu fufcipiat*
" *Quod fi prefumptum fuerit, irrita erit donatio hujufmodi*   Yet it is moft cer-
" tain that the practice was for divers years otherwife, and that the churches and
" tithes were moft commonly given by lay patrons, without the Bifhop's affent or
" inftitution, and that, as well by filling them with incumbents, as by appropri-
" ating them to Monafteries"   *Selden's Hift. of Tithes, p* 262.
    * The inftrument for affigning particular tithes to the church of Chale is now
in the hands of the Rector.

of Whippingham, to which he appropriated his own tithes
De Aula built the church at Yaverland, in the parish
of Brading, and endowed it with the tithes of his demefnes.

The tithes of a fingle parish have fometimes been portioned
out by various affignments. thus, in the parish of Godshill, the
tithes of Appuldurcombe, Week, and Heyno's lands, were
paid to Lyra; thofe of Lifle, of Wootton, to Quarr Abbey, the tithes of De Aula's lands at Spann, to the Rector of
St. Laurence, and the tithes of that branch of the Lifle family
that inherited De Eftur's lands at Whitwell, went to the
Rector of Gatcombe.

The Bifhop's licence was requifite for the acceptance of a benefice from a lay patron : feveral of thefe licences are entered in
the regifters of Winchefter Some were of a temporary nature,
for the celebration of divine fervice for two or three years, in a
newly erected chapel, within which time the Bifhop iffued a
commiffion of inquiry, whether a fufficient endowment was
fettled, and whether his licence might be continued, without
prejudice to the mother church : after a favourable return to this
commiffion the licence was made perpetual. Sometimes a licence was granted, *ad avdiendum divina in oratorio apud manfam
fuam pro fe et fua familia* *, and then no endowment was required, but when any perfon founded an oratory for perpetual
maffes, the Bifhop was obliged by the canon to take care that a
fufficient endowment was fettled for the maintenance of a prieft
to officiate. Several chapels in this ifland funk to ruin for want

---

* Among other inftances, the regifters mention a licence granted to John Paulet, Efq and his wife, to have a moveable altar for celebrating mafs by a prieft,
to be ufed in a proper and convenient place

of a fettled fupport, but they muſt have been created before the exiſtence of the canon, which obliged the biſhop to procure a fufficient eſtabliſhment for them. Thus alſo may the ſilence of the regiſters, reſpecting ſome of them, be accounted for; and the chapels which had no ſpecial endowment, were not under the neceſſity of a preſentation *.

Some

* The partition of pariſhes, and erection of chapels, are thus illuſtrated by Biſhop Kennet ‘ The firſt inſtitution of pariſhes in England, moſt of our writ- " ers have aſcribed to Archbiſhop Honorius, about the year 636, wherein they " build all on the authority of Archbiſhop Parker, but Mr Selden ſeems rightly " to underſtand the expreſſion, _provinciam ſuam in paroecias_, &c, of dividing ‘ his province into new dioceſes and this ſenſe is juſtified by the author of the " Defence of _Pluralities_. The like diſtinction of pariſhes, which now obtains " could never be the model of Honorius, nor the work of any one age Some " rural churches there were, under ſome limits preſcribed for the rights and pro- " fits of them; but the reduction of the whole country into the ſame limitations, " was gradually advanced, the reſult of many generations However, at the firſt " foundation of parochial churches (owing ſometimes to the ſole piety of the " Biſhop, but generally to the Lord of the manor), there were but few, and con- " ſeqiently at a great diſtance, ſo as the number of pariſhes depending on that " of churches, the parochial bounds were at firſt much large, and by degrees " contracted. For as the country grew more populous, and perſons more devout, " ſeveral other churches were founded within the extent of the former, and then " a new parochial circuit was allotted, in proportion to the new church, and the " manor or eſtate of the founder of it This certainly begat the increaſe of " pariſhes, when one too large and diffuſe for the reſort of all the inhabitants to the " one church, was, by the addition of ſome one or more new churches, cantoned " into more limited diviſions This was ſuch an abatement to the revenue of the " old churches, that complaint was made of it in the time of Edward the Confeſſor " _now_, ſay they, _there be three or four churches where in former times there was " but one, and ſo the tithes and profits of the prieſts are much diminiſhed_ When by " long uſe and cuſtom parochial bounds were fixed and ſettled, many of the pariſhes " were ſtill ſo large, that ſome of the remote hamlets found it very inconvenient " to be at ſo great a diſtance from the church, and therefore, for the relief and " eaſe of ſuch inhabitants, this new method was practiſed, of building private " oratories, or chapels, in any ſuch remote hamlet in which a _cappellane_ was " ſometimes endowed by the Lord of the manor, or ſome other benefactor, but " generally maintained by a ſtipend from the pariſh-prieſt, to whom all the rights
" and

Some chapels, involved in the fate of monaftic foundations, fell into the King's hands, under the denomination of chantries, and were either given away or fold *. The church of Eaft Standen, which ranked as a parifh church in Cardinal Beaufort's regifter †, fell under this predicament; when Kingfton, which in the fame roll is reckoned as a chapel, is now become a parifh church. other inftances of like nature may be obferved from the fame authority, the chapels at Knighton, Alverfton, &c have been deftroyed, when thofe of Yaverland, St. Laurence, and Brook have become parifh churches.

Diftinction
between a
chapel and a
parifh
church.

The chief diftinction between a parifh church and a chapel, confifted in the right of adminiftering the facraments, and burial of the dead ‡, which were to be performed only in the former, a diftinction which fubfifted in the days of King Edgar, when it was ordained by law that every man fhould pay his tithes to the mother church, except when a Thane or Lord fhould have a church with a burial-place within his own fee, in

" and dues were entirely preferved. John Peckham, Archbifhop of Canterbury,
" mentions this as a popular reafon why chapels were allowed in the larger pa-
" rifhes Capellæ parochianis ipfis ex gratia funt conceffæ, quia ad matrem eccle-
" fiam p. importunitate viarum et temporum et diftantiæ longitudine accedere fæpiffime
" nequeunt ullo modo nec infirmis periclitantibus commode providere." Kennet's Paroch
Antiq p 586, 587

   * There was a chapel built at South Baddefley, in the parifh of Boldre, in the New Foreft, by Henry Wells, Efq Lord of the manor of Baddefley, on his petition, ftating, that the place was three miles diftant from the parifh of Boldre, by reafon of which diftance, and the badnefs of the ways to the church, the inhabitants could not be prefent at divine fervice, &c. After the Bifhop had iffued a commiffion, of the nature before mentioned, to enquire into the truth of the allegations, the chapel was built and endowed But as it was the duty of the Chaplain to pray for the foul of the founder, that circumftance afforded a pretence for its being feized as a Chantry Reg Winton Joh Stratford epi a 1300

   † See Appendix, No LXXXII.

   ‡ Ad capellam non pertinet baptifterium neque fepultura. Selden on Tithes, p. 265

                                                        which

which cafe he might give to it, one third of his tithes, but if it had no burial-place, he was obliged maintain a prieft at his own chaige *.

The chapels, therefore, which were endowed with certain tithes by their founders, may be prefumed to have had licences for the appropriation of fuch tithes, in obedience to this old law of King Edgar, or under authorities derived from that fource; and it is to be obferved, that moft of the fmall parifhes in this ifland have been formerly prefented to, under the deno-mination of chapels; and that fome of them ftill retain a maik of fubordination, by paying an acknowledgement to the mother church. Bifhop Kennet obferves, that when an oratory had ac-quired the right of baptifm and burial, it was to be efteemed a parifh chuich : hence, at the fiift erection of thofe chapels, ex-prefs caie was taken in their eftablifhment that they fhould have neither font, bells, nor any thing that might piejudice the mo-ther church †.

T H E   P A R I S H   O F   B R A D I N G.

Brading, formerly written Brerding, is bounded on the noith   Limits. by the parifh of St. Helens, by that of New-church on the weft, by Shanklin on the fouth, and on the fouth-eaft by the fea· it is ftill a large parifh, notwithftanding St Helens, Yavei-land, Shanklin, and Bonchurch, have been taken from it, but as thofe churches weie built before any iegifter appeais to have been kept by the Bifhops of Winchefter, the times of their feparation are uncertain.

The church of Brading is fuppofed to be the oldeft in   Antiquity the ifland. The conveits, at the fiift intioduction of the

* Jo Brompton inter X Scriptoics, p 871.
† Paroch Antiq. p. 590.

Chriftian

Christian religion by Bishop Wilfred, are said to have been baptised there . and the annals of the church of Winchester relate, that King Ina [a] gave the church of Brading to the Bishop of Winchester.

The

[a] The reality of this donation is much to be doubted   In Wharton's Annals of the church of Winchester, it is said that King Ina, in 682, gave to the church of Winton, thirty hides of Land in Everland (Yaverland), and fifty hides in Bierding, in the Isle of Wight. The same writer says, that, in 735, Cuthred, a kinsman of King Ethelred, gave to the church of Winton, forty hides at Calbourn, twenty-five hides at Binewade, and twenty-two hides at Withenham, in the Isle of Wight   Farther, that in the year 800, King Egbert gave to the church of Winton, thirty hides of land at Calbourn, and forty-two hides at Shalfleet, in the Isle of Wight   Of all these donations, no more is found in the church, at the time of the general survey, than Calbourn; nor were the other lands, said to have been so granted, held by the church in the time of Edward the Confessor, as appears by Domesday-book   where Brading and Yaverland are recorded to have been held by a private person from that Prince, who was too remarkable for his piety to have either deprived the church of its possessions, or suffered them to be taken by others

Many of the charters of our Saxon Kings are strongly suspected to be forgeries   While the Normans were acquiring lands by violence, the Monks were active in procuring grants and immunities by fraud, and this might easily be done by collusion with the persons whose lands were seized by the Conqueror, these being prevailed on by the Monks to acknowlege that they held their lands from a Monastery, a deception by which they at once gratified their piety, and disappointed their plunderers   A charter then might be fabricated from some Saxon King in support of this declaration, without much danger of the forgery being discovered by the Normans

Bishop Stillingfleet, in his *Origines Britannicæ*, has examined into this matter with great accuracy, and produces some instances of Monkish forgery, pertinent to the present subject   He mentions a charter, supposed to have been made to the Abbey of Glastonbury   beginning with "A. D. 625," when, as this learned prelate observes, the Christians did not compute from the incarnation of our Lord, until the century succeeding that date   He also cites another charter to the same Abbey, supposed to have been granted by King Ina, which, by the manner and style, as well as other observable incongruities, discovers itself to be a forgery of later times   The Monks, he observes, have been much charged with this artifice by the bishops, and that there was a general suspicion of forgery in the charters of exemption extended to the Monasteries   He gives a full relation of the Monks of Canterbury, being convicted in the forgery of a charter of privileges, and quotes good authors, who, though willing to support the credit of ancient charters, yet own such forgeries to have been commonly practised in early times, and who lay

it

The advowson of the church was contested at law in the thirty-seventh year of Henry the Third, between the abbot and convent of Wenlock, in Shropshire, and Walter Lisle with Maud his wife, which suit terminated in favour of the convent.

In a letter from the Prior of Wenlock to the Bishop of Winchester it is stated, that the advowson of the church of Brading being claimed from them by Aymer de Valence, the said Prior and Convent resign their right therein to the Bishop, by whom it was with-held from Aymer, and continued in that see till John de Pontissera, at the request of King Edward the First, appropriated the church to the Convent of Breamore; in consideration, as it is recited, *of their great sufferings and losses, sustained chiefly by the means of the Lady Isabella de Fortibus**. The Prior of Breamore obtained a licence from the Bishop, to let the Rectory of Brading to farm, to the Prior of St. Dennis, near Southampton; with a condition, *that the alms to be given to the poor, should in no wise be diminished.* At the dissolution of religious houses it was granted to Henry Courtney, Marquis of Exeter: who presented to the church, in virtue of the right of the late Prior, then vested in him; but, by his attainder, this,

1332.

155.

it down for a rule, that the older the charter, the more they are to be suspected. He quotes the opinion of Papebrochius, that these forgeries were for the most part framed in the eleventh century, when there was ignorance enough to let them pass current, and occasion enough afforded to the Monks to contrive them for their own security against the incroachment of others upon their lands, and of the jurisdiction of the Bishops over their Monasteries. The same learned writer instances several forgeries of old charters to Monasteries, detected by blunders in the framing of them: and the supposed grant of Brading, Yaverland, and other lands, by King Ina, to the church of Winchester, may be referred to this class, from the great variation in the quantity and value of the lands, from what are specified in the grant.

* Ex Regist. Winton.

with

with his other poffeffions efcheating to the crown, was given to Trinity College, Cambridge

The church.   This church bears evident marks of great antiquity : it appears to have been erected in the eighth century ; little attention has been paid to fymmetry in its conftruction. The infide is very plain, has three ifles, and, in a chapel on the fouth fide of the altar, are two monuments, the one of the celebrated Sir John Oglander, and the other of his father, Sir William. On the tombs are their figures in armour, carved in wood *.

Bimbridge.   Bimbridge †, called the ifle of Bimbridge, is a peninfula formed by Brading Haven, wherein there were anciently three manors, Woolverton, La Wode, and Middleton or Milton, the two former of which belonged to the family of Glamorgan, in Somerfetfhire   On the death of Sir Nicholas Glamorgan, in the thirty-fixth year of Edward the Third, all his lands were divided among his fix fifters, one of whom marrying Thomas Hacket, he purchafed the remaining five fhares of thefe manors from the other fifters ‡ . and by a deed in the forty-fixth year of Edward the Third, fettled in his family the manors of Woolverton, La Wode, Middleton, and La Clyve, in the parifh of Woolverton, together with the advowfons of the chapels

* The family of Oglander is the moft ancient in the ifland, their anceftors came over at the time of the Conqueft, and the name is derived from their place of refidence in Normandy

† " Before Sir William Ruffel buylt the cawfey and the brydge, Yaverland " (as now by corruption), was called Overlond and after the buylding thereof, " the peninfula was called Within Brydge, now Binbrydge " Oglander's Manufcript

‡ Another fifter married Rowel, and afterwards to Hunfton, had the manors of Brook and Uggeton.

of Woolverton, La Wode, and Middleton[*]. This estate of
the Hackets came to Sir James Worsley, in the reign of Henry
the Eighth, by marriage with the only daughter of Sir John
Leigh, who married the Heiress of Hacket; and still remains in
the family of Worsley, of Appuldurcombe, as the lineal descendants of Sir John Leigh.

Brading Haven is a large tract of marshy ground, containing eight hundred and fifty-six acres, covered every tide by
the sea, which flows through a narrow inlet   The right to
the fishery was contested at law, by Sir John de Weston,
against Sir Peter D'Evercy and John de Glamorgan, Lords
of the adjoining lands.   Sir John de Weston claimed a third
part of the chalk of the three Lordships, a third part of the fishery,
and a third part of the half of the chance of the sea, or ship-
wrecks, the King being entitled to the other half; of which
rights his ancestors had been possessed beyond the memory of
man, though he was then disturbed in the enjoyment by the
other parties.   By the intervention of friends, the cause was
submitted to arbitration, in the sixth year of Edward the Second,
when the right of Sir John de Weston was affirmed[†]   The
property of the haven, with the right of fishery, is in the family of Worsley, of Appuldurcombe.

The recovery of so large a piece of land from the sea, had
been long an object in contemplation, and Sir John Oglander
has preserved accounts of several undertakings for this purpose.

Brading
Haven

Inland ed
from the
Haven
temp Ld L

---

[*] Each of these manors had a distinct chapel, but as no presentation to them
appears in the register of Winton, they may be presumed to have had no endowment, they are now so totally ruined, that little more than the foundations are to
be traced

[†] See a copy of this instrument, Appendix, No LXXXIII

C c 2   A part

A part of Brading Haven was taken in by Sir William Ruffel [*], Lord of Yaverland, at the time when Yar-bridge was erected In the year one thoufand five hundred and fixty two, another parcel of land was walled in from the fea, by Mr. George Oglander, and Mr. German Richards, when the North-marfh and fome adjoining lands were gained.   And again, in the year one thoufand five hundred and ninety-four, a third acquifition was made of Mill-marfh, and other meadows between the fluice and the bridge, by Mr. Edward Richards.

Sir Bevis
Thelwall's
attempt to
inclofe the
Haven.

The next, and laft attempt, was of a more extenfive nature.   A grant of Brading Haven was obtained from King James the Firft, by Gibbs, a groom of the bed-chamber. The owners of the adjoining lands contefted this grant, which the King was very earneft in fupporting.   After a verdict obtained in the Exchequer againft the gentlemen of the ifland, Gibbs fold his fhare for *two thoufand pounds* to Sir Bevis Thelwall, a Page of the King's bed chamber, who admitted the famous Sir Hugh Middleton to a fhare.   They employed a number of Dutchmen to inclofe and recover the Haven from the fea.   The firft taking of it in, coft *four thoufand pounds*; and *one thoufand pounds* more was expended in building a dwelling houfe, barn, a water mill, trenching, quickfetting, and other neceffary works; fo that, including the original purchafe the total expenditure amounted to *feven thoufand pounds*   But after all, the nature of the ground did not anfwer the expectations of the undertakers, for though that part of it adjoining Brading proved tolerably good, nearly one half of it was found to be a light running fand: neverthelefs an inconteft ble evidence appeared,

* Warden of the Ifle of Wight, in the reign of Edward I

by

by the difcovery of a well, cafed with ftone, near the middle of the Haven, that it had formerly been good ground. Sir Hugh Middleton tried a variety of experiments on the land which had been taken in, before he fold his fhare, fowing it with wheat, barley, oats, cabbage, and finally with rape-feed, which laft was alone fuccefsful. But the greateft difcouragement was, that the fea brought up fo much oofe, weeds, and fand, which choaked up the paffage for the difcharge of the frefh water; at length, in a wet feafon, when the inner part of the Haven was full of frefh water, and a high fpring tide, the waters met under the bank, and made a breach. Thus ended this expenfive project, and though Sir John Oglander, who lived in the neighbourhood, confeffes himfelf a friend to the undertaking, which, befides its principal object, tended to render that part of the country more healthy, he declares it as his opinion, that the fcheme can never be refumed to any profitable purpofe.

Sir Bevis Thelwall and his heirs laboured to afcribe this accident to other caufes, in order to preferve their claims, and to recover compenfation for their loffes; but the whole affair died away, and the fea ftill overflows the Haven. Neverthelefs among the papers of Sir Robert Worfley, there is found an eftimate, made in the year one thoufand fix hundred and ninety-nine, of the expences neceffary to recover it[*], which fhews that object to have been again in contemplation.

The northern fide of Bimbridge is low land, but adjoining to Yaverland is a fteep chalk cliff, called Culve.

* See Appendix, No. LXXXIV.

Clif,

Cliff *, formerly famous for a breed of hawks. In the reign of Queen Elizabeth an order was issued to search for some of them, which had been stolen †.

Cliff and West Nunwell.

There are two lordships in this parish of the name of Nunwell, under the distinctions of East and West, both which have been possessed by the Oglander family, from the earliest accounts of the landholders of the island. The seat of Sir William Oglander, Baronet, at Nunwell, is a large handsome mansion, with a fine lawn before it; the prospects from the house are beautiful and pleasing.

Kerne

Kerne, formerly written Curne, appears by the roll of the tenants of the island, to have been held by the Knights Templars, and by the chapel of Burton. The possessions of both having been granted to Winchester college, the manor is held under a lease from that body, by Mr. Bagster.

Alverston.

Alverston, formerly written Alfredstone, is recorded in Domesday-book among the extensive possessions of William Fitz-Stur; and in the reign of Edward the First, was held by William de Aumarle, of the county of Dorset; from his heir it came to Sir John Maltravers, whose daughter and heir married Humphrey Stafford, a younger brother of the Earl of Stafford, and by his daughter and heir it came to Sir Giles Strangeways. It was purchased by Richard Broad, Esquire, and afterwards by the late Lord Holmes, who devised it to the Reverend Mr. Holmes.

Langard,

Langard or Langed, called in Domesday Langareston, was formerly part of the possessions of the family of Russel, Lords

---

* Culver, from the Saxon culppe, a pigeon, and the number of those birds that harbour there will entitle it to the name of the Pigeon Cliff.

† Vide Appendix, No. LXXXV.

NUNWELL the Seat of Sr William

of Yaverland. It was held in the laft centuiy by that of Knight, from whom it was purchafed fome years fince by William Pike, Efquire, who bequeathed it to Mi. Bonham, the prefent poffeffor.

Whitfield is a manor that gave name to its propiietors, who anciently wiote it Witeville *. The eailieft tianfaction in which it appears, is the atteftation of Thomas Becket, Archbifhop of Canterbury, that Hugh de Witeville had given his manor of Witeville to the Monks of Quari, confirmed with his anathema againft the violators of the grant . it is probable that the heirs of Hugh difputed the authenticity of the conveyance; for the monks were deprived of it, and the manoi was afterwards held by the Ciown. It was given by Edward the Firft, with Freſh-water and othei lands, to his daughter Maiy, a Nun at Am-brefbury, for her fupport in that convent †.

THE PARISH OF ST. HELENS

This fmall parifh comprehends the noith-eaft extremity of the ifland: it is bounded on the weft by the parifh of New-church; by the fea, on the noith and eaft; and by the pa-rifh of Brading on the fouth The chief part of the parifh confifts of a manor and faim, called the Priory, formerly a cell to an Abbey in Normandy. The convent built a fmall church here, which they fupplied from their own body, until the canon required vicars to be conftantly iefident. It is recorded in the regifter of Winchefter, that, in confideration

---

* Two manors of the name of Witesfel, are mentioned in Domefday-book, which were together iated at four hides

† See Appendix, No. LXXXVI.

of

of the fmallnefs of this parifh the Bifhop licenced the Prior of St. Helens to celebrate mafs and adminifter the facrament, until a vicar fhould be eftablifhed. In Cardinal Beaufort's valuation of the fpiritualities in his diocefe, the church is rated at thirty marks.

St Helens was given to the college of Eton, and is held under it; a ftipend of twenty pounds a year being paid to the vicar, who alfo enjoys an addition of the fame fum from Queen Anne's bounty. The old church was fituated at the extremity of the parifh, fo near the fea, that the waves wafhed away great part of the church-yard, and even endangered the building itfelf; the inhabitants therefore obtained a brief for the erection of a new church, which was accordingly built on a more fecure fpot, and confecrated by Trelawney, Bifhop of Winchefter *, in the year one thoufand feven hundred and nineteen.

The Priory is now the feat of Nafh Grofe, Efquire. the fituation is remarkably pleafant, the gardens are laid out with tafte, and command a fine view of Portfmouth, and the road at Spithead.

St. John's, the feat of Lieutenant-general Amherft, commands a moft delightful profpect of Spithead, Portfmouth, and the coaft of Hampfhire.

Apley, the feat of Mis. Roberts, is a fmall elegant place, fituated about a quarter of a mile from Ride. From the houfe and garden, the road at Spithead and the town of Portf-mouth appear to the greateft advantage.

The Priory.

St John's.

Apley.

* St Helens appears to have been of more confideration in former times than at prefent, fee Rymer, vol ii p 728 10 Edw III. *Breve Regis majoribus et balivis de Yarmouth & Infula Elræ in Inf Vect de mutando naves fuas ad Portf-mouth*

                                                                        T H E

St John's in the Isle of Lieutenant

THE PARISH OF YAVERLAND.

This parifh, confifting of only one farm, and a few tene- Situation
ments, is fituated between Sandown-fort and Bimbridge-down:
it extends to Yar-bridge, on the north; and is furrounded
by the parifh of Brading, except on the fouth, where it is
bounded by the fea.

The church is fuppofed to have been built and endowed by one Hiftory.
of the Ruffel family. William Ruffel, by marrying Eleanor,
the daughter and heirefs of Sir Thomas de Aula *, in the reign
of Edward the Firft, became Lord of Yaverland, St. Laurence,
and feveral other manors. the particulars of which are feen in
the roll of thofe who held under the Countefs Ifabella de Fortibus. By an inquifition taken in the feventeenth year of Henry
the Sixth, Stephen Hatfield was found poffeffed of Yaverland, &c.
in right of Eleanor his wife, who was fifter and heirefs of Thomas Ruffel, fon of Sir Maurice Ruffel. The eftate again devolved
to daughters, and the Lordfhip of Yaverland was, in the firft
year of Queen Mary, purchafed by German Richards, Efquire,
in whofe family it continued till within thefe few years, when
it was devifed by Mr. Richards, the laft of the name, to the Reverend Mr. Wright; and in cafe of his death without children,
to go, with divers other lands, to Exeter College, Oxford.

The church pay sa penfion to the mother-church of Brading.
It is called a chapel in Cardinal Beaufort's rate, and exempted
from taxation on account of its inability.

---

* This family is of great antiquity, the name was often written de Hawles,
and fome of them are fuppofed to be ftill exifting under that of Hollis.

THE

THE PARISH OF SHANKLIN.

Situation.

The parish of Shanklin is bounded on the north by the parish of Brading, by the parish of Newchurch on the weft, by the parish of Bonchurch on the fouth, and by the fea on the eaft. This, as to parochial afseffments, is confidered as a diftinct parish; but is properly a chapel annexed to the Rectory of Bonchurch: it was formerly taken out of the parish of Brading, where the inhabitants ftill bury their dead; and a penfion of ten shillings is paid annually from the chapel to the Rector of Brading, as an acknowledgment to the mother church. The chapel was built by one of the Lifles, and endowed with fifty acres of land, together with the tithes of many tenants of the manor. This part of the ancient posseffions of the Lifles paffed through the Dennis family to that of Popham, with Bonchurch and other lands.

History.

Shanklin Chine.

The fituation of the Chine * (as it is called), at a fmall diftance from the village of Shanklin, is exceedingly romantic, overgrown with shrubs and bushes, and difplays a moft beautiful and picturefque fcene, the path down to the fea is very fteep;

---

* The term chine is applied to the back bone of an animal, both in the manege, and culinary language, which forms the higheft ridge of the body. Echine, in the French, is ufed in the fame fenfe, and Boyer has the word chinfienau for a great cut, or flash. Hence the word chine might be thought peculiarly expreffive of i high ridge of land cleft abruptly down, and the feveral parts of the fouthern coaft denominated chines, all correfpond with this defcription. A chine alfo appears to fignify the fame as a chafm, and both to be derived from the Greek word χαινω, or chainu, hifco, or dehifco, that is to cleave afunder, fo as to form a chafm, or chine. It is well known that the χ in the Greek alphabet is always expreffed in Englifh by ch, and that it is pronounced by the modern Greeks, as our ch, in church, chart, &c. and perhaps it was fo pronounced by the ancients

half

A Burgess Green telegraph ... Hill

half way down is a fisherman's cottage, placed in a most beautiful but secluded spot.

THE PARISH OF BONCHURCH.

The parish of St. Boniface, or as it is usually termed Bon- Situation.
church, is of a triangular form; it is bounded by Shanklin on
the north, by Newchurch on the west, and by the sea on the
south   In Domesday-book it is recorded as a manor, belonging History.
to William Fitz-Azor *, and by the rolls of the landholders
of the island, is found to have remained long in the family
of Lisle.   From the Lisles it came by marriage to the family
of Dennis; and from them descended to the Pophams.   When
the church was built is uncertain, but it was probably soon
after the general survey.

In the center of this small parish is the cottage of St. Bo- Col Hill's
niface: Colonel Hill, the proprietor of it, has made confiderable cottage.
additions there; and the garden is laid out with taste.   Nothing
can exceed the beauty of the situation of this cottage and the
small village adjoining.

THE PARISH OF NEWCHURCH.

The parish of Newchurch extends nine miles in length, from Situation.
Ride on the north shore, to Bonchurch on the south, it is
bounded on the east by the parishes of St. Helens, Reading,

---

* Two brothers, William and Gozeline, the sons of Azor, are mentioned in
Domesday-book, and many of the manors then possessed by them, being found
afterwards in two families of *the Insula*, or Lisle, affords room to conjecture that
the Lisles were their descendants

Shanklin, and Bonchurch; and on the weſt by Binſtead, Arreton, Godſhill, and St. Laurence.

Extent.

Newchurch ſtands in the middle of the pariſh, and probably gave name to the ſurrounding village. it was one of the ſix churches given by William Fitz-Oſborn to his Abbey of Lyra, in Normandy [*]. The following are the moſt conſiderable Lord-ſhips belonging to it.

Ride.

Ride, or, as it is called in old records, La Rye, is a populous village, ſituated on the north channel, oppoſite to Stoke's-bay, on the coaſt of Hampſhire. In ancient rolls it is mentioned as one of thoſe places where a watch was to be kept for the ſecurity of the iſland. It was part of the poſſeſſions of the family of Dillington, till Sir John Dillington ſold it to Henry Player, Eſquire, whoſe ſon Thomas built a chapel there, in the year one thouſand ſeven hundred and nineteen; and charged the manor with an annual rent of ten pounds, payable to the Vicar of Newchurch, to officiate therein, or provide ſome one to officiate for him. This village is of late much increaſed, both in buildings and trade. it is oppoſite the towns of Portſmouth and Goſport, at about ſix miles diſtance A conſtant intercourſe is carried on by packet-boats, which paſs and repaſs regularly ſeveral times in a week, to the mutual benefit of both places: Portſmouth is ſupplied with butter, eggs, and poultry from the iſland; and, in return, furniſhes the iſlanders with divers neceſſaries.

Aſhey.

Aſhey is a manor, but as it is not mentioned either in Domeſday-book, or among the landholders under the Counteſs

---

[*] When that Duchy was loſt to the crown of England, Newchurch was given to the Abbey of Beaulieu, near Southampton, the preſentation of a Vicar, by that Abbot and Convent, is ſeen in the regiſter in the year 1447.

Iſabella

View from the sea toward Pier Hill & Milton

Isabella de Fortibus, must have taken its name since the reign of Edward the First. At the dissolution of religious houses it belonged to the Abbey of Whorwell, in Hampshire, and was purchased by Giles Worsley, Esquire, a younger brother of the Worsleys in Lancashire, whose son, by his first wife, dying a minor soon after his father, a suit at law was commenced between his heir at law in Yorkshire, and his half-brother, the eldest son by a second wife, which was settled by arbitration, that the half-brother should retain possession of two thirds of the estate; and that the manor of Ride, the other third part, should be given to the heir at law, by him it was immediately sold to Mr. Dillington, of Knighton. Sir Bowyer Worsley, the grandson of Giles, sold his share of the estate, including Ashey, to Mr. Coteile, from whom it passed by inheritance to Lord Edgcumbe

On the highest part of Ashey Down, is erected a triangular truncated pyramid, of hewn stone, about twenty feet high, having the apex obliquely cut off; it serves as a mark for ships coming into St. Helens or Spithead, and was built, at the expence of the crown, for that purpose.

The manor of Knighton Gorges was held in the reign of Henry the Third by John de Morville, a younger brother of de Morvilles, a considerable family in the county of Cumberland. John de Morville dying in the fortieth year of Henry the Third, Ralph de Gorges, who married Elen, his daughter and coheir, enjoyed the manor in her right, and received the homage of his tenants at Bradpole in Dorsetshire. Sir Ralph de Gorges, the son of Elen, left only one daughter, Eleanor the wife of the celebrated Sir Theobald Russel, whose son Sir Ralph

Russel

Ruffel fucceeded to the Lordfhip of Knighton, and left Sir Maurice his heir : Thomas the only fon of Sir Maurice dying without iffue, his heirs general were John Hacket, fon of one of the daughters of Sir Maurice Ruffel *, and two of her daughters Margaret, who married John Keneys, and Eleanor the wife of Stephen Hatfield: Knighton fell to the fhare of Hacket, as appears by the return to an inquifition taken in the feventeenth year of the reign of Henry the Sixth, he alfo poffeffed Woolverton, Milton, and other eftates in this ifland † He left two daughters, Joan and Agnes; Joan married ——— Gilbert of Witcombe, in Somerfetfhire, and had Knighton with part of Woolverton for her portion ; and that manor continued in the Gilbert family until the fifth of Elizabeth, when George Gilbert of Witcombe fold the manor of Knighton, and his fhares of Milton, Woolverton in Bimbridge, and the manor of Cleavelands in the parifh of New-church, to Anthony Dillington, Efquire, of Pool, in Dorfetfhire. Mr. Dillington fold his fhare of Woolverton, Milton, and Cleavelands, to Sir Robert Worfley ; but Knighton continued for a long time the feat of his family, until by a failure in the male line the manor devolved to two fifters, coheireffes of Sir Triftram Dillington, Baronet, the laft of whom bequeathed it to Maurice Bocland, Efquire, on whofe deceafe, it defcended to the prefent proprietor, George Maurice Biffet, Efquire Knighton Houfe is an old building, containing feveral good apartments, beautifully fituated on the edge of a hill between fome fine woods, formerly remarkable for great plenty of pheafants.

The houfe.

---

* Dugdale has mentioned the Ruffel family as anceftors of the Dukes of Bedford ; but the Ruffels of the Ifle of Wight not only bore different arms, but appear plainly to have funk in female heirs.

† Efch 23 Hen. VII

The

Swainswick, the Seat of ... W ... M. Bassett Esq.

The manor of Apfe, is in fome ancient writings called *Apfe canonicorum*, from having belonged to the canons of Chrift-church, in Hampfhire, to whom it was given by Baldwin, the firft Earl of Devon of that name, when he new-modelled the monaftery, and placed regular inftead of fecular canons there. After the diffolution of religious houfes, the manor was pur-chafed by Mr. Dillington, and afterwards fold by one of his fucceffors to Mr Edward Leigh, of Newport, who left it to Sir John Chichefter, Baronet, from whom it has been lately pur-chafed by the Right Honourable Sir Richard Worfley.

Wroxall appears to have been always held in demefne by the lords of the ifland It was granted by Richard the Second, the laft year of his reign, together with all the other crown lands in the ifland, to Edward, Earl of Rutland, who was at the fame time created Duke of Albemarle. In an old rental of the crown lands in the ifland, taken in the twenty-third year of Henry the Seventh, Wroxall ftands firft on the roll at the rent of twenty-one pounds, eleven fhillings, and five pence. the manor came to Lord Edgcumbe, by inheritance from Mr. Coteile.

THE PARISH OF ST. LAURENCE.

This fmall parifh is bounded by that of Newchurch on the eaft, by Godfhill on the north, by Whitwell on the weft, and on the fouth by the fea; in old writings it is called St Laurence under-Wath, and was part of the poffeffions of the an-cient family de Aula, till the reign of Edward the Third, when the daughter and heirefs of Thomas de Aula, marrying William Ruffel,

Ruffel, carried it into that family, where it remained till the reign of Richard the Second, when it paffed to John Hacket and Stephen Hatfield, who married the daughters and coheireffes of Sir Maurice Ruffel; from Hacket it came to Sir John Leigh, and with his daughter and heirefs went, in the reign of Henry the Eighth, to Sir James Worfley, and ftill remains in the fame family.

The Clifts.

The fituation of this parifh is extremely romantic, the greateft part of it confifting of a flip of land extending about a mile and a half along the fea-fhore, and fecluded from the adjacent country, which lies very high above it, by a range of fteep rocky cliffs on the north, appearing in fome parts like an immenfe ftone wall. Huge fragments of earth and rock frequently fall from thefe cliffs. The village of St Laurence, compofed of a few ftraggling cottages, placed as the irregularities of the ground dictated, is fituated nearly in the centre of the parifh. The church is the fmalleft in the ifland. The foil is rich and loamy, highly cultivated where the uneveneffes of the ground will permit It is divided into fmall enclofures, interfperfed with large fragments of rock; the communication with the village is by a fteep road cut through the cliff at the weft end of the parifh.

The village of St Laurence

T H E   P A R I S H   O F   W H I T W E L L.

Situation.

The Parifh of Whitwell is of a very irregular figure, it is bounded by the parifhes of St. Laurence and Godfhill on the eaft, by the

parifhes

parifhes of Chale and Niton on the weft, and by the fea on the fouth. The manor of Whitwell and Weftover, formerly a part of Calbourn, were anciently included in the manor of Gatcombe, which, in Domefday-book, is faid to have been poffeffed by three brothers, in the time of Edward the Confeffor; each of thefe brothers had his hall, or capital meffuage. The firft mention of Whitwell is found in the roll of tenants, under the Countefs Ifabella de Fortibus, where de Eftur, Lord of Gatcombe, is faid to hold the manor of Whitwell in demefne. This, together with Gatcombe, came to the family of Lifle, by the marriage of Walter Lifle with Maud the daughter and heirefs of De Eftur: it came afterwards, by purchafe, into that of Worfley of Appuldurcombe, to which it ftill belongs. The church is properly a chapel belonging to Godfhill, but, on account of the feparate parochial rates, is deemed a diftinct parifh. The chapel of St. Radegund, which is now the chancel of the church, was built and endowed by De Eftur, Lord of Gatcombe, who is found in the regifter to have prefented it by the title of the Chantry of Gatcombe: the Rector of Gatcombe receives the rent of the lands with which the chantry was endowed, and is to officiate in the church at certain times, but this duty is compounded for.

There is in the parifh cheft, a decree, fomewhat mutilated, of John Dowman, Vicar-general and Chancellor of Richard Fox, Bifhop of Winchefter, in a caufe brought before him by the inhabitants of Whitwell, againft the Vicar of Godfhill, and Rector of Gatcombe. The decree * is in favour of the inhabitants. it appears from this deed, that what is now called the church

* The inhabitants allege, that from time immemorial, the Vicar of Godfhill, for the time being, " auxilio et juvamine rectoris de Gatcombe, pro tempore exiftentis fummam viginti et fex folidorum et octo denariorum, fingulis annis ad onus infra fcriptum contribuentis fumptibus et impenfis fuis, invenire et exhibere folebat, unum prefbyterum, habilem et idoneum, qui continue in dicta villam refidebat,

church of Whitwell, confisted of two chapels, the chapel of the
Blessed Virgin Mary of Whitwell, and the chapel of St. Radegund contiguous to it; that the former was to be supported and
repaired by the inhabitants of Whitwell parishioners of Godshill, the latter by the Rector of Gatcombe. that the inhabitants
of Whitwell parishioners of Godshill, were to be buried at Godshill, and the inhabitants of Whitwell parishioners of Gatcombe,
at Gatcombe.   There is a lease in the same chest (dated in the
year one thousand five hundred and seventy-four), of a house,
called the Church house, held by the inhabitants of Whitwell of
the Lord of the manor, and demised by them to John Brode, in
which is the following proviso · " Provided always, that if the
" quarter shall need at any time to make a quarter-ale or church-
" ale, for the maintenance of the chapel, that it shall be lawful
" for them to have the use of the said house, with all the rooms,
" both above and beneath, during their ale "

By an account of the number of inhabitants in the parish of
Whitwell, taken in the year one thousand six hundred and thirty-
two, and still preserved, it appears that they then amounted to *three
hundred and nine:* their present number will be found in the parochial table to be *three hundred and forty-four,* an increase of
thirty-five [4].

In the year one thousand six hundred and fifty, by a tax for
the relief of the poor, at the rate of two shillings for every ten

bat, in Eque et ra divina officia diebus Dominicis et festivis ac aliis diebus, hu-
manis more recebcic ri   et sacramenta et sacramentalia omnia et singula quotiens
necesse erit, ime tuum deputari duratis it excepta incolis de Whitwell prædicta
ministrant   magist r Bly vic rius de Godshill et Wilhelmus Hac-
ton rector de Gatcombe   per dictos incolas debite requisiti il-
lut sacerosrju egurus culta subsistente reuicrant " Dated A D 1515

[4] It may be presumed from this circumstance that the opinion entertained by some
persons, of a decay in the population of the island, is not well founded   Though
the towns of Carisbrook, Newtown, and Yarmouth have greatly decreased, Newport,
East Cowes, West Cowes, and Ride, have considerably augmented their numbers.

pounds, there was raifed the fum of eight pounds feven fhillings and eight pence. In one thoufand feven hundred and feventy-fix, at one fhilling in the pound, the tax amounted to feventy-eight pounds four fhillings and three pence halfpenny, fo that the annual value of the parifh, in the year one thoufand fix hundred and fifty, appears to have been eight hundred and thirty-eight pounds five fhillings and ten pence, and at prefent is computed at one thoufand five hundred and fixty-four pounds fix fhillings and eight pence; probably in both inftances under-rated.

The greateft part of this parifh produces fine corn, the line Under Wa. of cliffs from St. Laurence extends along the fhore through the parifh of Niton to Chale Bay, where they terminate. The country below this range of cliffs, is called, by the inhabitants, Under Cliff, or Under Way.

THE PARISH OF NITON.

This parifh, which is in old writings called Niewton, but Boundaries. now diftinguifhed by the name of Crab Niton, from the plenty of fea crabs on that coaft, is furrounded on the eaft and north by the parifh of Whitwell, by Chale on the weft, and by the fea on the fouth This was one of the old parifhes, whofe Hiftory. church was given by Fitz-Ofborn to the Abbey of Lyra; and in the claim of Ifabella de Fortibus, half a fee was held there by the Countefs in demefne. The church came to the crown on the diffolution of religious houfes, and was, with five other churches in Hampfhire, given to Queen's College, Oxford, by Charles the Firft, in exchange for the College Plate.

The manor of Niton, which had been held in demefne by Niton. the Lords of the Ifland, was purchafed by Thomas Coteile, Efquire, and defcended by inheritance to Lord Edgcumbe.

E e 2 The

Beauchamp. The manor of Beauchamp, so named from Beauchamp, Lord of Alcester and Powick, who, in the reign of Edward the Third, enjoyed it, with Fresh-water and another manor called Keineys Court, from a family of that name who resided at Tarant Keireys, in Dorsetshire, remained long in the ancient family of Meaux of Kingston. The grand-daughter and surviving heiress of Sir William Meaux, Baronet, married Sir Edward Worsley, Knight, of Gatcombe, on whose death these manors were divided, and afterwards sold to different persons.

THE PARISH OF GODSHILL.

Boundaries. The parish of Godshill is bounded by that of Newchurch on the east, by Arreton on the north, by Carisbrook, Kingston and Chale on the west, and by Whitwell and St. Laurence on the south. This is one of the ancient parishes that existed before the compilation of Domesday-book, and one of the six churches given by William Fitz-Osborn to the abbey of Lyra.

Godshill ma- The manor of Godshill, which gave name to the parish, be-
nor. longed to the Abbey of Lyra, till it was given to the Convent of Sheen in Surry, together with the Priory of Carisbrook, and manor of Freshwater, as appears by a lease from that Convent, in the twenty ninth year of the reign of Henry the Eighth, to Captain Richard Worsley, for the term of forty-six years, at the annual rent of *two hundred marks*. The remainder of this term, among other leasehold estates, came to Sir Francis Walsingham, by marrying Captain Worsley's widow: Sir Francis Walsingham soon afterwards obtained the manor of Godshill in fee. It has passed through several conveyances since, and has been lately purchased of Sir Thomas Miller, Baronet, by Sir Richard Worsley.

The

The church stands on the top of a steep hill, commanding a most beautiful prospect, and is an ancient well built edifice, with cross isles. several of the old tombs in it have had brass figures and inscriptions on them, which have been long since stripped off, but by the oldest accounts, they belonged to the families of de Aula, Heyno, and Fry Among the monuments remaining, are the following. a handsome tomb of Sir John Leigh, and Mary, his Lady, the daughter and heiress of John Hacket, Esquire, who died in the reign of Henry the Eighth; it is without inscription, but exhibits their figures in full length, of alabaster, with the arms of the family of Hacket on the border of the Lady's robe A monument of Sir James Worsley and his Lady, who was the daughter and heiress of Sir John Leigh· it is without any inscription, but the arms are those of Worsley, Leigh, Hacket, and Standish, the family of Sir James Worsley's mother. The next monument is to the memory of Captain Richard Worsley, son of Sir James; and the inscription on it supplies the deficiency of the others *.

On

* Richardo Worsley armigero nuper insulæ Vectis præfecto, unico fratri suo, filio primogenito Jacobi Worsley de Worsley-Hall in provincia Lanc sti oriundi, equitis aurati, ejusdem item insulæ olim præfect', ex Anna filia Johannis Ley equitis aurati, apud Appledercombe in eadem insula nata, Johannes Worsley Ar iger posuit.

En pia Worselei lapis hic tegit offa Richardi,
Vectis præfectum quem gemit ora suum
Et patriæ charus dum vixit, et utilis idem,
Mortuus in patria nunc tumulatur humo
Quem pater adversa materq. aspectat in urna,
Maris et in medio spectat uterq parens
Ad latus hîc nati pueri duo, forte perempti
Præpropera, infesti pulveris igne jacent.
Fælices omnes, vel quos fors dira coegit,
Tristia funestis claudere fata rogis
Appeldercombus genuit rapuitq sepulchrum
Ossa habet Hinc animas vexit ad astra Deus.

In the month of January, in the year one thousand seven hundred and seventy-eight, the church was struck by lightning, and considerably damaged; the particulars of this storm, and its effects, are described in a letter from the minister of the parish, in the following note *.

The

Obiit idem Richardus 12 die Maii A Dni 1565. Johannes et Georgius filii dicti Richardi, obierunt 6 die Septembris, A Dni 1567.

In the church porch are the following lines to the memory of Richard Gard, liberal benefactor to the parish school

> Ecce cubat Gardi corpus mortale Richardi
> Hoc tumulo, verum spiritus astra tenet
> Cujus dona scholis largita et munera egenis
> Annua, perpetuo non peritura manent
> Inclyta si pareret multos hæc insula tales,
> Qualem jam tandem protulit nunece virum,
> Tunc bene pauperibus, meliusq scholaribus esset,
> Sub pede quos pressos quisq. jacere sinit.

Dictus Richardus Gard, sepultus fuit 5 die Februarii, 1617.

* " Dear Sir, we had here on Monday last, about nine in the morning, very severe " lightning, with two of the loudest claps of thunder I ever heard. There was a " sensible interval between the first flash of lightning and its thunder. The second " flash of lightning and clap of thunder, seemed to be at the same instant My " house rocked as if it was tumbling down, and at first I thought it the effects " of an earthquake I concluded that the cloud would burst, and be attended with " fatal consequences it first made its appearance against the old tower, and " from thence, its zig zag, confused, and various directions are so perplexed that " they cannot be followed in any one continued line of description. It seems " to have commenced its rage near the middle of the wall, about four feet below " the dial place of the clock, where it tore off large pieces of massive stone, and " loosened many others, but did not penetrate quite through there. some of it " must have entered by the spindle, in the centre of the dial-plate, as it broke the " clock-case liquified the upper part of the pendulum, distorted the works of the " clock, and broke the piece of iron that regulates the striking

" It has done no mischief in the story where the bells are, except splitting the " wall on the south side, over the belfry, it has rolled up some of the lead, " leaving no marks on the boards or timber that supported it The battlements " are loosened, the spindle that supports the weather-cock is bent double, so is " the pinnacle on which it stands The pinnacle on the south east angle is in.

" the

The manor of Appuldurcombe belonged formerly to the
Abbey of Montſburg, together with Week and Sandford. It
was long enjoyed by the family of Fry, under a leaſe from the

" the ſame ſituation The cramp irons and lead that faſtened them in, are wrench-
" ed out of their places

" Near that part of the tower, where it ſtruck, it broke almoſt all the glaſs in
" the great window behind the gallery, entered the church in an angle be-
" tween the ſtone frame of the window and the wall, ſhivered and toe the whole part
" of the frame to which the glaſs was faſtened, and booked it from the build-
" ing.

" There is a large hole between the two roofs in the angle at the bottom of
" the weſt end, through which it muſt either have deſcended from the battlements
" of the tower, or come out from the ſtory where the clock is fixed In its eaſt-
" ward direction, it has grazed over the arches, deſcended to the battlement, doing
" no miſchief there, but tearing off ſome of the white waſh, it continued its courſe
" eaſtward, to the monument between the two chancels, ſtruck off a part or the
" moulding, and then laid hold of the iron work, when it became forky, con-
" ducted by the different pieces of the iron about the monuments One part of
" it entered cloſe by the corner of one of the hatchments, inſinuated itſelf with
" inconceivable ſubtility through the wall, and came out again in the upper joint
" of the window-frame over the communion table The other part entered the
" wall in the angle cloſe to the bottom of Mr Stuart Worſley's monument,
" pierced through the wall and the buttreſs on the outſide, threw a large piece
" of ſtone to a conſiderable diſtance, deſcended down the buttreſs, ploughed up
" a furrow a yard or more in length at the north eaſt corner of the buttreſs, and
" made its exit There are ſome ſtones looſened on the outſide of the opening of
" your family vault, which may, or may not be the effect of this ſhock—there
" is alſo, another furrow at the ſouth weſt corner of the church, near the place
" where it begun its violence

" This is but a very faint deſcription of the effects of the lightning, if it had
" happened the day before when we were aſſembled in the church, I believe many
" of the congregation would have been deſtroyed by it.

" I thought it right to inform you, Sir, of the truth and particulars of this
" event, therefore, choſe rather to expoſe my ignorance of technical terms,
" than betray the leaſt unwillingneſs to inform you of any thing in my power,
" that you would wiſh to know, a tribute of gratitude juſtly due to you from, Sir,

your much obliged,

and obedient humble ſervant,

DANIEL WALSH'

Godſhill, Jan 21ſt 1778.

To Sir Richard Worſley, Baronet.

convent

convent of Nuns, without Aldgate, London: the laft of that family dying without iffue left this leafe to his widow, one of the daughters and heirs of John Hacket, Efquire, of Woolverton. This lady marrying for her fecond hufband Sir John Leigh, of More, in Dorfetfhire, fhe left by him, an only daughter, Anne, poffeffed of a very large eftate derived from her mother. Anne, in the third year of the reign of Henry the Eighth, married Sir James Worfley, of Worfley Hall, in Lancafhire, defcended from Sir Elias de Workefley, Lord of the manor of Workefley, at the time of the Norman Conqueft: he is mentioned in an old chronicle as attending Robert, Duke of Normandy, in his expedition for the recovery of the Holy Land [*].

His fon and heir, Richard, fucceeded him: he left two fons John and George, who were unfortunately blown up in the porter's lodge at Appuldurcombe [†], in one thoufand five hundred and

---

[*] This family took its name from the manor of Worfley, fituated about feven miles from Manchefter, in the County Palatine of Lancafter, of which they continued Lords till the reign of Richard the Second, when Elizabeth, the daughter of Sir Geoffrey Workefley, as the name was then written, being found by an inquifition to have been born out of marriage, the Lordfhip came to Sir John Maffey, who had married the fifter of Sir Geoffrey Thomas Brereton, Efquire, of the county of Chefter, married the daughter and heirefs of Sir John Maffey, and recovered poffeffion of this Lordfhip from Robert Worfley, by a fuit in Chancery It was afterwards difpofed of to the Lord Chancellor Egerton, from whom it defcended to the prefent Duke of Bridgwater, who has made a navigable canal from the mill in the townfhip of Worfley over the river Irwell, at Barton-bridge, to convey the coals from his mines, to Manchefter by which undertaking, which was at firft thought impracticable and accomplifhed, at great expence and laudable perfeverance, his Grace has been able to reduce the price of the carriage of coals from ten fhillings to two fhillings and fix pence the ton This furprifing navigation is fometimes carried over public roads, fometimes over bogs, but generally by the fide of hills The Duke is extending it ftill farther, and, by this inland navigation, will (when his plan is accomplifhed) be able to open a communication from the Weftern to the German Ocean The family of Worfley, feated at Hovingham, in Yorkfhire, branched off, in the time of Edward the Second.

[†] Sir John Oglander furnifhes the particulars of this unfortunate accident in his Manufcript Memoirs, where he relates that "thefe two young gentlemen, being in

the

and fixty-feven. Richard's widow married Sir Francis Walfingham, Secretary of State to Queen Elizabeth, by whom she had a daughter Frances, fuccefively the wife of Sir Philip Sydney, of Robert Earl of Effex, who was beheaded, and of Richard de Burgh, Earl of Clanrickard and St Albans. John the fecond fon of Sir James, fucceeding his nephews, had a long conteft with Sir Francis Walfingham, for the chattel eftates; but Walfingham prevailing, enjoyed, in right of his wife, the leafes of Boucombe, the priory of Carifbrook, the manors of Godfhill and Frefhwater; which were then of great value John Worfley died in the year one thoufand five hundred and eighty-one, and left an only fon Thomas, who had two fons, Richard, and John. Richard fucceeded him, and was created a Baronet by King James, in the year one thoufand fix hundred and eleven. he married Frances, the daughter of Sir Henry Nevil, of Billingbere, in the year one thoufand fix hundred and twenty-one, and had by her Sir Henry Worfley, his heir, and feveral other children. Sir Henry married Bridget, daughter of Sir Henry Wallop, afterwards Lord Lymington: and, at his death, in the year one thoufand fix hundred and fixty fix, left Sir Robert his heir; and James, afterwards knighted. Sir Robert married Mary, the daughter of the Honourable James Herbert, fecond fon of Philip, Earl of Pembroke, Lord Chancellor to

the lodge at Appledercombe, or Gatehoufe, where they went to fchole, the fervants were dryinge of powder there againft the general mufter, a fparke flewe into the difh, that fett fire to a barrel which ftood by, blew up a fide of the gatehoufe, killed the two children, and fome others, hurt one James Worfley a youth, their kinfman and mine, that went to fchole there with them, who hath often told me this ftory "

Charles

Charles the Second, by whom he had iffue, Robert and Henry. Robert married Frances, daughter of Thomas, Lord Vifcount Weymouth, by whom he had feveral children, who died in his life-time. Henry was, appointed envoy extraordinary and plenipotentiary to the court of Portugal; and, afterwards Governor of Barbadoes. Sir James Worfley, of Pilewell, in Hampfhire, fucceeded Sir Robert: he had feveral children, but one only furvived him, Sir Thomas Worfley, who married the eldeft daughter of John, Earl of Cork and Orrery; by whom he had one fon, and a daughter, Henrietta Frances. On the death of Sir Thomas, in the year one thoufand feven hundred and fixty-eight, Sir Richard Worfley fucceeded him: in the year one thoufand feven hundred and feventy-five, he married Mifs Seymour Fleming, daughter and one of the coheireffes of the late Sir John Fleming, Baronet, of Brompton Park, in the county of Middlefex, by whom he has one fon, Robert Edwin Worfley.

Appuldur-
combe park

Appuldurcombe Park is the chief feat of the Worfley family: the old priory houfe, was fituated a fmall diftance from the prefent manfion It underwent a thorough repair in the reign of Queen Elizabeth, and was taken down by Sir Robert Worfley, in the beginning of the prefent century.

The entrance into the park, which is well flocked with deer, is through an elegant gateway of the Ionic order. The foil is very rich, and affords excellent pafturage: beeches of
uncommon

Appuldurcombe Hall, the Seat of the Right Honorable Sir Richard Worsley Baronet Governor and Vice Admiral of the Isle of Wight.

uncommon magnitude, interfperfed with venerable oaks form the back-ground above the houfe; the different eminences command moft extenfive and grand profpects. On the caft is feen St. Helen's road, Spithead, and Portfmouth; on the weft, the Cliffs at Frefhwater, the Dorfetfhire coaft, and the Ifle of Portland; on the north, is a view of the New Foreft and the channel, by which the ifland is feparated from the other part of the county; and on the fouth, is the Britifh Channel On the fummit of the park is an obelifk of Cornifh granite, near feventy feet in height, erected to the memory of Sir Robert Worfley; and on a rocky cliff, about a mile from the park, is the ruin of an ancient caftle, which ferves as a point of view from the houfe.

The houfe is pleafantly fituated about feven miles fouth of the town of Newport; it has four regular fronts of the Corinthian order, built of free-ftone; the pillafters, cornices, balluftrades, and other ornamental parts, are of Portland ftone: the roof is covered with Weftmorland flates. The grand entrance in the eaft front is through a hall fifty-four feet in length, by twenty-four in breadth, adorned with eight beautiful columns of the Ionic order, refembling Porphyry. On this floor are feveral handfome apartments, containing many valuable portraits, and other good paintings; the offices, are very commodious; on the firft and Attic ftories are upwards of twenty bed chambers, with dreffing rooms. The prefent houfe, was begun by Sir Robert Worfley, in the year one thoufand feven hundred and ten, but left in a very unfinifhed ftate; it has fince been completed by Sir Richard

The houfe,

F f 2

Worfley,

Worfley, who has made confiderable additions, and much improved upon the original defign.

Stenbury.

The manor of Stenbury was held by the family of De Aula, foon after the Norman Conqueft, from whom it defcended to that of Heyno *, who enjoyed it for more than two centuries, and lived at the manor-houfe which was furrounded by a moat †. It was purchafed of Ratcliffe, Earl of Suffex, by Thomas Worfley, Efquire, of Appuldurcombe, and continues in the fame family; under which it is now held by James Worfley, Efquire, who refides there.

Rockley.

Rookley, or Roucley, gave name to the family of Roucley, who were the ancient owners of this lordfhip, and refided on it: there is a licence mentioned in the regifter of Winchefter, for De Roucley to have oratories in his lordfhips of Roucley and Denmead. One of the family, in the reign of Edward the Third, married a daughter and coheirefs of Sir John Glamorgan, of Brook; and removed thither. The eftate came to the family of Coleman; the laft of whom devifed it, after the death of his fifter, to James Worfley, Efquire.

* Probably by marriage, as few purchafes are found in the ifland at that period.

† Upon digging down the bank, in 1727, in order to fill up the moat, there were found ten earthen pots, or urns, filled with coals and bits of bones; from the different compofition, fhape, and fize of thefe urns, the fpot might probably have been a family cemetary, before the cuftom of burying in church yards.

The

The Cottage at Steephill belongs to Sir Richard Worsley Stanley Governor of the Isle of Wight

The fmall village of Steephill, is fituated at the fouthern ex- Cottage at
Steephill tremity of this parifh, under the cliffs. The fingularity of the fituation tempted Mr. Stanley, foon after he became Governor of the Ifle of Wight, to build a cottage there, which is admirably contrived, and moft elegantly laid out. It devolved with Mr. Stanley's other eftates to his fifters, who have lately fold it to the Honourable Wilbraham Tollemache, of Calverly Hall, in the county of Chefter.

THE PARISH OF ARRETON.

The parifh of Arreton is bounded by Newchurch and Bin- Limits ftead on the eaft, by Wootton and Whippingham on the north, by Carifbrook and Gatcombe on the weft, and by Godfhill on the fouth. Though the name of Arreton does not occur in Domefday-book, it was one of the fix churches given by William Fitz-Ofborn, to his abbey of Lyra; and in the reign of Henry the Firft, when Baldwin de Redvers endowed the abbey of Quarr, he either gave the manor of Arreton, or Arreton procured it for his new foundation, in which it remained till the Abbey was diffolved. It was purchafed of the crown by Sir Levinus Bennet, whofe fon fold it to Thomas, Lord Culpeper, when Governor of the ifland; by a marriage with his daughter and heirefs, it paffed to Lord Fairfax, of Leeds Caftle, in Kent, in whofe family it ftill remains. In this parifh there were formerly feveral lordfhips, though fome of them are now difmembered; in Domefday-book two Standens are mentioned.

Eaft

East Standen.

East Standen is a lordship held at the time of the Conqueror's survey, by William Fitz-Stur, when it was rated at one hide and a half; and in the roll of landholders under Isabella de Fortibus, it was held by Thomas D'Evercy. Sir Peter D'Evercy built a chapel here, and endowed it with a moiety of the tithes of his lands in Standen; the rector of Aireton enjoying the other moiety: he gave also to the said chapel the tithes of his demesne lands at La Wode and Bimbridge. The lordship came afterwards to John Glamorgan, who married Anne, the daughter and heiress of D'Evercy, as appears by an inquisition in the escheat rolls of the county of Somerset, in the nineteenth year of the reign of Edward the Third Isabella, one of the daughters of Glamorgan, and Hacket, who married another daughter in the year one thousand three hundred and sixty-five, severally presented to the church of Standen. In the reign of Henry the Seventh, this place was honoured with the residence of Lady Cecilia, daughter of King Edward the Fourth, and sister of the reigning Queen. Her first husband was the Lord Welles, after whose death she married a gentleman of the name of Keynes, of the county of Lincoln: she died at Standen, and was buried in Quarr Abbey. The foundations of the chapel are still visible in the orchard behind the house This place is delightfully situated at the east end of St George's down, the top of which is a pleasant level, near a mile in length, commanding a fine view of the sea, and of the greatest part of the island. When the Earl of Southampton was Governor

The old bowling green on St George's down.

and resided here, a bowling green was made on St. George's down, and a house of accommodation built near it, where the Governor and the gentlemen of the island used to dine
together

together twice a week *. The manor of Standen, after having been difmembered, was difpofed of, to different purchafers.

Sir John Oglander, who was a member of the Society, has preferved a lift of their names in the following terms.

" The Gentlemen which lived in the ifland in the 7th year of King James his
" reign, thefe all lived well, and were moft commonly at our ordinary

" Sir Robert Dillington.   Mr William White.
" Sir Richard Worfley.   Mr Richard Bafket
" Sir Thomas Fleming, L. C J of England. Mr. Rice, of Bangborn
" Sir Thomas Fleming, his fon   Mr. Leigh, of Binding
' Sir Richard White, who married Sir Mr Hobfon, father and fon
       " Richard Worfley's mother   Mr Urry, of Thorley, now Gatcomb
" Sir John Mewx.   Mr Philip Fleming, of Cornley.
" Sir John Leigh   Mr John Worfley, of Gatcombe
" Sir William Lifle   Mr John Harvey, of Avington
" Sir Bowyer Worfley, of Afhey, who fold all. Mr. Emanuel Bad, High Sheriff, 1627
" Sir John Richards.   a brewer.
" Sir John Dingley   Mr John Leigh, fon of Mr. Barnabie,
" Sir John Oglander.   fince knighted
" Sir Edward Dennis.
" Old Mr Richards.   Farmers
" Old Mr Boreman
" Mr. Barnabie Leigh   Mr. Urry, of Awghton.
" Mr. Cheek, of Motfon, whofe fone fold all. Knight, of Langard.
" Mr Dillington, who will buy all.   Streaper.
" Mr. Boreman   Legg
" Mr. Cheek, of Merfton   Fitchet.
" Mr Lifle, of Briddlesford, went to daughters. Shambler.
" Mr Barnabie Colnet, of Pann, his fon fold. Wavell.
" Mr German Rychards.   Loving.
" Mr Wayght   Sampfon.
" Mr. Erlefman, of Calbron.   Champion "

Among a number of other circumftances mentioned by Sir John, as indicating a decline of the profperity of the ifland, in the year one thoufand fix hundred and twenty-nine, he inftanced the difcontinuance of this ordinary for want of company.

West

West Stan-
den.

West Standen is situated to the westward of St. George's down, and is now the seat of Henry Roberts, Esquire; who has made considerable improvements there; and the grounds about it are well laid out.

Hasely.

Hasely is a name not found in Domesday book, whence it may be presumed to have been part of Arreton, when the general survey was taken. It was given to Quarr Abbey at its first foundation, by Engler de Bohun, and by the Monks converted into a grange, and was one of the most considerable they enjoyed. At the dissolution of the Abbey it was purchased by Mr. George Mills, of Southampton, in whose family it remained during the reign of Queen Elizabeth. In the reign of James the First it was purchased, with several other manors belonging to the Abbey of Quarr, by Sir Thomas Fleming, Lord Chief Justice of England, and descended, through the female line, to John Fleming, Esquire, of Stoneham Park, near Southampton.

Merston.

Merston is, in Domesday-book, recorded as only one carucate of land; but this being very short of the present extent, it may be presumed that Prestitune, which is there mentioned, after Merston, and rated at two hides, has since been added to it, and has lost its original distinction: as there is no Lordship existing in the island under that name. They were then both in the possession of William Fitz-Stur; and in the roll of Isabella de Fortibus, Merston is held by Robert Giros: from him it passed to a younger son of Lisle, who, in the rolls of the landholders, and in the inquisition of the tenures of the island, taken the seventh year of the reign of Edward the Third, is called Lisle of Merston. It afterwards came into the family of Chyke: and, in the reign of Charles

the

the Second, was purchafed by John Mann, Efquire; from whom it defcended to Robert Pope Blachford, Efquire.

The manor of Bottebridge appears for the firft time in the roll of the Countefs Ifabella de Fortibus, William Uiry is mentioned as holding lands there, under the Abbot of Quarr. And in the roll of eftates bound to fupply men for the defence of the ifland, the manor of Bottebridge was charged with one bowman. It was purchafed by Sir Robert Dillington, and defcended by the female line to Mr Biffet. *Bottebridge.*

The name of Hale is not found in Domefday-book, but in the roll of landholders under Ifabella de Fortibus, the manor is faid to be held by William de Godditon. It has been for feveral defcents in the Oglander family. *Hale.*

Briddlesford was part of the ancient poffeffions of the Lifles; Sir John Lifle built a chapel there, and endowed it with the tithes of his demefnes at Briddlesford. *Briddlesford.*

THE PARISH OF BINSTEAD.

The parifh of Binftead is bounded by Newchurch on the eaft; it is feparated from the parifhes of Wootton and Arreton on the weft, by Fifhborn creek; and is bounded by the Channel on the north. This fmall parifh feems to have originated from the grants of William the Conqueror, and William Rufus, of half a hide of land to Walkeline, Bifhop of Winchefter, for the digging of ftone to repair that cathedral. The firft grant expreffes—*nec folum autem ibi, fed per totam terram meam in eadem infula,* " not only there, but throughout all my land in

G g

" that

" that ifland ;" which might have afforded the Bifhops of Winchefter opportunity to extend their limits beyond the firft expreffed quantity, at the time of this grant, the whole ifland was in the Crown, by the forfeiture of Earl Roger, the fon of William Fitz-Ofborn.　It is alfo found in the regifter of Winchefter, that when William of Wykeham rebuilt the body of that cathedral, he dug the ftone in the Ifle of Wight, and commiffioned the Abbot of Quarr to provide carriages to convey it to the fea. the pits from whence the ftone was taken, are ftill vifible.

The church.

Binftead church, was probably built by one of the Bifhops of Winchefter, having always belonged to that fee, and paid an annual penfion of two fhillings to the facrift of the Monaftery there : it is fubjected to the Rector of Calbourn, who formerly claimed archidiaconal jurifdiction over Binftead, and Brixton.　The church is a fmall plain building, having nothing remarkable about it, but a rude and very ancient piece of fculpture over the key-ftone of the north door, reprefenting a human figure, fitting with the feet on a kind of pedeftal, refembling a ram's head ; the whole is about two feet and a half high : it is vulgarly called the Idol, but probably was one of thofe ftrange figures, which the Saxon and Norman architects commonly placed on key ftones, and frizes. It is reported that upon the church being repaired fome few years ago, this figure was removed ; but the inhabitants were difpleafed at it, and procured its reftoration.

T H E

THE PARISH OF WOOTTON.

This parish is separated from Binstead by Fishborn Creek, Situ..in
which forms the eastern boundary; it has the Channel on the
north, a part of the parish of Whippingham, on the west, and
the parish of Aireton on the south. This small parish was
taken out of Whippingham, in the reign of Henry the Third,
when Walter de Insula built the chapel, and endowed it with
glebe, arable, pasture, and woodlands, adding the tithes of his
demesne lands at Wootton, and Chillerton, which is a part of
the parish, notwithstanding it lies eight miles distant, adjoining to Gatcombe.

The first church was consumed by fire, and the small
church now standing built in the same place: there are
therefore no monuments of the Lisles in it, the family
having removed to Thruxton and Mansbridge, near Southampton, before its erection * It may be noted, that there
was a chapel adjoining to the old church, dedicated to St Edmund the King, which had an independent endowment, and
it appears from the return of the Dean of the island, that it had
a chaplain distinct from the rector of the church.

The branch of the Lisle family settled at Wootton, in the
year one thousand four hundred and ten, were called *Lisle
de Bosco*, and sometimes de Bosco only, " of the wood,"
whence the place obtained the name of Wood-town, corrupted
to Wootton: in the roll of landholders under Isabella de For-

---

* The register of Winchester records a licence granted to the Lady Elizabeth
Lisle, widow of Sir Bartholomew Lisle, who died in the nineteenth year of Edward
the Third, to have a chapel at Mansbridge.

tilus,

tibus, we find the eighth part of a knight's fee in Whippingham, held by *Johannes de Insula, qui dicitur de Bosco*; and
Nicholas de Bosco was constituted warden of the island by patent, in the first year of the reign of Edward the Second *.

THE PARISH OF WHIPPINGHAM.

Situation

The parish of Whippingham is bounded on the north by
the sea as far as King's Quay † Creek; by Wootton on the
east; by the river Medina on the west, and by Arreton on
the

---

* Sir John Lisle, of this family, took so active a part against Charles the First,
that he was appointed one of the judges who tried and condemned him   He afterwards became one of Cromwell's Lords, and a Commissioner of his Great
Seal   On the Restoration, he fled to Lausanne, in Switzerland, where he
was assassinated by three Irish ruffians, who hoped to make their fortunes by this
action   His widow, many years after, met with a fate still more severe, being
tried by Judge Jefferys, on his memorable Western circuit, for harbouring, after
the battle of Sedgmoor, two of Monmouth's party, Mr Hicks, a presbyterian
minister, and one Nelthorpe, men whose names were in no proclamation, nor did
any proof appear of her knowing they had been engaged in the rebellion, but
though she was loyal herself, and had a son in the royal army, that fought against
Monmouth, she was obnoxious on her husband's account, and being then above
seventy years of age, obtained only the favour of being beheaded instead of burned
  By the death of Edward Lisle, Esquire, of Moyle's Court, in the county of
Southampton, the male line of this ancient family is extinct

† When King John retreated for security to the Isle of Wight, he probably resided in this neighbourhood   it being said that he kept near the coast, not caring
to venture far into the island, because William, Earl of Devon, then Lord of it,
had taken part with the Barons confederated against him   This conjecture is
strengthened by the country being open to the water on three sides, and by a landing-place here, still retaining the name of *King's Quay.*
  The retreat of King John, was after the signing of *Magna Charta*, and during
his negociations with the Pope for absolution from that engagement.   Rapin relates that—" after taking these measures with all possible secrecy, fearing, if he
" appeared too much in public, his designs might be discovered or guessed at, he
" chose the Isle of Wight for his residence, in this retirement he kept himself as
" it were concealed a good while, conversing only with fishermen, or sailors, and
" diverting

A North View of OSBORNE in the ISLE of WIGHT

the fouth   This is one of the old parishes given by William Fitz-Ofborn to the abbey of Lyra, and at that time included the parifh of Wootton, which now pays an annual acknowledgment of ten fhillings to Whippingham, as the mother-church.

The manor of Barton or Whippingham is the moft confiderable in the parifh; in the reign of Edward the Confeffor, it was held by Bolla; and at the time of the general furvey, it was among the large poffeffions of William Fitz-Stur, whofe eftate, in the reign of Henry the Third, fell to Walter de Infula, by marriage with the daughter and heirefs of the faid Fitz-Stur, then called De Eftur. It was granted in the year one thoufand two hundred and eighty-two, by Thomas de Winton and John de Infula, to the Oratory of the Holy Trinity, and is now held under the College of Winchefter, by the Earl of Clanrickard

Ofborne, formerly called Aufterborne, near Barton, is a manor that was held by the family of Bowerman; and, in the reign of Henry the Eighth, came to by John Arney, who married Alice, the daughter and heirefs of Richard Bowerman. The right of poffeffion was contefted in the twenty fourth year of the fame reign, between Nicholas Bowerman and Arney; when it was awarded to the latter. In the third year of the reign of Edward the Sixth, it paffed to John Lovybond by pur-

" diverting himfelf by walking on the fea fhore with his domeftics. When the
" King was known to be retired to the Ifle of Wight, people were in vain inquifi-
" tive about the caufe of his retreat fome joked, and faid he was become a fifher-
" man, others that he defigned to turn pirate. During three months he waited
" patiently for the return of his agents, and for the arrival of the foreign troops,
" which he was made to expect" Rapin, vol. 1 p. 277.

chafe;

chafe; and in the fifth of Charles the Firft was transferred in like manner to Euftace Man, Efquire, who lived during the civil war. He is faid to have buried fome valuable property in a wood on the manor, which he could not find again; after the Reftoration he applied to Charles the Second for a grant, and procured a very full one, of all wafts, eftrays, wrecks, treafure trove, &c with the privilege of free warren for the manor of Ofborne: this grant is now in the poffeffion of the Lord of the manor The place where the property is fuppofed to have been buried, is to this day called the Money Coppice. John Man, the fon of Euftace, was poffeffed of great property, and left feveral bequefts to charitable ufes, in the year one thoufand feven hundred and five. The manor defcended to Robert Blachford, Efquire, of Sandhall, near Fordingbridge, in Hampfhire, the fon of Elizabeth, fole heirefs of the above Man, and is ftill in the fame family. Robert Pope Blachford, Efquire, has built an exceeding good houfe at Ofborne, which commands a fine view of the road at Spithead and the oppofite coaft.

Pann.

Pann is a manor that was retained by the lords of the ifland in their own hands, as appears by the roll of the Countefs Ifabella, and which always went with the lordfhip, whether in the Crown, or in the hands of a fubject. In a rent-roll of the Crown lands, in the twenty-third year of the reign of Henry the Seventh, the manor was valued at feven pounds thirteen fhillings and eight-pence; it was granted, in the feventh year of Edward the Sixth, to Leonard Brown and John Tropps, as truftees for Thomas Carew, Efquire, who fold it to Colnett, from whofe fon it was bought by Thomas Kemp, Efquire: it then came to Henry Bromfield, Efquire, of Haywood, by marriage

FAIRLEE the Seat

riage with the daughter and heirefs of Kemp, who fold it to Gilbert, of whom it was purchafed by Mr. Rolefton, of Southampton.

THE PARISH OF NORTHWOOD.

The parifh of Northwood is fituated on the weft fide of the river Medina, oppofite Calfhot Caftle, at the entrance of Southampton river. It is bounded on the north and northweft by the fea; by the parifh of Calbourn on the weft; and on the fouth, by part of the parifh of Shalfleet, and the foreft of Parkhurft, which is extra-parochial.

Situation.

The church of Northwood is a chapel of eafe to Carifbrook; but fince the reign of Henry the Eighth has enjoyed all parochial privileges, and is exempted from contribution to the repairs of the mother church. When the Priory of Carifbrook obtained the rectory, and endowed the vicarage, the tithes of Northwood, both great and fmall, were affigned to the vicar, doubtlefs, becaufe they were at that time of very little value; the parifh being as the name imports, moftly over-run with wood. The Vicar of Carifbrook is Rector of Northwood.

When it became parochial.

The place of greateft confideration in this parifh is the town of Weft Cowes, which was, without a name, till Henry the Eighth built here, and on the oppofite point, at Eaft Cowes,

Weft Cowes.

Cowes, two forts, or blockhouses, for the security of the island and road [*]. The town of West Cowes stands on a rising ground, at the mouth of the river Medina; the view on approaching it by sea is very beautiful: it owes its origin and increase to its excellent harbour, where ships are not only secure from storms, but so happily situated, as to be able to turn out, either to the eastward or westward, whenever a fair wind offers. The town is well peopled, and enjoys a good trade for the sale of provisions, especially in time of war, when large fleets of merchant ships often ride here for several weeks, waiting either for wind or convoy. The town is but indifferently built, and the streets are very narrow.

The chapel.　　　　The chapel of West Cowes was erected in the year one thousand six hundred and fifty-seven: it is not dedicated to any particular saint; but was consecrated by George, Lord Bishop of Winchester, in the year one thousand six hundred and sixty-two, and endowed in the year one thousand six hundred and seventy-one, with five pounds per annum for ever, by Mr Richard Stephens. It was farther endowed in the year one thousand six hundred and seventy-nine, by Bishop Morley, with the sum of twenty pounds per annum; provided the inhabitants paid the minister (who is always a person of their own chusing) the sum of forty pounds per annum; but in case of a failure in their part, the said endowment of twenty pounds to be forfeited for ever.

---

[*] The late Dr Speed was of opinion that the place a little to the west of Cowes called the street, was a Roman way to Carisbrook, which he apprehended to have been a Roman camp: before Cowes became a port the passage to the Isle of Wight was from the opposite shore to Gurnet Bay.

THE

THE PARISH OF NEWPORT.

While the caſtle of Cariſbrook was inhabited by the lords of the iſland, and the priory retained its eccleſiaſtical dignity, the town of Cariſbrook was in fact the metropolis of the iſland, and Newport no more than a poor fiſhing village But when the lordſhip of the iſland was ſold to the crown, the caſtle loſt its conſequence, as the court of a potent baron, and drew no reſort to it ; and in the enſuing wars with France, the priory was ſequeſtered as an alien priory : the town of Cariſbrook thus deprived of its two principal ſupports, fell to decay, while Newport roſe by the ſuperior advantages of its ſituation, a cir-cumſtance that has in moſt towns been determined by political conſiderations at the time of their erection ; and ſo long as the cauſes that firſt drew inhabitants together continued to operate, their numbers increaſed : on any alteration in theſe circumſtances, they as naturally conformed to the alteration, and removed to more convenient ſituations.   In rude ages, the hill on which Cariſbrook Caſtle ſtands, was found well adapted for the erec-tion of a fortreſs, as an aſylum againſt hoſtile and civil inva-ſions ; and of courſe a town grew at the foot of the hill, and the reſidence of the lord of the iſland there, contributed to ren-der it the chief town of the iſland.   When government became more fixed and regular, civil policy improved, and public ſe-curity better provided for, men were directed by other views in the choice of their abode.   The land being extremely fer-tile, corn became the ſtaple commodity of the iſland, but Cariſbrook market proved inconvenient for trade, on account of its diſtance from a port.   Not far off, a fine ſtream from the ſouthern hills directed its courſe into the channel which ſe-parated the iſland from the Britiſh coaſt ; and the tide flowing

H h up

up almoſt to the center of the iſland, pointed out a deſirable ſpot, healthful, well ſheltered, well watered, and convenient for communication with every part of it. The freſh river worked mills to grind the corn, and the tide from the ſea, not only furniſhed a conveyance for it to any part of the world, but alſo for bringing back returns of ſuch foreign commodities, as the iſlanders might want for their own conſumption. Theſe circumſtances and conſiderations will account for the decay of Cariſbrook to an inconſiderable village; while Newport roſe to be the moſt flouriſhing town in the iſland.

When the townſmen firſt conceived the intention of building the church, which by its dedication to Saint Thomas Becket, is ſuppoſed to have been about the cloſe of the reign of Henry the Second: it was a work of progreſſive execution, according to their abilities; and thoſe mechanical profeſſions that contributed to carry it on, ſet up the inſignia of their occupations, as hammers, ſhears, &c to perpetuate their liberality. Some of theſe ſymbolical repreſentations are yet to be ſeen under a ſmall pediment in the center of the ſouth ſide of the building: ſucceſſive repairs have probably deſtroyed the reſt: the inhabitants had however no burial-place till the reign of Queen Elizabeth, when the plague being at Newport, they acquired that privilege, there not being ſufficient room to bury their dead at Cariſbrook, the mother-church. This church contains three iſles, and has in a ſquare tower a ring of ſix bells. The pulpit is a curious piece of antiquity, it is of wainſcot, richly ornamented with carved emblematical figures, diſpoſed in the pannels round it, repreſenting the liberal ſciences and cardinal virtues. The moſt conſiderable monument there, is that of Sir Edward Horſey, whoſe armed figure in marble lies on the tomb, under

under a decorated niche. the infcription is given in the following note.*

The appointment of the curate of Newport, is ftrictly in the vicar of Carifbrook, but as the inhabitants fupport their own minifter, he feldom interferes in their choice. By feveral entries in the town books, the allowance paid to the minifter appears to have been various and difcretionary, till the middle of the laft century, when a rate was firft eftablifhed for his fupport, a copy of which is given in the appendix. The town of Newport has extended beyond the limits of the parifh; Caftle-Hold is part of the parifh of St. Nicholas; Copping's Bridge is in the parifh of Whippingham, and Node Hill in that of Carifbrook.

Contents of the parifh.

THE PARISH OF ST. NICHOLAS.

The chapel of St. Nicholas in Carifbrook Caftle, was built either by William Fitz-Ofborn, or by his fon Earl Roger; but not many years after its erection, it was, with its lands, given by Baldwin de Redvers to Quarr Abbey, with the confent of thofe termed his Barons. This chapel was endowed with thirteen

Hifto.

* Edwardus qui miles erat fortiffimus Horfey,
  Vectis erat præfes, conftans, terraque marique
  Magnanimus, placidæ fub pacis, nomine fortis,
  Jufticiæ cultor, quam fidus amicus amico.
  Fautor Evangelii, dilectus principe vixit,
  Munificus populo, multum dilectus ab omni
  Vixit et ut fancte, fic ftamina fancta peregit.
  Qui obiit 28 die Martii
  An Dni. 1582.

II h 2

parcels

parcels of land in that part of the town of Newport, called Caftle-Hold; as alfo with lands at Shalcombe, Rowborough, Cofham and Luccombe. Caftle Hold is the moft populous part of the parifh. Sir John Oglander, in his Memoirs, affirms that a chapel once belonged to it, fituated in a field, ftill called the Chapel Field. The parifh has no place of devotion but the chapel in the caftle, and as no fervice is now performed there, the fmall living of St. Nicholas is a *finecure,* in the gift of the Governor. The chapel, being very old and decayed, was rebuilt at the expence of the Crown, in the year one thoufand feven hundred and thirty-eight, and is the place where the governor or his fteward adminifters the oaths to the Mayor of Newport. The Crown pays an annual penfion of three pounds to the vicar of Carifbrook, which probably was the original ftipulation with the Abbey of Lyra, as an acknowledgment to the mother church.

Caftle Hold the principal part of the parifh

THE PARISH OF CARISBROOK.

This parifh at the time of the general furvey was called Boucombe *, and was the largeft in the ifland, ftretching from the northern extremity, where Weft Cowes now ftands, acrofs to the fouthern point of the ifland at Chale Bay, an extent of more than twelve miles: the parifhes of Northwood, Newport, Kingfton and Chale, have been fince taken out of it.

Antient extent of the parifh

In its prefent ftate, the parifh of Carifbrook is bounded on the north, by the borough of Newport, part of the parifh of

Prefent boundaries

* Or Beuconbe, a pleafant valley. the town, which then confifted only of twenty cottages near the church, acquired its name from the Saxon word for a town, Caer, and its fituation on a brook.

Northwood,

Northwood, the foreſt of Parkhurſt, and a detached part of the pariſh of Shalfleet; it has Calbourn on the weſt; Brixton, Shorwell and Godſhill form its limits on the ſouth-weſt, and it has Arreton and Godſhill on the eaſt.

Boucombe is the moſt conſiderable manor on the iſland. it Boucombe. had been held by Edward the Confeſſor, and was with other crown lands there, given to William Fitz-Oſborn with the lordſhip of the iſland: but the whole returning again to the crown by the forfeiture of Earl Roger his ſon, for treaſon, it reſted there at the compilation of Domeſday-book. It is there ſaid to have been rated at four hides, though it was not charged at that time; the church was called the church of the Manor, and by the twenty cottages adjoining to the church, it is pointed out for the ſame church that was afterwards called Cariſbrook. This manor was always united with the Lordſhip of the iſland [*], till King James the Firſt, in the year one thouſand ſix hundred and twenty-five, granted it to Chriſtopher Villiers, Earl of Angleſea, the brother of his great favourite the Duke of Buckingham, under a fee-farm rent of eighty pounds five ſhillings and eight pence halfpenny, which ſum is ſtill paid to the crown; and in the year one thouſand ſix hundred and fifty-two, Villiers ſold it to Sir enry Knowles, or Knollis, of Grove Place in Hampſhire, whoſe ſon ſold the manor of Boucombe, with other manors, to William Stevens, LL. D. who compelled him to diſpoſe of it under its value, by telling him that he was appointed one of the commiſſioners of ſafety to the Protector, and that if he did not let him have it for the ſum offered, he would acquaint the Protector of his diſinclination to him, and that his eſtates would be forfeited of courſe; in which

[*] The lords of the iſland retained this Manor and Pann in their own hands, for the ſupport of their kitchen, even when they thought fit to leave out others

caſe

cafe he fhould be able to buy them of the commiffioners for a
much lefs fum than he then offered to him   Mr. Stevens, foon
after the Reftoration, was ordered to pay Mr Knowles two
thoufand pounds more for this manor . and the King afterwards
knighted him for complying with his requeft fo readily   Mr.
Stevens's grandfon difpofed of this manor to John Blachford,
Efquire, in the year one thoufand feven hundred and twenty-
eight, in whofe family it ftill continues.

Carifbrook
village and
church.

The fmall village of Carifbrook ftands at the bottom
of the caftle-hill, about a mile to the fouth weft from the
town of Newport, but retains no marks of its former confequence, excepting what may be difcovered by examining the
church.   This appears to have been formerly a very large
pile of building, but has fhrunk in proportion with the town.
Sir Francis Walfingham, Secretary of State to Queen Elizabeth,
having the leafe of the Priory by his marriage with the widow
of Captain Richard Worfley, and being thereby bound to repair the chancel, perfuaded the parifhioners that the body of the
church would be large enough for them; and gave them an hundred marks to fuffer it to be taken down, which was accordingly
done : it alfo appears to have loft one of the fide ifles.   The
building however ftill remains fufficiently large for the congregation , and the aged tower, which preferves a venerable
air of Gothic dignity, contains a peal of eight bells lately
hung there. The only monument of any confequence to be
found in the church, is to the memory of Lady Wadham, wife
of Sir Nicholas Wadham, Captain of the ifland in the reign of
King Henry the Seventh   There is indeed a fmall wooden
tablet hanging againft one of the pillars, having an allegorical
reprefentation and infcription painted on it, which however fanciful, has the merit of being fuited to the profeffion of the per-

fon

fon it commemorates. At the top is the figure of a fhip, with a man fitting on the deck, a crown of glory fufpended over his head; *fides* is written on the fails, *verbum Dei* on the compafs, and *fpes* on the anchor, &c. under this fhip is the infcription, given in the note below *. The whole is ftill frefh, and the letters fo well painted and fhaded as to appear carved in relievo.

The impropriation of Carifbrook is of much greater value than that of any other church in the ifland, as confifting not only of the great tithes of that parifh, but alfo of all fuch tithes in other parifhes, as had been at feveral times obtained by the Priory. Thefe having been collected by the procurator or proctor of the Abbey of Lyra, are from thence termed procuracies or proxies.

The Priory farm, which confifts of the demefne lands of the Priory Farm old Priory, came into the poffeffion of the Dummer family by

* " Here lyeth the body of the right worthy William Keeling, Efquire, Groom
" of the Chamber to our Soveraigne Lord King James, General for the Hon Eaft
" India Adventurers, whither he was thrice by them employed, and dying in
" this ifle at the age of 42, An. 1619, Sept 19 hath this remembrance here fixed
" by his loving and forrowful wife, Ann Keeling

    " Fortie and two years in this veffel fraile
    " On the rough feas of life, did Keeling faile,
    " A merchant fortunate, a captaine bould,
    " A courtier gracious, yet (alafs) not old
    " Such wealth, experience, honour, and high praife,
    " Few winne in twice fo manie years or daies
    " But what the world admired, he deemed but droffe
    " For Chrift without Chrift all his gaines but loffe,
    " For him and his dear love, with merrie cheere,
    " To the Holy Land his laft courfe he did fteere.
    " Faith ferv'd for fails, the facred word for card,
    " Hope was his anchor, glorie his reward,
    " And thus with gales of grace, by happy venter,
    " Through ftraits of death, heaven is harbor he did enter "

                purchafe.

purchafe. When the Manor of Avington was firft granted
from the Crown does not appear, but in the roll of the landholders in the eighth of Edward the Firft, it is found in
the poffeffion of William de St. Martin, who held alfo the
Manors of Shide, Northwood, and Fairlee, in the ifland, together with other lands in the county of Dorfet Sir Laurence St. Martin, his grandfon, who died in the eighth of
Richard the Second, leaving no iffue, his eftates devolved to
Sybil his fifter, married to Sir John Popham, of an ancient
family, named from Popham in the county of Southampton.
Stephen Popham, who died in the fixth of Henry the
Sixth, left his lands in the ifland to Elizabeth, one of his
daughters and coheireffes, the wife of John Wadham, Efquire,
which were enjoyed by Sir Nicholas Wadham his grandfon,
captain of the ifland. Sir Nicholas dying without iffue, left
his lands to his widow, by whom Avington was fold to a gentleman of the name of Harvey, in whofe family it remained
for more than two centuries From Harvey, it went by marriage to Leigh, whofe defcendants fold it to Sir John Miller,
Baronet, in whofe family it ftill continues; but the manfion-
houfe and the principal farm were purchafed by Mr. Pike,
and, on his death, defcended to Sir John Carter.

THE PARISH OF GATCOMBE.

S. ation

The parifh of Gatcombe is fituated on the eaft fide of Carifbrook,
and is furrounded by that parifh on the north, weft, and fouth, on
the eaft it is feparated from Aireton by the river Medina. In
the time of Edward the Confeffor, the manor of Gatcombe was
held

Gatcomb, in the
The Seat of

held by three brothers* at the time of compiling Domesday-book, Gatcombe was part of the possessions of William Fitz-Stur, and appears to be the same family in the roll of landholders under the Countess Isabella. But in the reign of Edward the Second, Lisle, by marrying the daughter and heiress of that family, became owner of extensive possessions held by them. That branch of the Lisles ending in the succeeding reigns, with John Lisle, this manor, with Whitwell, and Westover, came to John Bremshot, who married Lisle's daughter. The family of Bremshot ended in two daughters: it appears by an inquisition taken on the death of Edmund Dudley, in the second year of the reign of Henry the Eighth, that John Bremshot, Esquire, died in the eighth year of Edward the Fourth, seized of the manors above-mentioned, and the advowson of the church of Gatcombe, in the Isle of Wight; together with the manor of Bremshot, certain lands called Little Gatcombe, and twenty-two acres of land in Portsea, in the county of Southampton. That he left issue two daughters his heirs, Elizabeth and Margaret, Elizabeth married John Dudley, Esquire, by whom she had issue Edmund Dudley†, who was attainted for high treason in the first year of Henry the Eighth. Margaret married John Pakenham, Esquire, by whom she had issue Edmund Pakenham. That John Dudley and John Pakenham, in right of their wives, took possession of the aforesaid manors, and held them in copartnership. That Edmund Dudley, soon after (John first obtaining the wardship), marrying Elizabeth, daughter and heiress of Edward Grey, Viscount Lisle, settled his part on the marriage. Lastly, that Elizabeth, the wife of John Dudley, died in the fourteenth year of Henry the Seventh,

---

* *Inquif. p. m. Job. 23 Edw. III.*

† The infamous lawyer, who prostituted his profession to gratify the avarice of Henry the Seventh. His son, John Dudley, made Duke of Northumberland, was beheaded by Queen Mary.

I i   and

and Margaret, the wife of John Pakenham, in the first year of Henry the Eighth

Dudley's moiety of Gatcombe was purchased by Richard Worsley, Captain of the Island. John Pakenham left Sir Edmund Pakenham his son and heir, whose estate was inherited by two daughters. One of these daughters married Richard Earnley, of Cackham, in the county of Suffex, and the other married Sir Geoffrey Pole, the brother of Cardinal Pole, who had each a moiety by these marriages. Gatcombe was bought out of the hands of Earnley and Pole, by John Worsley, Esquire, of Appuldurcombe, whose son, Thomas, devised it to his younger son John. In this branch of the Worsley family Gatcombe still remains. In the year one thousand seven hundred and fifty, Sir Edward Worsley rebuilt the mansion-house, and made other considerable improvements, on his death he was succeeded by Edward Meaux Worsley, Esquire, the present proprietor.

The church. The patronage of the church of Gatcombe always went with the manor The Chantry, called in the Episcopal registers, *Cantaria Manerii de Gatcombe*, was at Whitwell, and was dedicated to St. Radigund The land adjoining to that chapel, which was the endowment of that chantry, is esteemed to be in the parish of Gatcombe, and pays a pension to it as the mother-church The vicar of Godshill officiates in the chapel of Whitwell, where the rector of Gatcombe is bound to assist him, but the distance rendering it inconvenient for the latter to discharge that duty, he pays four nobles annually to the vicar of Godshill to perform the whole. In the north side of the chancel of Gatcombe church, there is the figure of a man in full proportion carved in wood; which is called the old wooden knight, but must have been probably a representation of one of the family of the Lisles

THE

THE PARISH OF KINGSTON.

The parish of Kingston is the smallest in the island, it is Situation
bounded by the parish of Shorwell on the south, and by the
parish of Godshill on the east. It is in Domesday book called
Chingestune, probably from some old possessor of the name of
Chinge, was then in the king's hands, and had been held by
Ulric in the time of Edward the Confessor. It was soon after
in a family, who from it assumed the name of Kingston,
and who enjoyed it many years; several of them being subscribing witnesses to deeds of very ancient date. Sir Jordan de
Kingston held this manor in the reign of Edward the first, at
half a knight's fee. Sir John de Kingston was one of the jury
summoned before the escheators, in the seventh year of Edward
the Third, and was afterwards appointed one of the wardens
of the island. In another inquisition in the twenty-second year
of Richard the Second, Lewis Mewes is recorded to have held
the manor of Kingston in right of Alice his wife, daughter and heiress of William Drewe, who had married the
heiress of Kingston. It continued in the family of Mewes,
or Meaux, for more than three hundred years; Lady
Worsley, relict of Sir Edward Worsley, Knight, the last
survivor of that ancient family, devised it to Edward Meaux
Worsley, Esquire.

The church was built by one of the Kingstons, before the Church.
registers of the diocese; so that the founder and date cannot be
ascertained. but the Lords of Kingston appear by those registers
always to have enjoyed the presentation.

THE

THE HISTORY OF

THE PARISH OF CHALE.

The parish of Chale has Niton, Whitwell, and Godshill on the east, Godshill and Kingston on the north; Shorwell and Brixton on the north-west; and the sea on the south, which forms the dangerous bay, that takes its name from the parish. In Domesday-book it is called Cela, and there classed among the large possessions of William Fitz-Stur: it was rated at one hide, but contained only one carucate of land. In the reign of Henry the First, Chale belonged to Hugh Vernun, who built the church, upon which it became a parish distinct from Carisbrook This appears from the cartulary of Carisbrook, where William Gifford, Bishop of Winchester, confirms an agreement made between the church of St Mary of Carisbrook, the minister of that church, and Hugh Vernun, founder of the church of St Andrew of Chale, on the day of the dedication of the said church. The priest of Carisbrook claimed the church of Chale, as belonging to his parish: whereas Hugh Vernun alledged that his tenants did not belong to the church of Carisbrook; but by ancient usage could go to what church they pleased when living and bury their dead with equal liberty. In order however to terminate all animosity, he assigned to the church of Carisbrook a moiety of the glebe land and tithes of burials and oblations, excepting those of his own house, which he reserved entire, for maintaining the service and repairs of the church of Chale. The parson of Chale was bound to perform the whole service of his church; and on these considerations, the priest of

Carisbrook,

Carisbrook testified his consent to the new church having a cemetary, which agreement the Bishop confirmed under his anathema.

In the twenty-first year of Edward the First, Richard Barnevyle, with the assent of Adam Barnevyle, granted certain lands in Chale, with common pasture on Chale down to Richard the son of Sir Richard de Langford*, and in the second year of Edward the Second, Barnevyle granted all his other lands in Chale to John Langford, chief Lord of Chale. In the reign of Edward the Third, Sir John de Langford, then lord of Chale, was appointed Constable of Carisbrook Castle, and was one of the three wardens of the island, elected by the inhabitants. The frequent alarms occasioned by the French, who often threatened, and had several times actually made descent on the island, caused the family of Langford, with many others of good estimation, to seek more secure and quiet habitations; and Sir Thomas Langford is, after this removal, found of Bradfield in Berkshire, having leased out the manor of Chale. Reservation is made in this lease of wards, marriages, reliefs, escheats, wrecks of the sea, &c. with the advowson of the church of Chale. The tenant was to pay a rent of sixteen marks, at his manor of Bradfield, and to furnish a horse or horseman, whenever the King's service required. Chale continued in the Langford family till the first year of Henry the Eighth, when Sir John Langford dying, left an only daughter Anne, his heiress, who married Thomas Pound, Esquire, of Southwick, in the county of Southampton. The manor was sold by them to Captain Richard Worsley, and still remains in the family of Worsley of Appuldurcombe.

Cartas Ri. II. Bar.

Godyton, or
Gotton.

The manor of Godyton, in this parifh, gave name to its ancient poffeflors. Walter de Godyton, in the year one thoufand
three hundred and twenty three, built a chapel on Chale down,
dedicated to St. Catharine, affigning certain rents for a chantry
prieft to fing mafs, and alfo to provide lights, for the fafety of fuch veffels as chanced to come on that dangerous
coaft during the night *. At the diffolution of chantries,
it was perhaps found impracticable to divide the ufeful from
the fuperftitious part of the inftitution; fo that the whole
fell together, the chantry involving the light-houfe in its
ruin.

By an entry in the regifters of this diocefe, it appears
that eleven years before the erection of this chapel, there
was an hermitage ftanding on the fame fpot. the entry
is as follows: *Walter de Langftrell admiffus ad hermitorium
fupra montem de Chale, in infula Vectis, Idil. Octobris, A. D.
1312.*

The fituation pointed it out for a fea mark, it being about
feven hundred and fifty feet above high water level, half
a mile from the fhore, and commanding a moft extenfive
view. The tower of the chapel is yet ftanding, and is
known by the name of St. Catharine's Tower: it is thirty-five feet fix inches high; octangular without, and quad-
rangular within, finifhed with a pyramidical roof, each fide,
interior as well as exterior, being exactly four feet. From
this conftruction, the curious have found out fome re-

S. Cha-
rine's tower.

* Regift. Winton, 1323

femblance

semblance to the temple of the eight winds at Athens, a building, it is more than probable the architect never saw, or ever heard of *.

St Catharine's tower still remains, of most essential use by day to vessels navigating the channel · but having become extremely ruinous, its fall was to be apprehended ; and as its sudden disappearance might have been attended with fatal consequences, it was substantially repaired, and its angles strengthened with buttresses, at the expence of the Lord of the manor The foundation of the whole chapel is also cleared and levelled, by which, not only its figure was discovered but also the floor and stone hearth of the priest's little cell, at the south-west corner, close to the tower.

Looking eastward, from the elevated spot where the tower stands, two other hills are to be seen · the nearest, which is about three miles distant, is called Week down, over which, about a mile and a half farther, appears that called Shanklin down. Concerning these downs, a singular circumstance is remarked by the inhabitants of Chale, that may be mentioned for the gratification of those who are curious in natural enquiries, as the evidence of it seems unobjectionable. Shanklin down may now be guessed to stand about an hundred feet higher than the summit of Week down ; yet old persons

* In an ancient survey belonging to Sir Richard Worsley, Baronet, there is a small rude drawing of this chapel, when entire, from which it appears that it had only a body, without a transept, the tower stood at the west end A description of this tower, with four views of it, in its decayed state, is seen in the Gent. Mag. vol xxvii p 176.

G ll

still living affirm that within their remembrance, Shanklin down was barely visible from St. Catharine's; they declare moreover, that in their youth, old men have told them, they knew the time when Shanklin down could not be seen from Chale down, but only from the top of the Beacon; the old post of which stands near the chapel. This testimony, if allowed, argues either a sinking of the intermediate down, or a rising of one of the other hills; the causes of which are left for philosophical investigation.

Chale Bay.

Chale Bay, which opens from the most southern point of the island, westward from the shore called Underway, is about three miles in extent, and has at low water a fine broad beach, separated from the high country above, by a continued range of perpendicular cliffs, extremely dangerous to ships. The Black Gang way down to the strand at Black Gang is very awful, the descent being through an immense gully, among vast masses of broken ground and disjointed rocks, the ruins of the land above. In an arched excavation, at the bottom, under the projecting rock, from whence water is continually dripping, there issues a spring strongly impregnated with copperas. The surrounding scene from this depth is truly majestic.

Gold dust found in Chale Bay

Some years ago, it was discovered that the sand under the cliffs was mixed with gold dust: this for a while engaged the country people to wash it in bowls and pans, as is practised in Africa and South America, but from a number of dollars
occasionally

_Blackgang Chin a r Wet

occasionally found there, it appears likely that both were the contents of some Spanish ship wrecked in this dangerous bay, and in stormy weather thrown up by the violence of the waves.

THE PARISH OF SHORWELL.

Shorwell is bounded by the parish of Carisbrook on the north-east; has Godshill, Kingston, and Chale, on the south east, and Brixton on the south and west. Shorwell, anciently written Sorewell, is the name of two manors, distinguished by North and South : the former was in the King's hands, at the time of the general survey, and went in the grant of the island to Baldwin de Redvers : in his family it remained till the reign of Henry the Third, when Amicia, Countess of Devon, gave it to the Nuns of Laycock, in Wiltshire, which grant was con-firmed by her daughter Isabella. It was held by that Convent till its dissolution; and in the survey of the island, taken in the second year of Elizabeth, is found in the possession of Thomas Temes, Esquire. About the latter end of the same reign, it was purchased by Sir John Leigh, in whose descendants it still continues, being now the property of five young Ladies, coheir-esses of John Leigh, Esquire.

Limits.

North Shor-well

North Court-house, the seat of the Leigh family, was begun, in the reign of King James the First, by Sir John Leigh, Knight, who being then far advanced in years *, left the execution of it to his son Barnaby Leigh, Esquire. It was repaired and much improved by Barnaby Eveleigh Leigh, Esquire, at his first com-

North Court-house.

* Sir John Leigh died only in 1629, aged eighty-three

K k

ing

ing to the estate; and is one of the best houses in the island; the gardens are well laid out, and command an extensive view of the sea.

South Shorwell.

The manor of South Shorwell, or West Court, was many years in the Lisle family, from whom it descended to that of Dennis : and is now enjoyed by Colonel Hill, in right of his Lady.

Woolverton,

The manor of Woolverton was formerly held by a family of the same name; Sir Ralph de Woolverton gave the tithes of his demesnes to the Priory of Carisbrook; he also held lands called Little Woolverton under Wathe, where one of the family built a chapel, the ruins of which are still visible. The De Woolvertons had likewise a seat, near King's-Clere, in Hampshire, both which estates, in the reign of Henry the Fifth, are found in the family of Dingley, or Dinely; Robert Dinely appears to have been Sheriff of Hampshire, in the sixteenth year of Richard the Second. Woolverton continued in this family * till the Revolution, when it was sold to Maurice Hunt, and Anthony Morgan, Esquires; but the principal farm and manor-house has been lately purchased by James Joliffe, Esquire.

There was formerly a considerable family in the island, named De Shorwell, several of whom appear as witnesses to very ancient deeds among the tenants of the Countess Isabella, Robert

* In the survey of the island, taken the second year of Elizabeth, of which only the West Medine, in the possession of Sir Richard Worsley, Baronet, is extant, Woolverton is said to be held of the manor of Gatcombe, and that it contained three hundred acres of land.

de Shorwell is faid to hold lands in Clatterford; and William de Shorwell was joined with the Bifhop of Winchefter, in the office of Sheriff of Southampton for feven years, from the firft, to the ninth year of Henry the Third. The chapel of Shor-well, which feems to have been built after the foundation of Carifbrook, is confirmed to that Priory by the charter of William de Vernun. It belonged to that parifh till the reign of Edward the Third, when the inconvenience of burying their dead at Carifbrook (efpecially in winter time) occafioned its fepara-tion.

THE PARISH OF BRIXTON.

The parifh of Brixton is bounded by that of Mottefton on the weft; by Calbourn and Carifbrook on the north; by Shor-well on the eaft. The parifh of Brixton having been taken out of Calbourn, which was part of the moft ancient poffeffions of the church of Winchefter *, it is probable the church was built and made parochial by fome Bifhop of that fee. When the manor of Swainfton was granted to William Montacute, the firft Earl of Salifbury of that name, we find large franchifes, par-ticularly wrecks of the fea, beftowed on the Earl, without any mention of Brixton, which was that part of Swainfton adja-cent to the fea: at that time, therefore, the manor may be fuppofed not to have been divided, though the church had been built long before The Rectory of Calbourn formerly claimed archidiaconal jurifdiction over that of Brixton †; but

Boundaries.

Hiftory.

* Appendix, No LXXXVII contains an order of Edward the Third to Orle ton, then Bifhop of that fee, to array the clergy of the Ifle of Wight.

† In the return made by the Dean of the Ifland to Bifhop Woodlock, in 1305. It is faid that Brixton confuevit adjacere ecclefiæd, Calbourn ufq to n p an ecclefiæ

K k 2   it it appears in the registers of Winchester, that the Rectors of Brixton refusing to submit to the jurisdiction of the Rector of Calbourn, the contest rose to actual violence. A commission was therefore given to the Rector of Gatcombe, to exercise that authority until the right should be determined; but the claim was in all likelihood accommodated by the influence of the Bishop, who was patron of both churches.

Lemerston.

The manor of Lemerston, in this parish, gave name to its ancient possessors, soon after the Conquest; who built and endowed an oratory here for three priests. It came to the Tichbornes, of Tichborn in Hampshire, by a marriage with the daughter and heiress of Ralph de Lemerston, and they retained it four hundred years Sir Henry Tichborn, Baronet sold it some years since to George Stanley, Esquire, father of the late Right Honourable Hans Stanley, who devised it to his sisters.

Uggeton.

Uggeton was a manor given by Mascarell, Lord of Brooke, to the Knight's Templars, on the suppression of that order it was given to God's-house at Portsmouth, and on the dissolution of religious houses it escheated to the crown, where it continued till the reign of James the First, when it was disposed of. It was afterwards purchased by Stephen March, Esquire, and descended by the failure of issue male, to his grandson Harcourt Powel, Esquire.

T H E   P A R I S H   O F   M O T T E S T O N.

Boundaries.

This parish has that of Brixton on the east, Calbourn on the north, Shalfleet on the west, and occupies a small part of the

sea

fea coaft on the fouth. The manor of Motteſton is, in Domeſ-day-book, termed Modreſtone, and is enumerated among the poſſeſſions of William Fitz-Azor, being rated at two hides, and ſaid to contain four carucates of land. By a ſurvey, in the reign of Edward the Firſt, it is found in the hands of Robert de Glamorgan * : it was afterwards held by Sir John de Langford, and it appears that Dionyſia, his widow, preſented to the church of Motteſton, in the year one thouſand three hundred and ſixty-one: it came ſoon after to Edward Chyke, Eſquire, who preſent-ed to the church, in the year one thouſand three hundred and ſeventy-four; and it remained in the ſame family for above three centuries †. It was afterwards purchaſed by Sir Robert Dilling-

ton,

* It is probable that Glamorgan enjoyed this and other lands in the Iſland, as his part of the inheritance of Brian de Loula, who died in the nineteenth of Henry the Third, one of whoſe daughters and heirs married William Glamorgan, as appears by the following record cited by Madox. *Tho Brito et Alicia uxor ejus Will de Glamorgen et Radus de Scepham, haredes Briani de Loula, dederit 100 marcas de fine pro nulenda ſaſina de terris, &c. quæ fuerunt ipſius Briani, et de quibus idem Brianus obſit ſeiſitus.* Comput in quidem 100s p quos ſunt ſi erant fi is cum reſpo latendi ſi nia de terra que fuit ip as in Blancford Et mettered quietum clamaverunt regi mon d Kingſtrong cum poſſion &c 19 Hy III

† Of this family (whoſe eſtate Lloyd remarks to have been three hundred pounds a year three hundred years ago, and no more within thirty years of his time) was Sir John Cheke, a very learned and polite gentleman in the ſixteenth century. He was bred at St John's College, Cambridge, and was made Profeſſor of Greek in that Univerſity. In 1544, Sir John Cheke, and Sir Anthony Cooke, were appointed joint tutors to Prince Edward, in the Latin tongue. He was alſo made a Canon in New College, Oxford, now Chriſt-church, on the diſſolution of which College a penſion was aſſigned him in lieu of his Canonry. At the acceſſion of his pupil, Edward the Sixth, he obtained ſeveral grants, together with the Provoſtſhip of King's College, Cambridge. In 1549 he was one of the Commiſſioners for viſit-ing the Univerſity of Cambridge, and one of the thirty-two Commiſſioners appoint-ed to compile a body of Eccleſiaſtical Law. He alſo tranſlated the Common Prayer Book into Latin, for the examination and opinion of Peter Martyr, who did not underſtand the Engliſh language. The King made great progreſs in his ſtudies, under Sir John Cheke, who adviſed him to keep a diary of all the tranſ-actions of his reign, and, according to Lloyd, he was the promoter of the king's acts of charity. Edward beſtowed the honour of Knighthood on him, made him *Chamberlain* of the Exchequer for life, Secretary of State, and a Privy Counſel-

lor,

ton, of Knighton, and was fold by Sir Triftram Dillington, to John Leigh, Efquire, of Northcourt. It is part of the poffeffions of the daughters and coheireffes of Mr. Leigh.

The parifh is very fmall, and the church, which was built before the oldeft remaining regifter of the Diocefe of Winchefter, is fuppofed to have been founded by one of the Glamorgans.

THE PARISH OF CALBOURN.

Boundaries.   The parifh of Calbourn is bounded on the eaft by Northwood, a detached parcel of Shalfleet, and by Carifbrook; by Brixton and Motteſton on the fouth; by Shalfleet on the weft, by which it is feparated by the brook * which runs into Newtown-bay; and by the channel on the north. In Domefday-book Calbourn is called a hundred lying in Boucomb hundred: it was rated at feventeen hides, contained twenty-five carucates of land, wherein were feventeen villains, fifteen cottagers, eleven

lor. He attached himfelf to the intereft of the Lady Jane Grey, and, upon the King's death, acted as her Minifter, for which Queen Mary committed him to the Tower. He obtained a pardon, but difliking the reftoration of popery, obtained leave to travel; and fettled at Strafburgh, where the Englifh fervice was kept up, which he regularly attended in the mean time his eftate was confifcated, under the pretence of his not returning at the expiration of his leave of abfence. Being greatly reduced, he read Greek lectures at Strafburgh for his fubfiftence. Being prevailed on to return to England, he was feized, and again confined in the Tower He was by threats induced to conform to the Romifh religion, and received abfolution from the hands of Cardinal Pole, on which compliance, he obtained fome compenfation for the lofs of his eftate. But grief and remorfe fhortened his life, fo that he died in 1557, at forty three years of age he was author of feveral books, and was a diftinguifhed reviver of polite literature

* Calbourn is fuppofed to have received its name from the Brook. and of courfe, that the brook was anciently termed the Caul Bourn.

                                                        bondfmen,

Swainson, in the Isle of Wight the Seat of Sir Fitz Williams Barrington Bar.

bondfmen, and two mills. The whole manor, in King Edward the Confeffor's reign, had been worth fixteen pounds, at that time, the Bifhop's part was thirty pounds; the whole was farmed at forty pounds, but it is remarked that it could not produce that rent, becaufe feven pounds was held in fee, and the church had thirty fhillings.

By the contents and value of the land, this manor muft, at the time of the Norman Conqueft, have included Swainfton, and Brixton; neither of which names are found in Domefday-book. Thus it extended crofs the ifland, from the channel on north, to the fouth fhore at Brixton bay. The parifh ftill retains the old name, but the manor has long been known by that of Swainfton; for in the thirteenth of Edward the Second, the King confirms the grant of Ademarus, Bifhop of Winchefter, to the Burgeffes of Newtown, and feals his charter at Swainfton. This manor, with the advowfon of the church, remained in the fee of Winchefter until Edward the Firft, in the twelfth year of his reign, being difgufted at the Pope, for intruding John de Ponteffera into the Bifhoprick, contrary to his inclination, vexed the Bifhop many ways, and among the reft, deprived him of this manor. The Bifhop, to purchafe the peaceable enjoyment of the other lands belonging to his fee, relinquifhed the manor of Swainfton, and paid a fine of two thoufand pounds to the King, for confirming to him the temporalities of his Bifhoprick [*]: among thefe, the Bifhop was allowed to retain the advowfon of the churches of Calbourn, Brixton, and Binftead, which had always belonged to that fee [†].

Ancient extent.

Swainfon.

---

[*] See Appendix, No LXXXVIII.

[†] To this manor there formerly belonged half a Knight's-fee in Whippingham, and half a Knight's fee in Lemerfton. *Rot pat.* 12 *Edw I.*

King

King Edward the Second, in the firſt year of his reign, beſtowed Swainſton on his ſiſter Mary, a Nun at Ambreſbury, in
exchange for the Borough of Wilton, and other lands ſettled on
her by her father, Edward the Firſt*. The ſame King afterwards gave it to his ſon Edward †, then Earl of Cheſter; who,
in the fourth year of his reign, granted it to William, Lord Montacute, afterwards Earl of Saliſbury. It was forfeited by the attainder of John, Earl of Saliſbury, in the firſt year of the reign of
Henry the Firſt; but muſt have been reſtored to his ſon; for in the
following year, Thomas de Montacute, Earl of Saliſbury, granted
to his dear and beloved brother, Aleyn de Buxhall, for the entire affection, &c. ten pounds, to be annually taken of the
iſſues and profits of the manor of Swainſton ‡. By the marriage
of his daughter and heireſs, this manor went to Richard Nevill §,
Earl of Saliſbury, from whom it deſcended to his ſon, the famous Richard, Earl of Warwick, who was defeated and
killed by Edward the Fourth, at the battle of Barnet. Being
again forfeited, Edward granted it to George, Duke of Clarence,
and by his attainder it reverted again to the Crown. It was reſtored
to his ſon Edward, Earl of Warwick, by whoſe attainder it came
to Henry the Seventh; and when Henry the Eighth granted it

* See Appendix, No. LXXXIX.

† This King's order to the Earl of Saliſbury to put his lands in a ſtate of defence is contained in the laſt number of the Appendix.

‡ Madox's Form. Anglic.

§ Richard Nevill was ſon of Ralph Earl of Weſtmoreland, by his ſecond wife,
Joanna, daughter of John of Gaunt, Duke of Lancaſter, in conſequence of this
alliance he became poſſeſſed of the manor of Swainſton, and was ſoon afterwards
created Earl of Saliſbury. Richard Nevill, his ſon, married the daughter of Beauchamp, the laſt Earl of Warwick of that family, ſiſter to Henry Beauchamp, Duke
of Warwick, crowned King of the Iſle of Wight by Henry the Sixth; he ſucceeded to the title of Warwick by this marriage, and to that of Saliſbury on his father's
death. He left two daughters coheireſſes, Anne and Iſabella. Anne firſt married
Edward Prince of Wales, ſon of Henry the Sixth, and afterwards Richard the
Third, Iſabella married George, Duke of Clarence, brother of Edward the Fourth.

to Margaret, Countefs of Salifbury, fifter to Edward, Earl of Warwick, beheaded in the Tower, fhe married Sir Richard Pole, Knight of the Garter: fhe was alfo attainted and beheaded. Thus this manor was forfeited to the Crown for the fifth time. Queen Mary, in the firft year of her reign, reftored Swainfton to Winifrid, daughter and coheir of Henry, Lord Montagu, fon of the Countefs of Salifbury; Winifrid firft married Sir Thomas Haftings, brother of Francis, Earl of Huntingdon, who married Catharine the other fifter; and fecondly Sir Thomas Barrington, Knight, of Barrington Hall, in the county of Effex, by whom fhe had one fon Francis, created a Baronet by James the Firft, in the year one thoufand fix hundred and eleven; from whom the manor defcended to Sir Fitz-Williams Barrington, Baronet, the prefent reprefentative of that ancient family*. The horfe at Swainfton is pleafantly fituated, and commands a view of the channel between the ifland and the New Foreft The pleafure grounds and walks through the woods are extenfive and well laid out.

Manor-ncufe.

The manor of Newtown lies within that of Swainfton The chapel belongs to the church of Calbourn, and the glebe, with which it was endowed, is enjoyed by the Rector. In the regifter of Winchefter, in the firft of Edward the Sixth, there is an entry in the following terms: " For the fettling the matter " of variance between John Mewes, Efquire, and Mr. Ran- " dolph Howard, Parfon of Calbourn, the Bifhop, as arbi- " trator, awards, that Mr Mewes fhall pay his whole tithes " for his meifh, called Bernard-meifh, in Newtown: and " whereas the Parfon of Calbourn hath formerly paid only " twenty fhillings per annum towards the finding a Prieft for " the inhabitants of Newtown, it is ordered that he fhall from

Newtown.

* The reader is referred to the Baronetage of England, and the Hiftory of Effex, for a more full account of this ancient family, in which county they had large poffeffions, and frequently reprefented it in Parliament.

L l   " hence-

" henceforth, with the favourable aid of the inhabitants of New-
" town, at his own cofts, maintain a Prieft up rifing and down
" lying, to refide in the houfe adjoining to the church-yard at
" Newtown. The Mayor and Burgeffes, and the inhabitants
" of Newtown, do, on this confideration, quit their claim to
" Longbridge Croft, otherwife called Magdalen's Croft, which
" they will fuffer the faid Parfon of Calbourn and his fucceffors
" to enjoy · and the faid Mayor and Burgeffes, and inhabitants,
" as alfo the Parfon of Calbourn doe agree, that if any diffe-
" rence fhall hereafter arife touching this award, that they will
" refer themfelves to the determination of the Bifhops of Win-
" chefter for the time being."   Signed June the eighth, in the
firft of Edward the Sixth.

In the furvey of the ifland taken the fecond year of Elizabeth,
it appears that the Parfon of Calbourn held a grant of forty
acres, called Magdalen's-land, belonging to the chapel of Newtown, for which land he provided a reader for the chapel ·

There was another manor among the lands poffeffed by William Fitz-Stur, in Domefday-book, named Calbourn, now called
Weftover, which came with Gatcombe and other lands, to the
younger branch of the Lifles, called Lifle of Gatcombe   It was
purchafed by Erlefman, of Sir Geoffrey Pole's widow, and Earnley, in the beginning of the reign of Queen Elizabeth; Erlefman
fold it to Sir Robert Dillington, whofe defcendant fold it to the
father of Captain David Urry, whofe fon fold it to Lord Holmes.
It is now in the poffeffion of the Reverend Leonard Troughear
Holmes, who has a very pleafant feat there.

The patronage of the church at Calbourn, was confirmed to
the Bifhop of Winchefter, by Edward the Firft, when the
Bifhop relinquifhed the manor to the King; neverthelefs, Edward the Third contefted it with the Bifhop, prohibiting him
from

Westover Lodge A Hunting Box belonging

from admitting any perfon to that church, until the right of patronage fhould be decided: but this difpute was foon terminated,
and the Bifhop's collation took place *.

THE PARISH OF SHALFLEET.

The parifh of Shalfleet in the Weft Medina, like that of New- Situation.
church in the Eaft, extends acrofs the ifland, from the northern
to the fouthern fhore, being however very narrow at the fouthern extremity. Its northern fhore is extenfive, ftretching from
Yarmouth, eaftward to Newtown Bay : it is bounded by the parifhes of Calbourn and Mottefton on the eaft, a fmall extent of
the fea fhore on the fouth, and on the weft by the parifh of
Brook, a detached portion of St. Nicholas, and the parifhes of
Thorley and Yarmouth.

The manor of Shalfleet was held by Ediic, in the time of Shalfleet.
Edward the Confeffor ; and, at the general furvey, was among
the extenfive poffeffions of Gozeline Fitz-Azor : it had been
rated at fix hides, but at that time paid only for three; in the
Confeffor's time it was valued at twenty pounds, and at the
time of the general furvey, at twenty-five pounds, and had then
a church. The manor did not long continue in the laft mentioned family, being very early in that of Trenchard This family
came probably into the ifland, when Richard de Redvers had
the lordfhip; as the oldeft accounts inform us, that Earl Richard
gave to Pagan Trenchard, the manor of Hordhall, near Lymington, in the county of Southampton : to which is to be added,
that in the oldeft pipe-roll †, Pagan Trenchard is charged with
the levy of Danegeld, in the Ifle of Wight. King Stephen had
then taken the ifland from Baldwin, Earl of Devon. It appears

* Ex Regift. Adam Orleton, p. 9, 10.
† Ann 6 Stephen.

that

that neither hidage nor efcuage were collected by the crown, when it was held by the Lords of the Ifland.

Although this ancient family often refided at Shalfleet, they lived chiefly at Hordhall; in the regifter of the diocefe, a licence is mentioned for Richard Trenchard to have mafs celebrated for himfelf and family, in his houfe at Hordhall. In the fourteenth of Edward the Second, Ralph Gorges petitioned the Parliament againft Sir Henry Tyers, Conftable of Carifbrook Caftle, for maintaining Sir Henry Trenchard, at that time an outlaw *, in poffeffion of his lands, againft the rights of the King †; but this outlawry came to nothing, as Trenchard ftill retained his eftates. Soon after, John Trenchard fettled the manor of Shalfleet on the marriage of his younger fon Henry; from whom it defcended by female heirs, through feveral generations, till Thomas Worfley, Efquire, of Appuldurcombe, purchafed the manor from John Waller, Efquire. It is ftill in that branch of the Worfley family ‡

Ningewood   The firft account we have of the manor of Ningewood or Lingwood is, that it was granted by Baldwin, Earl of Devon, to the Monks of Chrift-church §, in which Priory it remained till its fuppreffion, when it was, with Shalcombe and other lands, exchanged by Henry the Eighth with Thomas Hopfon, Ef-

---

* This outlawry was probably on account of Trenchard having affociated with the male-content Barons againft the King, in the enfuing year, Sir Henry Tyers fuffered death for adhering to Thomas, of Woodftock, and other Barons, in an infurrection. Dugd. Bar. vol. ii. p. 21.

† Ryley's Placit. Parl. p. 426

‡ There is a farm in the manor of Shalfleet, called Wollerans, which received its name from Wolleran Trenchard, a younger fon of Sir Henry Trenchard, to whom it was given by his brother John, in the twenty-third of Edward the Firft, as appears by the deed ftill exifting

§ Monaft. Angl. vol. ii. p. 138

quire,

quire, anceftor of the famous Admiral, for the manor of Mary-bone, in Middlefex * Ningewood was purchafed from Hop-fon, by one of the family of Comber, and defcended from them to Sir Thomas Miler, Baronet, through the female line.

Wellow was held by the Lords of the ifland in demefne, and came to the Crown, when the Lordfhip of the Ifland was purchafed by Edward the Firft. It was granted with the other Crown lands to the feveral fubfequent Lords, and be-ing beftowed on George, Duke of Clarence, it continued in the Crown after his attainder, till King James the Firft grant-ed it away again. It was purchafed with other eftates by the family of Comber, from whom it came to Sir Thomas Miller, Baronet.

[margin: Wellow.]

The manor of Watchingwood is in Domefday-book termed Watchingwell, and belonged to the nunnery of Wilton; it was rated in the Confeffor's time at three hides, but in that of the Con-queror, at two and a half, *becaufe half a hide was then in the King's park.* This record falfifies the current affertion, that Woodftock park was the firft park made in England; for the park here mentioned was in being fixty or feventy years, prior to that of Woodftock. There is another manor of Watching-wood, which was held by the family of Trenchard; they are diftinguifhed as Upper and Lower Watchingwood, and together compofe that detached part of Shalfleet parifh, which lies between the parifh of Calbourn, and the foreft of Parkhurft. The upper farm is the property of John Bull, Efquire, of Strutton-ftreet, Lon-don; and the lower farm has been lately purchafed of Mr. Good-enough by Sir Fitz-Williams Barrington, Baronet.

[margin: Watching-wood]

The church of Shalfleet being mentioned in Domefday-book, muft have exifted at the time of the general furvey, but was

[margin: Church]

* Madox Firm Burg No. 488.

probably

probably founded after the death of William Fitz-Ofborn: for as he gave all his other churches to the Abbey of Lyra, it is natural to conclude he beftowed the whole. Edward the Third granted it to William Montacute, Earl of Salifbury, whofe arms are ftill to be feen in the painted glafs of the church windows; and the Earl gave it to his new founded Abbey of Buftlefham, or Bifham, in Berkfhire. The impropriation, after the diffolution of the Monafteries, was purchafed by Lord Chief Juftice Fleming, who devifed it to a younger branch of his family; and after paffing through feveral hands, it came to the family of Reeves, in which it ftill remains.

THE PARISH OF BROOK.

Situation

This fmall parifh is bounded by Shalfleet on the eaft; by Thorley and a detached portion of St. Nicholas on the north; and by Frefhwater and the fea on the fouth-weft. The manor of Brook was in the Conqueror's hands at the time of the general furvey, and had been part of the poffeffions of Earl Tofti, it had been rated at three hides, but then only at one: it contained fix carucates of land, and was valued at feven pounds per annum. It was foon after in the poffef-fion of Sir Ralph de Mafcarell, who gave the tithes of his demefnes at Brook, to the Abbey of Lyra *, this grant is confirmed by William his Grandfon, in as ample a manner as it was enjoyed under Robert his father, or under Ralph his grandfather By furveys taken in the reigns of the three Edwards, we find it occupied by the family of Glamorgan Nicholas Glamorgan, the laft male heir, who died in the thirty-fixth year of Edward the Third, as appears by the efcheat roll

---

* Cartul Crinb. penes R. W. Burt. cart 55

of the county of Somerfet, left fix fifters his heirs, Ifabella, Margaret, Petronella, Eleanor, Anne and Nicola. Ifibella, the eldeft fifter, married Roucle or Rookley, and afterwards Hanfon; for fhe appears in the regifters of the diocefe, to have prefented to the church of Brook, under both thofe names. Margaret married —— Rofe, and Petronella —— Uiry: who in her right had Laft Standen in the parifh of Arreton Eleanor remained fingle, Anne married —— Veer, and Nicola married Hacket There was another fifter married to Winford, and had iffue, but fhe died before her brother Nicholas. Roucle enjoyed this manor through feveral defcents, but the name became extinct in two daughters. The one married Bowerman, and the other Gilbert; who held the manor in common, till the third year of Edward the Sixth, when Nicholas Bowerman purchafed Gilberts moiety [*].

There was fome years fince, a difpute refpecting the patronage of the church of Brook, it being claimed by St. John's College, Cambridge, as a chapel belonging to Frefhwater; but was determined in favour of the Bowerman family, who continue to prefent to it The church was repaired and beautified by the late William Bowerman, Efquire, who alfo rebuilt the manor-houfe, which is pleafantly fituated in a rich vale.

Church

THE PARISH OF THORLEY.

The parifh of Thorley is fituated weft of Shalfleet, having that parifh partly on the north and partly on the eaft,

Boundaries.

[*] King Henry the Seventh, coming into the Ifle of Wight, in the fourteenth year of his reign, honoured Dame Joanna Bowerman, then Lady of the manor of Brook, with a vifit, and in acknowledgment of his entertainment, not only left behind him a drinking-horn as a prefent, but gave her a warrant for a fat buck of the feafon, to be yearly delivered out of his foreft of Carifbrook during her life, this warrant is dated at Brook, in Auguft, the fourteenth year of Henry the Seventh, and is now in the poffeffion of the family of Bowerman

on

on which fide it has alfo a portion of the parifh of St. Nicholas; the parifh of Yarmouth completes its northern boundary: it has part of the river Yar, and the parifh of Frefhwater on the weft; and on the fouth is bounded by the parifh of Brook. This was one of the manors held by Earl Tofti, but Alfi was the tenant at the time of the general furvey. It is mentioned as containing feven carucates of land, was valued at the time of Edward the Confeffor at eight pounds, but under William the Conqueror, at twelve pounds. Thorley was grant-ed to Richard de Redvers, Earl of Devon, by Henry the Firft, and was held by his defcendants till the Countefs Ifabella difpofed of the ifland to Edward the Firft. It was afterwards granted to Montacute, Earl of Salifbury, and being forfeited by the attainder of John, Earl of Salifbury, was granted by Henry the Fourth to Edward, Duke of York, in tail male, together with the reft of the ifland. Edward the Fourth granted it to George, Duke of Clarence, and when it was forfeited by his attainder, it remain-ed in the Crown till the reign of Queen Elizabeth, who grant-ed Thorley, Frefhwater, &c. to David Urry, Efquire; but held it at thirty pounds per annum, which was referved as a fee-farm rent, and is ftill paid to the Crown the fon of David Urry left a daughter his heirefs, who married Richard Lucy, Efquire, of the county of Warwick: he fold it to Sir Robert Holmes, Knight, then Governor of the Ifland, from whom it defcended to the Reverend Leonard Troughear Holmes through the female line.

Thorley is a very fertile parifh, and the manor one of the beft in the ifland, notwithftanding the greateft part of it was once a warren, as appears by a grant of the Countefs Ifabella, who gave to the Prior of Chrift-church, a fifth part of the coveys in her manor of Thorley. In the records of Parliament there is found a petition from the Prior and Convent of Chrift-church. Ifabella de Fortibus

had

had granted to the faid Priory the tithe of rabbits within the manor of Thorley, in the Ifle of Wight, but that William Ruffel, Warden of the Ifland, would not permit them to take the faid tithes: to which it was anfwered, that a writ fhould iffue to the Treafurer and Barons of the Exchequer, to enquire into that grant, and whether they were feifed of thofe tithes, and to order juftice to be done in it. The office of Warrener of Thorley and Wellow, is found to have been beftowed by Edward the Third on Walter White. there were formerly feveral rabbit warrens in the Ifland which have been deftroyed. Sir John Oglander mentions a rabbit dealer in his time, who carried great numbers to London every week, and adds, that there were very few hares in this country, till Sir Edward Horfey gave encouragement to ftocking the ifland with them.

The church.

The church of Thorley was probably built by Amicia, Countefs of Devon, who gave it to the priory of Chrift-church, in Hampfhire, in which convent it remained till its diffolution. This priory appears to have held out beyond the limited time; there is a remarkable entry in Bifhop Gardiner's regifter, of a prefentation to this church, in the year one thoufand five hundred and thirty-feven, by John Diaper, by divine fufferance prior of Chrift-church, and the Monks of his convent [a]. The church was, with other eftates of the priory exchanged with Thomas Hopfon, Efquire, in the year one thoufand five hundred and forty-fix, for his manor of Marybone, in Middlefex; the next prefentation is therefore recorded in his name [b].

[a] *Per religiofos viros Johem Draper Dei patientia priorem ecclefiæ conv. i ecclefiæ c prioratus Chrifti Ecclefiæ de Twynham, et ejufdem ibid. convertine.* Reg. Gard. fol. 31 verf. Maij 21.

[b] *Per difcretum virum Thomam Hopfon.* Idem. fol. 54 verf Jan. 18, 1546.

THE PARISH OF YARMOUTH.

Situation.

The situation of Yarmouth is implied in its name, and the town stands on the eastern point of land, at the mouth of the river Yar: the limits of the parish are very small, it has Shalfleet for its eastern boundary, it is terminated by Thorley on the west, and washed by the sea on the two other sides. This town, called in ancient charters Eremuth, is the first in the island that obtained a charter of franchises; which was granted to it by Baldwin, Earl of Devon, brother to the Countess Isabella, in the reign of Henry the Third, from this circumstance Yarmouth may be supposed to have been much larger formerly than at present. It is indeed said to have had three churches, but if these churches are understood to have been contemporary, it is a mistake, the truth is, that when the first church which stood at the east end of the town, was burnt or otherwise destroyed, a second was built at the west end, where the castle now stands. This church was also demolished by the French, in the thirty-fifth year of Henry the Eighth, on which event the King ordered a castle to be erected on the spot, part of which stands on the old wall of the church, as may be observed on the east side of the fortress: the present church was at the same time built in the middle of the town. The town of Yarmouth, from having been a place of some importance, is reduced to a small village. The endowment of the church being very small, was augmented by the bounty of of Queen Anne; which was added to a sum of money given by Colonel Henry Holmes, for the same purpose. the only object in the church worthy of attention, is a very elegant monument

nument of Sir Robert Holmes, in a small chapel, on the south side of the Chancel. Under the statue is the following inscription *.

THE PARISH OF FRESHWATER.

This parish comprehends the western extremity of the Isle of Wight, and consists in great part of a peninsula formed by the river Yar, joined to the rest of the island on the south side Situation.

* H. S. J.

Robertus Holmes miles,

Henrici Holmes de Mallow comitatus Corkensis in Hibernia armigeri filius natu tertius, ab ineunte adolescentia acquirendam armis gloriam intentus, militiae nomen dedit, et sub serenissimi regis Caroli vexillis tyrocinia ponens contra perduelles fortiter feliciterq. pugnavit. Pari deinde animo, pari laude, navalibus se immiscuit pretiis, et sub auspiciis celsissimi principis Ruperti, egregie meruit. Cum vero videret causam regiam armis ultra defendi non posse, ad exteros sese principes contulit, et in Gallia, Germania, Flandria, rebus belli pulchre gestis inclarui Rege Carolo 2do. fauste tandem prospereque restaurato, abeo castelli de Sandon in Vectis insula praefecturam (tanquam veteris meriti praemium) accipit et subinde militiae titulo ornatus est anno 1666. Copiarum navalium quae rubris revlis insigniuntur, legatus alter constitutus, portum Batavum de Uli exigua classe intravit, cumq illic naves centum et octaginta concremasict, in Scellengam descendit, et Branderium istius insulae primarium oppidum incendio delevit. Ob haec et alia multa praeclare acta cum serenissimus rex haud indebitus illius et virtuti et fidei praemiis honoravit, insulaeq Vectis ducem et gubernatorem durante vita naturali praefecit, quinetiam fecialium principi mandavit ut ipsius gentilitiis insignibus leo Anglicus adscriberetur, necnon crista nempe brachium armatum e navali corona porrectam et tridentam gerens. Hos honores qua arte acquisivit eadem etiam tuebatur, vir fortissimus nimirum bene merendo, fideli semper in regis et in patria n studio Obijt An. Dom. 1692, Nov. 18.

Honoratissimo patruo infra sepulto hoc monumentam posuit Henricus Holmes Armiger. Vectis insulae praefectus, authoritate regis locum tenens.

by

by a narrow isthmus, at a place called Freshwater-gate*, but
the parish extends beyond the river, over the lordships of Afton, Compton, Willingham, and other lands, and is bounded
on the east by the parishes of Thorley and Brook. Freshwater
being a large parish, is divided into six districts, namely, Easton,
Weston, Norton, Sutton, Middleton, and Willmingham Brook
was undoubtedly included in the parish at the time of the general
survey, though it afterwards attained parochial independence.

The church.
While the church of Freshwater remained under the Abbey
of Lyra, the Monks had spirited up the parishioners to op-
pose the Vicar presented by the Bishop, when the presentation fell to him by lapse, and several persons were excommunicated on the occasion. There is a raised tomb in one of the isles
of this church, [the burial-place of the lords of the manor of Afton,] exhibiting on a cross plate the representation of a man in
armour. this tomb having been opened some years since, was
found to contain the skeleton of a man, with the skull placed
between his legs, probably the remains of some Chief who was
beheaded The advowson of this church vested in the crown
as an appendage to an alien monastery, and was often granted
to the Captains of the island, but is now in St. John's College,

* In January, 1629, Sir Edward Dennis, Sir John Oglander, Sir William
Meux, Captain Cheeke, Mr Burnaby Leigh, and Captain Hopson, went to London, to petition Government to allow money to repair the forts, including a
proposal for making the peninsula of Freshwater, a place of retreat for the inhabitants of the island, with their cattle, upon any invasion which they could
not withstand, and Yarmouth for the more considerable inhabitants Freshwater was to be insulated, by cutting through the neck of land at Freshwater
gate, and the passages to be secured with draw-bridges, and half moons But
their solicitations were answered only by good words and promises. *Oglander's
Manuscript*

Cambridge

View from Freshwater Gate

Cambridge. There are two manors named King's Freshwater, and Prior's Freshwater in this parish.

King's Freshwater has been held by many great families, having been granted to some for the term of life only, while others enjoyed it in tail male. Under King John, it is found in the possession of Margery Vernun, who paid forty marks, and furnished two horses for the livery of the manor *. Edward the First, in the thirtieth year of his reign, bestowed this manor, among others, on his daughter Mary, a Nun at Ambresbury. It was held by Giles Beauchamp, Lord of Alcester and Powyck, in the time of Edward the Third, who, among other privileges, obtained a licence to fortify his house at Freshwater, and to embattle the walls †. In the thirteenth of that reign, the said Giles being beyond sea, on the King's service, had a special exemption from furnishing six soldiers for his lands in the Isle of Wight ‡. The manor after that time was granted, with the Lordship of the island, to several families; and reverting to the Crown, by the attainder of George, Duke of Clarence, it was by Queen Elizabeth, granted in fee-farm: being sold by the grantees to Thomas Urry, Esquire, it descended by a female heir to Thomas Morgan, Esquire, who disposed of it to the late Lord Holmes, from whom it descended through the female line, to the Reverend Leonard Troughear Holmes.

Prior's Freshwater, so called, is a small manor, it was purchased by the family of Comber, and descended from them to the present owner, Sir Thomas Miller, Baronet.

---

* Rot. Pip. 7 Joh. † Dugd. Bar. vol. 1. p. 249.
‡ Idem. ibid.

Affeton

Affeton was a manor that had belonged to Earl Tosti, but at the time of the general survey, was in the King's hands: it was rated at four hides in the time of Edward the Confessor, but in the general survey, at three hides only; and was valued at eight pounds; from whence it appears to have been one of the best manors in the island. It is found, soon after the compiling of Domesday-book, in the possession of a family who took their surname from it, there are two grants from Robert de Affeton, and William de Affeton, to the Abbey of Lyra, of the tithes of their fisheries: which deeds, though without date, seem to have been made prior to the founding of Quarr Abbey. After Baldwin de Redvers had founded that Abbey, it proved a formidable competitor with Lyra for pious donations. Sir Richard Affeton, is found to have been much intrusted by the Countess Isabella de Fortibus; and it may be inferred from a variety of circumstances, that he promoted the sale of the island to the King. In the twenty-third of that reign he was joined with Sir Adam Gourdon, in the office of Warden of the Island; and was allowed a sum of money to provide for the soldiers arrayed for the defence of the island, and for war engines. In the fifteenth year of Edward the Third, the manor is found in the family of Brokenford. In the survey, taken the second year of the reign of Elizabeth, the manor of Affeton was possessed by the ancient family of Bruen, or Bruin, Lords of the manor of Fordingbridge. It was afterwards purchased by the family of Urry, and is now in the possession of John Urry, Esquire, a Captain in his Majesty's navy: the house is pleasantly situated on the banks of the river.

The manor of Compton was also part of the possessions of Earl Tosti: it was in the King's hands at the time of compiling Domesday book, where it is called Cantune; was rated in the

The Cave under Fushwa'ert loff   Gul fg y Sculp

Confeſſor's time at three hides, but then only at one; and is ſaid to contain four carucates of land. It was very early in the poſſeſſion of a family who took their name from it, and who held this manor, together with Atherfield, till the latter end of the reign of Edward the Third, when they ended in a daughter, married to Lyete. Many of them were knighted, and in the reign of Edward the Third, Sir Adam de Compton commanded the band of Freſhwater. In the ſurvey taken in Queen Elizabeth's time, Compton is found to be held by three proprietors, who were probably deſcended from the daughters of Lyete. It is now in the family of Miller, who inherited this, with ſeveral other Lordſhips, from that of Comber *, but the principal farm has been lately purchaſed of Sir Thomas Miller, Baronet, by William Bowerman, Eſquire.

Wilmingham is mentioned in the general ſurvey, as a manor in the King's hands, and was rated at one hide: as it is not enumerated among the lands held from the Counteſs Iſabella, it may be ſuppoſed to have been held by her, and the ſucceeding Lords of the iſland in demeſne. It was among the lands exchanged by King Henry the Eighth with Hopſon, for Marybone; and was purchaſed by Thomas Coteile, Eſquire, by whoſe daughter and heireſs it deſcended to Lord Edgcumbe.

Wilmingham.

---

* The ſituation of Compton is elevated, and conſiderably above the level of the ſea, Sir John Oglander affirms, that in the year one thouſand ſix hundred and twenty four, a large pair of ſtag's horns was diſcovered there, about two fathoms deep in the ground, by the moldering of the cliff, which he conjectured to have remained there ever ſince the iſland had been ſeparated from the oppoſite ſhore. The country people in this part of the iſland, frequently dig nuts out of the ground, which they call Noah's nuts.

The late David Urry, of Afton, Eſquire, remembered one of the barrows on the downs at the weſt end of the iſland, being opened, which contained an urn full of bones.

The

Weston.

The manor of Weston derives its greatest consequence from having given name to a respectable family, the Lord of Middleton, or Milton, in Bimbridge; which manor, and that of Avicestone, by a survey taken in the reign of Edward the First, appear to have been held by De Weston: and Sir John de Weston was, by Edward the Third, appointed one of the Wardens of the island. It was among the possessions of Sir William Braybeuf, Sheriff of Hampshire, under Edward the First, and from him obtained the addition of Braybeuf, or, as it is corruptly called, Weston Braybrook.

Freshwater cliffs

The parish of Freshwater from the point where Worsley's Tower formerly stood, opposite to Hurst Castle, round to Freshwater gate, is fortified by those stupendous promontories of Chalk, known by the name of Freshwater Cliffs. The height of these cliffs is indeed prodigious, being in some places six hundred feet above the level of the sea. To form a just conception of their magnitude, they should be viewed from the sea, at the distance of about a quarter of a mile; when the most lofty and magnificent fabrics of art, compared with these stupendous works of nature, shrink in idea to Lilliputian size. These cliffs are frequented by immense numbers of marine birds, puffins, razor-bills, willocks, gulls, cormorants, Cornish choughs, daws, starlings, and wild pigeons, some of which come at stated times to lay their eggs and breed, while others remain there all the year. The cliffs are in some places perpendicular, in others they project and hang over in a tremendous manner, the several strata form many shelves, these serve as lodgments for the birds, where they sit in thick rows, and discover themselves by their

motions

The Modern House Cost by Men's of Symonton River

Godfrey sculp.

motions and flight, though not individually vifible. There are many chafms and deep caverns that feem to enter a great way into the rocks, and in many places the iffuing of fprings form fmall cafcades of rippling water, down to the fea, fheep and lambs are feen grazing in the lower parts of the cliff, near the margin of the fea ; the cliffs have fometimes proved fatal to them, as well as to other cattle who have ventured to graze too near the edge; from which, hounds in the ardour of the chace, have to their mutual deftruction driven and followed their game. The country people take the birds that harbour in thefe rocks, by the perilous expedient of defcending by ropes fixed to How caught. iron crows, driven into the ground . thus fufpended, they with fticks beat down the birds as they fly out of their holes; a dozen birds generally yield one pound weight of foft feathers, for which the merchants give eight pence ; the carcafes are bought by the fifhermen at fix pence per dozen, for the purpofe of baiting their crab-pots.

The foil at this end of the ifland is very different Alum Bay. Bay, on the north fide of the weft point of the parifh, derives its name from the alum found there The edges of the cliffs are beautifully variegated with a diverfity of colours, arifing from the different ftrata of earth, compofed of red and yellow ochre, fullers earth, and feveral kinds of fand of different hues. Copperas-ftones are found on the coaft, in fuch Copperas-ftones abundance, and of fo good a quality, that veffels are often freighted with them for London, and the cliffs belonging to Captain Urry, near Alum Bay, produce great quantities of white Sand for glafs works. fand, which is ufed at London, Briftol, and Worcefter, in the compofition of the finer forts of glafs and porcelain.

N n

The

The Needles. The Weſtern termination of this pariſh, and of the iſland, is an acute point of high land, from which has been disjoined, by the waſhing of the ſea, thoſe lofty white rocks, called the Needles, formerly three in number, but about ſeven years ago, Lot's wife the talleſt of them, called Lot's Wife, which roſe a hundred and twenty feet above low-water mark, and in ſhape reſembled a needle, being undermined by the conſtant efforts of the waves, overſet, and totally diſappeared.

T H E E N D

Godſhill Church

TABLE

OF

CONTENTS

OF THE

APPENDIX.

C O N T E N T S.

CONTENTS.

XXXVII.

C O N T E N T S.

CONTENTS.

CONTENTS.

CONTENTS.

CONTENTS.

A P P E N D I X.

Nº I.

Lift of the refpective LANDHOLDERS in the ISLE OF Wight, with the Valuation of the Lands; extracted from Domefday Book, 20 William I. with Notes.

Hic annotantur tenentes tiaf. in infula de With.

1. Rex Willelmus.
2. Epf. Wintonienfis.
3. Eccla. S. Nicolai.
4. Abbatia de Lire.
5. Abbatia Wiltunienf.
6. Wills. filius Sher.
7. Wills. filius Azor.
8. Gozelin filius Azor.
9. Goderic pbz. et alii plures.

Terra Regis *
Hæ terre infra fciipte jacent in infula de Wit.

REX ten. in dnio *Chenijtone* & *Done*. octo. libi. hoes tenuer. in alodiu. de rege E. Tc. geldav. p. ii hid. ✝ modo p. nichilo. Oda cu.
ii libis. hoib. habuit dimid. hid. & quarta parte uni. v. Alwold. i viig.

Kingfton and Dean.

Herould.

* The lands found in the poffeffion of the king, came to him by the forfeiture of Roger earl of Hereford, lord of the ifland

✝ Moft of the writers on antiquity, as well as the lawyers, having been mif-taken in the *hide*, which they all conclude to be a meafure of land, it may be neceffary to examine more particularly what is meant by a hide of land. If lord Coke and others, who think it was the fame with a carucate, had confidered duly how the hides and carucates appear in Domefday book, they never could have been betrayed into that error · it being obvious that hides and carucates are there diftinguifhed from each other. The order of that book is, I To note the pof-feffor 2. The name of the lands. 3 The rate or value of the lands in hides. 4 The quantity in carucates, or plough lands, virgates, or yard lands, bovates, &c. After thefe particulars, we fee the houfes, fervants, cottagers, woods, &c. The number of carucates almoft always exceeds that of the hides, in one place more carucates make the hide than another, which difference arifes either from the quality of the land, or perhaps fometimes from the favour of the commiffioners in making the rates We find alfo, that feveral manors are rated lower, or at a lefs number of hides, in this tax book, than they had been rated in the time of Ed-

a

ward

Herould. i virg. Goduin. i virg. Alric. una v. Biictric. dim. hid. un. quisq̃. hor. parte. molini que pars xxii denar. hor. v tainor tra. ten. rex in firma sua & ht. ibi ii car. in dnio & appciat. c. sol. & tam. redd. viii. lib. de firma.

Qd Oda tenuit xi sol Qd. Alwold. v sol Qd. Herold. v solid.

Longdown and Bingbourn.   *Ladone* & *Bedingeborne* ten. rex in dnio. Oda tenuit in alodiu. de rege E. Tc geldav. p. iiii hid. & mo p. dim. hida. Tra. e. iii car. Rex ten. in firma sua. Oda habeb. iiii lib. de firma.

Sandford and Week.   *Sandford* cu. *Wua* ten. rex in dnio. Rex E. tenuit tc. in hide qdo. viecom. recep. ii hide & una v. Tra. e. xii car. In dnio sunt iii car & x villi. & iii bord. cu. vi car. Ibi x servi & ii molini de lxx denar & vi ac. pti. De herbagio xx sol. Silva sine pasnagio T. R. E. xxv lib. ad pensu. & arsura. qdo. rex recep. xx lib. simili modo & nc. xx lib. ad pensu & tam. redd. de firma xxvi lib. ad pensu. & c denar.

Arreton.   *Adrington* ten. rex in dnio. Rex E. tenuit. Ibi iiii hide. Tra. e. v. car. In dnio. sunt iii car. & x villi. & xii bord. cu. x car. Ibi vii servi & un. molin. de xv solid. Huj. m. ecclam ten. abb. de Lira cu. una v. tre. & una ac. pti. & omi. decima m appciat. xx solid.

Totu. m. T. R. E. valb. x lib. & post. & mo. viii lib. Tam. redd. xii lib. blancas. de xx in ora.

Yaverland.   *Everelant* ten. rex in dnio Rex. E tenuit non suit hidata. Tra. e. v car. Ibi sunt xii villi. cu. v car. T. R. E. valb. c sol. & post. & mo. iiii lib. tam. redd. c solid.

Adgetor.   *Avedestone* ten. rex in dnio. Tres libi. hoes tenuer. in alodiu. de rege E. tc & mo. geldav. p. una hida. Tra. e. iii car. Ibi sunt xi villi. cu. iiii car. Val & valuit xl. solid. tam. redd. lx sol. albas.

In insula ht rex un. frustu tre. unde exeunt vi vomeres.

Scaldeford ten. rex in dnio. Savoid tenuit in alodiu. de rege E. tc. & mo. geldav. p dim. hida. Tra. e. i car. Ibi sunt iii villi. cu. i. car. & dim. Val. & valuit xiii sol. tam. redd. xvi sol. & viii den.

ward the Confessor. and some are said not to be rated, because they were in the king's hands For instance, the manor of Boucomb, one of the most considerable manors in the island, which had paid for four hides in the Confessor's time, is here not rated at all; and yet it is said to contain fifteen carucates of land. From hence the hide plainly appears to be the discretional rate, or valuation fixed to ascertain the Danegeld, which tax was also termed hidage, and the carucate, to be the content of the land in acres.

Lisielande

Lifcelande ten. rex in dnio. Quinq. libi. hoes. tenuer. in alodiu. p. v maner. de rege E. Tc. geldav. p una hida & dimidia viiga. modo. p. dim. hida & dim virga. Almar habuit dim hida, Ulnod dim. virg. Suaran dimid. v. Odeman dim. v. Godman una v. Tra. e. ii car Ibi funt iiii villi. hntes. in dnio. ii car. & dim. & v acs. pti. Val. & valuit xx folid.

Lovecumbe ten. rex. Sawin tenuit in alodiu. de rege E. Tc. geldav. p una hida. mo. p. ii partib. uni. v. Tra. e. i car & ibi e. in dnio cu. vi bord. & ii fervis. T. R. E. valb. iiii lib. & poft. & mo. iii lib. tam. iedd. de fiima iiii lib. — **Luccombe.**

Nonoelle ten rex. Ulflet tenuit de Tofti com fed n fuit alodiu Tc. geldav. p ii hid modo p. una v Tra e. i car. & dimid. In dnio. e car & i vills. & ii bord. cu. dim. car & iii fervis. T R. E. valb lx fol. & poft. & modo xl. fol & tam. redd. de fiima albas. — **Nunwell.**

Lacherne ten. iex. Herald com. tenuit Tc geldav p. una hida mo. p. nichilo. Tra. e i car. & ibi e. in dnio. cu. ii boid. & v fervis. T. R. E. xxv folid. & poft. & modo xx folid. — **Kerne.**

Ulwai tone ten. rex. Eddeva tenuit de Godvino com. Tc. geldav. p. dimid. hida mo. p. nichilo. Tra. e. i car. & ibi e. in dnio. cu. iii boid. & uno feivo. Val. & valuit x fol. — **Hulveiftone.**

Sande ten. rex Ulnod tenuit de rege E. in alodiu. Tc. geldav. p. ii hid. modo p. dimid. & dimid. v. tia. e. iii car. In dnio. e. una cai. & vii villi. & uno bord cu. iiii car. & iiii ac. pti. Valuit xl fol. mo. xxx — **Sandown.**

Waiocheffelle ten. rex. Gueda comitiffa tenuit de Godvino comite in alodiu. Tc. geldav. p. v hid. modo p. ii hid. & dimid. Tra. e x car. In dnio. funt iiii car. & x villi. & xxiiii bord. cu. vii cai Ibi xxvii feivi & molini de xx folid. & iii ac. pti. Silva de uno porc. T. R. E. valb. xxvii lib. & poft mo xx lib. tam. redd. xxii lib. — **Wioxall.**

Hafelie ten. rex Herald. com. tenuit, tc. geldav. p. iii hid modo p. una v. & dim. Tia e. iiii car. In dnio. funt ii & iii villi & iiii boid. cu ii car. Ibi xv feivi & x ac. pti. Silva de ii poic. T. R. E. valb. viii lib. & poft. & mo c fol tam. redd viii lib. de firma de xx in ora. — **Hafely.**

Benverdeftei ten. rex Godum. tenuit de iege in alodiu. Tc. geldav p. una hida mo. p. dim. hida & dim v Tra. e. ii cai. ibi funt iii villi. cu. una car. Silva de uno porc. Valuit xl. fol. mo. xx folid. — **Binnells**

Chochepon & *Ethoiii* ten. rex. Duo lib. hoes. tenuer p ii manei. in alodiu. de iege E. Tc. geldav. p. una hida mo. p. iii viig. Iia e.

ı caı. & ibi e cu. iii villıs. Valuıt xxx ſol. modo xx ſol. & tam. redd. xxx ſol.

Hoteleſton ten. rex. Alnod tenuıt de rege E. ın alodıu. Tc geldav. p tcıa. parte hıdæ modo p. dım. vırg. Tra e. dım car. & ibi e. cu. ıii bord. Valuıt x ſol mo. v ſol.

Stenburȝ ʌnd Whıppıng-hʌm.

Staneberıe & *Wıp.ngeba* ten. rex. Chepıng tenuıt ın alodıu. de rege E p. ıı maneı. tc. geldav. p. iii hıd. mo. p ıı hd. Tra e vii car. In dnıo. ſunt ıı & vıı vıllı. & x bord. cu. vi car. Ibi xii ſervi & v. ac. ph. Val. & valuıt ſep xıı lıb.

Wenechetone ten rex. Duo lıbi hoes. tenueı. ın alodıu. de rege E. p. duob. m. Tc. geldav. p. una hıda mo p. nıchılo. Tra. e. ıı car. & ibı ſunt cu ıı vıllis. Valuıt & val. ıiı lıb.

De his tam duob. m. exeunt de firma xviii lıb. de xx ın ora.

In *Soflet* eſt una v. de ıſto m. hanc tenuıt Bolla de rege E. ın alod. nc. het. ıex ın fııma ſua.

Nıton.

Neeton & *Abla* ten. rex. Duo lıbi. hoes. tenuer. ın alodıu. de rege E. p ıı mancr. Tc. geldav p. iii hid. mo. p. una hida & una v. Tra. e. viıı car. In dnıo. ſunt iıı car. & vii villi. & xviiı bord. cu. v car. Ibı ıx ſeıvi. T. R. E. valb. xvıı lıb. & poſt. & mo. xıı lıb. tam. redd. xvıı lıb.

Wootton.

Odetone ten. rex. Eddid regina tenuıt. Tc. mo. geldav. p. una hıda. Ibı ſunt iıiı vıllı. cu. iiı car. Val. & redd. iiı lıb.

Terra Regıs ın ınſula de With *.

In Bovecome hd.

Bıook.

Rex Wılˡelmus ten. ın dnıo *Broc*. Toˤti com. tenuıt tc. p. iii. hid. modo p. una hıda. Tra. e. vi car. In dnıo. ſunt iı car & iıı villı. & vıı boıd. cu. ıı car. & dımıd. ıbi ıx ſervi & molın de xv den. & vı ac. pti. T. R. E. ıalb. vıı lıb. & poſt. vi lıb. modo vii lib. & tam. redd. vıiˡlıb. plus.

---

* Domeſday Book beıng rather a roll of the landholders in each county than a regular ſurvey of the manors, the latter are to be ſought for under the names of theıı reſpectıve proprıetors Thoſe who held eſtates ın the Iſle of Wıght, are indeed claſſed apart from the reſt of Hampſhıre, ın the oıder hereafter copıed, the manors already recıted exıepted, whıch were found among the king's lands at the beginnıng of this county lıſt, and are not dıſtınguıſhed by the hundred they ſtand ın.

Ipſe

Ipfe **Rex** ten. in dnio. *Cantune.* Tofti com. tenuit. Tc. fe defd. p. iii   *Compton.*
hid modo p. una hida. Tra. e. iiii car. In dnio. e. una & vii villi. & iii
bord. cu. ii car. ibi un. ferv. & ii ac. pti. T. R. E. valb. vi lib. & poft.
& mo. c fol tam. redd. lx fol. plus.

Ipfe rex ten. in dnio. *Affetune.* Tofti com tenuit. Tc. p. iiii hid. mo   *Affeton.*
p. iii hid. una v. min. Tra. e. viii car. In dnio funt ii & xiiii villi & viii
bord. cu. vi car. ibi xii fervi & vi ac. pti. T. R. E. valb. x lib. & poft.
& modo viii lib. Tam. redd. x lib.

Ipfe **Rex** ten. in dnio. *Welige.* Coolf tenuit in paragio * de rege. Tc.   *Wellow.*
p. ii hid mo. p iii virg. Tra. e. iiii car. In dnio funt ii & vi villi &
iii bord. cu. i car. & dim. ibi iiii fervi & vi ac. pti. T. R. E & poft. &
mo. valb. x lib. Tam. eft ad firma de xv lib.

Ipfe **Rex** ten. in dnio. *Frefcewatie* Tofti com. tenuit Tc fe defd. p.   *Frefhwater.*
xv hid. modo p. vi hid. Tra e. xv car. In dnio funt ii car & xviii villi.
& x bord. cu. viii. car. ibi vii fervi & vi ac pti T. R E valb. xvi lib
& poft. xx lib. Tam. eft ad firma de xxx lib. De his xv hid. ten. abb. de
Lira iii virg. & Wills. fil. Azor una hid.

Ifd. **Rex** ten. in dnio *Wilmingeham* Ulviet venator tenuit in paragio.   *Wilming-*
Tc. & mo. p. una hida. Tra. e. i car. ibi iii villi. cu. ii car. & dim. ac.   *ham.*
pti. Val. & valuit xx folid.

De hoc m. regis ten. Raynald. fil. Croc una v. & dicit qd. Rogeri
com. dedit ea. patri fuo. Valuit v fol. mo. eft vaftata.

Ipfe **Rex** ten in dnio *Bovecome*, de firma regis E fuit. Tc. fe defd.   *Bovcombe.*
p. iiii hid. modo p. nichilo. Tra. e. xv car In dnio fuit iii car. & xxv
villi. & xv bord. cu. xv car ibi x fervi & viii ac pti. & molin. de xi den.
De theloneo † xxx fol. & falina fine cenfu. Silva de v porc.

De tra. huj. m. ten. Willi. f. Shei dim. v. ibi e. i car. cu. uno villo.
val. x fol. Gozelin. & Wills. fr. ej. ten. una v. que ante eos reddeb. ga-
blu. s. ifti n. reddider.

Huj. m. ecclam ‡. cu una v. tie. ten. monachi de Lire.

De

---

* This tenure *in paragio* is not clearly determined; fome confidering it as denoting an independent tenure, and others as the holding of lands in purpuity between two heirs. *Paragium* fignifies equality of name, blood, or dignity, but
more efpecially of land, in the partition of an inheritance between colers .
hence comes, to difparage, and difparagement *Co Li* 166

† Toll

‡ The church, which is here called the church of the manor of Bovcomb, is
the

De hac v. tre. ten. Hunfred. tant. ubi ht. viii hoes. redd. v. fol. & Wills. f. Azor ii acs & dim. ubi ht. iiii dom. hi ten. abſq. voluntate pbri. Ad hanc ecclam. adjacent xx maſure bordarior. & reddt. xiii fol. ibi molin. de vi ſolid. & oms decime Bovecome ſunt ipſius eccle.

Tot T. R. E. & poſt. & modo val. xx lib. Qd. ht. abb. iiii lib. Iſd. Rex ten. in dnio. *Heldelie*. Cheping tenuit de rege E Tc. ſe defd. p. vi virg modo p ii v. un ferding min. Tra. e. iii **car**. In dnio. e. una & iiii villi & un. bord. hnt. ii car. Silva de ii porc. & v ſervi. Val. iii lib.

Lemeiſtone.   Ipſe Rex ten. *Leviagtune*. Ulviet venator tenuit in paragio. Tc. p. una hida modo p. dim. Tra. e ii car. ibi iiii villi. & ii bord. hnt. ii car. ibi ii ſervi. Silva ad clauſura. Val. & valuit xx fol.

Shide.   Iſd. Rex ten. *Side*. Chetel tenuit in paragio. Tc. p. una hida & dim. mo. p. una tant. Tra. e. iiii car. In dnio. e una & v villi. & viii bord. cu. iii cai. Ibi un. ſerv. & iiii molini de xii ſolid. & vi den. & iiii ac pti. Silva ad clauſura. Val. & valuit iiii lib.

De his iiii pnominatis. m. iedd. Wills. f. Stui lx lib. quavis. min. valeant.

Shorwell.   Iſd. Rex ten. *Sorewelle*. Tres taini tenuer. in paragio & iii aulas habuer. Tc. p. una hida & dim. modo p. iii virg. Tra. e. iii car. In dnio. e una car. & dim. & ii villi. & viii bord. cu. i cai. ibi vi ſervi. Silva ad clauſura Val & valuit iiii lib.

Atherfield, Dunmoſe, and Wilpan.   Iſd. Rex ten. tria m *Auriſel, Duniorde, Valpedie*. Tres taini tenuer. Tc. p. iii hid. modo p. una hida. Tra. e. iii car. In dnio. ſunt ii & un. villi. & v bord. cu. ii car. ibi iiii ſervi & vi ac. pli. Val. & valuit iii lib. tam. redd. vii lib.

Kingſton.   Iſd. Rex. ten. *Chingeſtune*. Uluric. tenuit in paragio. Tc. p. una hida mo. p una v. Tra e ii car. ibi vi bord. hnt. una. car. ibi iiii ac. pti. Val. & valuit xv fol. tam. redd. xxx fol.

Avington.   Iſd. Rex ten. *Alwineſtune*. Donnus tenuit. Tc. p. duab. hid. & dim. modo p ii hid. ga. caſtellu. ſedet in una v. Tra. e vi car. ibi viii villi. & ii bord. cu. iiii car. ibi ii molini de v fol. & vi ac. pti Val & valuit iii lib tam iedd. iiii lib.

the ſame which has ſince obtained the name of Careſbrook, and as this latter name does not occur in Domeſday Book, the old received opinion that it was called Careſbrook from Whitgar the Saxon prince of the iſland, can have no foundation beyond the fanciful conjecture of ſome monkiſh etymologiſt.

In

In Cauborne hd. qd. jacet in Bovecome hund.

Walchelin. epf. Winton. ten. in dnio. *Cauborne.* Sept. fuit in monaf- terio *. Ibi funt xxxii hide. Sed. T. R E. & mo. n. geld. nifi p. xvii. hid. Tra e. xxv car. In dnio. funt vi car. & xxvii villi & xv bord cu. xiiii car. ibi xi fervi & ii molini de vi fol. & iii den. & viii. ac. pti. Silva de xx porc.

De hac tra. ten. vi hid. Herpul ii hid. & Alfi iii hid. & dim. Has hidas tenuer. vii alodiarii de epo. nec poterant recede. alio l. ab illo. Ibi funt iii car & dim. & iii villi & xxii bord. cu v car ibi xii fervi & xv ac. pti.

Ecclam. huj. m. ten. Malger. cu. dim. hida & ibi ht. i car cu. uno bord.

Tot m. T. R. E. & poft. valuit xvi lib modo qd. eps. ht. xxx lib. & tam. e. ad firma. p. xl lib. fed n. poteft pati nec redd. qd. hoes. ten. vii lib. eccla. xxx fol.

Calborn or Swey mefton.

Qd. ten. Ses. Nicolaus †.

Scs. Nicolaus ht. i hid. in *Efeldecome* de rege W. Alwin. forft. tenuit. Tc. fe defd. p. una hida. mo. p. nichilo. Tra. e. ii car. & ibi funt in dnio. cu. uno bord. Valuit iiii lib. mo. iii lib.

Shalcombe.

Qd. ten. Sca. Maria de Lire.

Abbatia S. Marie de Lire ht. in infula de Wit. vi ecclas. quibz. ptin. ii hide & ii virg. tre. & dim. & in plurib. m. hnt. v villos. qui ten. i hid. & dimid. qrta. part. uni. v min.

Decimas hnt. de omib. redditionib. regis. Tot. qd. hnt. appciat. xx lib. Geld. redd. de ii hid & dim. v. tre.

---

* That the bifhop of Winchefter fhould hold Calborn, which is faid to have been always in the monaftery, appears like a contradiction. But it muft be noted that thofe bifhops whofe cathedrals were conventual, held their lands in common, and undivided from the convents by whom they were elected At that time a grant to the church of Winchefter, was to the bifhop and his convent, and thus it remained until the reign of king Edward I. when the bifhop, John de Pontiffera, divided the revenues with the convent. This feparation of interefts in the church lands, was probably occafioned by the king withholding the temporalities of the church of Winchefter from that bifhop, which tranfaction is explained in the account of Calborn.

† This is the chapel in the caftle of Carefbrook, which was afterward given to Quarr abbey, as is recited in its proper place.

Tena

Terra Sce. Marie de Wiltune.

Watching-wood. Abbatia de Wiltune ten *Watangewelle*. Sep. fuit in monasterio. T. R. E. se defd. p. iii hid. modo p. ii hid. & dimid. ga. dimid. e. in parco regis *. Tra e. viii car. ibi vii villi. & xii bord. hnt. v car ibi salina fine censu Silva de ii. porc. phi. e. in parco. Val. & valuit iii. lib. qd. rex ht. v. solid.

Terra Willi. filii Stur.

In Bovecome hd.

Chale. Willelm. filii. Stur. ten in dnio. de rege *Cela*. Chetel fuit in paragio. Tc. p. una hida. mo. p. una v. Tra. e. una car. & ibi e. cu. iiii bord. hntib. i car. ibi iiii servi & una ac. pti. T. R. E. & modo val. xl sol. cu. recep. xx sol.

Gotton. Isd. Wills. ten. *Gadetune*. Bruning & fz. ej. tenuer. in paragio. Tc. & mo. se defd p. una hida. Tra. e i car. ibi e. cu. ii bord. & iii acris pti. Val. & valuit xx solid.

Appleford. Isd. Wills. ten. *Apleford* & Robt. de eo. Chetel tenuit in paragio. Tc. & mo. se defd. p. una hida. Tra. e. ii car. In dnio e dim. car. & iii bord. cu. i car. ibi iiii ac. pti. Valuit xvii solid. modo xviii solid.

Gatcombe. Isd. Wills. ten *Gatecome*. Tres frs. tenuer. in paragio de rege E. Tc. se defd p. ii hid. modo p. una hida. Qsq. habuit aula. Tra. e. iiii car. In dnio. funt iii car. & vi villi. & xv bord. cu. v car. ibi vi servi & molin. de iiii den. ibi xxvi ac. pti. Silva ad clausura. T. R. E. & mo. val. vi lib. cu. recep. c sol.

Witcombe. Isd. Wills. ten *Witecome* Godric. tenuit in paragio. Tc. p. una hida mo. p nichilo. Tra. e i car. Ibi e. in dnio. cu. iii bord & ii ac. pti. & dim. Valuit x sol. modo xv sol.

Calborne, now West-over. Isd. Wills. ten. *Cauborne*. Bolla tenuit in paragio Tc. se defd. p. iii hid. dim. v. min. modo p. una v & dim Tra. e. ii car. In dnio. funt ii car. & un. vills. & iii bord. cu i car. ibi iii servi & molin. de v sol & ii ac. pti. & dim. Silva ad clausura. T. R. E. & post valb xxx sol. modo xl solid.

Woolverton. Isd. Wills. ten. *Ulwarcumbe* & Luran de eo. Ipse tenuit in paragio de rege E. Tc. e mo se defd p una hida. Tra e. i car & ibi e. cu.

---

* Here we plainly fee the miftake of fome of our hiftorians, who tell us that Woodftock park, made by king Henry I was the firft park in England H. Knighton dates it in 1119.

uno villo. & ii bord. & molin. de xxxv den. & dim. ac. pti. **Val.** & valuit x folid.

Ifd. Wills. ten. dim. hid. in *Egrafel* & Travers ten. de Willo. Hanc tenuit Ulviet in paragio. Tc. & mo. fe defd p. dim hida. Tra. e. i car. & ibi e. in dnio. cu. i bord. & una ac. pti. & dim. Val. x fol.

Ifd. Wills. ten. *Cevredone* & Hunfrid. de eo. Turchil tenuit in paragio. Tc. & mo. p. una hida. Tra e. 1 car. & dim. In dnio. e. una. & iii villi & un. bord. cu. i car. Silva ad claufura. Valuit xx fol. modo xxx folid.   Chiverton.

Ibide. ht. ifd. Wills. de rege unu. villan. cu dimid. v. tre. & una. acra. tre. & dim. qs. tenuit Rainald. pifto. de Willo comite Furn. comitis fuit ibi. Val. xvi denar. Vills. redd. x folid. p. annu.

Ipfe Wills. fili. Stur. ten. *Hardelei* Godric tenuit in alodiu. de rege E. Tc. fe defd. p. una hida mo. p. dim v. Ibi e. i car. & iii bord. cu. dimid. car. & vui fervi. Silva parva fine pafnagio. Val. & valuit xl folid.   Hirdley.

Ifd. Wills. ten. *Orham.* Godric tenuit in alod. de rege E. Tc. geld. p. dimid. hida. mo. p. una v. Tra. e. i car. In dnio. e. una car. & dimid. & v bord. cu. dim. car. Valuit xl fol. mo. xx fol.

Ifd. Wills. ten. *Wipingeham.* Bolla tenuit de rege E. in alod Tc. & mo. geld. p. una hida. Tra. e. In dnio. e. dim. car. & iii villi. & ii bord. cu. i car. Val. & valuit x fol.   Whipping-ham.

Ifd W. ten. *Witesfel* & Rainald. de eo. Chetel tenuit in alod. de rege E. Tc. & mo. geld. p. una hida. Tra. e. In dnio. e. una car. & un. vills. & iii bord. & un. ferv. cu. dim. car. ibi falina de xiiii fol. & viii den. & una ac. pti. Val. xx folid.   Whitfield.

Ifd. Wills ten. alia. *Witesfel.* Godric tenuit in alodiu. de rege E. Tc. geld p. iii hid. modo p. una hida. Tra e. vi car. In drio. funt iiii car & iiii villi hnt. iii. car. ibi iii molini de xi folid. & viii ac. pti. T. R. E. valb iiii lib. & poft. iii lib. modo vii. lib.

Ifd. W. ten. *Ateballe* & Nigell. de eo. Godric tenuit in alod. de rege E. Tc & mo. geld p. dim. hida. Tra. e i car. In drio. e una & un. vills. & iiii bord. cu una car. & iiii ac. pti. Val. x folid.   Ihle.

Ifd. W. ten. *Beneftede.* Tovi tenuit in alod de rege E p. m. Tc geld. p. v virg. modo p. ii virg. Tra. e. ii car. ibi funt cu. ii villis. Val & valuit x folid.   Binftead.

Ifd. W. ten. *Mereftone* & Hunfrid. de eo. Brictuin. tenuit de rege E. in alod. Tc. & mo. geld p. dimid. hida. In dnio. e. i car. cu. uno villo. Val. & valuit x fol.   Merfton.

Periton. Ifd. W. ten. *Preffetone* Tovi tenuit in alod de rege E. Tc. & mo. geld p ii hid. & una v & dim Tra. e i car Ibi funt viii villi cu. i car & iiii ac. pti & pifcaiia ad aula. Silva de uno porc. Val. & valuit xx folid

Standen. Ifd. W. ten. *Standone* & Hunfiid. de eo. Bolla tenuit de rege E. Tc. & mo. geld. p. una hida & dimid. Tia e. In dnio. e. una car. & ii villi & iii boid. cu. una car Val. & valuit xx fol.

Moniſton. Ifd. W. ten. *Meffetoie* Rex. E. tenuit in dnio. de firma fua fuit nec geldavit Tia. e cai. In dnio. e. una car. & ii villi. & un. bord. & ii fervi cu. i car. Val & valuit xx folid.

Alverſton. Ifd. W. ten. *Alvieftone* & Tovi de eo. Ipfe tenuit de rege E. Tc. & mo. geld p una hida. Tra. e. ii cai. ibi e. un. bord. & molin. de xl denar. Valuit xx folid. modo v folid.

Teira Willelmi filii Azor.

Bonchuich Wills. fili Azor ter. de rege *Bonecerce*. Eftan tenuit de Godvino com. in alod. p. m. Tc geld p. una v. modo p. nichilo. Tra. e. dim. car. ibi funt iii boid. T. R. E. valb. xxx fol. & poft. & modo xx. folid.

Langard. Ifd. Wills. ten. *Leuegareftva*. Duo libi. hoes. tenuer. in alod. de rege E. Tc. geld p dim hida modo p. una v. Tra. e. i car. & ibi e. cu. ix bord Valuit xl fol. modo xxx fol.

Standen. Ifd. W. ten. *Standone*. Duo libi. hoes. tenuer. in alod. de rege E. Tc. geld. p v virg. modo p. una v. Tia. e. ii car. In dnio. e. una car. cu. uno boid. De hac tra. ten. qda. Peurel dimid. v. ibi ht. i car. T. R. E. valb. xxx folid. & poft xv fol. modo dniu. Willi xl fol. Peurel x fol.

Briddlesford. Ifd. W. ten. *Breiesforde* & Nigell. de eo. Unlof tenuit in alod. de rege E. Tc. & mo. geld. p. una hida. Tia. e. iiii car In dnio. e. una & v villi. & v bord. cu. iiii cai. Valuit xx folid. modo xl folid.

Yaverland. Ifd. W. ten *Evreland*. Almer & Soartin tenuer in alod. de rege E. Tc. geld. p. iii hid. modo p. una v. Tra. e. iii car. In dnio. e. una cai. cu. viii boid. & molin de xii foli. ibi una ac. pti. & dimid. Valuit iii lib. & poft. iiii lib. mo. c. fol.

Ifd. W. ten. *Selins*. Algar tenuit de rege E. Tc. geld. p. una hida. mo. p. iii virg. Tra. e. i cai. In dnio. e. dim. car. & iii villi. & ii bord. & ii fervi cu. una car. Silva de ii poic. T. R. E. & modo val. xl. fol. cu. recep. xx fol.

Brading. Ifd. W. ten. *Beraidin* & nepos ej. ten. de eo. Alnod tenuit in alod. de rege F. p. m. Tc. & mo. geld. p. tiib. partib. uni v. Tra. e. dim.

Cai

car. In dnio. e. una car. cu. iiii bord. & una ac. pti. Silva de ii porc. Valuit x fol. modo xx folid.

Ifd. W. ten. *Bourdourde* & *Brandeftone* & *Liteftand.* Duo libi. hoes. de rege E. p. duob. m. in alod. Tc. & mo. geld. p. una hida & uno v. Tra. e. ii car. & in uno m. In dnio un. vills. & ii. bord. cu. dim. car. & ii ac. pti.   Boidwood.

De hac tia. ten. nepos Willi. una v. & Peurel dim. hida & una v. Tot. T. R. E. valb. xxx fol. & poft. xx fol. modo xvi fol.

Ifd. W. ten. in *Bochepone* x acs. & ibi e. un. boid. Val. iii fol.   Blackpan.

Ifd. W. ten. *Scaldeford.* Ofgot tenuit in alod. de rege E. Tc. & mo. geld. p. una v. Tia. e. i car. & ibi e. cu. iii villis. Silva de ii poic. Valuit xvi fol. modo x folid.

Ifd. W. ten. *Witeftone* & *Wills.* & Ricard. de eo. Elmer tenuit de rege E. in alod. Tc. & mo. p. una hida geld. Tra. e. ii car. In dnio. e. una cu. iii villis. Valuit xxx fol. mo. xx fol.

Ifd. Wills. ten. *Benveflei* & Rogeri. de eo. Ulnod tenuit de rege E. Tc. & mo. geld. p. dimid. hida. Tra. e. i car. ibi eft un. boid. Valuit x fol. modo vii folid. •   Barnefly.

Ifd. W. ten. *Rodeberge.* Abb. de Winceftre tenuit in alod. de rege E. Tc. & mo. geld. p. una v. Tia. e. i cai. Ibi e. in dnio. cu. uno villo. cu. ii bord. & dim. cai. Valuit v fol. mo. xx fol.   Rowbury.

Ifd. W. ten. *Lamore* & Arfchitil. de eo. Tres libi hoes. tenuei. de rege E. Tc & mo. geld. p. dim. hida. Tia. e. i car. In dnio. e. una cai. & v bord. cu. dim. cai. Valuit xxx foid. modo xx fol.

Ifd. W. ten. *Aviceftone.* Godric tenuit de rege E. in alod. Tc. & mo. geld. p. una v. & tcia. parte uni v. Tia. e. i car. ibi manet qda. vavaffoii. hns. ii vac. Val. & valuit x fol.   Wefton.

Ifd. W. ht. in infula qdda. fi uftu. tre. unde exeunt iii vomeres.

Iteiu. Wills. filius Azor ten. de rege *Modreftan.* Quatuor taini tenuer. in paragio. Tc. p. ii hid. modo p. ii vi g. & divid. Tra. e. iiii car. In dnio. e. una cai. & vii fervi & vii boid. cu. i car. & xvi ac. pti. I. R. E. valb. x. lib. & poft. & modo vi lib.   Mottifton.

Ifd. W. ten. *Seureome.* Leving ten. in paragio Tc p. una hida mo p. dim. v. Tia. e. i car. ibi funt ii bord. & ii fervi & molin. & ii ac. pti. Val. xl. fol.

Ifd. W. ten. in *Hameftede* dim. hid. & Nigell de eo. Aluric tenuit in paragio. Tc. & mo. p. dim. hida. Tia. e. uni. car. & ibi e. cu. ii vill... & ii boid. Val. & valuit xx fol.   Hamftead.

     Ifd.

Chillerton. Ifd. W. ten. dimid. hid. in *Celatune* & Wills. foreſt. de eo. Aluric tenuit in parag. Tc. & mo. ſe defd. p. dim. hida. Tra. e. 1 car. Valuit x ſol. modo v ſolid.

Shide. Ifd. W. ten. in *Sida* una hid. & una v. Ednod tenuit in paragio. Tc. p. v virg. mo. p. iii virg. Tra. e. iii car. In dnio. nichil. ſed xv bord. & iiii ſervi cu. i. car. & dim. ibi mo'in. de x ſolid. & ii ac. pti. Silva ad clauſura. T. R. E. & poſt. valb. xl ſolid. modo lx ſolid.

Fichwater. Ifd. W. & Roger de eo ten. in *Freſcewatre* i. hid. & p. tanto geld. Hanc tenuit qda. ppoſit. Tofti in m. de Freſcewatre. Tra. e. 1 car. & ibi e. in dnio. cu. iii bord. T. R. E. & modo valb. xl ſol. cu. recep. xx ſol.

Chillerton. Ifd. W. & Goiffrid. de eo. ten. in *Celertune* una v. & p. tanto ſe defd. Blacheman ten. in paragio. Tra. e. i car. & ibi e. in dnio. cu. ii. bord. & uno ſervo. Valuit xx ſol. modo xxx ſolid.

Terra Gozelini filii Azor.

Gozelinus fili. Azor ten. de rege *Scaldeford* Oſgot tenuit in alod. de rege E. Tc. & mo. geld. p. una v. Tra. e. i car. & ibi e. in dnio. Azor ten. de Gozelino. T. R. E. valb. xl. ſol. & poſt. xx ſol. modo xxx ſolid.

Ifd. Gozelin. ht. in inſula un. fruſtu. tre. unde exeunt iii vomeres.

Roude. Ifd. Gozelin. ten. *Rode.* Alnod tenuit in alod. de rege E. Tc. geld. p. iii hid. mo. p. v viig. tie. & dimid. Tra. e. vi car. In dnio. ſunt ii car. & vi bord. & iiii ſervi cu. una car. & iiii ac. pti. De iſto m. ten. Azor una v. & Sauvin. dim. hid. & qrta. parte. uni v. & Nigell. iii partes uni. v. In dnio e. una car. & un. vills. & ii bord. cu. i car.

Tot T. R. E. valb. ix lib. & poſt. viii lib. modo viii lib. & x ſol.

Shanklin Ifd. Gozelin. ten. *Senchz.* Sex libi. hoes. tenuer. de rege E. in alod. Tc. geld. p. iii hid. & dim. modo p v. virg. tre. & dim. Tra. e. v car. In dnio. ſunt ii car. & iiii villi. & ii bord. & ii ſervi cu. ii car.

De iſto m. ten. Livol. i hid. & ibi ht. ii bord. cu. dim. car. Tot. T. R. E. valb. viii lib. & poſt. vi lib. modo vii lib.

Ifd. Gozelin. ten. *Weriſtetone.* Tres libi. hoes. tenuer. in alod. de rege F. Tc. & mo. geld. p. ii hid. & iii virg. & tcia. parte uni. v. Tra. e. iiii car. Hanc tra. tenent iiii hoes. de Gozelino, Wills. & alt. Wills. Goiffrid. & Dovenold. Ibi e. in dnio. una car. Tot. T. R. E. valb. c ſol. & poſt. & modo l ſol. int. oms.

Shide. Ipſe Gozelin. ten. de rege *Sida.* Ednod tenuit de rege E. Tc. ſe defd. p. ii hid. una v. min. modo p. una hida & dim. Tra. e. iiii car. In dnio.

e una

e. una car. & iii villi. & ii bord. cu. i car. & dim. ibi iii fervi & ii molini de v folid. & ii ac. pti. T. R. E. & modo val. l fol. cu. recep. xl fol.

Ifd. Gozelin. ten. una v. in *Celertune* & Goiffrid. ten. de Gozelino. **Chillerton.**
Blacheman tenuit in paragio. Tc. & mo. p. una v. Tra. e. i car. & ibi e.
in dnio. Val. & valuit x fol.

Ifd. Goz. ten. *Sorewelle.* Ulnod. tenuit in paragio. Tc. p. ii. hid. & una **Shorwell.**
v. modo p. dim. hida. Tia. e. ii car. & dim. In dnio. e. una & ii villi.
& vi boid. cu. una car. & dim. ibi iii fervi & molin. de xl den. & xiiii
ac. pti. T. R. E. & poft. valb. c fol. modo iiii lib.

Ifd. Goz. ten. *Seldeflet.* Edricus tenuit T. R. E. & tc. fe defd. p. vi **Shalfleet.**
hid. modo p. iii hid. & dim. v. Tia. e. xiiii car. In dnio. funt ii & xiii
villi. & xix bord. cu. ix car. & dim. ibi molin. de xi den. & iiii ac. pti.
ibi eccla. Silva de xx porc.

De hac tra. ten. Goiffrid. ii virg. & dim. & ibi una car. cu. ii villis.
& uno bord. & Tuigifus dim. hid. Liof. i hid. Hi hnt. in dnio. ii car.
& ii villos. & ii bord. cu. dim. car.

Tot. T. R. E. & poft. valb. xx lib. modo xv lib. int. oms.

Ifd. Goz. ten. *Hameftede.* Aluric tenuit in paragio. Tc. & mo. p. dim. **Hamftead.**
hid. Tra. e. i car. ibi ii fervi & un. vills. cu. dim. car. Val. & valuit xx
folid.

Ifd. Goz. ten. *Ulvredeftune.* Aluric tenuit in paragio. Tc. & mo. p.
una hida. Tra. e. ii car. In dnio. e. una & dim. & un. vills. & iii bord.
cu. i car. ibi iii fervi & una ac. pti. Val. & valuit lx folid. Turald. ten.
de Goz.

Ifd. Goz. ht. dimid. hid. in *Celatune* Aluric tenuit & tc. & mo. p. **Chillerton.**
dimid. hida fe defd. Tra. e. i car. & ibi e. cu. ii vil'is. & iiii ac. pti. Val.
& valuit x folid.

Terre Tainor. Regis *.

Godric pbz. ten. de rege *Meleusford.* Ipfe tenuit in paragio de rege
E. tc. & mo. p. una hida & dim. v. Tra. e. dim. car. In dnio. tam. e.

una.

* We here find fome few perfons who retained poffeffion of the lands they enjoyed in the time of Edward the Confeffor. Thefe were probably officers under
the crown, who acted as bailiffs over the king's lands, and might have been con
tinued by William the Conqueror, as better qualified for fuch fervice than ftrangers. The learned Selden, in his notes on Eadmerus, p. 170. clearly proves
that thefe *Taini Regis* were no other than the king's fervants, and they had their
refpective offices, though they are not here fpecified, as they are in fome other

una. car. cu. uno bord. & molin. fine cenfu. & pti. i ac. & dim. Val. & valuit x fol.

Thorley. Alfi fili. Briisi ten. *Torlei.* Tofti comes tenuit. Tc. fe defd. p. iii hid. modo p. ii hid. Tra. vii. car. In dnio. funt ii & x villi. & xi bord. cu. vi car. ibi vii fervi & vi ac. pti. T. R. E. & poft valuit viii lib. mo. xii lib.

Sheat. Alric ten. & tenuit in *Effuete* i hida. & p. tanto fe defd. Tra. e. dim. car. In dnio. e. una car. & ii fervi & un. bord. & molin. fine cenfu. Valuit x fol. modo xv. fol.

Hill. Ulnod ten. & tenuit *Alalei* T. R. E. & mo. geld. p. una v. In dnio. e. dimid. car. Val. v. fol. valuit vii fol.

Herbrand ten de rege *Lepene.* Godric tenuit de rege E. Tc. & mo. geld. p. una hida. Tra. e. iiii car. In dnio. e. una car. & iiii villi. cu. ii car. ibi ii ac. pti. filva fine pafnag. Valb. iiii lib. modo iii lib.

Wefton. Edric ten. *Avneftone.* Ipfemet tenuit de rege E. Tc. & mo. geld. p. dim. v. Tra. e. dim. car. ibi e. in dnio. cu. ii bord. & ii fervis. Val. & valuit v folid.

Bagwich. Oirant ten. *Celvecrote.* Pat. ej. ten. de rege E. Tc. & mo. geld. p. dim. v. In dnio. e. dimid. car. cu. uno bord. Val. & valuit v folid.

Alfi ten. de rege *Abaginge.* Ipfemet tenuit de rege E. in alod. Tc. & mo.

places in Domefday book, where Cela is mentioned as the king's huntfman, Godwin the falconer, Milo the porter, Herebert the chamberlain, &c. Yet it is to be obferved, that they are diftinguifhed into *thani majores*, and *minores*. The *thani majores* were fuch as ferved the crown in a fuperior capacity, and were efteemed next in degree to an earl. though both thefe were rather names of office than titles. Without a due attention to circumftances, William Fitz Ofborn might be charged with great injuftice and cruelty for having turned almoft all the people of the ifland out of their lands, who had made no oppofition to his taking poffeffion there. and this will appear the greater hardfhip, if, as fome authors have afferted, king William oufted none but thofe who had been in arms, or otherwife acted againft him. But to extenuate the conduct of Fitz Ofborn it muft be remembered, that at the coming in of the Normans, many of the greateft men held their lands from the crown by grant for life only, or a leffer eftate. and that no man under the rank of a thane, could difpofe of his lands without licence, while moft of the lower fort held their lands at the will of fome earl or thane. This being the cafe, Fitz Ofborn, who had an abfolute grant of the ifland from the Conqueror, (fuppofing a right in William to grant) might legally take lands from the tenants at will, and beftow them on his followers. nor could he in good policy leave the Englifh in poffeffion of the ifland.

                                                                              geld.

geld. p. una v. Tra. e. dim. car. ibi dimid. ac. pti. Valuit v folid. modo iii folid.

Ulward ten. de rege *Witingeham*. Ipfe tenuit de rege E. in alod. Tc. & mo. geld. p. dim. hida. In dnio. e. dim. car. cu. iii bord. Val. & valuit x folid.

Alric & nepos ej. ten. de rege *Hoteleftone*. Ipfemet tenuer. in alod. de rege E. Tc. & mo. geld. p. tcia. parte uni hide. Tra. e. dim. car. & ibi e. in dnio. Val. & valuit v fol.

Hunfrid. ten. de rege tcia. parte. uni hide in *Hoteleftone*. Godefa tenuit in alod. de rege E. Tc. & mo. geld. p. tcia. parte uni. hide. Tra. e. iii car. In dnio. e. una car. & ii ac. pti. Valuit lx. fol. modo xx folid.

Edwi ten. *Apledeforde*. Ipfemet tenuit de rege E. in alod. Tc. & mo. geld. p. dimid hida. Tra. e. i car. In dnio. e. dimid car. cu. uno bord. & ii ac. pti. & dim. Valuit xx fol. modo x folid.

Soartin ten. *Drodntone* de rege. Ipfe & alter lib. homo tenuer. in alod. de rege E. Tc. geld. p. una hida & dim. tcia parte uni. v. min.

In dnio. e. dim. cai. & un. vills. & un. bord. cu. i cai.

De ifto m. ten. Wills. ii partes uni hide ad firma. & ibi ht. i. car. Valuit xxxii fol. modo xlii fol.

Godric ten. de rege *Ovingefort*. Ipfe tenuit de rege E. Tc. & mo. geld. p. una v. ibi un. vills. ht. dim. car. Valet xl denar.

Tovi ten. de dono regis in *Cheniftone* dim. v. Bondi tenuit de rege E. in   Kingfton. alod. Tc. & mo. geld. p. dim. v. ibi e. un. vills. Val. & valuit iii fol.

In Hemrefwel hd.

Aluric & Wiflac hnt. i. hid. & ii virg. & dim. in *Ermud*. Ipfi tenuer. in paragio de rege E. Tc. & mo. fe detd. p. una hida & ii virg. & dimid. Tra. e. ii cai. ibi vii villi. & ii bord. hntes. ii car. Valuit xii fol. modo xxv fol.

Ulnod & Bruning hnt. dim. hid. in *Soete*. Ipfi tenuer. in paragio. Tc. & mo. p. dim hida. Tra. e. i cai. ibi iii villi. hnt. i car. & molin. de xl den. & ii ac. pti. Val. & valuit x folid.

Gerin ht. una hid. in *Lemmode*. Rex E. habuit in firma fui tc. & mo. p. una hida. Tra. e. iiii car. In dnio. e. una & vi villi. & x bord. cu. iii cai. ibi. dim. ac. pti. Silva ad claufura. Valuit vi lib. modo vii lib.

In Bovecome hd.

Ulfi ten. dim. hid. in *Cela*. Ipfe tenuit in paragio de rege E. Tc. &.   Chale. mo. p. dim. hidi. Tra. e. i cai. In dnio. e. dimid. cai. & ii bord. hnt. dim. car. & una ac. pti. Val. x fol.

Godric

Godric ht. de rege dimid. hid. in *Huncheford*. Ipfe tenuit T. R. E.
Tc. & mo. fe defd. p. dim. hida. Tra. e. i car. In dnio. e. dimid. cu.
uno bord. & molin. fine cenfu. & una ac. pti. Val. & valuit x folid.

Lemerftone. Elnod ten. in *Levingtune* i. hid. de rege. Ipfe tenuit in paragio T. R.
E. Tc. & mo. p. una hida. Tra. e. i car. In dnio. eft dim. car. cu. ii
bord. Valuit x fol. modo xii fol.

Ulnod ten. de rege dimid. v. & p. tanto fe defd. T. R. E. & modo.
Tra. e. dimid. car. ibi e. un. bord. Val. xxx den.

Aluric & Wiflac ten. dimid. hid. in *Heceford* & p. tanto fe defd. T.
R. E. & mo. Quatuor alodiarii tenuer. in paragio. Tra. e. i car. In
dnio. e. dim. car. & v bord. hnt. i car. & dimid. ac. pti. Val. & valuit
x fol.

Appleford. Bolle ten. de rege una v. in *Apleford* & p. tanto fe defd. T. R. E. &
modo. Tra. e. i car. & ibi e. in dnio. cu. iii. fervis & ibi v ac. pti. Val.
& valuit x fol.

No II.

Warrant to Mr. Richard Worfley to fearch for Allum Ore in the Ifle
of Wight.

1561.   AFTER my right harty Comendacons—Whereas the Queans Ma.
being infermyd that there is w'. in that Ile certen Oure of Alume. For
Trial and Profe wherof Her Highnefs purtly fendeth thider the Bearer
herof One Bendall. Thefe fhall be in her Ma'' name to require you
w'. your Authorite and favi'. fo to affift him in that behalf, as he may
revife fyche partes there as he fhall thynk to be meete for the pr. pofe and
bring w'. him fume part of the fayde Oure to th'end he maye therof make
fume Profe here w'. in the Realme. In this part, as her Highnefs trufteth,
You will give Order that no man there fhall impede and refift him;
So he hath Charge to ufe himfelf with fyche moderation and refpect
of behavio' as fhall apperteyne. And thus I byd You hartely well to
fare—Fro the Court at Weftmynfter the 7th. daye of Marche 1561.

Your Affured

Frend,

W. CECILL.

No III.

N° III.

Carta W. regis junioris de Hid. in infula Vecta.

W. Rex Angl. W. vicecomiti de infula fal. Notum fit t. et omnibus baronibus meis quod ego conceffi Walkelino epō dimidiam hidam terræ in Vecta Infula ad opus Eccl. fuæ, ficut eam fibi pro anima fua concefferat pater meus, die qua erat vivus et mortuus. Nec folum autem ibi fed et per totam teiram meam in eadem infula, falvo gablo meo. Per planū et Silvam fibi lapides fodiendi dedi licentiam, fi in filva tantæ parvitatis fuerit ut per eam tranfeuntis cornua cervi appareant. Hoc factum d. apud Kenefare. T. Ranns. Captt. Uifo de Abelot. Croco Venatore.

N° IV.

De Quadraria in Infula.

H. rex Angl. Ric°. de Redverijs. fal. Præcipio tibi ut permittas Eccle. fcti Petri de Winton. et epō et monachis tram qãm habuit ipfa eccle. tpiē patris et fratris mei. Ubi ē quadraria in infula ita habere pacifice ficut unquam melius habuit et ficut brev. fris mei precepit. Quod fi non fecis Alneraldus de Lincol. faciat ecclæ et epō habere. T. Rogo'. Canō. et E. Dap'.

N° V.

H. rex Angl. Ric°. de Redverijs et miniftiis ejus fal. Præcipio vobis ut pmittas monachos fcti, Swithi de Winceftra omnino in pace et quietam tenere hidam trãe de infula de Wight in qua folebat capi pēt ficuti unqm. melius et quietius tenueiunt tprē. patris et fiatris mei, et prohibeo ne aliquis fe intromittat de tiã illa. Quia volo ut ita quieta fit trã illa ficuti te tpr. fuit. Et monachi prædicti fcti Swithi et feivientes eoium ita quiete et pacifice capiant petram ad opus ecclæ fcti Swithi, ficuti te tpre. facere folebant, et fine aliqua diftuibācone, T. Eud. Dapi. apud Suttonā.

N° VI.

PAROCHIAL TABLE,

ISLE OF WIGHT.

Parishes.		Dedication	Patrons	Kings books			Year. tenths			Number of Inhabitants	
				£	s	d	£	s	d		
Arreton,	vic	St George	John Fleming, Efq				2	2	0		
Binftead,	rect	Holy Crofs	Bifhop of Winchefter					2	8½		
Bonchurch,	rect	St Boniface	W Hill, Efq and Mr Popham					2	8½		
Brading,	vic	St Mary	Trinity College, Cambridge				2	0	0		
Brixton,	rect	St Mary	Bifhop of Winchefter	32	3	4	3	4	4		
Brook,	rect	St Mary	William Bowreman, Efq					3	10½		
Calborn,	rect	All Saints	Bifhop of Winchefter	19	17	8½	1	19	9		
Carefbrook,	vic	St Mary	Queen's College, Oxford	23	8	1½	2	6	9¼	{ Parifh at large { At Nodde Hill	995 } 250 }
Chale,	rect	St Andrew	Rt hon. Sir Rich Worfley, Bart	14	3	11½	1	8	4¼		
Frefhwater,	rect	All Saints	St John's College, Cambridge	19	8	4	1	18	10		
Gatcombe,	rect	St Olive	Edw Meux Worfley, Efq	25	18	9	2	11	1½		
Godfhill,	vic	All Saints	Queen's College, Oxford				3	15	9		
Kington,	rect		Edw Meux Worfley, Efq	5	6	8		10	8		

Parish		Church	Patron			Inhabitants
Newport*,	cur	St Tho Becket	Under Carisbrook			2317
Niton,	rect	St John Bapt ft	Queen's College, Oxford	20 7 1	2 0 8½	267
Northwood,	rect	St John Baptist	United with Carisbrook			{Parish at large 420, At West Cowes 1660} 2080
Shalfleet,	vic		The King		1 17 2½	599
Shanklin,	vic		W. Hill, Esq and Mr Popham			100
Shorwell,	rect	St Peter	Coheiresses of John Leigh, Esq	20 0 2¾	2 0 0¼	524
St Helen's,	vic	St Helena	Eton College			417
St Lawrence,	rect	St Lawrence	Rt hon Sir Rich Worsley, Bart.			77
St Nicholas,	vic	St Nicholas	Governor of the island		0 14 0	{Parish at large 52, In Castle Hold Newport 124} 176
Thorley,	vic	St Swithin	Miss Gother		0 13 10½	143
Whippingham	rect		The King	19 1 5½	1 18 1¼	{Parish at large 435, At East Cowes 257, At Coppings Bridge-Newport 87} 779
Whitwell,	vic	St Mar & St Radegund	Queen's College, Oxford			344
Wootton,	rect	St Edmund	Rev Mr Walton	7 16 0½	15 7¼	42
Yarmouth,	rect	St James	The King			268
Yaverland,	rect		Rev. Mr Wright	6 6 10½	12 8½	81
			In the House of Industry			530

Total Parishes 30, Inhabitants 18024

* If to the number of inhabitants in Newport parish we add those residing in such parts of the town as lie in Carisbrook, St Nicholas, and Whippingham parishes, the town of Newport will be found to contain 2778 inhabitants

Nᵒ VII.

See p. 28.

Inquiſitio 7ᵒ Edwardi Tertij.

Inquiſitio capta apud Newport in inſula Vecta in vigilijs nat. ſcti Joh̄ Baptiſta anno regno Regis Edwardi Tertij a conqueſtu ſeptimo, coram Johē Titchborn et Laurentio de ſc̄to Martino ſcutag. Dni Reg's in com Southton. de anno regni Dni Edwardi nuper regis Angliæ patris Dni regis nunc quarto aſſig. ad inquirend. Feoda militaria prædict. anno quarto aut aliquam partem feodorum eorundum ut de corona Angliæ ſeu de Rege vel de progenitoribus Dni Regis vel de Archiepātibus Epātibus Prioratibus aut alijs Dignitatibus quibuſcunq. quæ in cuſtodia Regis tunc fuerint. Et qui tenuerunt Feod. de hereditatibus heredum tunc infra etatem, et in cuſtodia Regis tunc exiſterunt. Et quot Feoda et quam partem Feodi quilibet tenens hujuſmodi tunc tenuit, et in quibus villis, et qui fuerunt anteceſſores eorum qui tenent per deceſſam heredit. et qui alio modo, et qui heredes fuerint infra etatem, in cuſtodia Regis eodem anno quarto. Et qui Archiepāt. Epātus Abbatiæ Prioratus et aliæ Dignitates quæcunq. tempore illo vacabint temporalium quorum cuſtodia ad Dnm Regem pertinuere, per ſacramentum.

Johis de Inſula, mil.	Robi de Inſula de Meiſhton
Johis de Glamorgan, m.l.	Robti Fryland
Johis Heyno, mil.	Walteri de Sydeling
Johis de Kingſton, mil.	Johis le Martre
Robti Doglandie	Johis alle Moure et
Jacobi Chamberlain	Laurentij le Norreys.

Qui dicunt ſuper ſacramentum ſuum qd. non ſunt aliqui milites ſeu aliqui alij tenentes in inſula Vecta qui tenent Feoda militaria aut aliquam partem Feodi militis ut de corona Angliæ nec tenuerunt prædicto anno quarto, ſeu ab aliquo tempore cujus coutume memoria non exiſtit Dicunt tamen quod in eadem inſula ſunt et alij liberi tenentes qui tenent et ſemper hactenus tenuerunt terras et tenementa ſua tam predicto anno quarto quam aliquo alio tempore tranſacto de honore caſtri de Careſbroke per certa ſervitia militaria, viz. per ſervitium cuſtodiendi dictū caſtrum tempore guerre, ſumptibus proprijs per xl. dies p. defenſione dictæ

insulæ.

infulæ. De quibus vero militibus et libere tenentibus, Baldwinus de Infula de Gatecomb, tenuit eodem anno quarto de caftro prædicto quinq. feoda milit. de quibus Dñus Rex nunc tenet duo feoda.

Johannes de Infula, tenuit eodem anno, quarto de caftro predicto feptem feoda milit. et dimid. et 8ᵃᵐ. partem unius feodi in inf. predicta.

Willielmus Ruffel tenuit eodem anno quarto de dicto caftio vj feoda et ij as partes feodi. in inf. predicta.

Robertus de Glamoigan. et Petrus D'Evercy tenuerunt eodem anno quarto iiij feoda militai. in inf. predicta.

Radulfus de Goiges tenuit eodem an. in forma predict. ij feoda militar. viz. in Knighton et alibi.

Galfridus de Albermarlia tenuit eodem modo unum feod. mil. eodem anno quarto in infula prædict.

Henricus Tienchard tenuit eodem modo unum feod. milit in Schaldeflet in inf. predict.

Adam de Compton ten. eodem modo de dicto caftro unum feod. milit. in Compton et Atherfield.

Reginaldus de Scto Martino tenuit in forma prædicta dimid. feodi militis in Alvington de dicto caftro

Willielmus de Heyno tenuit eodem modo de eodem caftro, unum feod. milit. in Stenbuiy.

Johannes de Langford tenuit in forma prædicta unum feod militis in Chale.

Willūs, filius Walteri de Infula, et Baldwinus de Neweton tenuerunt eodem modo de dicto caftro dimid. feodi in Neweton.

Jordanus de Kingfton tenuit eodem modo de dicto caftro, un. feod. mil. et viij partem uni feodi in Kingfton et Mollefby.

Henric. D'oglandre tenuit eodem modo ij partes dimid. feodi mil. in Nunnewell et Buggebury, de caft predict.

Hugo de Chekenhull tenuit eodem mo. de dicto caftio viij partem unius feodi mil. in Wippingham.

Will de la Clyve tenuit eodem modo de caftio predict. xiij partem undus feodi in la Clyve.

Henricus Touloufe ten. eodem mo. de dicto caft. viij parte. feodi apud Bulnere.

Rogerus de Chellingwode tenuit eodem modo de caftro pred ct. xiij parts. unius feodi in Chellingwood.

Johes

Johēs Aurifaber tenuit eodem modo de dicto castro xiij partem unius feodi mil. in Clatterford.

Willielmus de Whitfield tenuit eodem modo de castro predicto xl partem unius feodi mil. in Aucheston.

Nicolaus de la Hy de tenuit eodem modo xxij partem unius feodi mil. de dicto castra in la Hyde.

Robtūs Morin tenuit eodem modo de dicto castro xiij partē feod. in Edweton.

Hen. de Stella tenuit eod. mo. xij parte. feodi mil de dicto cast. in Debborn et Gurnore. Et quod Rich de Affeton tenuit eod. an. quarto de cast pred. un. feodi in Affeton.

Dicunt etiam qd. predicti milites et liberi tenentes nullum aliud servitium aliquo tempore retroacto fuerint aliquibus comitibus seu comiteff. quondam Dominis insulæ predictæ. nec Dño Regi, avo Dni Regis nunc, seu Domino Edwardo Regi patri Regis nunc, aut Dno nostro Regi nunc extra insulam predictam in aliquo exercitu seu guerra Dni Regis, preter quod dicti milites et libere tenentes conducere solebant comites et comitiffas quondam Dominos insulæ in recessu eorundem cum in partibus dictæ insulæ aliquo tempore comōraffent ufq. ad mare transeundo de insula predicta ad aliquas partes exteras. Et dicunt quod dicti milites et libere tenentes aliquod scutagium Dno Regi seu progenitoribus suis aut aliquibus Dominis insulæ predictæ nullo tempore hactenus solverint: nec aliquod scutagium de eisdem militibus seu tenentibus predictis ante hæc tempora levatum extiterit Et dicunt quod nulli Archiepiscopatus, Episcopatus aut aliæ Dignitates superius nominatæ tempore illo vacabant, nec aliqui heredes infra etatem seu in custodia Dni Regis predicto anno quarto fuerint in insula predicta in cujus testimonium jurati predicti huic inquisitioni sigilla sua appofuerunt. Dat. die, loco, et anno supra dicto.

<hr>

Nᵒ VIII.

Inquif. ann 18 Edw. II. num. 216, in Turri Lond.

Inquificio capta apud Schidham brigge die Jovis prox. post festum sancti Petri quod dicitur ad Vincula, anno regni regis Edwardi filii regis Edwardi decimo octavo, coram Johanne de la Hoese & Johanne de Insula custodibus portuum, litorum, et terrarum maritimarum in Insula Vecta, tam infra libertates quam extra per dominum regem pro defensione

dictæ

dictæi nsulæ tempore guerræ ab antiquo tempoie debitis et oidinatis, ab abbatibus, prioribus, rectoribus, et militibus terras feu redditus infra dictam infulam habentibus, necnon de aliis liberis tenentibus et aliis, fi jurati fuerint et ariaiati in armis, et arma habeant juxta formam per dictum regem ultimo ordinatam, per facramentum Roberti Urry, Walteri de Goditone, Roberti Doglandre, Johannis le Femers, Johannis de Comptone, Willielmi le Taillour, Ricardi de Donewyvile, Walteri de Kyngeftone, Rogeri le Wyte, Thomæ de Colevile, Roberti de Fielende, Johannis de Comptone (and 33 others.) Et eciam de ignibus loco communium fignorum quot debent effe ab antiquo; per quot homines vigilæ debent fieri de nocte et die infra dictam infulam. Qui dicunt per facramentum fuum, quod comites, abbates, priores, rectores, milites, et alii liberi tenentes qui viginti libratas terræ feu redditus habuerint, cujufcumque ftatus extiterint, habebant equitaturam et arma competencia et omnes homines qui plus habuerint, plus habeant, et qui minus minus fecundum ordinacionem factum in ftatuto domini regis Wynton. Item dicunt quod omnes liberi tenentes et alii tocius infulæ predictæ jurati fint in armis et arreati per conftabularios pacis domini Regis, fecundam formam a curia domini regis ultimo ordinatam et ibidem miffam. Item, dicunt quod in hundredo de Eftmedine eft unus ignis infra pontem fuper Pintoheftone, et debet ibidem vigilia fieri per quatuor homines de nocte, et per duos homines per diem. Item, alius ignis juxta finctam Helenam apud Yarnesforde, et debet vigilia fieri ficut prius. Item tercius ignis apud Sandham fuper Rotuburgh, et debet vigilia fieri ficut prius. Item quartus ignis apud Schenehundred fuper montem, et fuper la Chyne, et debet vigilia fieri per duos homines de nocte et per hundredum de die. Item quintus ignis fuper Smeredone, et debet vigilia fieri per quatuor homines de nocte et per duos homines de die. Item, fextus ignis eft apud L Hinis, et debet vigilia fieri per duos homines de nocte, et per unum hominem de die. Item, feptimus ignis eft apud la Wytedich apud Apuldercombe et debet vigilia fieri per tres homines de nocte, et per unum hominem de die. Item, octavus ignis eft apud Nywerone apud la Wirdet, et debet vigilia fieri per tres homines de nocte, et per duos homines de die. Item, nonus ignis eft, apud Athertone fuper Bertedone, et debet vigilia fieri ut prius. Item decimus ignis eft apud Staundene et debet vigilia fieri per duos homines de nocte, et per unum hominem de die. Item, undecimus ignis apud Woditone apud le Coc, et debet vigilia fieri per quatuor homines de nocte,

nocte, et per duos homines de die. Item duodecimus ignis apud Wer-
pingham fuper Redmerefdone, et debet vigilia fieri per tres homines de
nocte, ac per duos homines de die. Item trefdecimus ignis eft apud la
Rye, et debet vigilia fieri per fex homines de nocte, et per duos de die.
Item in hundredo de Weftmedine eft unus ignis fuper Chaledon, et debet vigilia fieri per quatuor homines de nocte, et per duos homines de
die. Item fecundus ignis eft apud Atheipewe, et debet vigilia fieri ficut
prius. Item, tertius ignis eft fuper Lourkedone, et vigilia debet fieri ut
prius. Item quartus ignis eft apud la Wyide, et debet vigilia fua fieri
ut prius. Item quintus ignis eft fuper Bertelmeworth, et debet vigilia
fieri ut prius. Item, fextus ignis eft apud Lufburgh et debet vigilia
fieri ut prius. Item feptimus ignis eft apud Gerthell, et debet vigilia
fieri ut prius. Item octavus ignis eft apud Hamftede et debet vigilia
fieri ut prius. Item nonus ignis eft apud Havedburgh et vigilia debet
fieri ut prius. Item decimus ignis eft apud Thorneheye, et vigilia debet fieri ut fupra. Item undecimus ignis eft apud le Ferthelonde et
vigilia debet fieri ut prius. Item, duodecimus ignis eft apud Herte-
poll et vigilia debet fieri ut prius. Item, trefdecimus ignis eft apud
Wyghtbergh, et vigilia debet fieri ut prius. Item quatuordecimus
ignis eft apud Lavendone et vigilia debet fieri ut prius. Item quinque-
decimus ignis eft apud Emedone, et vigilia debet fieri ut prius. Item,
fextufdecimus ignis eft apud Holebergh, et debet vigilia fieri ut prius.
In cujus rei teftimonium prædicti jurati figilla fua appofuerunt. Dat.
die, loco & anno fupradictis.

N° IX.

Alia Inquif, anno 18 Edw. II. n. 416.

Inquificio capta apud Schidhambrigge die Lunæ prox. poft feftum
fancti Petri quod dicitur ad Vincula, anno regni regis Edwardi filii regis Edwardi 18. coram Johanne de la Hoefe et Johanne de Infula
cuftodibus portuum litorum et terrarum maritimarum in infula Vecta,
tam infra libertates quam extra per dominium Edwardum de auxiliis
pro defenfione dictæ infulæ tempore guerræ, ab antiquo tempore debitis
et ordinatis, ab abbatibus, prioribus, rectoribus, et militibus terras, ten.
redditus infra dictam infulam habentibus necnon de aliis liberis tenentibus et aliis, fi jurati fuerint et arraiati de armis, et arma habeant juxta

formam

formam per dominum regem ultimo ordinatam, per facramentum Simonis Gilberd. Ad. Afrith. Johannis le Clerke, Nicholai Joh. & Roberti Fynden, Walteri le More, Willielmi atte Brigge. Ad. Jorfal, Warini Treffant, Willielmi le Savage, Walteri Legiftie, et Stephani Bigges. Et eciam de ignibus loco communium fignorum quot debent effe ab antiquo et in quo loco et per quot homines vigiliæ debent fieri de nocte et die infra dictam infulam. Qui dicunt per facramentum fuum quod omnes abbates, priores, rectores, milites, et alii libere tenentes qui viginti libratas terræ habuerint cujufcumque ftatus extiterint, habebunt equitaturam et arma competencia pro homine; et qui plus habuerit plus habeant, et qui minus minus, fecundum ordinacionem factam in ftatuto domini regis Wynton. Item dicunt quod omnes libere tenentes et alii tocius libertatis de Frefhwatere jurati funt in armis, et arraiati per conftabular. pacis domini regis fecundum formam a curia domini regis ultimo ordinatam et ibidem miffam. Item dicunt quod in dicta libertate de Frefhwatere eft unus ignis fuper Schirpenorde et debet vigilia fieri per tres homines de nocte, et per duos homines tota die. Item alius ignis eft fuper Hetdere, et debet vigilia fieri ficut prius. In cujus rei teftimonium prædicti jurati præfentibus figilla fua appofuerunt. Dat, die, loco et annis fupradictis.

N° X.

Lift of the Men at Arms furnifhed to Edward I. for the Defence of the Ifle of Wight. From Irquif. 16 Edw. III.

From the bp. of Salifbury	5	From the abbot of Walton	1
From the abbot of Glaftonbury*	7	From the preceptor of Shalford	1
		From	

* Copies of two certificates of difcharge for the Abbot of Glaftonbury —
Ex Regiftro Abbatiæ Glifton. in Biblioth. Dñi Vicecom Weymouth. Fol 128, 129 Johan Hacket leutenint le conte Arundel pour la guide de Portfmouth & coneftible de Porceftie as vefcontes de Wiltfhire & Berlfhire, & a tous autres que ceftes lettres verront ou orront fol en Dieu Voilles favoir le ferice l'Abbe de Glaftinglurgh etre bn et fuffinient fait par tout le temps qu'ils befogne de morer pour la dite garde, pour toutes fes terres en les dites contees, tanqu'a la date de ceftes In temoyance de queux chofes aux ceftes lettres ouvertes jay mis mon feal Efcriptes a Porceftie le Lundy prochein apres la Circumcifion. L'an du regne du roy Edward tierce apres la Conquefte, comme

d   N. B This

From John Mandut	1
From Emmeline Longefpey	1
From the abbot of Stanley	2
From Beatrice de Winterfhall	1
From the abbot of Gloucefter	1
From the abbefs of Godeftow	1
From Robert de Keynis	1
From the abbot of Malmfbury	3
From the abbot of Cirencefter	2
From Tho Warblington	1
From the prior of Hurle	1
From Tho de Ambrofbury	1
From the abbot of Abygdon	3
From Elia Molendinari	1
From John Daudele	1
From Wm Pagham	1
From Rich. Wynton	1
From Peter Coudray	1
From Hugh Taylour	1
From the abbot of Romele	1
From Lucia de Grey	1

From the preceptor of Conele	1
From Nic Burden	1
From Roger de St Martin	1
From Mary the king's daughter a nun at Ambrefbury	2
From the bp. of Worcefter	1
From Hamon de Parles	1
From the bp. of Bath and Wells	1
From Robt. Kingborne for William de Cotes	1
John Grey for Walter Skydemour	1
John Blaine for the abbot of Thukefburgh	1
Rich. Selby for the hundred of Herewalkeden	1
Henry Hemenhall for Chipham and Malmefbury	1
Walter Cornifey for the hundred of Warham	1
John Carrile for Chalk & Domerham	1
Geoffry de Calne for Heightfbury	1
From Roger de Stoke for Weftbury	1
From the abbefs of Whorwell	1
From Hugh Peverell	1
From Will Ires for the abb. of Shafton	1
From Maurice de Wileb for Matthew Fitz John	1
From —— Serne	1
From the community of Wilts	6
From Alife de Bavent	1
From the prior of ——	1
From Adam de Breton	1
From Richard de la Rivere	1

Prynne on the IV Inft. p 211.

(N B This John Hacket was probably the father of Thomas Hacket, who is feen in the fubfequent roll of landholders in the Ifle, and anceftor to that John Hacket who was found one of the heirs of Ruffel that died 10 Henry VI.)

Ex Regiftra Glafton

P. 129. Richard count de Arundel affigne par noftre feignr le Roy pour la garde de la mer, en Hampfhire, as vifcontes & autres miniftres noftre dit feignr. le Roy en la conte de Wiltfhire & Barckfhire fal. pour ceo que Johan Abbe de Glaftenburgh

Nº XI.

Ex Rot. Antiq. Hominum Armatorum et Sagittariorum Infulæ Vectis.

	Arm.	Sag.		Arm.	Sag.
The abbot of Quarr	4		Edward Barnaby	1	
The lord of Woodyton	6		The Man of Nunwell	2	
The abbefs (i e. of Laycock) for Sherwell	3	2	Richard de Hale	2	
			Ralf Overton for Horringford	1	
The prior of Chriftchurch	2	2	Thomas Hacket	1	
The lord of Yaverland	2	2	William Urry	1	
The lord of Apuldurcomb	2	2	The Lady Mary Buteler for Hale	1	
The lord of Kingfton	1		The prior of Portfmouth	2	
The lord of Wonfton	1		Geoffry Rouelle	2	
The lord of Standen and Wode	1		The man. of Bathingborne	2	
The manor of Whitefield	1		John Palmer of Wotton and Jo. Stone	1	
The man. of Stenbury	1		Roger Baker	1	
The lord of Nyton and Chale		1	William Stouer	1	
The man of Bottebridge		1	Ifabell Keynis for Niton	2	
The prior of St Helen's		1	John Waite	1	
The prior of Burton		2	Henry Pedder for Weftbroke	1	
The lord of Alverfton		2	Sr. Theobald Gorges for Chillingwood	1	
The man. of Milton		3			
The Vavafor		2	The Tenant of ———	1	
John Malterfon for Wood Aufterborn (Ofborne) and Chillingwood		3	Robert Syngdone	1	
			Sr John de Kingfton for Lucclo and Priffloe	1	
The man of Pagham		2			
The man. of Nettlefton		2	The Churches of Eaft Medne		
The abbot of Beauly		2			
John Wyvill		4	The Church of		
John Noireys		1	Brading		2

burgh fait trouve pleinement et fuffiament gents d'armes pour la garde de la mer en Hampfhire a Porcefter pour toutes les tems qu'ils tient en les avait dites contees de Wiltfhire and Barkfhire felon ce que ces predecefleurs en temps de neceffire folent faire Si comme par temonyance vous mandons que au dit Abbe, ne a fes tenants bondes par refon de la dite garde ne face mal ne molefte tranqu comme il continue la dite garde en la maniere comme il fait, c'eft a fcavoir pour fes terres in Wiltfhire treys hommes d'armes & pour fes terres en Barkfhire un homme d'arme, &c En temoyance de quelle chofe a cette lettre patente avons mys noftre feal. Donnè a noftre chaftel de Arundel 9 Mart l'an du regne le Roy Edward le tierce apres la conquefte treifieme.

	Arm	Sag.
Yaverland		1
Newchurch	2	
Arreton	1	3
Whippingham		2
Niton		1
Benstede		1
Shentlyn		1
Bonechurch		1
Wootton		1
Wathe		1
Appulduiford		1
Stownam or Standen		1
Knighton		1
Alverston		1
The vicar of Brading		1
The vicar of Arreton		1
The vicar of Goddeshill		1
The chapel of St. Edmund at Wootton		1

The West Medine.

	Arm	Sag.
The prior of Carisbrook	6	
The procurator of Lyra	1	2
Giles Beauchamp for Freshwater	2	
Gilbert de Spencer	1	2
The Lord of Affeton	1	
The erle of Salisbury	3	2
Sr John de Kingston	1	2
John de Compton		2
Sr. Thomas Langford		3
The manors of Gatecomb, Whitwell, Caulborn, and Mersten		3
Thomas Rale	1	
Sr. Laurence de St. Martin	1	1
The lord of Motteston	1	

	Arm	Sag.
Ralf de Woolverton		2
Nicholas de Woolverton		1
Ralf Dicton and Tho. Hacket for Hatherfield		2
Sir John Tychborn		2
Thomas le Wayte		2
Will Passelew & Geoffry Roucle		2
John Berle		2
John Fauterby		2
Lady Isabella Hunston		2
Henry Tailour		1
The abbess of Laycock		1
Park		2
Laurence Russel		3

The Churches of the West Medine

The Church of	Arm	Sag.
Freshwater	1	
Schaldeflet	1	
Caulborn	1	
Brixton	1	2
Shorewell		2
Gatecomb		3
Chale		2
Motteston		2
Broke		1
Lemerston		1
Kingston		1
Yarmouth		1
The vicar of Shorewell		2
The vicar of Shaldeflet		2
The vicar of Thorley		1
The vicar of Caresbrook		2
The prior of Christchurch, who is rector of Thorley		1

N° XII.

Difpofition of the Militia in the Ifle of Wight, *temp.* Edw. III.

The Eaft Medine.

I. William Ruffel Ld. of Everland, had under his command Ever-land, Binbridge, Northil, and Brading. The Ld. of Woolveten in Binbridge his Vintener.

II. Peter de Heyno Ld. of Stenbury, had under his command Sten-bury, Whitwell, Wioxal, Bonchurch, Cliff, Apfe, Nyweton (Crab Knighton) and Sandham : the Ld. of Wathe his vintener.

III. Theobald de Gorges, Ld. of Knighton, had under his com-mand, Knighton, St Hellens, Kern, Ryde, Quarr, Binfted, and New-church : Reynold Oglander, Ld. of Nunwell, his vintener or lieu-tenant.

IV. The Bailiffs of Newport, had the command of the town.

V. John Urry lord of Eaft Standen, commanded Eaft Standen, Ai-rerton, Whippingham, St Katherines, Rookly, Nettlecomb, and Woot-ton. The Lord of Wootton his vintener.

The Weft Medine.

VI. John de Kingfton had the command of Kingfton, Shorwell, Carefbrook, Paik, Northwood, and Watchingwell. The Ld of Wooton, Sir John Lifle for his manor of South Shorwell (or Weft Court) his vintener.

VII. The Ld. of Modefton (Tho. Chyke) had the command of Mo-defton, Newtown, Caulboin, and Buixton. Tho Langford Ld. of Chale, his vintener

VIII. The Ld. of Brook had the command of Brook, Shalfleet, Tho-ley, and Yarmouth. The prior of Chriftchuich, for his Manor of Ninge-wood, vintener.

IX. Adam de Cumpton Ld. of Compton, had the command of Compton, Affeton, and Frefhwater. The Ld. of Affeton, Robt de Affeton, vintener.

N. B. It is probable, that perfonal merit was confulted more than their feveral eftates in beftowing the command of thefe companies

N° XIII.

N° XIII.

Brev. Regis de Morando in inf. Vecta, 51 Edw. III.

Rex dilectis & fidel. suis Johi de Cavendish & sociis suis justiciariijs ad placita coram nobis tenenda affignatis sal. &c. Cum insula Vecta quæ infra littus maris in comitatu Southamptoniæ situatur, hostibus nostris publicis maxime sit propinqua, quam etiam insulam ijdem hostes multam desiderant, et cum infra breve tempus appropinquare et debellare proponunt ut audivimus, & se parant. Nos licet de avisamento concilij nostri sessiones nostras in com. prædicto ad placita coram nobis tenenda quamdiu nostræ placuerit voluntati ordinaverimus; volumus tamen et jubemus qd. omnes et singuli residentes et habitantes in insula Vecta cujuscunq. fuerint status et conditionis, salvationi et defensioni ejusdem insulæ continue intendant et ibidem moram faciant et remaneant absq. eo qd. ipsi seu eorum aliquis coram nobis in sessionibus nostris in comitatu prædicto comparere seu venire vel in affisis juratis seu recognitionibus aliquibus ibidem (quanquam nos specialiter tangant) poni seu panellari non compellatur, aut tenentur quocunq modo vel colore quousq. aliud inde duxerimus demandandū. Et ideo vobis mandamus qd. ipsos homines residentes et habitantes eadem insula coram nobis in sessionibus nostris prædict. in com. prædict. comparere seu venire vel in affisis juratis seu recogn. aliquibus ibidem (licet nos specialiter tangant) poni seu panellari nullatenus compellatis, &c.

Ejusdem Brevia mittuntur vicecomiti Southamptoniæ et Hugoni Tyrrel custodi castri de Carefbrook in inf. Vecta et Johī Griffith constabulario ejusdem castri.

Rymer, vol. vii. p. 147.

N° XIV.

Nº XIV.

A true Noate of the ſtrenght of the Iſland, taken by Sir John Oglander, liſtennant the 12th. of May 1625, and by him delivered to the Counſell.

In Sir John Oglanders Band

Officers	7.
Muſkettes	60.
Corſlettes	21
Bare Pickes	9.
Soom 97	

In Sir Edward Dennis Bande

Officers	10
Muſkettes	103
Corſlettes	13
Bare Pickes	23
Men unarmed	61
Som 210	

Apeldorcoombe Bande

Officers	9
Muſkettes	150
Corſlettes	45
Bare Pickes	37
Men unarmed	40
Som 261	

Mr Dillingtons Band

Officers	12
Muſkettes	60
Corſlettes	20
Bare Pickes	15
Men unarmed	15
Som 122	

Sir John Rychardes Band.

Officers	6
Muſkettes	61
Corſlettes	14
Bare Pickes and men unarmed	28
Soom 109	

Mr Checkes Band

Officers	7
Muſkettes	113
Corſlettes	21
Bare Pickes	13
Som 154	

Sir William Meux

Officers	12.
Muſkettes	156
Collivors	29
Corſlettes	44
Men unarmed	20.
Som 261	

Mr Leyghes Band

Officers	6
Muſkettes	63
Corſlettes	16.
Bare Pickes	10
Som 95	

Mr Boormans Band.

Officers	13.
Muſkettes	65
Corſlettes	17
Bare Pickes	20.
Som 115.	

Mr Hobſons Band

Officers	18
Muſkettes	83.
Corſlettes	38.
Men unarmed	31.
Soom 170.	

Mr. Urrie's Band.

Officers	11
Muſkettes	80
Corſlettes	22
Bare Pickes	9
Soom 122.	

Nuport Band.

Officers	22
Muſkettes	94
Collivors	4
Corſlettes	12
Bare Pickes	32.
Holbertes	10
Men unarmed	130.
Som 304.	

Muſkettes	1088.
Collivors	33.
Corſlettes	263.
Bare Pickes	196.
Holberdes	10.
Men unarmed	297.
Officers	133.

Som totoll of all the able men within the iſland is 2020.

Since they arr all armed.

Nº XV.

N° XV.

A Lift of the Captaines of the Ifle of Wyght as they are to take place and be ranked when they fhall appeare in the field with their companies, and in all meetings upon martiall bufineffes.

Sir Edwaid Dennis } Knights my lieutenants of the Ifland.
Sir John Oglander }

The Weft Medham.

> Sir William Meux, knight.
> Sir John Leygh, knight.
> Mr. Booreman, efq.
> Mr. Hobfon, efq.
> Mr. Haivie, efq.
> Mi. James.
> Mr John Urrey
> The town of Newport.

The Eaft Medham.

> Bairronnett Worfley.
> Bairronnett Dillington.
> Sir William Liflie, knight.
> Mr. Edward Cheke, efq.
> Mr. Bafkett, efq.
> Mr. Thomas Ryce.

Whereas theie hath ben fome queftion and difference moved by fome of the captaines above mentioned foi piecedencie upon feveral pretences, which beinge leaft unfettled might hazard the iayfinge of fome mifchiefe oi diforder for pievention wheieof, I doe hereby require that all the cnptaines doe conforme themfelves to the oider of this lift, and take their places accoidingly until fuch time as I fhall find juft caufe to alter the fame. And whereas it is requifite that Sir Edwaid Dennis and Sir John Oglander doe one of them take the chaige of the one divifion and the other of the other divifion, and that I do not underftand how it may ftand with either of their conveniencies in iefpect of their refidence to bee appointed to either of the divifions, I doe leave that to bee accommodated by themfelves with their own beft comoditie. Expecting that upon all mufters and other occafions for the fouldiers ryfeinge, one of them bee in the head of the troopes of each of thofe divifions.

March 24, 1628.

CONWAY.

N° XVI.

The Watches and Wardes that ar now kept in our Ifland, Sept. 20. 1638.

Eaft Meden.

Cap. Rice.	⎰At St. Caterons, a ward with 2 men. ⎱On the Hatton Nyghtonfyld, a watch with 2 men.
Sir Ed. Dennys.	⎰A watch at Lanes, 2 men. ⎱A ward at Roxall Down.
Sir John Oglander.	⎰Afhenr Down, a ward one man, and a watch 2 men ⎱At St. Hellen's Poynt, a watch, 2 men.
Sir R. Dillington.	⎰On Knyghton, a watch, 2 men. ⎱At Ryde, a watch, 2 men.
Sir Henry Worfeley	⎰On Apeldercoombe, a watch, 2 men. ⎱At Criple at Nyghton, a watch, 2 men.
Cap. Cheeke.	At St. George's Down, a watch, 2 men.
Cap. Bafket.	⎰On Bindbridge Down, a ward, one man, and a watch 2 men.
Sir Wᵐ. Liflie.	⎰At Eaft Cowes, Wootton Povnt, and at Fifchovfe, a watch, 2 men a peece.

Weft Meden.

Mr. Mewx.	⎰At Ramfe Down, a watch, 2 men. ⎱At Chale Down, a watch, 2 men.
Sir John Leygh.	⎰On Laidon Down, a watch 2 men. ⎱At Atherfylde, a watch 2 men.
Cap. Uiry.	⎰On Harberoe Downe, a waid 2 men. ⎱On the feac fhoie at Brixton, a watch 2 men.

e   Cap.

Cap. Harvye.	{	On Avington Downe, a watch 2 men.
		At Northwood, a watch 2 men.
		On Gatcome Downe, a watch 2 men.
Cap. Booreman.	{	On Freſchwaltor Downe, a ward and watch, 2 men a peece.
		On Motſon Downe, a watch 2 menn.
Cap. Hobſon.		At Hamſtede, a watch, 2 men.
Newport, 2 companies.	}	They only watch in the towne.

N° XVII.

Inſtructions to be obſerved by the Militia of the Iſle of Wight. May 17. 1651.

Imprimis, upon the diſcovery, at either of the forelands, or at any other watch of the iſland, of ten ſhipps and ſoe to twenty making towards the iſland out of the roadeway, then the ſearchers to hange up the gare to inform the centoner.

Item, upon notice thereof, the centoner to repaire to the ſea ſide, and yf he find thoſe ſhipps bound for land in the iſland, and they thought to be enemies, then to give notice to the captaine of the iſland, or in his abſence to his deputie, and the centoner to raiſe his companie, and to ſend to as many of the next centoners for to raiſe their companies, as ſhall be thought fitt for the hinderance of their landinge, by raiſinge the gare, by ringinge all the church bells, and alſoe by ſendinge about all the hoblers to give the alarum to all companies to repaire to the randezvous, and to ſtay untill they have further order

Item, yf the watch at the forelande, or at any place of the ſaid iſland, diſcover a greater fleet of ſhippinge making towards the iſeland out of the roade way, then to give notice to the centoner who is preſentlie to repaire to the ſea ſide, and yf he finde them enemies, determininge to land in the iſland, then preſentlie to give notice to the captaine of the iſland, or in his abſence to his deputie, that order may be given for the firinge of the beacons; and the ſaid captaine is in meane time to make what reſiſtance he can by his company, and the

companies

companies adjacent, to the end to hinder or retarde the landinge of the enemie as abovefaid, which faid adjacent companies are to be accordinglie affiftant.

Item, upon the firinge of a beacon, yf yt be in the Eaft Medine, then all the centoners there are to repaire with the feverall companies towards Bradinge Downe, and there to expect further directions, and all the companies in the Weft Medham are to repaire towards St. George's Downe to expect further directions. And yf the beacon be fired in the Weft Medham, then all the companies there to repaire towards Yarborrowes, and to receive further directions, and all the companies of the Eaft Medham to repaire to Avington Downe, and there to receive further directions from the governor, or in his abfence from his deputie.

Item, every centoner to choofe the moft fufficient man in his companie lying convenient for yt to be his fearcher, or to caufe the old fearcher, beinge not able himfelf, to finde a fufficient man. And efpecially care is to be taken, both in havinge the beacons well fearched, warded, and watched, and a fufficient quantitie of wode to lay by them if occafion ferve.

Item, every centoner is to charge every mufketteere in his companie to have in a readinefs three pounds of powder, and forty bulletts

Item, every watchman, both by day and night, is to come unto his watch with a mufkett loaden and a match lighted.

Item, the fearchers to come at fun rifinge, and at fun fettinge to charge the watch, and not findinge the watchmen there readie to doe their duties then to appoint fufficient men to fupply their places, and to complayne to the centoner, who fhall pay them (foe placed) their wages, which the offenders fhall repay, and be punifhed for the firft tyme in the ftocks, and the fecond time by being fent to the captaine of the ifleland to receive further punifhment.

Item, yf the fearcher doe not his dutie in truelie fetlinge the watch, and alfoe for fearchinge of yt, thrice in the night, and twice in the day, then the watch to give notice of his negligence to the centoner, who fhall fend the faid fearcher to the caftle to be there punifhed by the captaine of the ifland.

Item, every mafter that will appoint his fervant to watch for him in the night fhall forbeare his fervice and labour for the half day before

his watch, that he may take his reſt and be thereby the better ena
to doe the ſaid dutie.

Item, yf the watch perceave any ſuſpicious perſon, either by n
or by day, drawinge neere unto them, with whome they may no
probably able to make their partie good, then one to repaire
them to knowe what they are, and the other to keep further ou
danger, ſoe that he may eſcape them, and fly to the ſearcher for
And alſoe that the watch apprehend all rogues and idle perſons
are ſtrangers to be brought before ſome juſtice of peace to be puni
and ſent out of the cortry.

Item, the ſearchers are to reade their orders once or twice a weel
the watch, to the end they may the better underſtand their duties;
every captaine by himſelf or his lieutenant frequentlie view the w
by night, to ſee how the ſearcher perfoims his dutie, and to pu
him yf he find any neglect in him.

That noe perſon refuſing to ſubſcribe the late engagement*,
beare his owne armes but ſhall find ſuch an able man or men as
centoner ſhall approve of, according to that proportion as was uſu
impoſed on them And that they ſhall pay unto ſuch as ſhall b
their armes 12 d. a day for every day they ſhal be ymployed for th
And the ſaid perſons ſhall alſoe find ſuch able ſpare men as the cent
ſhall like to bear ſuch other armes beſides their trained armes, as
and have been uſually impoſed on them, or the eſtates which
enjoye.

That noe perſon ſoe refuſinge to ſubſcribe, ſhalbe permitted to
a watchman or ſearcher of the watches, but that the ſervice be
neglected, all ſuch perſons ſhall procure ſuch able perſons as the
toner ſhall approve of, to be watchmen and ſearchers in their ſte
giving ſuch ſatisfaction as hee ſhall be able to agree for.

That noe perſon whatever whoe ſhall ſoe neglect, or refuſe to
ſcribe the engagement, and to conforme to the preſent governm
ſhalbe permitted to keepe any ſort of armes in his cuſtodie, but
either bringe in their armes to Cariſbrook caſtle, there to be ſecured
depoſited as a magazine for the iſland, or be otherwiſe ſecured in
handes of ſome officer of the militia within the limitt of that c
pany, where the ſaid perſon doth inhabit to be appoynted by
centoner.

* To be true and faithful to the commonwealth, as eſtabliſhed without ki
houſe of lords.

That all others not refuſinge to ſubſcribe, ſhall accordinge to ancient cuſtome of the iſland beare their owne armes, without a diſpenſation from the centoner under whome they ought to ſerve, to the contrary. And that all perſons who are charged with other armes, beſides thoſe they beare themſelves, ſhall find ſuch able men and noe other who ſhall be approved of by the centoner.

That every centoner ſhall take care to have in a readines, what horſe hee can get furniſhed of ſuch perſons of qualitie within his lymmitts, who ſhall rather chooſe to ſerve on horſeback then on foot, and whome he ſhall think fitt to diſpenſe with, of all which horſe the ſaid centoner ſhall take a liſt and retorne yt fayrlie written togeather with the liſt of his company unto the captaine of the iſland, at every general muſter, when they are to cauſe the ſaid horſe to be brought forth furniſhed, to be viewed and exerciſed, that they may be fitt for ſervice yf any occaſion ſhall happen.

And that noe perſon within the ſeveral companies of the iſle, who ſerveth or ought to ſerve in his owne armes, or is appoynted to beare the armes of others, ſhall wilfully abſent himſelf from his muſter upon payne of ympriſonment.

That all ſuch who ſhalbe allowed by the centoner to beare armes for other men who have ſubſcribed the engagement, ſhalbe payed by them for whome they beare the ſaid armes, fix pence a day for every day when they ſhall appeare upon private muſters, and 12 d. a day at general muſters, or in caſe of any ſpeciall duty or ſervice.

That every centoner trayne his company at leaſt every month untill he receave order to the contrary.

That at every generall muſter every centoner doe take care to have all his muſketteris to appeare in the field on horſe back, to the end that they may be in the better readines for that ſort of ſervice very much conducinge to the ſafetie of this iſle as there ſhalbe occaſion.

That every centoner take care that the pariſh guns belonginge to the ſeverall companies be kept compleat, and provided with ſufficient wheeles and carriages, togeather with neceſſarie ſtores of powder, bulletts, and caſe ſhott, to be in a readineſſe for ſervice.

Every centoner is to cauſe theſe inſtructions to be diſtinctlie read at every private muſter in the head of his company.

N° XVIII.

N° XVIII.

Woorkes and Repacons done upon her Graces Caſtles and Forts within the Iſle of Wighte, viz. at

Careſbrooke, Yarmouthe, Freſhwater.

The duplicamente of thaccompte of Thomas Worſeley and John Dingley eſquiers appoynted by the lords of the queenes majeſties moſte honorable privie counſell to receave and defray diverſe ſomes of money for the repayringe and mendinge of her graces caſtles and forts there and the ſame woorkes to be appoynted by thadviſe and direccon of Sr. George Carewe knighte capten of the ſaide caſtles in places moſte neceſſarie as by the privie ſeale remayninge with Roberte Peter eſquier may appeare. That is to ſaye aſwell of all ſuch ſomes of money as the ſaide accomptauntes any maner of waye hath hadd and receaved of her majeſties treaſure out of her highnes receipte of the xchequier for the woorkes and repayres of the ſaid caſtles and forts as alſo of the yſſuinge and defrayinge the ſame in repayringe and mendinge her graces caſtles and forts at Careſbrooke Yarmouthe and Freſhwater viz. making 249* perches of wall of twoe and three foote thicke uppon the ſouth raveline at Careſbrooke 92½ perches uppon the eaſte raveline there, making a treade whele for the well with the gudgeons ſhafte and other yron and carpentrie woorke aboute the ſame and a plattforme over the wellhouſe, chardges of the maſons woorke of the ſoutheaſte and ſouthweſt knights the kepe a raveline in the northe parte of the caſtle, takinge doune two towres and making the loopes for the ſame agreable to tholde walls of the caſtle ſtoppinge all the loopes of the walls with plancks and makinge a newe bridge at the caſtle gate with ſondrie other neceſſarie reparacons and fortificacons done there within the tyme of this accompte as well at thaforeſaid caſtle of Careſbrooke as alſo in woorkinge and repayinge the ſaide fortes and holdes of Yarmouthe and Sharpnode in Freſhwater aforeſaide. To witt in and for diverſe and ſondry empcons and proviſions boughte and provided to and for the ſaide woorkes, with the lande and water carriadge of the ſame togeather with wages of artificers workmen and labourers occupied and imployed in and about the ſaide reparacons and for ſondry other taſkewoorkes done by greate with ſondrie other neceſſarie

ceffarie chardges incident to the fame woorkes viz. from the 25th of March 1587 annoq. 29 dne. Eliz. nunc regine untill the 24th day of November anno 30 dne. regine being by the fpace of 245 dayes then ended. As by a booke of payments thereof fubfcribed with the handes of the before named George Carewe knighte and the faid accomptaunts hereuppon being cafte tryed and examined may appeare which faid accompte was taken and declared before the right honourable Willm. baron of Burghley lord high thiear. of Englaund the feconde day of November in the 31 yere of the raigne of our foveraigne ladie Eliz. by the grace of God quene of Englaunde Fraunce and Irelande defender of the faithe &c.

That is to fay

The faid accomptauntes are charged with arrerages.

None for that the faid Mr. Worfeley upon his *lafte* accompte was even.

But the faide accomptauntes ar chardged with money by them receaved out of her highnes receipte of the xchequier by them to be imployed about the fortefyinge of the caftle of Carefbrooke in the ifle of Wyghte and other places and fortes in the fame ifle by warraunte of Sir George Carey knighte capten and governour thereof viz. of Henrie Killegrewe one of the tellors of the receipte aforefaide 100 *l.* and of Roberte Freake one other of the tellors of the fame receipte 566 *l* 13 *s* 4 *d.* by vertue of a privie feale dated the 23d day of February anno 29 dne Eliz. regine. In all as by certificat under thande of Robt. Peter efquier doth and maye appeare the fome of

666 13 4

Whereof the faide accomptauntes ar allowed for money by them iffued payde and defrayed for woorkes and reparacons done upon her majefties caftles and fortes within the ifle of Wighte viz. at

Carefbrooke viz.

Firfte the faide accomptauntes are allowed for money by them faid to be layed out and difburfed for woorkes and reparacons done uppon her majeflies caftle at Carefbrooke aforefaide within the tyme of this accompte viz. makinge 269 perches of wall of twoe and 3 foote thicke uppon the fouth ravelin and 92½ perches uppon the eafte ravelin, making a treade whele for the well with the gudgeons fhafte and other yron and carpentry woorke aboute the fame, and a plattforme over the wellhoufe, chardges of the mafons woorke of the foutheafte and fouthweft knightes, the kepe a ravelin in the northe parte of the fame caftle takinge doune two towers and makinge the loopes of the fame agreeable to tholde walls, ftoppinge all the loopes of the walls with planks and makinge a newe bridge at the caftle gate with fondrye other neceffarie repacons and fortificacons done there within the tyme of this accompte. The particuiaretyes whereof with there feverall natures and quantetyes are fett downe as hearafter followeth, viz. for

Empcons and provifions, viz. for

Boordes, 103 foote	0	5	5
Carriadges, 2, viz. one for the cannon pewtrell with yron woorke to the fame 1l. 4s. 7d. and one for the culveringe 16s. 8d. in all	2	1	3
Lyme, 315 quarters, viz 276 quarters 5 boz. at 2s. 8d. the quarter 36l. 17s. 8d. and 39 quarters at 2s. the quarter 3l 18s. in all	40	15	8
Brickes one thoufande with carryadge 4 myles		13	0
Fire boordes viz. 2 at 12d. the pece 2s. and 3 at 6d. 18d. in all		3	6
Lathes 700 at 8d. the 100.		4	8
A myll to grynde corne bought of Frauncis Porke of Wynchefter	6	6	8
Heare one quarter		2	0
Joyned table one		6	0
Treftles 3 at 12d. the pece		3	0
Whelebarrowes 50 at 1s 6d. the pece	3	15	0
Bafkets 12 doz. ½ at 2s the doz.	1	5	0
Pypes to kepe water for the morter, 2 at 2s. 6d. the pece		5	0
Bowdg barrel one and for mendinge and hoopinge a water tubbe		2	0

Wellropes 2 poiz. 300 ½ at 1l. 1s. 6d per medm. 4l. 16s. makinge out newe rope and tarringe of the fame 17s. 4d.

and

and for a rope for the watch bell 12d. in all with
1l. 7s. for a newe rope for a gynne the fome of 7 1 4

Cafementes for the chappell 3 .... 13 4

Tombrell, one 18 0

Lambſkinres for fponges, 6 .... 2 6

Sande, 486 lodes at 10d. the lode for digginge and carriadge 20 5 0

Wyninge of roughe ſtone for the woorkes viz. 334 lodes
at 3d. the lode 4l 3s. 6d and 1261 lodes at 4d. the
lode 21l. 4d. in all 25 3 10

Wynnynge and carriadge of hard plattner ſtone 126 tonnes
at 8d. the tonne 4 4 0

Wynninge and ſtapelinge of 11½ lode of freeſtone at 2s.
the lode 1 3 0

Hoopes 12 doz. at 6d. the doz. 6s. and for fettinge them
on 2s. in all 8 0

Bucketts for the well 2 .... 6 8

Ironwoorke of diverfe and fondry fortes with mendinge of
woorkemens tooles 4 2 1½

Nayles of feverall fortes and pryces 1 7 2

Glaffe and glafinge 2 5

——————
122 5 6½
——————

Land carriadge
Of diverfe and fondry provicons aforefaide from feverall
places to the faide caſtle of Carefbrooke with 9l 8s. 6d.
for carriadge of 387½ tonnes of freſh water for morter
for the woorks diſtincte a quarter of a myle at 6d the
tonne, and with 6l. 6s. for the like carriadge of lyme
from Newporte and Shyde pitt to the faid caſtle at diverfe rates, the fome of 20 13 4

Wages of artificers and laborers, viz. of
Mafons at 12d p diem 3 8 6
Carpenters at 12d. and 10d. per diem 2 9 2
Sawyers fawinge of planckes and boordes at 2s. 8d. the
100 .... 3 6 8
Plaſterers for plaſteringe 42 yeardes at 2d. the yearde 7 0
Joyners woorkinge uppon the modle of the caſtle, the

barbican,

barbican, ravelyns, kepe, ditches, banks, and other neceſſarie places at 10*d*. per diem 1 18 4

Laborers occupied aboute the fillinge of the ſouth and ſoutheaſte ravelins makinge the trenches and ditches about the ſame, filling the ſoutheaſte and ſouthweſt knights, helpinge to wyn lade and unlade ſtones with other neceſſarie woorks at 8*d*. per diem 128 6 4

139 16 0

Taſkewoorke, viz. to

Thomas Maſon and others for makinge 249 perches of wall of 2 and 3 foote thicke, every perche conteyning 18 foote in lenghte and one foote in heighte uppon the ſouth ravelyn at Careſbrooke at 1*s*. 6*d*. the perche, 18*l*. 13*s* 6*d*. for makinge 92½ perches of wall 3 foote thicke uppon the eaſte ravelyn at 1*s*. 6*d*. the perche 6*l*. 18*s*. 9*d*. and for woorkinge 24 foote of quoynes at 2*d*. the foote 4*s*. in all 25 16 3

John Mathewe maſon for lyme and woorkmanſhippe makinge 8 yeardes of wall of 2 foote thicke in the ſouthweſt knight at 2*s*. 4*d*. the perch 18*s*. 8. for takinge downe and newe makinge a ſtone dore and the wall to the ſame 10*s*. and for woorkinge and ſettinge a ſtone dore in the garden wall to paſſe to this knightes 10*s*. in all 1 18 8

To the ſayde John for lyme and woorkmanſhippe takinge downe and newe makinge one ſtone dore in the wall to the ſame in the ſouthweſt knighte 1*l*. for lyme and woorkemanſhippe makinge 10 perches of wall 5 foote thicke at 4*s*. 2*d*. 2*l*. 5*s* 8*d*. for lyme and woorkmanſhippe for makinge 45 perches 6 foote of wall 2 foote thicke at 2*s*. 4*d*. the perche 5*l* 5*s*. 8*d*. and for wynninge and ſtapelinge of free ſtone for lyme and woorkmanſhippe for copinge the two knights conteyninge 309 foote by greate 12*l* 6*s* in all 20 13 4

John Haſell for makinge a treade whele for the well with the gudgeons ſhafte and other iron and carpentrie woorke about the ſame and a plattforme over the wellhouſe by agreemente 16 0 0

John

John Mathewe for pavinge the wellhoufe and makinge the fynke through the wall   2 0 0

John Hazell for digginge the trenches for the well whele and frame thereof and for the key boltinge of the whele removing the frame of the whele to ferve for 2 bucketts and makinge a great duble doore to the kepe   1 5 0

John Mathewe aforefaide for the mafons woorke of the foutheft and fouthweft knightes, the kepe and a ravelyn in the north parte of the caftle, takinge downe two towers and makinge the loopes of the fame agreable to tholde wall of the caftle accoidinge to a plott thereof drawen and faid to be remayninge with the right honourable the lord high thear. of Englaunde   90 0 0

To him more for makinge a fynck in the kitchen and removinge certen ftones from the chapel to the woorke   3 0 0

John Hazell aforefaide for ftoppinge all the loopes of the walles with planks 4l. and for makinge a newe bridge at the caftle gate 2l. in all   6 0 0

                                       166 13 3

Rewardes and enterteignments, viz. of

John Daniell havinge the overfighte and chaidge of the faide woorkes and woorkmen and difburfement of there paye by the fpace of 13 weeks at 6s the weeke   3 18 0

34 men fent out of the mayne lande to have bene imployed in her majefties woorkes and difchardged to ietourne home, fome beinge unable to endure the woorkes others for that the nombei was full and fo for theie chardges to and from   1 6 4

John Hafell for his enterteynment attendinge to kepe notes of the carriadges of ftone fande lyme water and tymber by the fpace of 171 dayes viz. 18 dayes at 1s. and 153 dayes at 10d. per diem   7

Capten Peers for his paynes and expences cominge fiom Portefmouth to diiecle and fett out plotts foi the places to be fortefied

Willm Nutre foi fpoyle made in his coine in the wynninge and carryadge of rough ftone woine in his grounde

John Leigh gen. for the expences and chardges of himfelfe
    fyve men and fix horfes for 12 dayes travellinge from
    the ifle of Wighte to London, ftayinge there and
    bringinge downe the thoufande markes appoynted for
    the fortifications   4   0   0

                                                                      21 10   4

In all the chardges of the faid works and fortifications
    done at Carefbrooke aforefaide within the tyme of this
    accompt as by the booke thereof figned with thands of
    Sir George Carey knighte the faid accomptauntes and
    John Daniell hereuppon duly perufed cafte tryed and
    examyned may appear, the fome of   470 18   5

Yarmouth, viz.

Alfo the accomptauntes ar allowed for makinge of forti-
    ficacons of earth and turffe at the faide caftle of Yar-
    mouthe with other neceffarie reparacons done there
    within the tyme of this accompte as hereafter is parti-
    cularly menconed and declared, viz.

Empcons and provifions with other chardges, viz.

Fellinge and fquaringe of 2 elmes for plancks for ftocks
    carriadges and wheeles 7s. 6d. makinge 2 paire of
    wheles for culveringe and for facre and for fpokes and
    exinge them with carriadges and yronwoorke for the
    fame 2l 3s. in all   2 10   6
Mendinge the powder houfe in the caftle   7   6
Mendinge the gutters and leades in the faid caftle   16   0
Spade fhoes 16 at 8d. the pece   10   8
Pickaxes 6 at 8d. the pece   4   0
Spades 3 at 6d the pece   1   6
Mountinge thordinaunce upp into the plattforme   5   0
Yronwoorke of diverfe forts with mendinge of woork-
    mens tooles   9   4
Other neceffaries, viz. a fmall lyne to meafure the plotts
    1s 3d a grynde ftone and a wenface 1s. 2d. and a hat-
    chett 1s. 4d in all the fome of   3   9
Landcarriage of 2 culverings from Newporte to Yar-
    mouth   8   0

Laborer.

Laborers woorkinge uppon the foitificacons of earth and turfe at 8*d.* per diem   44 11 4

In all the chardges of the foitificacons done at Yarmouth within the tyme of this accompte as by the perticular booke thereof fubfcribed as aforefaid and hereuppon duly perufed caft tryed and examyned may appear the fome of   50 7 7

Frefhwater, viz.

And the fayde accomptauntes likewife ar allowed for woorkes and reparacons done at Frefhwater afoiefaide within the tyme of this accompte viz. makinge a fhonce of earth and turfe at Sharpnode in Frefhwatei, fellinge of trees hewinge fawinge woorkinge and fettinge of poftes and rayles about the fame at Sharpnode conteyninge 39 perches with othei woorkes done theie within the tyme of this accompte as heicaftei more particulerly is mentioned, viz.

Empcons and provifions with other chardges viz.

Boordes for carryinge of tuife and eaith 200 at 6*s.* 8*d.* the 100   13 4

Settinge of pykes and hedges to kepe of the force of the fea fiom the fkonce   1 4 0

A greate levell to be ufed about the woorkes with 3*s.* for a fmall coide   5 6

Yronwooike and mendinge of tooles with clampinge of whelebarrowes and with 2*s.* 9*d* for nayles   18 8

Wages of laboiers making a fkonce of turfe and eaith at Shaipenode in Fiefhwater at 8*d* per diem.   117 0 8

Tafkewooike, viz to John Brett caipenter for fellinge of trees hewinge fawinge wooikinge and fettinge of poftes and rayles aboute the fkonce at Shaipenode contejninge 39 perches at 1*s* 8*d* the perch   3 5 0

Heniye Hall havinge the diieccion of the earth woorkes and overfighte of the labomeis for 98 days at 1*s.* per diem   4 18 0

Rowlande

Rowlande Regles for his paynes taken in directinge the woorkes and feinge to the woorkmen at Freſhwater   2   0   0

In all, the chardges of the woorkes done at Freſhwater aforefaide within the tyme of this accompte as by thaforefaide booke ſubſcribed with the ſame handes hereuppon tryed and examyned maye appeare the ſome of   130   5   2

Some totall of the peticons and payments aforefaide   651   11   2½

And ſo the ſayde accomptauntes uppon the determinacon of this there accompte doe remayne in debte the ſome of   15   2   1

Whereof the ſayde accomptaunte is allowed for his rydinge chardges from his houſe at Appledercombe unto the quenes majeſties foreſaide caſtles and forts at feverall tymes within the tyme of this accompte for the like chardges of twoe of his men rydinge from his ſaide houſe to London for the declaringe and finyſhinge his accompte and for the travell and paynes of one clarke havinge the chardge of the foreſaide money and payinge and defrayinge the ſame at fondrie tymes and for kepinge and wiitinge the particuler booke thereof the ſome of 6l. And John Conyers one of her majeſties auditors is allowed for the travell and expences of himſelfe and his clarkes during the tyme of the ratinge, caſtinge, tryinge, and examyninge of the particulers of the ſaid booke and reducinge the ſame into an accompte and ingroſſinge the ſame accompte in parchment the ſome of 5l. and ſo he oweth 4l. 2s. 1d. ½. whiche ſome is payde into the receipte of her majeſties exchequier as appeareth by a tallye thereof leavyed the third day of November anno 31 dne Elizabethe regine and uppon this accompte ſhewed and remayninge maye appeare. And ſo theſe accomptauntes uppon this accompte doe remayne quyte.

W. B U R G H L E Y.
J. F O R T E S C U E.
Jo. C O N Y E R S, Aud.

N° XIX.

Ex Baronagio Johan Ci

Richard the 1ſt Duke of Normandy, great-gran

Godfrey, Earl of Ewe, a

Gilbert Criſpan Lul(

Baldwin de Lyuan,
alſo de Molis and d
ceſtre, came over at the
queſt

Gauger, a baſe ſon,
a Monk at Bec in
Normandy

Robert, Governor
of Brion, an. 1090

Richard de Redvers, [
to whom Hen y I g r
Wight, and the Mai
church, ob 1137 id
rſt at Brighte Abbey
tranſlated Ford oil

Robert de
Sanctæ Mariæ
Ecclesiæ.

William de Redvers,
called alſo William de
Vernon, to whom his
father gave the church
of Redvers, with the
tithes of that town, &c

Lucia dr of Dru,
Baron de Balun.

Richard de Redvers, Earl of
Devon, Lord of the Iſle of
Wight, confirmed the foun-
dation of the Priory of
Carisbrook, 7th Hen II
died at the city of Cenoma
nia in France, an 1162, 8th
Hen II

Dioniſia, da
and coheir of
Reginald, Earl
of Cornwall,
baſe ſon of
Henry I

Henry died
young vita
patr buried
a Quarera.

William de Redvers,
called de Vernon, Iſ
Iſle of Wight, and
church Twinehima
nephews, ob 14th
r Hen III buried at
in co Devon

Baldwin de Redvers,
Earl of Devon, and
Lord of the Iſle of
Wight, ob ſ p

Avicia dr and heir
of Ralph de Dols in
Berry, mar 2dly, at
Salisbury, an 1189,
to Andrew de Cha-
verni.

Richard de Redvers,
Earl of Devon, brother
and heir, ob ſ p 30
Hen II 1184 buried
at Montbroge in Nor
mandy Lord of the Iſle
of Wight

Emma
dr of
Roger
dePont
Arches

Baldwin de Redvers, ſon
and heir-apparent, ob vita
patris, 1ſt Sept 1216, 18
Johis bur at Chriſtchurch-
Twineham, where his tomb
yet remaineth near the high
altar

Margaret, dr and heir
of Warine fitz Gerald
Lord of Harwood and
Eb ſhe had the ma
nor of Chriſtel uch
dowe Ob 20 Lds
1252.

Baldwin de Redvers, Earl
of Devon, and Lord of the
Iſle of Wight, of which he
was created Earl at Chriſt-
mas, 1240 24 Hen III ob
1245, 29 Hen III bur at
Bromere, Hants

Amicia eldeſt daugh of
Gilbert de Clare, Earl
of Gloucester and He
reford Foundreſs of the
Abbey of Buckland ob
12 Ed I 1283

Baldwin de Redvers, Earl
of Devon, and of the Iſle of
Wight, born on the eve of
the Circumciſion 1235, poi-
ſone in Sept 1262, 46 Hen
III buried at Bromere

Avice a Savoyard,
related to queen
Eleanor.

Margaret a nun at
Laycock in Com.
Wilts Living 1278,
8 Ed I.

Iſabel de Redvers, ſſter and ſole heir
of Baldwin, Counteſs of Albemarle,
and Counteſs of Devon, and Lady of
the Iſle of Wight, which ſhe ſold or
over to the King Ob 1293, 2 Ed
I bur at Bromere, Hants

John de Redvers,
Ob inf in France
Vita Patris

John,
ob ſ p

Thomas de Fortibus,
ob ſ p buried in the
church of the Fryers
Preachers at Stam-
ford.

William de Fortibus,
ob ſ p buried in the
church of the Fryers
Preachers at Oxford.

Avice de Fortibus
died young, buried
in Meux Abbey in
co Ebor.

Ingram de Percy,
1ſt huſband

Aveline de Fort
ſole heir, Counte
her own right
huſband 6th of
ſame year, and at
minſter Abbey
remaineth

APPENDIX

Nº XX.

The king's Writ of Protection of the Abbey of Quarr, againſt the Counteſs Iſabell. directed to the Sheriff of Southampton.

REX dilecto et fideli ſuo Willō. de Braybofe ſalutem. Cum nos nupei ex occaſione quarundam diſcordiarum inter Iſabellam de Foitibus comiteſſam Albemarlæ & abbatem. et conv̄. de Quarrera ſuboiturum, ſuper quibus placitum pendet coram nobis, per breve noſtrum inter eos ſufceſſimus in protectionem & defenſionem noſtram ipſos abbatem et conventum, homines, terras, res reddibus et omnes poſſeſſiones, inhibentes omnibus et ſingulis ne quis eis injuriam moleſtiam damnum infeiret aut gravamen. Ac eadem comiteſſa nihilominus prædictis abbati et conv. damna graviſſima contra protectionem noſtiam præd. & contra pacem noſtram inferie non deſiſtat ut accepimus: nos ipſorum abbatis et conven̄ quieti in hac parte providere volentes vobis mandamus qd. ad abbatiam præd. perſonaliter accedentes eam in manum noſtram capiatis et ſalvo cuſtodiatis donec præd. placitum inter ipſos terminetur, & aliud a nobis ſuper receperitis in mandatis ſalvo dictæ comiteſſæ hoc qd. tenet ibidem p. aſſenſum prædictorum abbatis & conv. ut dicitur. Teſte Rege apud Dymbey 27 Oct. Pat. 10 Edw. I m. 3.

Nº XXI.

Charta Iſabellæ Comitiſſ. Alb. et Devon, Novo Buigo de Medina.

SCIANT preſentes et futuri, quod ego Iſabella de Foitibus comitiſſā Albemarl. et Devon, ac Dn̄a. Inſulæ in ligea viduitate et plena poteſtate mea, dedi et conceſſi, et hæc preſenti charta mea confirmavi burgenſibus meis de novo burgo meo de Medina omnimodam libeit.. tem de theolonio *, et de omnibus alijs conſuetudinibus unde libeii

---

* This *theolonium*, or toll, was a payment made for the libeity of ſelling in the market, and for freedom and protection in coming to, and going from the market The proportion was rated according to the value of the goods brought for ſale; an eighth, a twentieth, a fortieth part, was paid by the Romans, Germans, and Saxons. Madox. Firma Burgi Horn, in his Miroii des Juſtices, ſays, that by the ancient law of the land, buyers of corn and cattle in fairs and markets, ought to pay toll to the lord of the market for the legality of their contracts in the open market, private contracts being held unlawful.

burgenf_s libertatem habeant *, quantum in me pertinet; per totam terram meam, in villis in vijs, in terra, in mare, in portu †, in nundinis, in mercatis, in venditionibus, in emptionibus, in burgo et extra burgum ‡, et in omnibus locis, et omnibus rebus suis.

Conceffi etiam prætatis burgenfibus meis qd. fint quieti et liberi de fcutis et hundredis, et de omnibus fect. ad fcu. et hundi. in infula. Conceffi quoq, yfdem burgenfibus qd. habeant comia pafturæ ad omnimodo animalia fua p totam pafturam in landis meis in Parkhorft extra bofcum quietam de herbagio in perpetuum. Præterea conceffi ipfis burgenfibus, quod omne placitum quod in predicto burgo ortum fuit, quod ad me pertinet in ipfo burgo inter ipfos et per ipfos placitetur et amerciamentum inde proveniens, per ipfos amercietur et taxetur. Et

---

* The common liberties of a borough were of the following nature, a liberty of trade, under the protection of its lord, which was granted by the lord, whether he was the king, or a fubject, and for this licenfe every burgefs paid a yearly rent. The Saxons had this method of trading from the other Germans, who ftill retain the fame cuftom. 2. To pay this rent *per manum fuam*, that is, by an officer of their own chufing, either mavor, bailiff, or other compeer. This privilege fprang from the like cuftom in Normandy, and was granted by William the Conqueror and his fucceffors in their borough charters for, before the Conqueft, the king, or other lord of a town, had a *præpofitus*, or fteward, to collect rents for the lord of the borough. 3. A liberty of receiving toll for all goods fold in the town; with many other privileges, as markets, fairs, fifheries, &c. The farm, or rent, of the borough, arofe from the iffues and profits of thefe liberties, and this rent was generally fo eafy, as to leave a great furplus to the community of the borough.

† Under colour of thefe words *in portu*, in the grant, it is likely the bailiff of Newport might formerly exact a duty from veffels anchoring in the mouth of the river there, and this is rendered probable, becaufe it appears, by an entry in their books, that fuch a duty is claimed by the town. nor can any other foundation be found for the duty now paid at Cowes, by fhips which caft anchor in that road. It muft be from hence alfo, that they claim an exclufive privilege of fifhing in that river, which might prove but a weak pretenfion, if the right was controverted.

‡ From the latitude here given the town of Newport had ufed to exact a toll in all places within the ifle, and had conftituted five bailiffs for the levy of it by diftrefs. This franchife was brought in queftion, by a *quo warranto*, and being tried, 8 Edward I. the grant was adjudged to be illegal, being contrary to the laws of the kingdom, and made without the king's licence. *Ex antiquo Rotulo Placit.*

volo

volo et concedo pro me et hæredibus meis qd. nullus eorum cum amei-
ciari debeat de amerciamento qd. ad me pertinet, ad plus quam ad triginta denarios amercietur; et hoc judicis et confideratione ipforum
burgenfium conceffi infuper prædictis burgenfibus qd. nullus in dicto
burgo fit præpofitus aut balivus nifi ipfe quem ijdem burgenfes ex communi electione et affenfu eligerent; et præfati burgenfes et hæredes eorum reddent fingulis annis mihi et hæredibus et affignatis meis pro omnibus meffuagijs fuis in eadem villa exceptis meffuagijs ædificatis in tredecim placeis et dimid. placea quorum reditum una cum efcheata et
omnibus alijs rebus adhuc unde contingentibus dedi et conceffi Deo et
capellæ beati Nichi. in caftro meo de Carefbroc et vicario ejufdem capellæ prout carta ejus plenius proteftatur, ad duos anni terminos decem
et octo marcas duos folidos et duos denarios, viz. medietatem ad Paf-
cham, et alteram medietatem ad feftum fancti Michis: et leprofis hof-
pitalis fancti Auguftini ad prædictos terminos fingulis annis unam marcam argenti de libera et perpetua eleemofina mea, videlicet ad quemlibet terminorum prædictorum dimid. marc. Dedi infuper et conceffi
prædictis burgenfibus meis ad feodi firmam perpetue duratur unum
molendinum aquaticum fitum juxta prioratum fcti. Crucis qd. appella-
tur la Weft Mill, cum omnibus ptinentijs fuis, et medietatem unius
molendini aquatici fiti juxta la fo.d quod vocatur Le Ford Mill, cum
omnibus ptinentijs fuis. Conceffi etiam qd. præfati burgenfes quiete
habeant omnia et fingula amerciamenta de omnibus querelis et placitis
ortis in prædicto burgo quæ inter ipfos placitantur vel placitare poffint.
Et etiam qd. habeant totum theolonium et cuftumam quæ ad me pertinent in prædicto burgo et extra burgum, fimul cum poteftate diftrin-
gere pro eifdem theolonis et cuftuma, in omnibus locis ubi ea aliquando
tempore confueverunt, exceptis tredecim placeis et dimid fupradictis
et falvis libertatibus a me conceffis abbati et conventui de Quarr. et hominibus fuis, priori Xti ecclefiæ de Twynham et hominibus fuis, et priori de Appledurcombe et hominibus fuis, prout cartæ eorum plenius et
melius reftantur, habendum et tenendum omnia premiffa data et con-
ceffa prædictis burgenfibus et eorum hæredibus, cum omni comoditate
et incremento quæ in prædicto burgo acceffere poterint; fine contra
dictione reclamatione feu impedimento mei, vel hæredum aut affignatorum meorum, libere, pacifice, quiete, et integre, reddendo inde annuatim mihi et hæredibus vel affignatis meis pro prædicta feudi firma mo-

g   lendin.

lendɩn. thcolon cuſtum. et amerciament. decem et octo maɩcas argenti ad quatuoɩ anni tempora, viz ad feſtum ſcti. Michɩ̄s fexaginta folidos, ad nat. Dnɩ. fexaginta folidos, ad feſtum Paſch. 60s. et ad nat. ſcti Johis. Baptiſtæ 60s. Et pɩɩoɩɩ et monacis de Careſbɩoc duas marcas annuatim ad cofdem teɩminos per æquales portiones de perpetua eleemofina pro omuɩbus fervitɩɩs ſæculaɩɩbus exactionc et demandis. Et ego Ifabella et hæɩedes et affignati mei hæc omnia data conceſſa et confiɩmata pɩædictɩs burgenfibus et corum hæɩedibus in omnibus et per omnia waɩɩantizabimus et contɩa omnes gentes defendemus in perpetuum : ut autcm hæc noſtra donatio et hujus caɩtæ meæ confirmatio perpetuæ firmatis robur obtineat, prefentem cartam figilli mei impɩeſſione ɩoberavi Hɩjs teſtibus, Willō. de Sancto Martino, Henɩico Trenchard, Thomɩ de la Haulde, Tho. de Evercey, Wɩllō. Eſtur, Jordō. de Kingeſton militibus, Johē de Patghgrave tunc conſtabulaɩɩo infulæ, Johē. de Heyno, Wɩllē. de Nevile, Galfɩido de Infula, Hugone la Vavaſur, Walt. Barnard, et alɩis.

N° XXII.

Proceedings in Parliament, on the Petition of Hugh Courtney, Earl of Devon, claiming the Iſle of Wight as next Heir of Ifabella de Fortibus

Rot. Parl. 8 & 9 Edw. II.

POSTEA in paɩliamento ɩegis habito apud Lincoln. in quindena s. Hɩlarɩj anno &c 9°. prædicti thefaurɩj et cameraɩɩj ɩetuɩnaverunt coɩɩam concilio regɩs breve qd. ipfis fuper dicto negotio miſſum fuit, et fimiliteɩ quafdam evidentias pɩo jure ɩegɩs in terɩɩs et tenementis ɩn dicta petitione contentis quæ hic infeɩɩus continentuɩ.

Edwaɩdus Dei gr. &c. thefauɩaɩ. et camerarijs fuis fal. fupplicavit nobis dilectus et fidelɩs noſter Hugo de Cuɩteney per petitionem fuam coɩam nobis et concilio noſtro exhibitam, de quibufd. teɩɩis et tenementis cum pertɩnentijs quæ fueɩunt Ifabellæ de Fortibus quondam comiteſſæ Devon. ɩn infula Vecta ; et fimiliᵗer de manerio de Chriſtchurch cum pertineñtɩjs in comitatu Southampton de quibus quidem teɩɩis et tenementis præfata, comitiſſa, cujus propinquior hæres idem Hugo exiſtit ut aſſeɩɩt, feiſita fuit in dominio fuo, ut de feodo, die quo obɩɩt, ut jus et hereditatem pred. Hugonis reddere velimus eɩdem. Et quɩa

tam

tam nobis, quam prefato Hugoni juſtitiam fieri volumus in hac parte vobis mandamus qd. ſcrutatis libris, chartis, rotulis, et alijs monumentis in theſauraria noſtra et in cuſtodia veſtra exiſtentibus, vos ſuper jure noſtro in terris et tenementis predictis et qualiter et quo modo et qua cauſa terræ et tenementa illa ad manus Dñi Edwardi nuper regis Angliæ patris noſtri devenerunt, reddatis in proximo parliamento noſtro ſub ſigillo ſchaccarij prædicti diſtincte et aperte certiores remittentes nobis hunc hoc brevium. Teſte meipſo apud Weſtm. 30 Maij anno regni noſtri octavo.

Rot. Parl. 9 Edw. II.

Examinationes quorundam ſuper confectione chartæ comitiſſæ Albemarlæ factæ Dño Regi de quibuſdam terris de quibus infra ſit mentio et de redditione earundem facta Dño Regi

Walterus Covent. et Lichfeld. epiſcopus dicit, qd. epiſcopus Dunelmenſis mandavit ei qd. ſtatim occurreret ei apud Stokewell, viz. die Lunæ ante feſtum S. Martini anno &c. ob qd mandatum idem Walterus ibidem venit eodem die circam horam primam et ibi ex mandato præd. epiſcopi Dunelmenſis fecit et ſcripſit quandam chartam in quodam ga dino que in ſe continebat qd. Iſabella de Fortibus comitiſſa Albemarle conceſſit et reddidit Dño ſuo Dño Regi Angliæ inſulam de Wight, manerium de Chriſtchurch et manerium de Faukſhall cum pertinentijs, et quietem clamavit de ſe et hæredibus ſuis præd. Dño Regi et hæred ſuis in perpetuum. Et chartam illam liberavit præf. epo Dunelmenſi qui cum eadem adivit præd. comitiſſam ad confirmandum, et poſtea reportavit eadem chartam ipſi Walterio ſigillo præd. comitiſſam ſignatum. Et dicit qd. poſtea quando præfatus epiſcopus Dunelmenſis returnavit ad præd. comitiſſam ad licentiam ſuam de ea capiendam ipſe Walterus cum præf. epiſcopo intravit cameram ubi præfata comitiſſa jacuit, circa horam tertiam, et audivit eam loquentem cum præd. epiſcopo.

Frater Willus de Gainſborough dicit qd ipſe fuit confeſſor præd. comitiſſæ per quatuor annos ante mortem ſuam. Et qd ipſe ad mandatū præd. comitiſſæ venit ad quoddam manerium de Sutton extra Detford, ubi eadem comitiſſa in veniendo ad Cantuaria cepit infirmari et ſic fuit continue cum eadem ibidem et apud Stokewell uſque ad mortem ipſius comitiſſæ. Et dicit qd fuit præſens præd. die Lunæ quando præd. epūs Dunelmenſis venit ad comitiſſam apud Stokewell, et vidit et audi-

vit vbi præd. episcopus allocutus fuit eandem super quadam prælocu-
tione inter Dñum Regem et ipsam prius habitam de insula de Wight,
maneriis de Christchurch, et de Fawkshalle, cum pertinentijs et quæsivit ab eodem, si adhuc esset in eadem voluntate reddendi præd. insulam et maneria Dño Regi. sicut antea prolocutum fuerat. Quæ dixit
qd. sic Quæsita etiam per ipsum episcopum si vellet qd. charta inde
fieret; dixit qd. sic. Et tum præd. episcopus fecit præd. Walterum
scribere præd. chartam, qua scripta, idem episcopus reportavit eam
coram eadem comitissa, et eum coram ipsa comitissa, in presentia ipsius fratris Willielmi, Gilberti de Knovill, Galfridi Capellani, (hic
dicit ut credit) Agnetis de Mountcals domicelle ejusdem comitissæ &
plurium aliorum de familia comitissæ Chartam illam fecit legere,
et a præd. comitissa quæsivit si vellet qd. charta illa sub illa forma signa-
retur ; quæ dixit qd. sic : et præcepit præd. Agneti qd. sigillum suum
deferret, ad chartam illam consignandum ; qd. sic factum est. Post
cujus consignationem in præsentia prædictorum factam, eadem comitissa
tradidit præf. episcopo prædictam chartam, et seisinam prædictorum
insulæ et maneriorum præd. charta contentorum in manus ipsius epis-
copi, nomine Dñi Regis, et ad opus ejusdem, per chirothecas ipsius
ēpi quas eadem comitissa in manu sua tenuit, ex mera voluntate sua et
sponte reddidit ; et postea circa horam 3am. quando idem episcopus sic
recesserat, et eadem comitissa sic requievit. Et postea idem frater Willielmus post horam nonam rogavit prædictam comitissam qd. testamentum suum faceret. Quæ respondit qd. ita fatigata fuit qd. si multum in
loquendo laboravit, timebat sibi per hoc gravari multum et debilitari.
Sed postea ipsa comitissa post horam vesperarum, per ipsum fratrem
iterum requisita de eodem faciendo, fecit testamentum suum, et nomi-
navit per digitos suos executores suos, viz. abbatem de Quarrera, priorem de Brummore, priorem de Christchurch, Gilbertum de Knovill,
et sic fatigata quievit. Et postea per aliquod tempus, fecit se commu-
nicari per ipsum fratrem Willielmum, ad hoc faciendum revestitum,
et toto tempore prædicto erat bonæ et sanæ memoriæ : et postea inter
mediam noctem et auroram expiravit.

Walterus episcopus prædictus, comes Lincoln. et comes Warren.
testantur, qd. epūs Dunelmensis coram eis dixit qd. præd. charta facta
fuit in forma prædicta, et qd. redditio sibi nomine Dñi Regis de prædictis insula et maneriis cum pertinentijs, factum fuit ut prædictum est,
et ex bona voluntate dictæ comitissæ ; et quod ipsa comitissa fuit bonæ

memoriæ

memoriæ et fanæ mentis. Et quia a quibufdam dictum fuit qd. præd. epūs Dunelmenfis coram archiepō Cantaur. dixiffe debuit et cognoviffe contrarium facti prædicti; ipfi quæfierunt ab eodem epifcopo qui fic dixiffet, qui hoc omnino negavit, nec fuit intentionis fuæ aliquid dicere coram dicto archiepō. aut aliis de prædictis infula aut maneriis, nec dixit nifi de aliis terris quæ fuerunt dictæ comitiffæ et de hereditate Hugonis de Courtney, ut de terris Devon.

Ricardus de Afton miles dicit, qd. ipfe fuit fenefcallus hofpitij dictæ comitiffæ, per magnum tempus ante mortem fuam et tunc, et qd. per decem annos et amplius prælocutum fuit inter dictum Regem et ipfam, de redditione præd. infulæ et maneriorum cum pertinentiis, præd. Dño Regi facienda, pro quatuor millibus librarum; et fic femper continuavit voluntatem illam ita qd. caufa illius voluntatis fuæ perficiendæ arripuit iter fuum verfus Cantuariam per London. ubi Rex tunc fuit, et fuper hoc locuta fuit cum Rege; et Rex ei refpondit qd. fatis tempeftivè hoc facere poffit in reditu fuo de Cantauria, et fuit apud Stokewell die Lunæ prædicto. Omnia prædicta quæ frater Willielmus dixit, et modo quo dixit ipfo et aliis prænominatis præfentibus, fcientibus, videntibus, et audientibus, factu fuerunt Et qd. præd. comitiffa bonæ mentis et fanæ memoriæ fuit. Dicit etiam qd. audivit dictam comitiffam fæpius in vita fua dicentem qd. eo libentius redderet, pro eo qd. hæredes fui ita remoti a fanguine fuo fuerint, qd. propinquior hæres ejus ipfam potuit defponfare fi virum vellet habere, et qd. propter hoc aliquando locuta fuit cum comite Marefcallo fuper venditione præd. terrarum et aliarum.

Gilbertus de Knouill dicit, qd prima locutio facta fuit apud Briftol, quando comitiffa de Bares defponfata fuit, inter Dūum Regem et Ifabellam comitiffam Albemarlæ, per epūm Dunelmenfem et epūm Coventr. tunc thefaurarium de garderoba, mediatores de terra de infula de Wight et Chriftchurch cum pertinentiis, et fimiliter de Fawkfhall, de quibus prius habita fuit locutio inter eadem et comitem Marifcallum. Et dicit qd. poftea in vigilia s Martini, eodem anno quo comitiffa obijt, apud Stockwell, venerunt præfati epifcopi, et arrenarunt præd. comitiffam, ex parte Regis fuper præmiffis, ita qd. convenit de prædicta terris, qd. Rex folveret eidem comitiffæ fex mille marcas pro prædictis terris, et eadem comitiffa eodem die, reddidit in manus præd. epi Dunelmenfis præd. terras ad opus Dñi Regis, et remifit et quietum clamavit de fe et hæred. fuis, Dño Regi et hæred. fuis in perpetuum prout
charta

charta quam Rex inde habet teſtatur.   Et dicit qd prædicti denarij ſol-
vebantur in feſto s. Martini ſequenti in domo epī Dunelmenſis London.
mercatoribus de Spina, ita qd. ipſi inde reſponderent executoribus dictæ
comitiſſæ, cum illos peterent.   Et de eo tempore redditionis in manum
epiſcopi et conſignationis chartæ, et etiam de memoria, et de bona voluntate, et de tempore mortis præd. comitiſſæ concordat cum præfato
fratre Willielmo. Præterea dicit qd præfata comitiſſa dixit, qd. ſi ipſa
virum habere vellet, qd. pro parentela bene poſſit habere in virum
præd Hugonem de Curtney, ſi ipſe eſſet plene ætatis.   Et dicit qd.
tempore redditionis fuerunt preſentes omnes prænominati, Agnes de
Mounteals, Johanna de Marroys, et Rogerus de Gardino, et alij de
quorum nominibus ignorat.

Et quia totum negotium factum fuit, per epūm Dunelmenſem et de-
ductum, et in præſentia præd. Gilberti de Knouill et Galfridi capellani, ut prædictum eſt, neceſſe eſt ut veniant et audiantur ad informan-
dum animum Dñi Regis et ſimiliter qd. charta comitiſſæ videatur ſub
ccra.

Iſta examinatio præſcripta facta fuit in præſentia Dni W. Coventr. et
Lichfeld. epī comitis Lincoln. comitis Warenn. Johīs. Berewick, Rogeri le Brabazon, Johīs de Mettingham, Johīs de Drokensford et Gilberti de Roubery, &c. Unde miſſum fuit breve eidem Gilberto ſub tenore qui ſequitur.

Edwardus Dei gracia, &c. Dilecto et fideli ſuo Gilberto de Roubery
ſal.   Quia intelleximus qd. quædam ſcripta munimenta et memoranda
terras et tenementa quæ fuerunt Iſabellæ de Fortibus, quondam comitiſſæ Devon, inſulam Vectam et maner. de Chriſtchurch cum pertinen.
in comitatu Southampton, tangentia; quæ quidem terras et tenementa
cum pertinen. dilectus et fidelis noſter Hugo de Curtney ſibi ut hæredi-
tatem ſuam, per petitionem ſuam, coram nobis et concilio noſtro exhibitam, petit liberari, in cuſtodia veſtra exiſtunt: vobis mandamus qd.
ſcrutatis ſcriptis munimentis et memorandis in cuſtodia veſtra exiſtentibus, omnia hujus modi ſcripta munimenta et memoranda terras et ten.
prædicta qualitercunque tangentia, theſaurario et cameariis noſtris in
theſauraria noſtra cuſtodienda, ſine dilatione qualibet liberetis, et hoc
breve; et hoc nullatenus omittatis.   Teſte meipſo apud Thunderle 14.
Maij, anno regni noſtri octavo.

Et prædictus Hugo venit ad idem parliamentum apud Lincoln et por-
rexit ibidem quandam aliam petitionem in hæc verba.

A noſtre

A noſtre ſeignr. le Roy et à ſon conſeil monſtre Hugh de Courtney, que comme il ad longement ſuiz a divers pailements pur ſon droits, et ſon claim qu'il ad en L'iſle de Wight, en le manoir de Chriſtchurch et les appurtenances en la conte de Southampton et a darrein parlement tenuz a Weſtminſter en l'an de noſtre ſeignr. le Roy, qui ore eſt 9time. Fuit le dit Hugh reſpondu à ſa petition, qu'il ſueroit bref al treſoier et as chamberlayns noſtre ſeignr. le Roy que eux feiſſent ſercher, libres chartres muniments et tout autres remembrances as dits tenements touchants, et en leur garde eſteants. Et que le dits noſtre ſeignr. le Roy fut certifié à ſon prochein pailement ſuant deſſous le ſeal del Eſchequer. Et le dit Hugh ad ſuy quant en luy, eſt pur quoy il prie à dit noſtre ſeignr. le Roy qu' veille commander à ſon conſeil de veuer les dites charties, muniments, &c. touchant le Roy de ſon droit, et ſur cel la commander à eux que al dit Hugh ſoit fait ley et droit.

Unde lecta coram concilio Regis petitione prædicta et recitatis ibidem brevi et evidentijs ſupra dictis, ut ſecurius in eodem negotio procedi poſſit præceptum fuit qd. diligentius fieret ſcrutinium tam in theſauraria quam in garderoba Regis et alib', ſi aliqua chaita præd Iſabelle vel aliqua alia ſcripta vel memoranda negotium illud tangentia inveniri poſſint, et qd. Rex et concilium ſuum inde certificarentur, a die Paſchæ in 15 dies apud Weſtminſtr. et ſuper hoc emanarunt brevia theſaurario et camerarijs et ſimiliter cuſtodi garderobæ Regis, &c. Et inde dictum fuit præd. Hugoni qd. expectet diem ſuum coram Rege et concilio ſuo apud Weſtm. in quindena præd. &c. Ad quem diem cuſtos garderobæ Regis miſit coram concilio Regis apud Weſtm. chartam per quam præfata Iſabella conceſſit, reddidit, et quietum clamavit Dño Edwardo Regi patri Regis nunc, inſulam de Wight et manei. de Chriſtchurch ſupra dicta. Quæ quidem charta hic in ſequenti rotulo continetui in hæc verba.

Omnibus Chriſti fidelibus ad quos preſens ſciiptum prevenerit, Iſabella de Fortibus comitiſſa Albemaile et Devon. et domina inſulæ, ſalutem in Domino ſempiternam. Noveritis nos conceſſiſſe, reddidiſſe, et quietum clamaſſe, pro nobis et hæred. noſtris, egregio piincipi et Dño. noſtio chariſſimo Dño Edwardo Dei gr. illuſtri Regi Angliæ et Dño Hiberniæ, et Duci Aquitaniæ, totam inſulam de Wight in com. Southampton, cum advocationibus de abbatiarum, prioratuum eccleſiarum, homagijs redditionibus libeioium hominum, villenagijs, cum villanis eadem villenagia tenentibus, ac eorum. catall. et ſeqielis ſe.

quicquid

quicquid nos habuimus die confectionis præfentis fcripti in dicta infula, tam in dominico vel in dominio, fine aliquo retenemento, cum omnibus fuis pertinentijs, tam infra dictum comitatum quam extra. Conceffimus etiam et reddidimus et quietum clamavimus pro nobis et hæred. noftris præd. Dño. noftro Regi manerium Chrifti Ecclefiæ de Twynham in dicto comitatu, ac etiam manerium de Lambhith in comitatu Suir. fimul cum manerio quod vocatur la Sale Fawks in parochia de Lambheth cum omnibus fuis pertinentijs tam infra eundem comitatus quam extra, una cum homagijs, fervitijs, liberorum hominum, villenagijs, cum villanis eadem villenagia tenentibus, ac earum catallis et fequelis cum omnibus fuis pertinentijs fc. quicquid habuimus in præd. manerijs die confectionis præfentis fcripti, tam in dominico quam in dominio, cum omnibus fuis pertinen. fine aliquo retenemento Habend. et tenend. præd. Dño Regi et hæred. feu affignatis fuis libere et quiete et hæreditatie in perpetuum. Ita quod nec nos, hæredes noftri feu aliquis nomine noftro, in prædictis terris et tenementis, cum fuis pertinen. nominatis, feu non nominatis, aliquid juris vel clamij de cætero exigere feu vendicare poterimus in perpetuum. Pro hac autem conceffione, redditione et quieta clamatione, dedit nobis præfatus Dñus. Rex fex millia marcas argenti præ manibus Et ut hæc noftra conceffio, redditio, et quieta clamatio rata et ftabilis permaneat in perpetuum, huic fcripto figillum noftrum appofuimus Hijs teftibus Dño Antonio Dunelmenfi epifcopo, dñis Rico de Afton, Gilberto de Knouill, Rico de Waldgrave, Jordano de Kingfton, Roberto de Glamorgan, et Johē de Heyno, militibus; Johē de Grimftede, Philippo de Tangle, Rogero de Gardino, Waltero de Langton, clericis, et alijs. Dat apud Stokewell prope Lambheth, die Lunæ proximo ante feftum s. Martini in hyeme. Anno Dñi 1293. Et prædictus Hugo venit apud Weft. coram concilio Regis in quindena præd. et petijt ficut prius infulam et maner. prædicta cum pertinen. fibi reddi tanquam propinquiori hæredi præf Ifabellæ. Et fuper hoc Johīs de Stoner, pro Dño Regi dicit, qd. ex quo præd. Ifabella confanguinea præd. Hugonis, cujus bæres ipfe eft, ut dicit, infulam et maneria prædicta, Dño Edwardi Regi patri Dñi R. nunc (de quo eadem Ifabella infulam et maneria præd. tenuit in capite) per præd. chartam conceffit, reddidit, et de fe et hæred. fuis qui et. clamavit dicto Dño. Edwardo &c. in perpet. petijt judicium pro Dño Rege, fi præd. Hugo contra factum anteceffons fuæ præd. aliquid juris in præd. tenementis clamare poffit. Et præd. Hugo

dicit

dicit qd. præd. Ifabella confanguinea fua, cujus hæres ipfe eft obijt feifita de prædictis tenementis in dominico fuo ut de feodo et hoc petit verificare per patriam.　　Et quia dictus Hugo nihil refpondit ad factum prædictum dictum fuit eidem Hugoni qd. ulterius diceret fi quæ contra dictam chartam dicenda haberet, fi fibi viderit expedire.　　Et eidem Hugo pertijt qd. fuper hoc deliberare, et avifamentum ufq. ad prox. parliamentum habere poffit, et conceffum fuit ei et qd. negotium prædictum fit tunc in eodem ftatu quo nunc exiftit; propter qd. dictum fuit fibi qd. fequatur ulterius in prox. parliamento, &c.

N° XXIII.

A Grant of the Lordfhip of the Ifle of Wight to Philippa, Duchefs of York.　Dated 10th December, 3 Hen. V.

REX omnibus ad quos &c. faltem. Sciatis quod cum Dñus R. nuper Rex Angl Secundus poft Conqueftum per lras fuas patentes conceffifet cariffimo Confanguineo ñro Edwardo nup Duci Ebor' per nomine Edwardi Comitis Roteland. Infulam de Wyght Caftrum de Karfbroke infra eandem Infulam & totum Dominium ad dcam Infulam & Caftrum pertinens cum feodis Militum, Advocationibus Ecclefiarum, Vicariarum Capellarum & Hofpitalium, Wardis, Maritagijs, Relevijs, Efcaetis, Foreftis, Parcis, Bofcis, Warennis, forisfacturis catallis felonum & fugitivorum, Moris, Marifcis, Pifcarijs, Pratis, Pafcuis, Wrecco, Maris, Franchefiis, Libertatibus & Reverfionibus cum omnibus alijs pertinentijs fuis ac proficuis & commoditatibus quibufcumque · Habend. & tenend. eidem nuper Duci ad terminum Vite fue, abfque aliquo eidem nuper Regi reddend.　Ac idem nuper Rex per alias lras fuas patentes conftituiffet prefatum nuper Ducem Juftic. & Cuftodem tam Nove Forefte fue quam omnium aliarum Foreftarum fuarum citra Trentam Habend. occupand. & excercend. officia predca cum omnibus & fingulis libertatibus, privilegijs, juribus, feodis, proficuis, & commoditatibus ad officia illa pertinentibus ad terminum vite ipfius nuper Ducis　Ac Dominus H nuper Rex Angl. pater nofter voluiffet & conceffiffet quod fi contigeret prefatum nuper Ducem vivente Philippa uxore ejus obire tunc eadem Philippa haberet dcm Caftrum & Dominium de Karefbrok cum pertiñ excepta Conftabularia ejufdem Caftri.　Ac eciam cuftodiam Forefte predce ad terminum Vite fue cum feodis Militum & Advocationibus Ecclefiar' ac alijs proficuis & commoditatibus quibufcumque

Rich. II.

Hen. IV.

h　　　　　　　　　　　　　　　　　que

que ad eadem Caftrum Dominium & Cuftodiam fpectantibus, adeo integre & eodem modo quo prefatus nuper Dux illa tenuit ex conceffionibus fupradcīs. Ac infuper idem pater nofter quinto die Decembris anno regni fui undecimo per alias hās fuas patentes de uberiori grā fua conceffiffet prefato nuper Duci & heredibus fuis de corpore fuo legitime procreatis Infulam Dominia & Caftrum predcām cum omnibus pertineutiys fuis Habend. & tenend. prefato nuper Duci & heredibus fuis de corpore fuo legitime procreatis imperpetuum dcām Infulam & predcm Caftrum de Karefbrok infra eandem Infulam & omnia Dominia ad eadem Infulam & Caftrum pertinencia, adeo integre ficut idem pater nofter ea habuit feu habere poterat, cum feodis Militum, Advocationibus Abbatiarum Prioratuum tam alienigenarum quam indigenarum, cum omnibus Redditibus & Poffeffionibus quibufcumque, ac feodis & advocationibus ad eadem pertinentibus, Ecclefiys, Vicariys, Capellis & Hofpitalibus ac cum Advocatione Ecclefie de Fiefshewatie in Infula predcā, fimul cum Wardis, Maritagiys, Releviys, Homagiys, Fidelitatibus, Foreftis, Chaceis, Warennis, Parcis, Bofcis, Molendinis, Efcaetis, Reverfionibus, Waifs, Straifs, Redemptionibus cum Exitibus, Finibus & Ameiciamentis, Catallis fugivitorum felonum Utlagatorum & omnibus aliys forisfactuiis quibufcumque tam tenencium quam refidencium & non refidencium, retorno omnium brevium & executione eorundem, Wrecco Maris, Pifcariys, Pratis, Pafturis, Redditibus, Serviciys, liberis confuetudinibus & omnibus aliys proficuis & emolumentis quibufcumque de & in eadem Infula aliqualiter emeigentibus & provenientibus de omnibus & fingulis gentibus & tenentibus tam tenentibus qui de dicto patre noftro quam de prefato nuper Duce aut de aliys conjunctim vel divifim tenebant; licet ijdem tenentes vel refidentes tenuiffent de ipfo patre noftro aut de aliquibus aliys in capite aut aliter extra Infulam fupradcām. Et quod bene liceret dicto nuper Duci & heredibus fuis predcīs feipfos in feifinam ponere per fe aut Miniftros fuos in omnibus premiffis & qualibet parcella eorundem abfque impedimento vel perturbacōe dicti patris noftri vel heredum fuorum Vicecomitum, Efcaetorum, Ballivorum aut aliorum Miniftrorum fuorum quorumcumque; prout in literis tam dicti Domini R. nuper Regis, quam predcī patris nri fupradcīs plenius continetur. Nos de grā nra fpeciali & pio eo quod predcā Philippa Duciffa Ebor' que predcm nuper Ducem virum fuum ipfo fine herede de corpore fuo legitime procreato nuper decedente fupervixit ftatum quem in cuftodia dicte Nove Forefte virtute predce conceffionis prefati patris noftri fic habuit feu habere potuit nobis ad manda-

tum noſtrum ſurſum reddidit ac lr̃as patentes dicti patris noſtri eidem
Duciſſe ut eſt dictum factas in Cancellariam noſtram reſtituit cancelland.
Dedimus conceſſimus & confirmavimus & per preſentes damus concedimus & confirmamus pro nobis & heredibus m̃is quantum in nobis eſt
eidem Duciſſe Inſula, Caſtrum & Dominia predc̃a cum omnibus ſuis
pertin. excepta Conſtabularia ejuſdem Caſtri . Habend & tenend. prefate Duciſſe a tempore mortis prefati nuper Ducis ad totam vitam ipſius
Duciſſe predc̃m Inſulam ad dictum Caſtrum necnon omnia Dominia ad
eadem Inſulam & Caſtrum pertinencia, excepta Conſtabularia predc̃a, adeo
integre ſicut prefatus nuper Dux ea habuit ſeu virtute conceſſionis dicti
patris noſtri ſibi ut premittitur facte habere potuit aut debuit, cum feodis
Militum Advocationibus Abbatiarum, Prioratuum tam indigenarum
quam alienigenarum, cum omnibus Redditibus & Poſſeſſionibus quibufcumque ac feodis & Advocacōibus ad eadem pertinentibus, Eccleſijs, Vi-
carijs, Capellis & Hoſpitalibus ac cum Advocatione Eccleſie de Friefshe-
watie in eadem Inſula ſimul cum Wardis, Maritagijs, Relevijs, Homagijs, Fidelitatibus, Foreſtis, Chaceis, Warennis, Parcis, Boſcis, Molendinis, Eſcaetis, Reverſionibus, Waifs, Straifs, Redemptionibus cum exitibus, finibus & amerciamentis catallis fugitivorum felonum & urlaga-
torum & omnibus alijs forisfacturis quibuſcumque tam tenencium
quam reſidencium & non reſidencium, returno omnium brevium & executione eorundem, Wreccos Maris, Piſcarijs, Pratis, Paſturis, Redditibus, Servicijs, liberis conſuetudinibus & omnibus alijs proficuis &
emolumentis quibuſcumque de & in eadem Inſula aliqualiter emergenti-
bus & provenientibus de omnibus & ſingulis gentibus & tenentibus tam
tenentibus qui de nobis quam de ipſa Duciſſa aut de alijs conjunctim
vel diviſim pro tempore tenent, licet ijdem tenentes vel reſidentes teneant
de nobis ſeu de aliquibus alijs in capite vel aliter extra Inſulam predc̃m.
Et quod liceat prefate Duciſſe ponere ſe in ſeiſinam de tempore in tempus per ſe aut Miniſtros ſuos in omnibus premiſſis & qualibet parcella
eorundem abſque impedimento vel perturbatione noſtri vel heredum
noſtrorum Juſticiariorum, Eſcaetorum, Vicecomitum, aut aliorum Bal-
li orum ſeu Miniſtrorum noſtrorum vel heredum noſtrorum quorumcumque, eo quod expreſſa mencio in preſentibus lr̃is, ſeu in petitione nobis inde porrecta de vero valore annuo dictorum Caſtri, Inſule, & Dominorum ac aliarum rerum jurium & poſſeſſionum ſupradictorum eidem
Duciſſe per preſentes conceſſorum, aut de eo quod prefata Duciſſa habuit
ſive habet de dono Domini E. nuper Regis Angl. proavi noſtri ac dic-

torum Regum Rici & Henr. patris noftri necnon Johis nuper Ducis
Lancaftrie & ñro, aut de fumma five valore dictorum rerum jurium
proficuorum & commoditatum cafualium eidem Duciffe per nos ut premittitur concefforum facta non exiftit, juxta formam ftatutorum in hac
parte editorum non obftante.   Provifo femper quod eadem Duciffa durante vite fua Conftabulai. Caftri predci qui pro tempore fuerit Viginti
Marcas pro feodo fuo annuatim perfolvat.   In cujus &c.   Tefte Rege
apud Weftm. x die Decembr Anno regni fui tercio.

    Rex Vic Southampt. faltm   Cum decimo die Decembris ultimo
preterito per lias noftias patentes dederimus, concefferimus, & confirm-
averimus pro nobis & heredibus noftris quantum in nobis fuit Philippe
Duciffe Ebor' Infulam de Wyght, Caftrum de Carefbroke infra eandem
Infulam & omnia Dominia ad dcām Infulam & Caftrum pertinen. cum
omnibus fuis pertin. excepta Conftabular ejufdem Caftri.   Habend. &
tenend prefate Duciffe a tempore mortis Edwardi nuper Ducis Ebor²
ad totam vitam ipfius Duciffe predcām Infulam ac dcūm Caftrum, necnon omnia Dominia ad eadem Infulam & Caftrum pertinencia, excepta
Conftabularia predcā. adeo integre ficut prefatus nuper Dux ea habuit
feu virtute conceffionis Domini H. nuper Regis Angl. patris noftri fibi
facto habere potuit aut debuit, cum feodis Militum ac alijs liberitatibus
& liberis confuetudinibus in lris noftris predcis fpecificatis prout in eifdem lris plenius continetur : tibi precipimus quod ipfam Duciffam, Infulam, Caftrum & Dominia predcā cum pertinen. excepta Conftabular.
predcā, habere & eam omnibus & fingulis libertatibus & liberis confuetudinibus in hīs predcis contentis uti & gaudere permittas, juxta tenorem litterarum noftrarum predictarum ipfam contra tenorem earundem
non moleftans in aliquo feu gravans.   T. R. apud Weftm. xx die Febr.
anno tercio.

N° XXIV.

Petitions of the Inhabitants of the Ifle of Wight, to the King, and
Parliament, *anno* 28 Henrici VI. 1449.

Ifle of Wight.

    TO the kyng oure foveraigne lord. Pleafe it unto youre moft excel-
lent grace to be enfourmed how that youre ifle of Wighte ftondeth in
the grettyft juperdye and daunger of any parte of youre Realme of Ing-
lond;

Iond; the whiche Ifle withynne five yeres was at the nombre of x m.
fenfable men and xxx Knyghtes and fquyers dwellyng withynne; the
whiche x m. abovefeid are anentifed through peftellence and Werres, and
fome voyded becaufe of oppreffion of extorcioners, that nowe there is
fkante xii c. of fenfable men, and Knyghtes never one, and fquyers no
mo but Herry Bruyn fquier of youre Howfhold, that may labour aboute
Werres. And youre Caftell withynne youre feid Ifle is not repeired, nother the walles, garriettes and lopes, nother ftuffed with men and har-
neys, nother with gonnes, gonnepowder, croffe bowes, quarelles, longe
bowes, arrowes, longe fperes, axes and gleyves, as fuche a place fhuld
be in tyme of Were. wherfore youre feid fubgettes ben fo difconforted,
and thorought the grete clamer noyfe and enformacion that they heren
daily of youre trewe lige men, that ben diftruffed and comen owte of
Normandye, that youre adverfaries of Fraunce ben fully purpofed and
fette, and other youre enemyes, for to conquere the feid ile, whiche
God defende. Befechith mekely youre full humble fubgettes of the
feid ifle, that it may like unto youre Highneffe to ordeyne and appoynte
other elles to commawnde fuche as fhall occupie the faid Ile through vertue of youre graunte, to ordeyne and appoynte fuche fufficiante of men
and ftuffe above wretyn, as it may be fufficiant for the defence of the
faid Caftell and Ile, as youre faid fubgettes fhall have no caufe for to
voyde owte of youre faid Ifle; and youre feid fubgettes fhall pray to
God for you.

Refponfio. The kyng woll that the Lord Beauchamp fee to the rule
thereof.

Inhabitants of the ifle of Wight.

UNTO the wife and difcrete comens of this Parlement affembled :
Prayen the poure peple inhabitant within the Ile of Wyght in the Counte
of Hampfhire unto all the Commons affembled in this prefent Parlement, to confidere the gret noyfe that daily goeth uppon the fee by
owre enemyes, and the adverfite that thei fhewen daili unto the faid
Ile, the whiche Ile is undirtaken by certiyn warriours of owre ennemyes
of Fraunce to be conquerid into there handes bi fhorte time, the
whiche God defende; upon the whiche the poure peple of the ile ben
difcomforted and amayd, feyng the febelnyffe within themfelves. Certefying your wyfdoms that whereas the faid Ile hath ben hereafore at the
nomb're

.iombie of giet peple fenfable, hit hath ben fo pelyd and oppreffid now
of late bi one John Newport fteward of the faid Ile made bi the Duke
of York, for the wh che myfgovernaunce was by hym difcharged
and put oute of his office; and then after his difcharge the faid John
Newpoit and otheis of his fecte the laft fomei uppon the fee, fo thret-
enyng the Kynges peple of the Ile and diftreffing them, their bodies
their harneis and then godes, bothe bi londe and bi fee, that the peple is
forfaken the ile, fo at this dai there is not xv peple fenfable, the whiche
is unto us al enhabitantz in the Ile grete hevyneffe, feyng no more ftuf of
men nor no ftuf of archeric fenfable left within the Ile, nor within the
Caftell of the fame Ile, hit hathe cawfid us alle to make fupplicacion unto the Duke of Yorke and his counfaile foi fupportacion and aide of the
faid Caftel and ile bothe for men and archerie in falvacion of the Ilonde,
and of the Kinges peple theie Ceitefying unto youre allei wifdoms of
no relief by caufe of doubtze of iefumpcion; and that it is noifed here,
that by the iefumpcion thys Ile fhal ftond in the Kinges hand *, and that
the foifaid John Newport fewith dailli to the King oure foverayne lord
to be lewtenant, ftewaid, reffeyvour, and baylly within the faid Ile,
the whiche God defende, confideiyng the giet oppreffion bifore rehcr-
fid . and alfo it is openli fpoken and noyfed, that the faid John Newport hath fold the faid Ile and defireth to have the hed offices theie to
the entent to hurt the poure peple to ther otteraunce ondoying and dif-
truccion of the faid Ile; the whiche God of his hie mercy defende.
Moreovei certefying your wifdons, that the faid John Newpoit hath at
this day no lyvelode to mentayne his giet countenance but bi the op-

* It appears here that Richard Plantagenet, duke of York, fathei of king Edward IV. was one of the lords of the ifland , and though we aie deficieat in other
evidences to eftablifh the fact, this may be deemed fufficient, confidering the con-
fufions in this reign The inhabitants mention him as appointing to offices in the
ifland , they add, that they had applied to him to put the caftle in a ftate of
defence, and to provide for their fecuiity but the duke was at that time engaged
in greater purfuits, though he had not as yet publicly avowed his pietenfions to
the ciown, the queen and her favouiites giowing jealous of him, he was iemoved
to Ireland, with a commiffion to fupprefs the rebellion there. The inhabitants of
the ifle of Wight we fee could obtain no affiftance of the duke of York, perhaps
becaufe he was apprehenfive of the ifland being refumed by the crown; and not
without reafon, for it was afterward conferred on the duke of Somerfet, who had
before fupplanted him in the iegency of France.

pieffing

preſſing of the peple in the contray that he ſitt in, thoiw the whiche he
hath gretli empovred and huit the poure Ilond redy, for what time he
was ſteward of the Ile he had but x marcs of fee, and kepte an houſhold
and a countenance like a Loid, with as iich wynys as coulhe be imagened, namyng himſelf Newport the galaunt, otherwiſe called Newport the riche, whom the country courſon dayly that ever he com theie.
And after time the ſaid John Newpoit was ſo diſchaiged bi the Duke of
Yorke, the ſaid Duke ordayned and made one Harri Bruyn ſquyer to be
lewtenaunt and ſteward of the ſaid Ile; whoſe iule hath bea honourable there both to God, the Lord, and the peple of the Ile, as law ard
rygth at al times hath iequiied, and well yrulyd in his litil time the
contray, and were like to biing hit into his ſuiſt aſtate if he weie like
to contynew and abide within the Ile, foi he hath beſtowed a giet good
of his own bothe in gonnys and in aicherie lying within himſelf within
the ſaid Ile, the which is at this day a gret ſtienthe, iiches, ſocoui and
comfort to al the Iſle. Praying ſpecialli to your allei wiſdoms, in ſalvacion of the ſaid Ile, and in ſalvacion of the Kinges peple theie, that
forafmoche as the ſaid Hairi Bruyn is the Kinges houſhold man, and
boine to giet ieputacion ard wel enheiited, and at no time coiupte
but egalli iulith the ſaid Ilond after juſtice withoute complaynt, and
eniichid the contiay with his gret ſtuf if nede of the Waiie iequiied,
that he might contenew ſtille in his good rule, keping the contice undii the forme as he hath bigonne, to the ioſt ſalvacion of the ſaid
Ilond, and of the Kinges peple theie; foi whoſe good iule we al wul
ondurtake to the King our foveiayne lord And alſo that al othei officeis of the Ile, that is to ſay, Haiii Tienchaid Conſtable and Poiiei,
may have ſtraytely in comiaundement by the Kyng to abide iiſiiini
within the ſaid Ile duiyng the time of the Wei. ceitefying at al times
the Kinges Hieneſſe that ard John Newpoit ſhold come to goveine the
ſaid Ile, hit wul be the cauſe of diſtiuccion of the contiay, to whom
no man wul obeye excepte ine Knige oure foveiayne loides pleiuie, foi
he and his hath don ſo many giet offencis in the iee aboue the Ilond
in moithering the Kinges peple and his frendes, caſhiig them oute of
ther veſſelles into the iee, as thei have be comyng to the poit of Hampton, bi the whiche the Kinges cuſtomes of his poit of Suthampton
hath be loſt by his riot kept upon the iee of voiiim. maiks a ieie.
And alſo the ſaid Newport hath   the King oi foveiayne lord, and defiauded him in giavnting x maiks woith of liſt de

gret hurt and trouble hereafter
for the faid liflode is entailed; the whiche is hid fro the Kinges hie-
neffe; bi the whiche menes he defireth to be recompenfed by the offices of the Ilonde aforefaid. And alfo the faid Newport hath taken the
fame yer extorcionoufli in Hampfhire, gret multitude of diverfe graynes
of corne in the Kinges name of the poure peple of him that had but
iiij quarters of corne toke one, and made him carie hit to Hampton,
fome men x miles and fome men xx miles at ther own coft, and there
as was plenty of corne he toke money to his owyn ufe, to the fum
within the fhire of an c markes; the whiche the peple of the contrai
curfe him daily therfor. And to the witnyffe herof for the more cre-
dance we have fet to oure felis.

Refponfio. Le roy s' advifera.

Records in the Tower of London.

N° XXV.

The Annual State of the Crown Lands in the Ifle of Wight.
23 Henry VII. 1507.

Infula Vecta.   THE extent and clere valewe of all the Manors,
Lands, Rents, Fines, and all other Profits growing there
from the Feft of faint Michell tharchangell in the xxiij
yere of the reyne of our foverayn Lord King Henry the
vijthe, above all charges, unto the fame feft of faint
Michell in the xxiiijthe yere of our faid foverayn lord,
that is to fay by the fpace of oon hole yere.

Fyrft the maner of Wioxfale	xxj*l.* xj*s.* v*d.*
The maner of Whytefelde	xiiij*l.* ix*s.* iij*d.*
The ferme of Bordewode	lxvj*s.* viij*d.*
The ferme of Bowcombe	iiij*l.* ^xx
The ferme of Thorney	viij*l.*
The ferme of Nyton	xvij*l.* x*s.* viij*d.*
The ferme of Fiefshewater	xxxj*l.* xiij*s* iiij*d.*
The ferme of Panne	vij*l.* xiij*s.* viij*d.*

The

The maner of Swaynſton .... iiijvl ijs. xjd.

The maner of Bryxton .... xxxvjl. xvjs. iiijd. ij

The maner of Thorley .... xxxl. vijs. vd.

The maner of Wellowe .... xvl. xijd.

The fee ferme of the towne of Newport .... xxiiijl. ijs. ijd.

The fee ferme of the towne of Bradyng .... liijs. iiijd.

The fee ferme of the towne of Yernemouth .... xxs.

The juſtement of the foreſt .... liijs. iiijd.

The ferme of the conyes at Urreys grove .... iiijs.

The liberte of the Iſland .... xviijl. xvijs. iiijd.

The rent of Whytehedd's lands there, waid to the King which is by the yere ixl. xvijs nowe being in the hands of my lord of Cantbury } —

The rent of Grace Haynowe's lands, ideot .... vil. ijs. vijd. ob ij.

Sm. totlis. ccccvijl. vs. ijd.

Payments in the ſaid yere.

Fyrſt to the ſteward and receyvor for his fee there .... xvl.

Itm. to Richard Weſton ranger of the foreſt there .... vjl. xiijs. iiijd.

Itm. to Thomas Darell (lxs.) and William Clyfton (xls.) kepers of the foreſt } cs.

Itm to the keper of the king's oold parke there by the yere } lxs.

Itm. to Stephyn Bulle keper of the caſtell there .... xijl. ijs. viijd.

Itm. to Thomas Moreyne firme bayly .... iiijl.

Itm. the auditors fee .... xxs.

Itm. for mete and drinke of Grace Haynowe ideot for lij wekes every weke xijd. for the ſaid Grace Haynowe } lijs.

Itm. for kyrtylles ſmokks and kerchowes and other neceſſarie gere for the ſaid Grace Haynowe } xiijs. iiijd.

Itm. for the repācons. of the caſtell with the expences of Sr. Amys Pawlet and other the kings cōmiſſions. in the ſaid Ile this yere as hit appereth by divs. pcelles in a quer hereunto annexed } xxvl. jd. ob.

i

Itm.

Itm. deliued. to the said Sr. Amȳs Pawlet by the
  hands of Thomas Moreyn firme bayly of the Ile
  as appeieth by a bill indented hereunto annexed } vjl. xiijs. iiijd.
  being date the xxixthe, day of Jule, the xxiij
  yer. of the reyne of our souayn. Lord King Henry
  the vijthe

Itm. payed unto Sr. Amȳs Pawlet forsaid by the
  hands of the Ryve of Swaynston of the Law Day } xxiijs. iiijd.
  money there holden at hoktyde last past to the
  kings ufe with a fyne of xs.

Itm. for the cofts in the tyme of declaracon of the } xlvjs. viijd.
  accompts

                            xx
    Sm. of the payments   iiijxl. iiijs. ixd ob.
    Refteth due   cccxvijl. viijd. ob.

Memor. of a fcape of a fellon by the conalte. of
  the towne of Yernemowth which refteth uppon } cs.
  theym as appereth in the court rolles.

———————————

Nº XXVI.

The State of the Fee Farm and other Rents in the Ifle of Wight, pay-
  able to the Crown, and granted by Patent to the Governois of the Ifle
  of Wight.   The 20th George III. 1780.

Yearly Payments.

	£.	s.	d.
1. The Town of Yarmouth	1	0	0
2. The Town of Brading	2	13	4
3. George Maurice Biffett Efq. for Afhey tenths	1	6	8
4. Colonel Hill and Mrs. Popham for Shanklin farm	1	0	0
5. The Revd. Andrew Gother for Thorley tenths	0	10	0
6. Sir Thomas Miller, Bart. for Ningewood tenths	4	7	2
7. The Rt. Hon. Welbore Ellis and Chriftopher D'Oj-ley, Efq. for Shalcombe	1	0	0
8. The Heirs of John Leigh, Efq for Shorwell	1	12	7
9. The fame for Weftcourt	1	6	8

                                   10. The

	£.	s.	d.
10. The Right Hon. Sir Richard Worsley, Bart. for Roud, Rew, and Middleton	2	2	6
11. John Fleming, Esq. for Newnham.	1	12	8
12. The same for Combley tenths	2	10	0
13. Sir John Carter for the Rectory of Brading	0	10	0
14. Mr. Thomas Hastead for Lamplight at Stone Place	0	3	0
15. Daniel Collins, Esq. for Clatterford	0	2	0
16. Mr. John White for a Tenement at Princelade	0	1	0
17. Lord Edgcumbe for the Tenths of Ashey	2	13	0
18. The Heirs of John Leigh, Esq. for Rowborough	0	6	8

Total 24*l.* 17*s.* 3*d.*

Half Yearly Payments.

	£	s	d
19. Sir William Oglander, Bart. for the Manor of Whitfield and the woods	20	3	8
20. Sir Thomas Miller, Bart. for the Manors of Carisbrooke and Freshwater, and the Right Honourable Sir Richard Worsley, Bart. for the Manor of Godshill	56	1	10
21. The same for the Rectories of Carisbrooke and Godshill	49	6	3
22. The Heirs of Mill Baxter, Esq. for the Tenths of Cosham	1	0	1
23. John Fleming, Esq. for the Chauntry of Newport	12	5	9
24. Robert Worsley, Esq for Bordwood Tenths	3	8	4
25. Mr. Matthew Trickett for Great Thorness	8	1	8
26. The Corporation of Newport	24	2	2
27. Robert Pope Blachford, Esq. for the Manor of Bowcombe	80	5	3½
28. The Rev. Leonard Troughear Holmes for the Manor of Freshwater	32	17	10
29. The Rev. Leonard Troughear Holmes for the Manor of Thorley	32	0	0
30. The Right Hon Lord Fairfax for the Manor of Arreton	45	6	10
31. Sir Thomas Miller, Bart. for the Manor of Wellow	15	3	5
32. Lord Edgcumbe for the Manor of Wroxall	23	15	4

33. Mr.

		£.	s.	d.
33.	Mr. Thomas Bagſter for a Moiety of the Manor of Uggaton	5	2	9
34.	Harcourt Powell, Eſq. for the other Moiety of the Manor of Uggaton	5	2	9

Total 414l. 4s. 5d.

Free Chapel Rents payable half yearly.

		£.	s.	d.
35.	Mr. Sanders for Eaſt Standen	3	0	0
36.	Mr. Fallick for Maudlin's Chapel	4	3	4
37.	Mr. William Hearne for Briddlesford	1	8	8
38.	The Right Hon. Sir Richard Worſley, Bart. for the Manor of Apſe	20	4	4
39.	Mr. Thomas Dickonſon for Bagwich	2	0	8
40.	Mr. William Thatcher for Blakedown	1	6	8
41.	Lord Edgcumbe for Bottoms in Niton	0	13	4
42.	Lord Edgcumbe for Harvey's land Dᵒ.	0	5	0
43.	Lord Edgcumbe for Cheeks land Dᵒ.	0	14	0

Total 33l. 16s. 0d.

The Park Farm at Rack Rent, payable half yearly, 200l.
Total of Fee Farm and other Rents   672l. 17s. 8d.

N° XXVII.

Brev. Regis Ann. 31 Edw. I. de Auxil. ad Maritand. Primogen. Fil. Regis in Turri Lond.

EDWARDUS Dei gratia rex Angliæ, dominus Hiberniæ, & dux Aquitaniæ, tenenti locum theſaurarii & baronibus ſuis de ſcaccario ſalutem. Ex parte dilecti & fidelis noſtri Radulphi de Gorges nobis eſt oſtenſum, quod cum ipſe et tenentes ſui infra inſulam Vectam, ſeu cæteri homines et tenentes de eadem inſula auxilium aliquod ad primogenitam filiam noſtram maritandum de feodis ſuis militaribus ſeu terris et ten. ſuis in eadem inſula ratione conceſſionis nobis nuper de hujuſmodi auxilio factæ facere non debeant, nec ipſi ſeu aliqui alii hujuſmodi feoda,

da,

da, vel terras et tenementa in dicta infula tenentes, aliquod hujufmodi auxilium progenitoribus noftris quondam regibus Angliæ ad primogenitas filias fuas maritandas facere confueverint temporibus retroactis, collectores nichilominus auxilii prædicti in infula prædicta auxilium prædictum a præfato Radulpho, et aliis hujufmodi feoda et terras et tenementa in infula prædicta tenentibus exigunt, et ipfos ea occafione aliter quam hactenus fieri confuevit, graviter diftringi faciunt minus jufte. Et quia fuper præmiffis plenius certiorari, et præfato Radulpho et tenentibus prædictis de infula prædicta quod juftum fuerit fieri volumus in hac parte; vobis mandamus, quod fcrutatis rotulis noftris de eodem fcaccario de hujufmodi auxiliis progenitoribus noftris prædictis conceffis utrum videlicet tenentes de infula prædicta hujufmodi auxilium eifdem progenitoribus noftris vel eorum alicui, ficut tenentes de regno noftro facere confueverunt, necne; et fi fic, tunc quibus vel cui de progenitoribus noftris prædictis, et quo tempore? Et fi inde fuerint exonerati, ex qua caufa et qualiter, et quo modo? De eo quod inde inveneritis nobis fub figillo ejufdem fcaccarii diftincte et aperte conftare faciatis citra feftum Pentecoftes proximo futurum, hoc breve nobis remittentes. Tefte meipfo apud Ceftrehunte, 14 die Marcii, anno regni noftri triceffimo primo.

Per breve de privato figillo.

The certificate returned, is not found.

Prynne on the IVth Inft. p. 214.

Nº XXVIII.

The Draught of a Bill intended to have been brought before Parliament, 16 Car. I. to afcertain the true State of the Tenures in the Ifle of Wight.

WHEREAS Henry the firft of that name King of England after the Conqueft did graunte the feigniorye dominion or lordfhip of the Ifle of Wight in the Countie of Southampton, (among other things) unto Richard de Ripariis earle of Devon, to hould of him the faid King his heyres and fucceffors Kings of England, in chiefe by knights fervice as of his crowne of England, the faid Ifle after the death of the faid Richard,

defcended

defcended and came unto Baldwine his fonn and next heyre, which Baldwine had iffue Richard his eldeft fonn, Henry that died without iffue,
and William furnamed de Vernon, Richard fonn of Baldwine had iffue
Baldwine and Richard, they were both fucceffively earles of Devon,
and both died without iffue, after whofe deceafe the feigniorye of the
Ifle of Wight defcended and came to the faid William de Vernon their
uncle, fonn of Baldwine the *fecond**; which William had iffue Baldwine his eldeft fonn, whoe had iffue Baldwine Marie and Jane, and
died before his father, and then William died. after his deceafe the
feigniorye of the faid Ifle defcended to Baldwine his *nephew* † by his fonn
Baldwine, which Baldwine had iffue Baldwine, Ifabel married to William de Fortibus earle of Albemarle, and Margarite a nunn at Lacocke;
this laft Baldwine was the fifte of that chriftian name earle of Devon, and
created Earle of the faid Ifle of Wight by King Henry the third, and
did hold the faid Ifle and the honour of Chriftchurch in the faid countie
of Southampton in right of the fervice of xv knights fees, as appeareth
by the book of knights fees pertayning to the caftle of Carefbrook remayning in the Exchequer, and died without iffue: by and after whofe
deceafe, the faid Ifle, and other his inheritable lands defcended unto the
faid Ifabel his fifter, then the wife of William de Fortibus, whoe by
reafon that Margarite her yonger fifter had entered into religion, became
fole heyre to her brother, then William de Fortibus died, and the faid
Ifabel him furvived And that after the death of the faid William de
Fortibus without iffue by the faid Ifabel, being fole and in her pure
widowhood, Edward the firft of that name after the conqueft King of
England, about the 22nd. year of his reign, being lord paramount of
the faid Ifle, did purchafe the mefnaltie of the feigniorye of the faid Ifle,
of the faid Ifabel de Fortibus, and that by and after the faid purchafe,
all the knights, lords of mannors and free tenants of the faid Ifle, that
at that time and ever fince the conqueft untell the faid purchafe, had
holden of the faid earles of Devon and fome other lords meane, between the Kings of England and them, did then after the faid purchafe
become imediate tenants to the King, and to hold of the faid King by
fuch fervice as they before held of the faid earles of Devon. And the
knights, lords of mannors, and other the free tenants that now are, fay,

* The *firft*, Baldwine the fecond being faid juft before to die without iffue.
† Formerly ufed for grandfon.

they

they will averr maynteyne and prove, that before the said purchase soe made of the mesnaltie of the said Isle from the said Isabel de Fortibus, by the said King Edward the first, it cannot be proved by any record or otherwise, that any mannors lands or tenements within the said Isle, were holden imediately of any of the Kings of this realme in chiefe by knights service or otherwise, or that any the knights, lords of mannors or free tenants of the said Isle before the said purchase, did hold any their lordships mannors lands or tenements within the said Isle of any other then of the said earles, and of the earles of Hereford before them; or that the said knights, lords of mannors, and free tenants of the said Isle, did doe any service in any of the retroacted or former tymes, either unto the said earles or countesses, lords or owners of the said Isle before the said purchase, or since the said purchase unto the said King Edward the first, King Edward the second, or King Edward the third unto the seaventh yeare of his raigne, out of the said Isle in any of the said Kings armies or wairs, or were charged or did pay charge to any of the said Kings or their progenitors after the said purchase · neither was any escuage ever leavied uppon any of them, as may appear uppon a presentment then made of all the tenures and service then due to the said King by any the said then knights, lords of mannors, and free tenants of the said Isle, or any other service other then that the said knights, lords of mannors, and free tenants did use to conduct the said earles and countesses lords of the said Isle, when at any tyme they came into the said Isle unto the sea, *ad partes exteras*, and did deferr and keep the lords castle of Carebrooke within the said Isle, and the lands of the said Isle by the space of xl days in the tyme of war, and make and doe their free suite at the lords court of the burroughe of Newporte, from three weeks to three weeks And the said knights, lords of mannors, and free tenants now being, doe further shewe, that it doth appear to be the use and customes of those tymes, uppon all evidence, writings, surveyes and presentments, made after the death of any knight, lord of mannor, or free tenant, that died seized of any lands within the said Isle before the said purchase, to fynde that the said mannors and lands, whereof the said tenants so dyed seized, were holden *de comite, vel de comitissa in capite*; and that by the subtiltie of the escheators of those tymes that imediately followed the said purchase, the jurors upon inquisitions taken after the deathes of divers knights, lords of mannors, and free tenants, that dyed seized of any mannors,

cr

or lands, that before the faid purchafe of the faid Ifle by the faid King Edward the fiift as aforefaid, were prefented and found to hold the fame mannors and lands *de comite vel de comitiffa in capite*, did find thofe very lands to be holden *de domino rege in capite* fimply. And although afterwaids tyme and experience in the next fucceeding age did make the jurois of that tyme to fynde their error, and that then they did beginn to fynde thofe mannois and lands that by former inquifitions taken imediately after the faid purchafe were found by former jurois to be holden *de domino rege in capite*, fimply, to fynde that thofe very mannois and lands were thereaftei holden of the King, *ut de caftio fuo de Carebrooke*, in the faid Ifle. Neverthelefs, divers feodaries, informeis, called perfecutors, and evil difpofed perfons belonging to the court of Wards, by rewaids and encouragements ufed to be given and allowed unto them by the faid court, taking advantage of the ignorance of the jurois and their eironeous veredicts given upon the faid inquifitions taken imediately after the faid purchafe of the faid mefnaltie of the faid Ifle, by the faid King Edward the firft, by colour of the faid eironeous veredicts given upon the faid inquifitions, taken immediately after the faid purchafe of the mefnaltie of the faid Ifle as aforefaid, have grievoufly vexed divers of the faid knights, lords of mannois, and free tenants of the faid Ifle, by intituling his majeftie to the meane iates of all fuch of the faid ifland lands as by the faid eironeous inquifitions were found to be holden of the king *in capite*; although it doth playnly appear by that which hath bynn before declared, that the intention of the faid jurors upon thofe inquifitions taken foe immediately after the faid purchafe, was noe other than that thofe lands were holden of the King by the fame feivice they were formerly held of the earles of Devon, lords of the faid Ifle, before the faid puichafe, and noe otherwife. By reafon of which inquifitions the moft of the knights, lords of mannors, and fiee tenants of the faid Ifle, doe lye open and are fubject to moft grievous vexations, and fuither to be ruined and undone. For prevention whereof, and for fettling the feveial eftates of all the knights, lords of mannors, and fice tenants within the faid Ifle, concerning their tenures, ard of the grievous mifchiefs and oppieffions that have already happened to fome of them, by long and tedious fuits in the faid court of Waids, wherein the relatoi or profecutoi hath always the advantage and favour of the court againft the defendant. May it pleafe, &c.

That

That it may be enacted, &c.

That if it cannot be made appeal to this most high Court of Parliament that any mannors, or lands within the said Isle, were holden immediately of any the Kings of this realm in chief by knights service or otherwise, which may amount unto a tenure *in capite* (other then the whole seignorye, dominion, and lordship thereof granted to the Earles of Devon), during all the tyme the said Earles and their heyres were lords thereof, and before the purchase of the mesnaltie thereof by the said King Edward the first, that then the inquisitions and the erroneous veredicts upon them given may be vacated; and that the said knights, lords of mannors, and free tenants of the said Isle may be restored to their auncient terures, and by the same rents and services they held their said mannors and lands of the said Earles of Devon, owners of the said Isle. The knights, lords of mannors, or other the free tenants, for any their mannors, lands and tenements within the said Isle, did doe no other service to the lords of the said Isle, save that the knights and freeholders of the said Isle did use to conduct the said Earles and Countesses, lords and owners of the said Isle, when they came into those parts, unto the sea passing over the same into forreigne partes.

Nº XXIX.

Warrant of the Duke of Suffolk, Justice of the King's Forests in the Reign of Hen VIII. to the Warden of Caresbrook Forest, to return the Books of Swanmote. Dated 11th Dec 36 Hen. VIII.

CHARLES Duke of Suff' Presedent of the Kyngs most Honorable Councell, also Gret Master of His Hvgnes Houshold, and Justice of all and singler His Ma.ᵗⁱᵉˢ Forests, Parks, and Chaces on this side Trent. To the Warden, Leuteunt and Quarter Kepers of the Forest of Caresbroke, in the Isle of Wyght, in the Countie of Southt', and to evȳ of them, and all other the Kyngs Subjects w' in the sayde Countie Greting, For as muche as you have not as yet certefied us, nor yet o'. Right Trusty and Right welbeloved the Lorde Seint John, o'. Deputie in the office of the Justice of the Forests in the Counties of Southt', Wiltes, and Somers, The Books of your Swainymotes kept yerely, as ye were by

1546.

k   o'.

o͞r. former wryting to you in that behalf willed and charged to do, which is and hathe bene gretly to the Decaye and alfo to the Dyforder of the Kyngs Forefts, and the Game w't.in the fame. We therfor will and charge you on the behalf of the Kinges Ma.͞tie, all Excufes and Delays fet apte, to certefie unto us, or to the feid Lorde Seint John, The Kynges fev' Records, w't. the names of the Pryfoners taken in the feid Foreft, and their Offences, (yf any be) together w't. as moche matter as ye know worthy Reformacon w't.in the Kyngs faid Foreft. Befides yo͞r. ftrcits, The firft day of Hyllary Tearme next, as you tendre the contynuance of y͞r. office, and to w't ftand, that may to you folow upon y͞r. defalt. Geven under the Seale of o͞r. office of Jufticefhip of the Forcfts, the 11th day of Decembre, the yere of the Reigne of o͞r. Sovereigne Lorde Henry the Eight, by the Grace of God Kynge of England, Fraunce, and Ireland, Defender of the Fayth, and of the Churche of England, and alfo of Ireland, in Either the Sup͞me hedd, XXXVI.

William Seint John.

N° XXX.

Liberties claimed by Ifabella de Fortibus, Lady of the Ifland, and allowed her, 8 Ed. I by the itinerant Juftices.

LIBERTATES allocatæ com'tiffæ Ifabellæ d͞næ de infula Vectis coram jufticiarijs itinerant. quæ clamat habere.

Plenum returnum brevium D͞ni Regis. Placit. naemij vetiti et de tene. averiorum, vici franci plegij, emendationem panis et cervifiæ, foke, fake, toll, et theme, infangthef, fourchefs, pillori, tribuchet, tumbrel, wreccum maris, waif, liberam caceam. Ita qd. nullus debet capere vel fugare cervos vel biflas damos vel damas, nifi comitiffa, et habere menfam vetitam in cacea fua, et in moris ex antiquo in defens. tentis. Ita qd nullus poffit in eis ingredi aut operari fine voluntate et licentia ejufdem comit'flæ vel ballivorum fuorum. Item habet liberam warrenam per totam infulam ex parte occidentali ripe de Medene. Item liberum mercatum in burgo de Newport, per diem Sabbati qualibet feptimana et nundinas in eodem per iij dies in feptimana Pentecofte. Item liberum
mercatum

mercatum in burgo de Eremuth per diem Lunæ in qualibet septimana
et nundin. in eodem per iij dies in festo sctī. Jacobi, et quicquid ad
mercatum pertinet in utroq. burgo.   Item comitissa clamat ex antiquo
constabularium suum esse coronatorem insulæ ad presentandi adventuras
coronatori comitatus et ipse justiciariis itinerantibus

Mem. quod dñus Johannes de Insula et omnes dñi de Insula que tenent de comitissa facere debent sectam ad curiam suam militum de Newport de tribus septimanis in 3 septimanis.   Et pro illa secta habebunt
curiam suam de omnibus hominibus de feodo predicto p. quib. faciunt
sectam facient sectam de omnibus transgressionibus et debitis nisi trans-
greffio tangat personam comitissæ vel domini insulæ vel de velito nac-
mio aut de plaga facta cum armis violentur vel de ijs. quæ pertinet ad
coronam dñm Regis   Et dabunt rationabile auxilium ad militum filium
suum faciendum, vel filiam suam primogenitam maritandum.   Item
quilibet eorum debet servitium unius servientis tempore gueiræ per xl
dies ad terras insulæ custodiendum, et nullum aliud servitium.   Et te
nent terras eas ex conquestu.

Feoda militar. pertinent. ad castrum de Carefbrook in inf. Vect.

I. Dñus Johannes de Insula tenet vij feoda et dimidium et viij partem
   unius feodi de Isabella de Fortibus comitissa Devon et domina insulæ,
   in capite, unde tenent in dominio maneria de Roude, Apulderford,
   Woodyton, Chellerton, Shorwell, Rewe, Bonechurch, Holeway,
   Shentling, et Whippingham.   Tenentes ejusdem Johannis.
Johēs. de Weston tenet de eodem dim. feodi in Middleton et Anchefton.
Johēs. Colombe ten. quartam partem feodi in Brerding juxta Bernard-
   fhe.
Radulfus de Gardino ten. dim. feodi in Truckton qd. Tho. de Pylly
   tenuit.
Johēs. le Flemming et Willus le Marter tenent per partes dim. feodi
   in Blakepann et Roucle.
Johēs. de la Brugge ten. dim. feodi apud Wackland et Lefleland.
Henricus de Bottebrigge et Robertus de Roucle tenent 4am. partem
   un. feodi in Roucle
Will de Honningford ten 4am. partem un. feodi in Honningford.
Prior Domus Dei Southton. ten. dim. feodi apud Cofham.
Gilbertus Rcope ten. dim. feodi apud Cottesford et la Shete.

Wil. de Cockevill ten. dim. feodi in Hamſtede et Shete.

Robertus de Glamorgan et Johēs de Paſſelewe tenent 4am. partem feodi in Humfredeſton.

Robertus Haſkard ten. xxam. partem un. feodi juxta Careſbroke.

Gerardus de Hathon ten. xxam. partem un. feodi apud le Snape et Blakeland.

Hugo de Braybent ten. dim. feodi in Freſhwater.

2. Domina Matilde de Eſtur dña de Gatecomb ten. de dicta comitiſſa in capite V. feoda, unde ten. in dominio maneria de Gatecomb Whitwell et Caulborn, quod Willus de Eſtur filius et hæres ejuſdem ten. de dono ejuſdem Matilde.

Abbas de Quarrera ten dim. feodi in Shete.

Prior Chriſti Eccleſie de Twynham ten. 4am partem feodi in Whippingham et tenementum qd. Hen. Hurſt tenet in Freſhwater.

Dña de Whitfield ten. de Matilda de Eſtur. dña de Gatecomb un. feod in Whitfield, Brerding, Merſton, Weſtbroke, Goditon et Weſt Appleford.

Abbas Montiſburgi ten. un. feodum in Witecomb.

Willūs de Godditon ten. dim. feodi apud Hale.

Odo de Compton ten. 3am. partem unius feodi in Atherfield.

Johēs atte Brugge ten. 4am partem un. feodi apud le Brugge.

Will. le Martre ten. 4am partem un. feodi in Honningford et Alverſton per iiijd ad marcam.

Will. de Aumarle ten. un feodum in Afredeſton et iijs. ad marcam p. terr. Galfredi Piot, Chalecroft et Will. Randolf.

Will. Mallet ten. dim. feodi in Apeleigh juxta Sandham

Robertus Giros nunc Galfridus de Inſula ten. iiijam partem un. feodi in Merſton. et Sweyland.

Will. Urry ten. v. partem un. feodi de abb. de Quarreria in Bottobridge.

Will Spillman ten. v. partem un. feodi in Honningford.

Will. Ruſſel dñus de Overland ten xiij partem un. feodi in Newnham ad xijd. ad marcam.

Johēs de Woolverton ten. viij partem un. feodi in Suthwath.

Petrus de Coſham ten. p. fine ijs. ad marcam in Dencomb.

Henricus de Oglandre ten. p. fine xijd. ad marcam in Clatterford.

Johēs le Frye ten. viij partem un feodi in Gatecomb.

Robertus de Shorewell ten. p fine vjd. ad marcam in Clatterford.

3. Will. Ruſſel dñus de Everland qui filiam et heredem Tho de Hawle duxit

duxit in uxorem, ten. vj feoda et ij partes feodi de comitissa in capite, unde tenet in dominico man. de Everland et Suthwath Scti Laurenntij.

Johēs de Ripeijs nunc Richūs Ruffel ten. dim. feodi de eodem Willō. in Roughbery West Standon et le Spann.

Will. de Nywille et Mariella uxor ejus tenent dim. feod. apud Parcam et Teuckle.

Johēs Morin, Tho. Westbroke, et Johēs Wynyle ten. dim. feodi in la Moreton.

Will. Roberts nunc Johēs de Kene ten. dim feodi in Brerding.

Johēs de Kingston ten. dim feodi in la Shorde et Chillerton.

Johēs Flemming ten. dim. feodi in Horringford.

Prior Domus de Portfmouth, Walterus de Horringford et affign. Willī Leon, ten dim. feodi in Freshwater.

Idem Prior et Jordanus de Kingston ten. 4am partem un. feodi in Whippingham.

Hugo de Chekenhull ten. 12 partem feodi in Lortington.

Dnūs de Whitfield ten. 3am partem unius feodi in Brandeston.

Johēs Aurifaber ten. 3am. partem unius feodi in Quodhampton.

Nichūs de Motteston et Ad. Paulin ten. 3am partem feod. inter Carefbrook et Newport.

Dnūs Johēs de Infula et Prior Christi Ecclefie ten. 2as partes et dimidium unius feodi in Briddlesford et Hamstede.

Dnūs Johēs de Infula ten. 3am partem unius feodi in Shentlyn.

Rich. de Affeton ten 12 partem unius feodi in Celleiton.

Templarij ten. 4am partem de Curne in eleemofina.

Et Capellani de Burton tenent aliam partem in Curne in eleemofina.

4. Dnā Elena de Gorges ten 3 feoda de comitissa in capite, unde tenet in dominico man. de Knighton Johēs de Northwood ten. de eadem Elena dimidium feodi in Northwood.

Johēs. de Kingston ten. de eadem dimid. feodi in Chiverton. Rich. Coudroy ten. dimid. feodi in Bathingborne. Johēs Aurifaber ten. 8am. partem un. feodi in Venycombe, quam dicta Elena nunc tenet in dominico. Will. Gilbert ten. Hardley et Roughrigge p. dim. marc. per ann.

5. Robertus de Glamorgan ten. un. feodum et 6am. partem unius feodi de comitissa in capite, unde ten. maneria de Motteston et Burton, Capellani nunc tenent. Capellani de Burton de eodem Roberto tenent

nent 6am partem unius feodi in Burton in eleemofina. fine feivitio. Heredes Richī Mallet tenent 8am partem unius feodi in Hortingfbete.

6. Will. de Aumaile ten. unum feodum de comitiffa in capite in Wal-
panne et Honneyhull et Cokepul. Heredes Rogeri Scures tenent de
eodem Willō. 4am partem unius feodi apud Cadeland. Johēs Cokepull ten. 10am partem un feodi apud Cokepull. Heredes Rob. de
Crus tenent 10am. partem un. feodi in Honyhull cum molendino
quod capellani de Burton tenent. Heredes de Rogeri de Ampedene
ten. 3am. partem unius feodi in Cadeland.

7. Henricus Trenchard ten. unum feodi de comitiffa in capite, unde
tenet in dominico maneria de Shaldeflete, Cheftell, et Watchingwell.
Idem ten 12am. partem unius feodi in Bernardfley ut invenitur in
quodam Rotulo.

Johēs Trenchard tenet de eodem Henrico 7 partem unius feodi in Shald-
flete. Dnūs de Whitfielde tenet 7 partem unius feodi in Bernardfley.

8. Odo de Compton ten. unum feod. de comitiffa in capite in Compton
et Atherfield, unde tenet in dominico man. de Compton.

Abbas de Quarrera tenet unam virgat. terræ in Compton in eleemofina
fine fervitio. Willielmus le White ten. unam virgat. terræ in Compton per fervitium unius paris calcarum. Adam de Compton tenet de
eodem Odone per idem fervitium.

9. Robertus de Glamorgan ten unum feod. de comitiffa in capite in
Broke et Uggeton, unde tenet in dominico man. de Broke. Johannes
de Paffelew ten. de Roberto de Glamorgan dimid. feodi in Broke.

Templarij tenent 3am. partem unius feodi in eleemofina fine fervitio in
Uggeton. Heredes Barth. de Broke tenent unam virgat. terræ per fervitium unius libræ piperis p. añ

10. Tho. D. Everey ten. unum feodum de comitiffa, unde tenet in dominico man. de Standen et la Wode Rogerus Vavafor tenet de eodem Thoma 4am partem unius feodi in Wefton.

11. Abbatiffa de Laycock tenet de comitiffa in capite unum feodum,
unde ten. in dominico manerium de Shorwell et unam virgat terræ in
Walpan quam capellani de Burton nunc tenent.

12. Willielmus de Sčto Mutino tenet de comitiffa in capite dimid.
feodi et 4am. partem unius feodi, unde tenet in dominico maneria de
Alvyngton, Shide, Northwood, et Farlee.

13. Rogerus de Langford tenet de comitiffa in capite dimid. feodi et
4am. partem feodi, unde tenet in dominico man. de Chale. Gil-
                                                        bertus

bertus de Hofkeifwell tenet de eodem Rogero 3am partem unius feodi in Chale.

14 Robertus de Pimeley tenet de comitiffa in capite dimid feodi in Newcton, quod comitiffa nunc tenet in dominico.

15. Will. filius Willi. de Infula tenet de comitiffa in capite 4am partem unius feodi in eadem Neveton.

16. Baldwinus de Neweton tenet de comitiffa in capite 4am partem unius feodi in Neweton.

Robertus de Glamorgan (de quo prius) tenet de comitiffa unum feodi in Woolveton, Hardeley, Langrede, et Scottesford, unde ten. in dominico man. de Woolveton. Heredes Richi Mallet tenent de eodem Roberto 4am. partem unius feodi in Sandham.

17. Johannes de Heyno tenet unum feodum de comitiffa in capite in Stenbury, et tenet man. de Stenbury in domirico

18. Jordanus de Kingefton tenet de comitiffa in Kingefton dimidium feodi, et tenet illud man. in dominico.

Abbas de Tutchfield tenet de comitiffa 3am partem unius feodi in Cadland et pertinet ad Bouecomb.

19. Henricus D'Oglander tenet 2as partes feodi in Nonewell et Cotebear.

20. Hugo de Chekenhull ten 8am partem unius feodi de comitiffa in Wippingham et in dominico.

Johes de la Brigge tenet de comitiffa 8am partem feodi in Mollefiey.

Johes de Infula qui dicitur de Bofco, tenet de comitiffa 8am partem unius feodi in Wippingham.

Will. de la Clive tenet de comitiffa 10am partem unius feodi apud la Clive

Henricus Tolvas tenet de comitiffa 4am partem un. feodi, ad marcam 40d

Roger Coin tenet de comitiffa ad marcam 4d. vel per 40am partem feodi *in Wroxale.

Johannes Aurifaber ten de com. xijam partem feodi in Clatterford.

Rogerus de Chellingwood tenet xiij partem unius feodi de comitiffa in Chellingwood.

---

* Ad marcam was a rate to be paid by the tenant, when the tax of hidage was laid on the land, viz when a mark was impofed on each hide of land, this ifcertains the proportion the tenant was to pay which is evident by this inftance, where the rate of 4d ad marcam is explained to be the 40th part.

Edwardus

Edwardus de Whitefield tenet de comitiffa 40am partem un. feod. in Avecheftone.

Nich. de la Hyde ten. de comitiffa xxam partem feodi apud le Hyde, et debet effe bedellus, modo tenet Will. Danielles.

Robertus Moien tenet de comitiffa xiij partem unius feodi in Hodyneton modo tenet Hugo Godefhull in dominico

Heredes Hen. de Stella tenent de comitiffa 12am. partem unius feodi in Erthnote, quam nunc tenet Prior Chrifti Ecclefiæ.

Rich. Affeton tenent unum feodum in Affeton.

Abbas Montefburgi tenet unum feodum in Wyke, Sandford, et Appuldurcombe.

Prior Chrifti Ecclefiæ tenet unum feodum in Ningewood. Idem prior tenet xvjam partem unius feodi in Wynfton.

Pann * tenetur in dominico.

N° XXXI.

Limits of the Foreft of Parkhurft, and the Right of Common there.
38 Edw. III.

Extent. de comm. paftur. Man°ij de Aluyngton in Infula Vecta juxt. foreftu de Parkhurfte p. metas et būdas Limitat.

QUI dicunt Sup Sacrmd. Suid. qd Reginaldus de Sco. Martino hcāt. & here. debeat ad Man°m. Suid. de Aluynton Conam cu. oibz. audijs Sujs & aialibz in campo vocat. Woodfeld ipeq. et omēs. anteceffores Sui & oēs. alij quoi. Statu. ipe het. a tempore quo no existat memoria Conam pd. dcām. here cofueveiunt v̄z. a teira de Werrar p.

---

* Pann is the only manor mentioned to be held by the countefs in demefne; feveral other manors and lands held by her are not here mentioned, the manors of Boucomb, Thorley, Wilmingham, Wroxal, and Thorney, with many others, were parts of her demefnes This roll being the claim of franchifes allowed by the juftices itinerant, it was neceffary only to afcertain the lands held of the countefs Swainfton was at that time in the bifhop of Winchefter, and not held of the countefs. It is feen at the foot of this roll that thefe liberties were allowed by Solomon Roffs (or Rochefter) and his companions, juftices itinerant. at their feffions at Winton 8 Edw I.

foffatu

foſſatu Pōris. Sce. Crux uſq. ad Graſland & uſq. ad Seÿnt Auſten. Et hic a Scynt Auſten p. via vocat. Merkeway, Et a met. pdtis. uſq. ad queicu vocat Chane Oke dm̄ Rege de Parkehurſte. Et ulterius dicunt qd. Solu. quod quōda. fuit Robti Uriey extendit ſe a teia. mand'ij ſui per uſq. ad porta p vocat. Wolde Parke et ſic a porta piedicta p foſſatu de ſithelfield Yon̄ge Woode et ſic a Younge Woode uſq. ad tia. de Thoiney et ſic de Thorney uſq. ad Rederyſe et ſic de Redeiyſe extendit ſe in longitudine & via vocat. Meikeway uſq ad Seÿnt Auſtevn ptinet. ad Man̄m pdictu.

Extent foieſt. p. metas & bundas eiuſdem.

Sſ. facta die Meicui. in Vigilia nativitate bt̄e Marie in Inſula Vcc̄ta Anno Reg Eı. trij. xxxvijo. cora. John̄e. Kyıkeby Magrō. John̄e. Gerberd & aliỳs. Qui dicūt. p. ſac̄im. Suu. ut patet extr. q Reginaldus de Sco. Martino hēt Con̄am. paſtura. ext. cooptu. cu dmimodis audiỳs. p. totu ann. Et q. ide. Reginaldus poteſt cāpe ībm. Jon̄ne pro volutate Sua. Quia dicunt etiam qd. in ſithelfeld cot. clxv aci. ten. et valet quelibet acr. iijd. Sm xljs. iijd. Itm in eadē. poſſunt vendere quōlt año quiq acr. ioune. et valet acr. iiijd. Sm. xxd. Item Coopt. foieſte con̄.. cccxv acr. Boſci ſive Subboſci. Et valent panagij in eodē Boſco coībz. Annis xxs. Et ideo mino. qr. pōr. de Cariſbroke, Reginaldus de Sco Martino, et poi. Sce. cruex et oēs. Lurgenſs de Newport trent. Con̄am. in eadem paſtur extr. Cooptu. ad omimodis aidiỳs. Suis pei totū ann. Itm poſſunt vendere xxx acr. jouncar. picij. acr xvjd. Sm. xls. Ideo mino. vendi quia pid. Prior et Reginaldus poſſunt inde cāpe pro volūtate ſua &c. Item ut pz p. feodariū. Iuſule Willmo. de Sco. Martino tenet de Com. in capit Dimid feod. et quarta p. viii. feod. vnde tenet in Dom. Maniū. de Alfington, Shide, Noithwood, et fauelee, ut claiius patet p. feodaru ejuſdem Inſule.

The Extent of the Foreſt by the Markes and Boundes of the ſame taken on Wenſdaie ye Eve of the Natiuite of or. bleſſed Ladye in the Iſle of Wight the xxxvij yere of the Reigne of Edward the thiide before John Kyrkeby, John Gerberd, and othei. wch. dothe ſaÿe upo ther Othe as els where hit dothe appere yt. Reynold of St. Martyne hathe Com. of Paſture wthout the Wood couture for all his Beaſts

through

throwgh the hole Yere. And y'. thefaid Reynold maye take there
fyrfes at his Will. Alfo they fayeth y'. in Fithekfield are coteyned clxv
acr. of Land and evry ac. is woith iijd. Alfo y'. may fell yerely in the
fame v acrs. of fyrfes and the ac. is worth iiijd. Sm. xxd. Alfo the
Cont of the Foreft coteineth ccccxv Acr. of Wood or Underwood
comelye ye Panage of thefaid Wood is worth yerely xx^s. and therefore
leffe becaufe y' P'or of Carefbioke, Reynold of St. Martyns, and the
P'or of St. Cioffe and all the Buigefs. of Newport hathe Com. in y^e
faid Pafture w'h out the Cout. for all ye Beafts throwgh the hole yeie.
Alfo they may fell xxx Acr of ferfes pc. ye Acr xvjd. Sm. xls therefore
the leffe fold becaufe thefaid P'oi and Reynold may take there at ther
will and pleafuie, &c. Alfo as it appereth by the Feodarie of ye Ifle
W^m of St. Martyn holdeth of the Counties in Chefe D a fee and y^e
iiij p'. of a fee whereof he holdethe in Chefe ye Man^s. of Alfington,
Shide, Noithwood, and Fayrelec as hit dothe appere clearly by the
feodaiie off thefaid Ifle.   Old Cout Book of Newport, p. 7.

N° XXXII.

Carta Thomæ de Aula de Teira in Biiddlesford.

NOVERITIS, &c quod ego Thomas de Aula conceffi ecclefiæ
fctæ. Mar. de Quarrara donationem quam Willi de Parco fecit in manerio dc Briddlesford   Tefte Wallerano Teutonico, cuftode infulæ,
Gaufrido de Infula, Robeito filio Biieni, Willo Soiewell, Phillipo de
Glamorgan, Odone de Cumpton.

N° XXXIII.

Nomina quorundum Tenentium Infulæ, extracta ex rotulo, 17 Hen. VI.

JOHES de Wefton tenuit de comitiffa (fc Ifabella) et modo Johes.
Hacket tenet dimid. fcodi in Milton et Auchefton.
    Dna. Matilda Le Eftur, dna. de Gatecomb, tenuit de dicta comitiffa
in capite, et modo tenet Johes. Bremfhot, quinq. feoda, unde tenet in
maneria de Gatecombe, Whitwell, et Caulborne.

                                        Willielmus

Willielmus Ruffel dnus. de Everland, qui filiam et heredem Thomæ de Hawle duxit in uxorem, tenuit fex feoda et 2as partes unius feodi de comitiffa in capite; et modo tenet Stephanus Hatfield qui alianorum filiam et heredem Mauritij Ruffel militis duxit in uxorem, unde tenet in dominico maneria de Everland et Suth Wath fcti Laurentij

Dna. Elena de Gorges tenuit tria feoda de comitiffa in capite, et modo tenet Johes Hacket, unde tenet in dnico man de Knighton.

Robertus de Glamorgan tenuit unum feodum et 6am. partem unius feodi de comitiffa in capite, et modo tenet Johes Chyke, unde tenet in dnico. maneria de Mottefton et Burton, quod capellani nunc tenent.

Henricus Trenchard tenuit unum feodum de comitiffa in cap. et modo tenet Edwardus Brutenell, qui Agnetam filiam Thomæ Dupedene duxit in uxorem; unde tenet in dnico. maneria de Schaldeflete, Chefthull, et Whatchingwell.

Odo de Compton tenuit unum feodum de comitiffa in capite, et modo tenet Johes Lifle, unde tenet in dnico. man. de Compton et Atherfield.

Robertus de Glamorgan tenuit unum feodum de comitiffa in capite in Broke et Uggeton, et modo tenet Johes Roucle; unde tenet in dnico. man. de Broke.

Thomas de Evercy tenuit de comitiffa &c. unum feodum, et modo tenet Georgius Bramfhot de jure Eliz. uxoris fuæ filiæ et hæred. Willi. Urry; unde tenet in dominico man de Standen

Willus. de Scto. Martino tenuit de comitiffa in capita &c. et modo tenet Johes. Popham miles, unde tenet in dnico man. de Alvington, Shyde, Northwood, et Fairlee.

Robertus de Glamorgan tenuit de comitiffa &c. et modo tenet Johes. Hacket, maneria de Woolveton, Hardley, Langred et Scottefford.

Jordanus de Kingfton tenuit de comitiffa &c. et modo tenet Ludovicus Mewes, ut de jure Aliciæ uxoris fuæ, filiæ et hæredis Willi Drewe.

N° XXXIV.

A Difpenfation granted by Henry VII. to Sir John Leigh, &c. to
hold the Manor of Appuldurcombe, the Priory of Caiesbrook,
Cleveland, and Waitefhale, by Leafe, at the fame Time contrary to an
Act of Parliament. Dated at Weftminfter, 3d Nov. 20 Hen. VII.
A. D. 1505.

1505.

HENRICUS Dei Gra Rex Angliæ & Franciæ & Dominus Hib-
niæ Omibs ad quos pfentes Lie nre pveniint Saltm, Cum Johes Leye
alias dcus Johes Leigh de Infula Vecta in Com' Sutht' miles & Agnes
Ux' ejus ac Johes Frye Fil ejufdem Agnetis huint & tenuint ac habeant & teneant Maniu five Prioratum de Appuldurcombe cum ptin. fuis
infra dcam Infulam ad t'minu' triginta & quinq annor nondum Completor ex dimifsione & concefsione Abbatifsæ & Conventus Monafterij
Ordinis Scæ Claræ extra Aldgate Civitatis London cujus Quidem dimif-
fionis & Concefsionis dat' eft in Fefto fci Michis Archi Anno Regni nri
quarto decimo ac cum ijdem Johes Leye alias dcus Johes Leigh &
Agnes ux. ejus tenuint & tenuint ac heant & teneant Prioratum de Caiefbroke infra dcam Infulam cum Omibs & Omimod Manis Tris ac Ten'
reddit & Svicus pratis pafcuis & Pafturis Libtatib'. Franchefiis forisfact.
Rectoriis Penfionib'. Porcoibs Decimis, Oblacoibs pficius & Emolumentis cum Omib' & Singlis Comoditatib'. & ptin. quibufcumque tam infra dacm Infulam qm ext' eidem Prioratui, de Caiefbroke qualit'
cuinq fpectan five ptinen Advocacoibs. Ecchai Dumtaxat except' ad
Tminu' Vigmti & quinq. Annor' nondum Completor ex dimifsione &
concefsione Prioris & Conventus Domus Jhu de Bethelem de Shene in
in Com' Surr' Ordinis Cartus cujus vero dimifsionis & Concefsionis
Dat'eft Vicefimo tcio Die Menfis Junij Anno Regni nri decimo nono ac
etiam cum pfati Johes Ley alias dcus Johes Leigh & Agnes Ux' ejus &
Johes Frye pdict huint & tenuint ac heant & teneant Quandam Pafturam vocatam Clyvelonde infra dcam Infulam cum ptin' fuis ad
Tminu' Vite eor' & altius ear Dnicuis vnientis ex dimifsione & concefsione Thome Cooke & Johanne uxis ejus Johis Gilberte Armig' &
Johanne uxis ejus ac Robti Gilbte Fil. & hered. apparentis eordem Jo-
his & Johanne quar' quidem dimifsionu' una dimifsio Videlt pdict Thome
Cooke & Johanne Uxis ejus data eft feptimo die Marcij Anno Regni
Regis Edwardi Quarti Vicen no primo et alia vo dimifsio videlt pdcor'

Johes

Johis Gilberte & Johanne uxīs ejus ac p̃dci Robti Gilberte data eſt ia Feſto ſci Michīs Archi Anno Regni Regis Rici tc̃ij Secundo. Necnon cum p̃dci Johēs & Agnes ac dc̃us Johēs Frie hūnt & tenūnt ce hēant & teneant duas paſtuias vocatas Southale, Wabaruys cum ptin' ſuis infra dc̃am Inſulam ad Voluntatem Edwardi Waite Geñ & Galfii Gryme & Alicie uxis ejus de irſula p dca Novitis Nos de gia m̃a ſp̃iali ac ex c̃ta Scientia & mero motu nr̃is licenciam dediſſe & conceſſiſſe p. p̃ſentes p nob & heiedib'. nr̃is p̃fat Johi Leye alias dco Johi Leigh ſeu quocumq alio Nõie cenſeat & Agneti Uxi ejus ac dco Johi Fiye ut ip̃i ſimul poſſunt & quilt eor' ſepaiitim p ſe poſſit hc̃e tenei e gaudere & occupere dict Mañiu' ſive Priorat'de Appulduicombe & dcam Prioiatum de Careſbroke cum ptin' & cetis p̃miſſis ac Paſturas p̃dcas cum õmib'. & ſinglis eoi' ptin' Juxta Vim foimam & Eſc̃am pdcai' dimiſſionu' & conceſſioru eis aut eoi' alcui ante Datam P̃ienc̃u factar' conceſſar' abſq aliquar' Pecuniai' Su̅m̅s p. Occup̃icoe dc̃i fiimai' aut alicujus eaſdem Nob vel Heiedib'. nr̃is debit ſeu Foiiſiciendis durantib'. Tñiuiis ſupdeis licet Valoicm decem Maicai' excedant p. annu' cont. formam cujuſdam Actus in Parliaieuto n̄io apud Weſtmonaſteriu̅ tc̃io decimo Die Januarij Anno Regni nii quarto Su̅monit & tent. inde pviſi & editi aut aliquo alio actu Statuto ieſtituc̃coe ſive Oidinacoe inde pnos ante hec tempoia in cortiu̅m fact iut impoſtūm facieud. aut aliqua alia ie cauſa vel mat̃a quacumq. non obſtantib'. In cujus rei Teſtiuoniu̅ has Liãs m̃as fieii fecius Pieotes Teſtc̃me ip̃o apud Weſtm̄ tc̃io die Novembi' Anno Regi nii Viceſino.

P ip̃m Regem & de Data pdca Auctoiitate Pariameiti

B rotis.

No XXXV.

Extract from the Account-Book of Sir James Worſley, Keeper of the Wardiobe of King Heniy VIII. in the Tower of London, with an exact Copy of the King's Signatuie of Diſcharge.

Cootes Jaquetes, Dobletts, and Hoſes.

Item delyverd by the kings comaundement unto M. Ratclyſ a jaquet wt. de ſlyves of cloth of ſylv. lyned wt. blake ſc̃act wt. doblet and hoſe to the ſame.

Mens Auguſi 2°. a°. °,

Item

1° xvi xxx°.
die Novebr. Item delyverd by the kings comaundement unto M. Care a de. cote of ryffet faten garded wt. ruffet velvete furred wt. blake coneye.

ar. xvj xxviij°
d're Dec. Item delyverd by the kings comaundement unto Richard Longe a jaquet doblet and hofe of blake tylfent lyned wt. blake faten y° buttons and agletts rem.

Item delyverd by the king's comaundement unto M. Carewe a jaquet doblet and hofe of tawny cloth of gold tiffewe lyned wt. blake faten.

2° xvj xx
d're Dec. Item geven to James Worfley by the kings grace a cote of blake velvete with ij gardes of blake faten furred with blake conye.

Item delyverd by the kings comaundement unto mafter Norres a jaquet of cmofyn cloth of golde tiffewe lyned wt. blake fatten.

Item delyverd to mafter Bullayn by the kings comaundement a jaquet of cloth of fylv. tylfent wt. dropes lyned wt. blake faten wt. a payr of hofe to the fame.

Item delyverd to mafter Norres by the kings comaundement a doblet of rufset fatten garded wt. ftole work with hofe to the fame.

Item delyverd unto yonge Wefton a doblet of crimofyn faten enbrauderd lyned wt. white fcenet with hofe to the fame.

Item delyverd by the kings comaundement to my lorde of Suff. a jaquet of cloth of gold of damafke coved wt. cmofyn velvete enbrauderd and cutte open the fame lyned with cmofyn faten.

Item delyverd to my lorde of Devonfhire a jaquet of cmofyn cloth of golde tiffewe enbrauderd with white cloth of filv. lyned wt. cmofyn faten

Item delyverd by the kings comaundement to M. Care an armyng doblet and hofe of white faten quylted wt. Venyfshe golde.

Item delyverd by the kings comaundement to M. Bullayn an armyng doblet of cmofyn faten quylted wt. Venys golde wt. hofe to the fame.

Item delyverd to my lorde of Suff. a doblet of cloth of golde of damafke coved wt. cmofyn velvete enbrauderd cut opon y° fame lyned wt. fcenet wt. hofe.

Item delyverd to my lorde of Devon a doblet of cmofyn cloth of golde tiffewe enbrauderd wt. white cloth of filv. lyned wt. cmofyn fcenet wt. hofe to it.

N° XXXVI.

N° XXXVI.

Fees paid to different Officers in the Isle of Wight in the Reign of Henry VIII. extracted from a List of the King's Officers, with their Fees, &c.

	£.	s	d.
CONSTABLE of Carisbrooke Castle, fees	12	2	8
Keeper of the Park there	3	0	0
Herbage and Pannage	11	0	0
Parkhurst Forrester his fee	10	0	0
Ranger of the Forest	6	13	4

Per diem.　　　　Sandham Castle, Sandham Bay.

4s. Captain
2s. Under ditto
6d. Soldiers 13
8d. Porters 1　　　　　} Fee 363　6　8
8d. Master Gunner
6d. other Gunners 7

West Cowes Fortress.

1s. Captain
6d. Soldiers　2
8d. Porter　1　　} Fee 103　8　4
6d. Gunners　6

Captain, Steward, and Receiver of all the Possessions
in the same Isle, and 3 under him at 8d. per diem,　} 47　7　6
in all *per. ann*

N° XXXVII.

Henry R.

Order from Henry VIII. under his Sign manual to Richard Worsley, Esq. Captain of the Isle of Wight, to prevent any Pheasants or Partridges being killed in the Isle of Wight.

TRUSTY and welbeloved we grete you well and being credible enfourmed that o^r. Games of Partriche, and Fesant w^t in that our Isle of Wight is muche decayed by the pmission and sufferaunce of suche lewd

P^rsons

P~fons as for their pryvate Lurres contrary to our Lawes and Pleafure doo dailye w'. Netts and other Engyns take the fame. Yo" fhall undreftande that myndyng to havie the fayd Games of Ptriches and Fefant cherifhed w'.in our fayde Ifle as wel for our Difpoite and Paftyme if we fhuld chaunce to repayre thither. As for our Furniture at Sundry our Hono". Manors and Houfes which from tyme to tyme We entende to replenifhe w'. the Score of the fame Ifle as nede fhall requyre Our Pleafure and Comaundement is that yo". fhall not only uppon Monîcon to be by yo", hereof gyven to the inhabitaunts of the fayd Ifle have diligent Regarde and Vigilant Eye that no man of no Degree or Condicōn kill any Fefant or Partriche w'. Net, Engyne, or Hawke on any our propre Lands in the fame Ifle, taking the Netts and Engyns of all fuch as fhall attempte the contrary and further punifheng the Ptyes foe offending as to your wifdom fhal be thought convenyent. But alfo that yo". fhall advife all the reft of the Owners and Inhabitaunts there at o' Contemplācon alfo to fpare the fame Games in their owne Grounds, fpêally abfteyning to take or fuffre to be taken any Fefant or Partriche w'. Netts and fuch Engyns as totally deftroyeth the Brede of the fame wherein yo". fhall doo unto us acceptable fervice. And thiefe our Lrēs fhall be your fufficient Warraunt and Difcharge in that Behalf. Geven undre our Signet at o'. Manor of Otland the 19th daye of Decembie the 32 yere of o'. Reign.

Nᵒ XXXVIII.

Extract from a Manufcript Book in the Poffeffion of Guftavus Brander, Ffq. being an Inventory of the Jewels, Plate, Stuff, Ordenaunce, Munition, and other Goods, belonging to King Henry the Eighth, perufed and examined by certain Commiffioners appointed for that Purpofe by King Edward the Sixth, by Letters patent, dated at Weftminfter, the 14th. of September, in the firft Year of his Reign. A D. 1547.

Th' Ifle of Wighte.

The caftell at } ORDENAUNCE artillery and other munycions of Yarmouthe. } warre remaynyng at the faide caftell in the cuftody and chardge of Richard Ewdall captⁿᵉ. there the xxviᵗʰ. of Decembre anno regni Regis nunc Edwardi fexti primo.

Curtall

Curtall cannon of braffe furnyfhed   Oone,

Demy culveryne of braffe furnyfhed   Oone.

Demy culveryne of cafte irone furnyfhed   Oone.

Fowlers of irone with iiij chambers, their ftocks broken ij.º

Sacres of cafte yrone furnyfhed   ij.º

Doble barces of yrone with iiij chambers   ij.q

Single bafes of yrone with iiij chambers   ij.q

Demy culveryne of cafte yrone   Oone, broken,

Cannon fhotte of yrone   xv.

Demy culveryne fhott of yrone   xlvj.

Sacre fhotte of yrone   c

Fowler fhotte of ftone   lti.

Shotte of doble bafes of diece and lead   lti.

Shott of fingle bafes   xxxti.

Serpentyne powder   viij di. bar.
                                    iij doble,

Hagbuttes furnyfhed   xix.

Corne powder for the fame   di. bar.

Bowes   cxlti.

Sheiffs of arrowes   ccxlviij.

Bowftrings oone firkyne, conteyning   ij groffe.

Billes   ccxxiij.

The Blockhous at Sharpnode within the faid Ifle of Wighte, in the chardge of Nicholas Cheke.

Demy culveryns of braffe furnyfhed   Oone.

Sacres of braffe furnyfhed   Oone

Demy culveryne fhotte of yrone   xvj.

Sacre fhotte of yrone   xxiij.

Serpentyne powder   Oone doble bar.

The Caftell of } Ordenaunce, artyllery and other munycions of warre Caryfbroke } remaynynge at the faid caftell in the cuftody and charge of Richard Worfley gentilman, captayne of the faid ifle.

Slynges of yrone furnyfhed   ii.º

Fowler of yrone furnyfhed   Oone.

Doble baffys of yron furnyfhed   ij.º

Hoole culveryne fhotte	xxx^{ti}.
Demy cannon fhotte	l^{ti}.
Yron for dyvers peices	xxx^{ti}.
Demy culveryne fhotte of yrone	xxx^{ti}.
Sacre fhotte of yrone	cciiij.
Fawcon fhotte of yrone	cxl^{ti}.
Doble bafis fhotte	xl^{ti}.
Serpentyne powder	xxiij. doble bar, iij firk.

Hagbuttes furnyfhed, lacking xx flafks & xx touch boxes cxl.	
Coilles of lyntte	Dc.
Corne powder	iiij doble bar.
Cheftes of arrowes	lix.
Cheftes of bowes	xxj.
Bowftringes	iij bar.
Morispickes	D.
Javelyns	c. iiij. iiij.ˣˣ
Billes	Dccl.

The Caftell of Sandhambaye.

Ordenaunce, artillery, and other munycions of warre remaynyng at the faid caftell in the cuftody and charge of Peter Smythe captayne there.

Demy culveryns of braffe furnyfhed	Oone.
Saker of braffe furnyfhed	Oone.
Fawcone of braffe furnyfhed	Oone.
Porte peices of yrone with ij chambers furnyfhed	Oone.
Hoole flinges of yrone furnyfhed	Oone.
Demy flinges of yrone with vj chambers	v.
Quarter flinges of yrone with oone chamber	Oone
Demy culveryn fhotte of yrone	iiij.ˣˣ
Demy culveryn fhotte of dice and leade	xv.
Hollow fhottes for wild fier	xij.
Sacre fhott of yrone	lxij.
Sacre fhott of dice and leade	iiij.ˣˣ xiiij.
Fawcon fhotte of yrone	xxxvj.

Fawcon

Fawcon fhotte of dice and leade	cxvj
Shotte of ftone for port pieces	xxiiij.
Cafes of haile fhotte for the fame	xxviij.
Sling fhotte of yron	xx.
Slynge fhotte of dice and leade	xij
Demy fling fhotte of dice and leade	c.
Quarter flynge fhotte of dice and leade	xlvj.
Serpentyne powder	iij doble bar.
	j firk.
Hagbufshes wanting flafks and touch boxes	lxxviij.
Corne powder	Oone firkyne.
Bowes	Oone cheft.
Sheiff arrowes	Oone cheft.
Pickes	cl.
Billes	cxx.

The caftell at the Wefte Cowe.

Ordenaunce, artillery, and other munycions of warre remaynyng in the faid caftell in the charge or cuftody of Robert Raymonde captayne.

The Barbycan.

Curtoll cannon of braffe furnyfhed	Oone.
Baftard culveryne of braffe furnyfhed	Oone.
Porte pieces of yrone furnyfhed with iiij chambers	ij.
Three quarter flinges with ij chambers	Oone.
Porte peices not hable to ferve	Oone.
Cannon fhotte of yrone	xvij.
Baftard culveryn fhotte of yrone	xiij.
Baftard culveryn fhotte of leade	lvj.
Shotte for port peices of ftone	xxx.
Slinge fhotte of irone	xxxij.

The weft wynge.

Doble bafes with ij chambers not hable to ferve	Oone.
Single bafes with iiij chambers not hable to ferve	ij.

The eafte winge.

Doble bafes with iij chambers not hable to ferve	ij.

The

The mayne Towre.

Doble bafes with ij chambers furnyfhed	Oone.
Three quarter flinges with ij chambers a peice, whereof oone is not hable to ferve	} iij.
Single bafes with viij chambers not hable to ferve	iiij.
Three quarter fling fhott of leade	cxlvj.
Shotte for doble bafes	lxiiij.
Serpentyne powder	j doble bai. ij firk.
Hagbutts not hable to ferve	x.
Corne powder	iiij lb.
Bowes	xix.
Chefts of airowes	xxxij.
Pickes	xxij.
Billes	xx.

N° XXXVIII.

P A R T II.

The Weft Meden.

A note as well of all fuch plate, bells, veftmts. and other implemts. as hathe bene taken and folde owte of the churches within the Ifle of *Wight* by the parifhioners of the fame, as alfo of the names of thofe perfons wiche are appointed and bownde to appere for the anfwer of the fame.

Carifbroke.

Nicholas Baker, and Raffe Harvey, bound and appointed for the anfwer.

	£.		
Itm. folde in ann pmo. Edw. vj. one fenfor a fhipe and to crewats of filver, the weight appeareth not	vj.		
Itm. folde in ann. iij Edw. vi. one challes a paxe and a crofe of filver, weighing cxiiij oz for	£. xxviij	s. x.	
Itm. folde in ann. iij Edw. vj. to bells weighinge xvi c. for	£. xix.		

Som. £. liij.

Newport.

Newport.

Wm. Newman & Wm. Burrell bownd and appointed for the anfwer.

Itm. folde in ann. pmo. Edw. vj one fhipe to fenfors to paxes a pixe ij crewats ij candlefticks ij challefes and a crofs of filver, for } £. liiij. s. xviij. iiijd.

Itm. folde the fame yere to bel's weinge xvj C. & ½, at xxiiijs. the hondrith } £. xix. s. xvj.

Itm. veftments and other implements folde in ann. v & vj Edw. vj } £. xxv. s. xi. ijd.

} £. c. s. v. d. vj.

Shorwill.

Bryffifh Jones bownd and appointed for the anfweie.

Itm. folde in ann. j Edw. vj one ciofe one fenfor of filver weinge lxxiij oz. } £. xv. s. xviij. d. vj.

Itm. folde in ann. R. Edw. vj. ij. one challes of filvei weinge xvj oz. for } £. iiij. s. v. d. iiij.

Itm. folde in ann. R. H. viij. xxviij. a fhipe a chall. to crewats & j paxe of filver weinge xxxvij oz. & ½ } £. vij. s. xj.

} £. xxvij. s. xiiij d. x.

Brixton.

Anfwered unto the comyffioners by a fawconet of braffe wych remayneth with the pfhoners. untill the king's māts. plefuie be ferder knowen

Itm folde in ann. R. H. viij. xxxvj. one challes weing vj oz. for } xxvjs.

Itm. folde in ann Edw. vj v. one veftmt of iede vellct } xiijs. iiijd.

Itm. fold in ann. iiij Edw. vj 2 veftmts. of velvet with the appurtens. } lxxs. ijd.

} £. v. s. ix. d. vj.

Motftone.

Anfwered unto the comyfhioners by a fawconet of cafte yron remaining in the pifh. until the king's plefure be farder knowen.

Itm. folde in ann. pmo. Edw. vj a pixe of filver weinge v oz. } s. xxvj d. viij.

Fiefhwater.

Anfwered unto the comifhioners by a fawconet of braffe wch. remayneth with the pifh. until the king's plefure be faither knowen.

Itm. folde in ann. iiij Edw. vj a paxe & oz. broken filver weinge ij oz. } ixs. ijd.

Itm. one challes of filver takine out of the church by Walter Ruffel the mth. May in ann. xxxvj H. viij and went owt of the ifle x yeres paft, and hath nothing heie anfwerable.

} ixs. ijd.

Shalflete.

Shalflete.

Anſwered by a fawconet of braſſe remayning with the piſh. until the king's pleſure knowen.

Itm ſolde in ann. 1550 one paxe of ſylver weinge iiij oz. for } xviijs.

Itm. ſolde in ann. 1546 one challes ſilver. } xliijs. iiijd.

} £. d. iij. xvj.

Chale.

Anſwered by a fawconet of braſſe remayning with the piſh. until the king's pleſure knowen.

Itm ſolde in ann. pmo Edw. vj one challes and a little paxe of ſilver. } ls.

Calborne.

Itm. ſolde in ann. 1549 one croſs of ſilver weinge xlix oz. for } £. xiiij xxd.

The Eſte Meden.

Godeſhyll.

Chiſtopher Perkyns bownd and appointed for the anſwer.

Itm. ſolde in ann. R. Edw. vi. v. 2 crewats i challes ij candleſticks one pixe of ſilver weinge x C. oz. ½. } £. xxij. vijs. vijd.

Itm. ſolde in ann. R Edw. vj. vj. a croſſe & a paxe of ſilver, weinge xlvj oz. } £. s. d. xj. ij. iiij.

Itm ſolde in ann R. H. viij xxxviij 2 challes & one ſenſor of ſilver weinge xxxv. oz. } £. vij.

Itm. ſolde in ann. R. Edw. vj ij one ſenſor a ſhipe and to images of ſilver weinge xxxij oz. & 90. } £. s d x. ix. iiij.

Itm. ſolde one veſtmt. & other implemts. for } xliijs. iiijd.

} £. s. d. liiij. ij. vij.

Whitwell.

Richard Newman bownde and appinted for the anſwer.

Itm. ſolde in ann. xxxviij H viij one challes of ſilver weinge xij oz qto. } ls. vjd.

Itm. ſolde in ann. ij Edw. vj. one challes of ſilver weinge viij oz for } s xliiij. iiijd

Itm. ſolde in ann. R Edw. vj. vj. farten broken braſſe for } s vij xd.

} £. s d. v. ij. viij.

Sainte Lawraunce.

Richard Newman bownd & appointed for

Itm. ſolde in ann. xxxviij. H. viij one challes of ſilver weinge viij oz for } s xxxiii xd.

Arreton.

Arreton.

Steven Thorman bownd & appoint-ed for

Itm. folde in ann. pmo Edw. vj a croffe & challes a paxe & a fenfor of fylver weinge cxxxij oz. — £. s. d — xxxij. vj. viij.

Itm. folde the fame yere to hondrith and di. weight lacking iiij of brafie — s d — xxxvj. viij.

£. s. — xxxiiij. iij & iiijd.

Newchurche.

Thomas Ryce bownd and ap-pointed for the anfwer.

Itm. folde in ann. primo Edw vj. one croffe a chales a fenfor a paxe and a payer of crewats of fylver weinge cxl. oz. — £. xxx.

Itm. folde the fame yere one fewte of veftmts. for — £. vj.

£. xxxvj.

Neyghton.

Richard Yeds bownd and ap-pointed for the anfwer.

Itm folde in ann xxxvij. H. viij one challes of filver weinge xiiij oz for — s. lx.

Brardynge.

Harry Stowers bownd and ap-pointed for the anfwer.

Itm. folde in ann. 1549 one croffe a fenfor a fhipe a paxe and two erew-ats of filver for — £. xxxviij. iijs. & iiijd.

Itm one littel bell for — ijs.

£. xxxviij. s. v. iiijd.

RICHARD WORSLEY

GEORGE MILLE

JOHN MEWYS.

JOHN WORSLEY.

Richard Worfley capt. of the ifle of Wight and one of the king's majties. commiffioners for the church goods there, afketh allowance for his chardge comynge up with the fame with iiij horfe by the fpace of ij daies at xxs the daie, and lying here by the fpace of iiij daies about the delivery of the fame.

£. vij.

RYCHARD COTTEY.

The

The note of all fuch pcels. of plate as came unto the
commiffyoners hands to the king's mties. ufe owt of the
churches & chappels within the Ifle of Wight as alfo
of fuch fomes of money as they made of the veftmts,
& or. impliments of the faid churches.

Itm. Challes of filver   ix. ⎫
Itm. Pixes of filver   vi. ⎬ weinge clv. oz.
Itm. one Paxe of filver   ᵧ. ⎭

Itm in money made of the fale ⎱   £.   s.
of veftments & or. implemts. ⎰   lxxvj. xv.

RICHARD WORSLEY.

GEORGE MILLE.

JOHN MEWYS.

J O H N   W O R S L E Y.

Mfs. Harl. vol. 604. p. 83—89.

N° XXXIX.

A Copy of the Patent of Captain of The Ifle of Wight to Richard
Worfley, Efq.—Dated 8th. of April, 2d of Elizabeth, Together
with Articles of divers Things given in Charge by the faid Queen to
Captain Worfley. Alfo the Ordinary Charges appointed to continue in the Caftles and Forts within the faid Ifle.

ELIZABETH Dei Grā Angliæ Frauncie et Hibñie Regina Fidei
Defenfor' &c' omnibus ad quos p.ʳfentes Lr̄e pervenerint Salutem.
Sciatis qᵈ. Nos fidele Servicin̄ tam pʳ chariffimo Prī nr̄o Henrico nup.
Regi Anglie Octavo quam Chariffimo Frī nr̄o Edwardo nup. Regi
Angl' Sexto p. ditēm Serviente nr̄m Richm̄ Worfley Armigerū im-
pēns in tunc confiderantes ac p confimili fideli fervicio nobis p. eundē
Richūm Worfley. armigeru' impofteru' impēdend. de grā n̄ā fpāli in
ex certa Sciencii & mero motu nˀis Dedimus et conceffim' ac p.
pʳfentes pro nobis Heredibˢ. et Succefforibˢ. nˀis Damus et Concedimus
Eidem Rico Worfley Armigero Officiū Capitanij totiˢ. Infulæ nr̄e Vecte
in Com' nr̄o Southt', ac Officiu' Capitanij Caftri nr̄i de Carefbroke ac
Omnˢ

Omn' Alioru' Caftror' et fortalicior' nror quorucuq. in eadem Iofula Necnon officiu Conftabul' et Janitoris p'd. Caftri nri Carefbroke ac etiam Officia Senefcalli Supervifioris Receptor' et Ballivi omn' et finguloru' duor' manerior' Terraru' ten' poffeffionu' et Hereditametor' nroru' quorucuq. Nec non omn' et Singuloru' Bofcor' et Subbofcoru' nror' quorucuq. ac alioru' Revencionu' p ficuroru' et comoditat nroru' quorucuq modo in manib'. nris quocuq. modo Exiften' in Infula pd. ac omnium alioru' manerioru' Terraru' Ten' bofcor' poffeffionu' et Hereditametoru' quorucuq. quæ ad manus nras aliquo modo quocuq. impofterum devenire contigerint in eadem Infula ac ipm Ricm Worfley Armig' Capitaneu' totius pd. Infu' Vectæ ac Capitaneu' pd.ci Caft i de Carefbroke et Omn' alioru' Caftioru' et fortaliciaru' quorucuq. in eadem Infula Nec nō Conftabulai' et Janitore ejufdē Caftri de Carefbroke ac etiam fenefcallum fupervifiorem Receptore et Ballivu Omniu' et finguloru' Duoru' Manerioru' Terraru' ten' Bofcor' Subbofcoru' poffeffionu' et hereditametor' noftroru' ac alioru' Revenconiu' Pficuoru' et Comoditatu' meoru quorucuq modo in manib'. nris quocuq modo exiften' in Infu' pd. ac omn' alioru' Manerior' Terraru' Ten' bofcoru' Subbofcoru' Poffeffionu' et Hereditametoru' quorucuq quæ ad Manus nras aliquo modo qcuq. impofteru' devenire contingerint in eadē Infula pro nob's Hered. et Succefforib'. nris facimus, ordinamus, Conftituamus et Auctorizamus per Prefentes Quæ quidē Officia oña & Singula manib'. et difpofitioñs nris jam exiftunt Habend. Tenend gaudeid Occupand. et Exercend. oña et Singla p'd. Officia et eo u' quedit' cū oñib'. et Singulis Juirib'. auctoritatib' p'eminencijs et p' una' quibi feto. eifd Officijs et eoru' cuilib't aliquo modo pertinen' fpectan' five neden' aut cu' eild. Officijs feu eoru' aliquo ad aliquod temp'. ufitat p'fit Richō Worfley Armig' p. fe vel p. fufficient' Deputi' iua' five Deputat' fuosfufficient' ad Terminu' et pro termino Vitæ ejufd Ricii Dedia us etiam et Conceffimus ac per pñtes p nobis Heredib'. et Succeffiorib' nris dam'. et cōcedim' p' fato Ricō Worfley Armigeio p. occupatōe et exercicio omn' Officioru' pd vad et Feod. Sex Solidor' et novē Denarior' p. diem Habend Tenend. gaundend. et Annuatim levend et perpirand. ac in Manib'. pd Ricii Worfley Annuatim retinend. ead. Vad. et feod. fex Solidorum et novem Denanoru' per diem p' fit Ricō Worfley ad Terminu' et pro termino Vitæ fuæ de reddir' Exit Proficuis et revencoib'. Quibufcuq omn' et Singuloru' deoru' duoru' Marenor' Te raru' Ten' Poffeffionū et Hereditametorum quorucuq nioru modo in Manib'. nris

N quo-

quocquo modo Exiſten' in Inſula pᵈ·d. Ac omn' alioru' manerioru' Ter-
raiū ten' poſſeſſion' et Hereditamētoru' Quorūcumq. quæ ad manus nᵗᵃs
aliquo modo quocūq. ı npoſteru' devenıe contīgerınt in eadem Inſula
tam p. munus ſuas p. pɿıas et in manıbˢ. ſuis p prıjs retinends q. p. manus quoɾūcᵘuq Ballıvoru' ſɪɪmar' tenend et alioru' Occupatoıu' eorundē
p. tempoɾe exiſten' ıc de Reddit' exit' p ſic' et Revencoıbₛ omū et ſing-
loɪ' manerıoɪ' Teɪɪaru' Ten' poſſeſſıonu' et Hereditamētoɪ' nᵗᵒr quoɪū-
cūq modo ın manıbˢ. nᵗıs aliquo mᵒ. exiſten' ın Com' nᵗ·o Southt' ac
omū alıoɪ' manevıoɪ' Teııaıu' Tenet' poſſeſſıonu' et Hereditamᵉt' quorū-
cuq quæ ad Manus nᵗᵃs aliquo modo ımpoſteıū devenıe contıgerınɪ
ın eod com p maous gen'alıs Receptor' ac alıcujus alteɪius Receptoɪ'
eoɪūdē pro tempore exiſten' ſi exit' ıeddıt' Profıc' Revencōes Manerᵉ
teiɪ' ten' poſſeſſı' et Heredıtam' noſtɪ' pd. ıu Inſula pd. ad Solucō'em
feod. pd. ad alıquod Tempꝰs ımpoſte ɪu' non ſuffıcıant' ad Feſta Pache
et ſcı Mıchᵗıs Archı p. equales Poɪcōes Annuatım Solvend. Unacū'
omᵗbˢ et ſingulıs alıjs Pɪofıcuıs Comᵗodıtat' et Emolumᵉt'ˢ Quıbuſcuᵗq.
pd. Offıc' et coıu' cuılıbᵗt alıquo modo p tinen' ſpectan' ſive ıncıden'
aut cu' cıſd. offıc' ſeu alıquo ad alıquod tempᵒ uſıtat' ac ın tam Amplıs
modo et forma prout alıquıs alıus ſive alıquı alıj Offıc' pd aut eoɪū alıquod ante hac Henᵗꝗ et Occupans ſive habentes et Occupantes habuıt et
peıcepɪt hueɪunt & peıcepeıunt aut habuıſſe et Peıcıpıſſe debuit vel de-
bueɪunt Et ulteɪıˢ. de amplıorı gɪā nᵗ·a ob fidelı Servıcıū pd. Ricᵗı
Woıſley Arɪmıgeıı dedımus et conceſſımus aᵗc p. pᵗ·ſentes pro nob. He-
ᵗedibᵗ. et Succeſſoɪıbˢ. nᵗ·ıs Volumus Damus et concedimus eid. Ricᵗo
Woıſley Aıᵗ' qd. ıdem Rıᵗus Woıſley hᵉᵗbit duɪante Vıta ſua quēdā De-
pııotu' ſub ıpſo ın pd. offıcıjs Capıtanj pd. Seıvıtur' ac peı eundē Rıᵗm
ad ıd de tempoıe ın tempus appunctuand. & aſſıgnaıd. et ab eod. Seıvıcıo p. ıpᵗm ıemonend. Et qd. ıdem Rıᵗus hᵉᵗbit p. dᵗcto Deputato ſub
ıpᵗo ın pd. Offıc' Capıtan j ın Vad. duos Solıd. p. dıem Dedımₛ. et con-
ᵗceſſıᵗmˢ etıam ac p pᵗntes pıo nobis Hcıedıbˢ. et Succeſſoribus nᵗ·ıs p.
Servıcıo pd. volumus Damˢ. et concedimus pd Rıᵗcō Woıſley qd. ıpᵗē
hebit' duıante Vıta ſua tɪeſdecım Hom·nes ſub eod. Rıᵗcō Seıvıtur' ın
Inſula pd de tempore ın tempꝰs p eundē Rıᵗcus appunctuand. et aſſıg-
nand. et ab eod. Seıvıcıo ıemovendᵗ·s Et qd. ıdem Rıᵗus hᵉᵗbit p. quoɪt
coıu' treſdecım Homı' ın vad. ſex denaɪıoı' p. dıē pıo termıno Vıtæ
ᵗquıd. Rıᵗcı. Et ulteɪıus p. Majoıı Securıtatı ejuſd. de Vad. ıllıs eıd.
Rıᵗcō Solvend. dedımus et Conceſſınᵗ' ac peı pᵗntcs pıo nobis Heɪedıbˢ.
Succeſſoııbˢ. nᵗ·ıs damus et coıcedımus I ıd. Ricᵗō Woıſleȷ Armıge' p.
pd.

pd Deputat' fub fe vad. et feod duorū Solidor' p. diem ac p. quolt pd
trefdecim Hominu' vad et feod. fex denarior' p. diem Habend. et an-
nuati pcipiend. ead. Sepalia vad. et feod. duor' folidor' p die p. pd.
Deputat' et Sex Denarioi' p. diēm p. quolt' dctoi'm trefdecim Hominu'
ad Ternii et p. termino Vitæ pd. Rici Worfley Armig' de Reddit'
Exit' p.fic' et revencoïbˢ pd. in Inful' pd. ac in Com' nïo pd in forma
pd. tam p manus fuas p pãs et in manibus fuis retinend q. pei manus
Ballivoi' Firmar' tentiu' et alior' Occupatoiu' quocūq. pd. et ceteroiū
pʳ.miffor' p. termino. Exiften ac p. manus Receptor' pd. ad Feftı pd. p.
equales Poicoïcs annuatim Solvend Et ultei ius giã nã fpãli ac ex cetcia
Scientia et mero motu nʳis dedimus et conceffimus ac p pñtes p nobis Heiedibˢ. et Succeffoiibˢ. nʳis damus et concedimus pʳ.fat Ricō
Woifley Aimig' Officiū Cuft' et Cuftod. Parci nïi de Carefbroke in Infula nʳa pd. Nec non Herbãg et Panagiū ejufd Parci ac etiam officiū
Magïi deduct' feiaiū tam infra idem parcūq' infia Foreftam nʳa ib'm
ac infia et p. totam Infulā pd. cū Vad. feod. regaid. et conïoditatib.
eid officio ptinen' fpectan' feu inciden' ac etiam Vad. et feod. duoi'
Denai' p. diē p. Execucō et Occupacōe pd. officij Parci pd. Et ipïm
Ricūm Worfley cuftod. pd. Parci de Carefbioke et Magïim de duct' te-
iai' ib'm ac infra Foieftam et totam Inful' nʳam pd. p nob. Hered. et
Succefforibus nʳis facimus Oidinamˢ. et conftituimˢ. p.pʳ fentesHabend.
gaudẽd. exercend. et Occupand. idē officiū Cuftod et Cuftod. pd. Paici nïi de Caiefbioke ex pd. offic' magïi deduct feiaiu' ut pd. eft Unacū
oñibˢ pʳ eminencijs confuetudinibus et Comïoditatibˢ. eifdm offic' et cuft'
et coium cuilt' ptinen' aut cu' eifd. Offic' ad aliqd. tempˢ. ufitat. eid Ricō Woifley p. Se vˡ. pei fufficient' deputat' fuu' pro teimino Vitæ ipïius
Ricï ac Hẽnd. & gaudend. Heibagiu' et Pannagiu' ejufd. Poici cu'
oñibˢ. et finglis fuis ptinen' pʳ.fat' Ricō Woifley Aimig' p teimino
vitæ ejufd. Ricï abfq. Compoto feu aliquo alio nob. Hered. vel Succeffoiibˢ. nʳis p. pd. herbãg et Pannage ieddend. folvend vel faciend.
Ac hẽnd. et annuatim pcipiend. pd Vad. et feod. Duoi' Denai' per
Diē p Execucōe ejufd. Officij cuftod. et Cuftod. paici pd eid Ricō
Worfley p. teimino Vitæ fuæ de ieddit' Exit' et ievencoïbus pd tam
p. manus fuas proprias ac in nianibˢ. fuis ietinend. quā per manus Bal-
lioi' fiimaiioi' tenend. et alioi' Occupatoi' quorūcūq et iecept' pd.
Manei' Teii' ten' et Heieditamēt' et ceteroi' p'miffoiu' p tempoie Exiften' ad Fefta pd. p Equales Poicoïes annuatim folvēd Et pieterea de
amplioii giã nã ac in Confideiacōc pdca dedimus et conceffimus pei

n 2 pʳ.fentes

pᵣ fentes·p. nobis Heredibꝰ et Succeſſor' nᵣis damus et Concedimus pᵈ.
Ricō Worſley tot et tantas Denaɪ' ſuɪas ad quot et quantas Oꝰɪa pd.
ſepᵃlɪa Vad. et ſeod. ſupᵗɪus ſpecificat. a Feſto Scɪ Michis Archi Año
Regni pᵣ·mo huc uſq inteɪ ſe attingunt eᵗ eoru' quodlt. ab eod Feſto
hucuſq. attɪngɪt Habend et Percɪpiend eid. Rɪco et Aſſɪgnatɪs ſuɪs ex
dono et regaɪd. nᵣis de reddit' Exit' pſic' et revencōɪbꝰ. pd. tam p manus ſuɪs p pɪɪas et ɪn Mɪnɪbus ſuɪs p. prɪjs ɪetɪnend. q. p. manus Bal-
lɪoru' Fɪɪmarɪor' tenenc' et alɪoɪ' Occupatoɪ eorundē quorū̄cuɪq pɪo tempore exɪſten' abſq. cōpoto ſeu alɪquo modo reddend. ſolvend. vel facɪend'
Et ulterɪus nōs nō ſolu' fidele ſerɪvɪcɪū pfatɪ Rɪcɪ Worſley Aɪmɪger' ɪn-
tɪme conſidera̅tes veru' etɪam induſtrɪa et provid. cɪrcū̄ſpectɪone ɪpɪus
Rɪcɪ plene Confidentes de uberɪorɪ gɪa̅ nɪa dedimus & Conceſſimus ɑc
per preſentes p nobis Heredibꝰ. et Succeſſorɪbꝰ. nᵣis Damus et conce-
dɪmus eid. Rɪcō Worſley Armɪg' durante Vɪta ſua plena̅ Poteſtatem et
Auctorɪtatē ad Omnɪa et Sɪngula Scɪtus et Capɪtalɪa Meſuag' ac Teɪras
Dꝰɪcales quaſcuɪq Qou ū̄cuɪq. Dꝰɪoɪ' et Manerɪoru' nɪoɪ' ac alɪa teɪɪ'
ten' et heɪedɪtamc̅t' nɪᵃ quecū̄q cū̄ eoɪ' ptɪnen' quocū̄q modo ſive Juɪe
eadem Maꝰɪa teɪɪ' tent' et Hereditamc̅t' ɪn manɪbꝰ. nᵣis modo exɪſtꝰt ſive
nobis alɪquo modo pertɪnen' ſeu ſpectan' ɪn Inſul' pd. ac Omnɪa alɪa Scɪt'et
Capɪtalɪa Meſuag' ac Teɪras Dꝰɪcales quaſcuɪq Dꝰɪoɪ' ɑlɪoɪ' et Manerɪoɪ'
ac alɪa teɪɪ' Ten' et Heredɪtamenta Quecuɪq cū̄' eoɪ' ptɪ' que ad Manus
nᵣas alɪquo modo impoſteru' devenɪɪe ſeu nobis alɪquo modo ptɪneɪe vel
ſpectare contingerɪnt ɪn eadē Inſul' Vec' et Vɪs' franc. Pleg̅ ac alɪjs Cu-
rɪɪs Quɪbuſcuɪq. except' pro nobis et nōɪe nrō pro nobis Heredibꝰ. et
Succeſſorɪbꝰ nᵣis concedend. tradend. et ad firma' dɪmɪtt' locand' et aɪ-
quo alɪo modo exponend. cuɪcuɪq. perſonæ et quɪbuſcuɪq. perſonɪs con-
jū̄ctɪm ſeu conjū̄ctu vel dɪmɪſim' ſcɪtus et Capᵗla Meſuagɪa ac Terras
Dꝰɪcales nec non Terræ Ten' & Heredɪtamēt ɪlla cu' eoɪum ptɪnenc'
ſive eoɪ' alɪqua vel alɪquod aut alɪquas vel alɪqua' coru' percell' vel pcell-
lam hɪe Volentɪ et volentɪbꝰ. p. Indentuɪ' ɪnde ɪnteɪ nos et noɪe nɪō de
Aɪɪſamc̅to pd. Rɪcɪ Worſley Aɪ' Capᵗɪnɪɪ nɪe Inſulæ pd. et ſupᵗɪus
oꝰɪu' duoɪ' Manerɪoɪ' teɪɪa' ten' et Heɪedɪt' nᵣoɪ' quoɪūcuɪq ɪn eadē Inſula et ɪpᵃm pſona̅ ſɪve ɪpᵃs pſonas conjū̄ctɪ' ſeu conjunctɪm et dɪvɪſim
Scɪtꝰ et Capɪtalɪa Meſɪuagɪa ac Teɪɪ' Dꝰɪcales nec nō Teɪɪ' ten' et He-
redɪtamc̅t' ɪlla cu' eoɪu' pᵗɪn. habere Volentem et Volentes de tempore
ɪn tempꝰ. p. Teɪmɪno Vɪgɪntɪ unɪus Annoɪ' conficɪend. aut p Copɪam
Rotuloɪ' Cur' pro termɪno Vɪtæ ꝰ Vɪtaɪ' aut in Feod. vel alɪter Scdm
Conɪuetudɪne eoɪund, Maner' Teɪɪ' Ten' et Heredɪtamēt vel eoɪū̄

Alɪquoɪ'

Aliquor' five alicujus concedend. res'va'd. nob. Heredibs. et Succefforibs.
ni is añuatim fup. oñibs conceff dimiff et locacōibs. ac copijs fic ut
p'fert' dimiff five conceff p. pd Ricm Worfley Aimig' antiquu' Reddit'
Confuetud. et Servic' inde debit vl confuet' vel plus falvis nob. Heredibs. et Succefforibs. ñis oñibs. et oñimod. finibs. pficuis denior fuñis
fervicijs et confuetud. Quibufcu'q. nob Hered et Succefforibs. ñis p.
conceffionibs. edicōibs. ad firmam dimiffionibs loca'coibs et copijs pd.
five eorum alicui hend. pvenient ac pioventur' five debend. Et Volums.
ac Nobis Heredibs. et Succefforibs. ñis p. p'fentes concedimus qd ones
et fingule hmoi conceffiones Tiadicōes et ad firma dimiffiones et loca-
ciones aliquor' Statutuu et Capital' Mefuag' ac Terr' Dñical Dñioi' et
Maneiior' ac alior' Teñ. et Heieditamētoi' ñioi' pd. vel eor' alicujus
eoi' pcell p. Indentur' in Forma pd. cōficied. et concedend ac omnes
et fingule conceffiones eoiund. ftatutum et Capital' Mefuag' ac Terr
Dñicall' et alioi' teir' ten' et Hereditamēt p. Copiam Rotulor' Curiæ in
forma fupiadcla ad aliqd. temps conficiend. hmoi perfone et perfonis
cui et quibs. eadem Scitus et Capital' Mefuag' ac Terr' Dñical' et alia
teri' ten' et Heieditamēta ñia cu eor' ptin' vel eor' aliquod aut aliqua
eoi' pcella infoima pd. conceff tradit et ad firma dimiff five locat eiunt
done Valide et Sufficient' in Lege v'fus nos Hered ei Succefs ñios p.
terminis et Statubs. in eis fpecificat eiunt aliqua Amb guitate inde non
obflant' Provifo femp qd he Liē ñie Patēn aliqualt' non extend ad
auctoiizind. pd. Ricñi Worfley Aim' ad aliquod integru Manci' in-
tegie neq Aliqua' revercōem aliq°. Maneioi' teir' ten' five Heredia-
mēt dimittend. locand. ad firma' tradend. nec aliquo modo concedind
Et Uiteiius Nos accipentes Capitaneu Inful' pd p tempoie exiften'
Execu'coes quorucuq. proceff iu et Mandator' progenitoi' ñioi pio eis
aliafq. Jurifdic' Tempoiibs. retio Acts infia Inful' pd. huifle volentefq'
inhTiātes infra Inful' pd p. Vic'aut per aliquos alios Officiaiios feu Mi-
ftios extia Infui' illam nō moleftaii hmoi tamē Proceffus et Mandat' de
Tempoie in Tempus dbīe execut' foie acut pifat Seiviens ñr' ut Capi-
taneus Infu'æ pd. eafdē Execucōes fecuie uti valeat de gra ñia fpali ac
ex cetera Sciencia et mero motu ñis concedimus pifat Rico Worfley
Aimig Capitaneo Infulæ ñrē pd. qd ipe durante vita fua heat ei teneat
retura' oñia' et oñimod. Bñvis picept' Biliar' et Alioi' Mandatoi' ñior'
Heied. et Succeffor' ñior'quoiucuq. nec non Sumoiicōes Extract' &
picept' Scciō ñrō Heied et Succeffor' nīoi Ac Extract pi cept et mand.
quoiucuq. Jufticiar'nrōi Heied. et Succeffoi' nīoi Ac Extiact. pi cept'
et

et Mand. Quorucuq. Jufticiar' nroī' Hered. et Succeffor' nioī' itinānciu'
tam ad plita Corone Cōia Plita & Plita Foiefte & alioru' Juftic et Co-
miffionaī' q°.ruᷓcuᷓ'q. Attachiament' tam de Plit' Coionæq alioi' plitor'
quoiucuq. infra Inful' pd. ac in oñibᵇ. et Singlis Dᷓnijs Maneiijs Teii'
teñ' Poffeffionibᵇ. Feod. et Hereditamet' quibufcuq in eadē Infula ac
Oñia alia q̄cuque faciend. et Exequend. que ad officia Vic' in pmiſs'
ptinet ac ipoftei' peitinere poterit q nullus Vicecomes Ballivus feu aliᷓs
Miniftr' nī' Heied vel Succeffor' nroī' Infulam pd. aut aliqᷓⁿ. Dñia Ma.
neiia Teii' Ten' poffeffion' feod. et Hereditamēt' in ead. Inful' ingreda.
hᷓ. ad diftrucōes & Attachiamēts feu Execuecōes Bru' pcēpt' Mandat' Billar' Sumoñicon' et Extract' pd fiᷓe eorum alicujus nec pio
aliq°. officio nec aliq̄ ie officiu' in pñiffis tanquend. faciend. feu
Exequend. durante Vita pd Rīci Woifley fe intromittent nifi in'
defᷓu ejufd' Rīci Woifley ac miniftioru̅ fuoi' Et Ulteiius conceffimus et pei pntes pro nobis Heied. et Succeffoiibᵇ. nᷓfis concedimus
pᷓ fat' Ricō Woifley Aim' Capitaneo Infule nᷓe pd. qd ipē durante
Vita fua in Infula pᷓdᷓcta ac in oñibᵇ. Manijs Teii' Ten' Poffeffion' feod.
et Heieditamēt' in ead Inful' heat' et teneat p fe feu deputat. fuos five
Deputat' fuu' Affifam et Affaiam Panis, Vini, et Servicie ac oñimod.
alioi' Victualiu' menfuraiu' et pondeiu' quorucuq. et omniu' alioru' que
ad officia Clici mēati Hofpicij nᷓi Heied. et Succeffoi' noftioi' ptinet et
que impofteium Pertineie poterit faciend. et exercend. q°.ciens et
quandocumq opus fuit et neceffe adeo plene feut idē Clīcus meati nᷓi
Heied. et Succeffoi' nᷓoi' facēt vel iaceie debeiet in pᷓ.fentia niā̃ Heied. feu Succeffor' nioi' facēt vel faceie deberet in pᷓ.fentia nrā̃ Hered.
feu Succeffoi' nᷓoi facēt vel faceie debeiet in pᷓ. Sentiañrā̃ Heied. feu
Succeffor' nror fi prefens conceffio pᷓ.fato Ricō minime facta fuit Itaq.
Clīcus Mēati Hofpitij nᷓi Hered. Succeffoi' noftioi' non ingiediat' Infulam pd. nec aliqua Dominia Maneiia terr' teñ' poffeffiones Feod. et
hereditamēt in ead Inful' ad aliquod ibm̃ faciend' feu Exercend' quod
ad Offic' fuu' ptinet aut impofteru̅ pertinere poterit quoiifmodo Salvis
tame nob Hered. et Succefforibᵇ nᷓis oñibᵇ. finibᵇ. Ameiciamēt et
alijs pficuis inde pvenien' Ac inluper Nos confideiacōe pd. conceffimus
ac p pñ es pro nobis Heied. et Succeffoiibᵇ. nᷓis concedimus pᷓ fat'
Ricō Woifley Aimigeī' durante Vita fua Officiu Coionatoris nᷓi Hered & Succeffoi' nᷓoi' in Inful' nᷓia pd Ac ipᷓm Ricᷓm Woifley Coio-
natoiᷓ nᷓm Heied et Succeffoi' nioi in Inful' pdᷓcta faciamᵇ. oidinamus
et conftituimᵇ. p. pñᷓes ad Oñia et fingula in ead Inful faciend. exercend.
et e .eqᷓend que ad Coionatoiē et ad offic' coionatoris ptinet et impofteru'

pert.neie

pertinere potuit Qᵉciens et Quandocuᵗq opus fuerit et necesse adeo
plene ficut aliquis alius Coronator' nʳ' Hered. vel Succeffor' nᵗor' rōne
Officij sui five ione aliqᵒ i' Statutor' faceret vel facere deberet si pʳ sens
Conceffio minime fact' fuit' Cumq sint plurima Quoru' Declaratio ad
Gubernacōem dcte nie Insul' neceffar' futur' et quæ n hijs Literis nᵗis
Patent' nō exprimutur Nos ex fidel' servicio prᵗfat' servient' nᵗi tum ea
Omnia tum illos Que ad ea oīa affignat' erunt ad nōicōe affigna-
cōem et ordinem quocuq. modo ejufd. Servients nᵗi de tempore in Tem-
pus durante Vita sua efſe Volentes Volumus ac p. Pntes Ordinans. Af-
fign' Auctorizam' & conftituimus prᵗfat' Ricᵐ Worfley Armigᵘ ad ei
Oīa et fingula agend faciend et exequend. que in Schedula manu nᵗa
fignat' et hijs Literis Patentibˢ. annexa fpecificat et expreſſ. erut ac ad
omnes et Singulas hᵘꝛoi perſonas que ad aliqua Servic' feu aliqua Opera
five aliquod opus vel aliquod officiu in ead Schedula fpecificat erunt
Affignat' nōand affignand. & appunctuand. ac easd. perfonas ab eisd.
Servic' opibˢ. et officijs de tempore in tēpus removend. alias in cert'
Locis et Servic' de tempore in tempˢ. nōand affignand et appunctuand.
Et pro Solutᶜoe oīu' et Singuloru' huᵣoi feed Vad. et alioru' Denarior
Sumar Que in pd. Schedula exprimut. pd Ricᵒ Worfley pro Solutōe
et alijs Propofitis & Sᵛvic' nᵗis in eadē Schedula declarat de tempore n
tempˢ fiend. Volumus ac per pntes concedimus eide Ricō Worfley ple-
nam Praeᵐ et Auctoritatē qd. ipe durante Vita sua Virtute hᵘ' Litera-
ar' nᵗar' Patenciu' abfq. aliquo Warranto Oīa et Singla huᵐoi Vads.
feod et alias Denari' Sumᵉs que in pd. Schedula declaratr. de Exit'
Reddit Revencōibˢ & Proficuis quibufcuq. oīu' et Singloru' Dñior'
Minᵣior terrai' ten' poffeffionu' et Hereditametor' niam Quoruᶜuq.
Jam in Manibˢ. nᵗis quocuᵗq modo existen' in Infula pd. ac oīu' alior'
Dñior maneriou' Terr' Ten' poffeffionu' et Hereditametᵗ' quorcumq.
que ad manus nᵗas aliquo modo imposteru' devenire contigint in eid.
Inful' tam per manus ſuas Pᵗ. pias ac in Manibˢ. ſuis retinend. qⁿ. p. minus quoruᵗcuq. Balliol' firmarior' tenenc' et alior' Occup'. eorund. pro
tempore Existen' Annuatim et de tempore in tempus p. Solucōibˢ alijs
Propofitis et Servicijs in pd. Schedul' hijs Literis nᵗis patentibˢ annex'
fpecificat' hēt recipiat' ꝑcipiat et in Manibˢ ſuis Proprijs retineat ac
hēe recipere et ꝑcipere ac in Manibˢ ſuis Proprijs retinere valent et
poffit Et pro majori Securitate pd Ricᵒ Worfley de Annuali Solicie
ram pd. Vad. et allocacon eid. Ricō concefs qⁿ alior' oīu feod Vad.
et denari ꝛ' Sumar' in hijs Iꝛ̄s Paten' et in pd Schedula fpecificat et
declarat

declarat pd. Ricō Worſley annuatim durante Vita ſua pro propoſit' cu
Servic' nr̄is faciend. Volumus ac pro nobis Hered. et Succeſſoribs. nr̄is
per pr̄ſentes concedimus pd. Ricō Worſley q°.d ſi Exit' Reddit' Revencōes et Proficua pd. Dn̄ior' Manerior' Terra' Ten' Poſſeſſionu' et He-
redu̅ nr̄or' in Inſul' nr̄a pd. Annuatim pvenien' et Creſcen' ad Solu-
cōem pd. vad. Feod. et Denarior' Su̅ma' ſive earu' aliquor' juxta tenorem harum Literar' Patenc' & Schedul' eiſd' Literis Paten' Annex̄ non
Sufficere continguit Tunc pd Ricu̅s Worſley Virtute har' nr̄ar' paten'
alio Warranto ſive mandato oı̅a & ſingula pd. vad. feod. et Denar' Su-
mās in hijs Lr̄is Patent' et in Schedula pd. ſpecificat de Exit Revencōibs.
et pſicuis on̅iu' Manior' Terrar' Ten' poſſeſſionu' et Hereditamc̄t' nr̄or
quoru̅cu̅q. in Com' nr̄o Southt' p manus geneal' Receptor' ſive alterius
Receptoris cujuſcu̅q. eorud. exiſten' p tempore Annuatim et de Tempore in Temps. heat recipiat et percipiat et hēre recipere et pcipe valeat et poſſit Quodq ide' Receptor' gen̄al' p tempore Exiſtens Annuatim et de Tempore in temps. plenam et integı̅ā Allacacōem de on̅ibs.
Denarijs Su̅mis p ipm̄ pr̄fat' Ricō Worſley p. vad. feod. et Denarior'
ſu̅mis pd. ſolut' Ptextu har' Literar' nr̄ar paten' aliq'. alio Warranto
ſive mandato nr̄o Hered' vel Succeſſoru' nr̄or heat Quare Volumus et
per Partes pro Nobis Hered. et Succeſſoribs. nr̄is concedimus qd. pr̄fat'
Ricu̅s Worſley Ar' durant' Vita ſua on̅ia et ſingula pr̄miſſa ei Juxta te-
nore̅ haru' Lr̄aru' Patenc. plene heat' teneat gaudeat et Utatur abſq.
impeticōe impedime̅to pturbacc̄e moleſtacōe ſeu gravamine nr̄i Hered.
et Succeſſor' nr̄or Juſtic' Eſcaet' Vic' Comit' aut Alior' Ballior' ſeu Mi-
niſtror' nr̄or vel Hered. ſeu Succeſſor' nr̄or' quoru̅cu̅q Volentes ac per
pr̄ſentes p. nobis Hered. et Succeſſoribs nr̄is concedimus et firmiter in-
jungend Pcipimus tam Cancellar' qm̄ Theſ et Baronibus Sccij nr̄i Hered et Succeſſoru' nr̄or' ac receptor' nr̄o general' in Com' pd. p o tempore Exiſten' ac on̅ibus et ſingulis alijs offic' et Miniſtris nec non tene̅n.
firmar' pr̄miſs. quibuſcu̅q nr̄m Hered. vel Succeſſor' et alijs quibuſcuq.
quibus aliquo modo pertinet ſive impoſteru' ptinere poterit et eoru' cuilt
ſupm̄. Demōſtracōem haru' Literaru' nr̄ar' Paten' aut irrotulament' ea-
rund. abſq aliqo alio br̄i Warranto ſeu Mandato Nobis Hered vel
Succeſſoribs nr̄is impetrand. ſeu Pſequend. plena debitmq. ſolucēm
Allocac̄ in deducc eis Acquietanc' et exoneracōem de et in on̅ibs. et
ſingulis pr̄miſſ. pr̄fat' Ricō Worſley et Aſſignatis ſuis de tempore in
temps. faciet et fieri cauſebant, qdq ipr̄ed Ricō vel Aſſignatis ſuis contra tenore haru' Lr̄ 1' Patenc' Aliqualit' non moleſt'ent aliqua Varietate
incertitudine

incertitudine contiietate Omiffioe non iecitacōe vel aliq alia re caofa vel
materia quacuq̄. in aliq°. non obftan̄ et demonftracō ha.' n̄rai' Lr̄ar
patenc' aut inotulamēt eafᵈm eiit annuatim et de tempoie ~ teṗ pd.
Cancellai' et Thes' et Baronib, Sccṛ pd. ac Receptori genā li in Com'
pd. p. tepie exiften' et omibs alijs miniftris et Offic' n̄iis Hered' et fucceſ-
for' n̄ior. et oriib, alijs quibus aliquo mod ptiret feu impofter' ptine' potii
et eor' cuilt' fufficiens Warrant et Exoneiacō in hac parte Eo q°.d. ex-
preffa mencio de vero valore aut ceititudine pr.miffor' five eoi' alicujus
aut de alijs donis five conceffionib. p. Nos feu p. alique͂ pgenitor' n̄ioi'
pr fat. Ricō Woifley ante hec tempora facta in pr̄fentib, minime fact'
Exift' aut aliquo Statuto Actu Oidinacōe pvifione five Reftricōe incou-
trm̄ inde ante hac hīt, fact. edit oidinat feu prīs aut aliqua alia ie caufa
vel materia quacuq' in aliquo non obftan'. In cujus rei Teftm̄ has Lias n̄as
fieri fecimus Patentes. Tefte me ipā apud Weftm' Octavo Die Apilis
Año Regni noftri Secundos.

Pei bieve de pivato Sigillo et de Dat. prediē. &c.

*Articles of diveife Things geven by the Quene's Ma.ᵗⁱ in Chaidge to Richaid
Woifley Efquire Capp.ᵐᵉ of the Ifle of Wight to put in Execuion in fuch foire
as by his D fuie on fhall feme mete to tend to ile Wealth and Stiength of the
feid Ifle.*

IMPRIMIS the faid Capp.me fhall forthwith put in oider and aiey the
tviole People of the Ifle as fhall feme meteft for the Defence of the faid Ifle and
the Lacks which he fhall finde aid may by the auctoiitie of his office oi by Confent of
ile Fiecholders and Inhītants theieof iemedye he fhall foith wh endivoi his
whole induftrye aboute the fame and fuch as he cannot iediffe he f'a'l fignify
to her Ma.ⁱ wh his opinion how the fame ai to be iemedied whein hei
Maⁱⁱ will accept his good will in acceptable paite.

Item after this pi fent time he fhall caufe yeeily et ⁱ Seafons in Jeyaie oi
oftei' yff nede fo iequiie duiinge Peace Eveiy Centoiei to caule the whole Cen-
ioite togethei and bringe them to fuch place wh in the foid Ifle as by the faid
Captaine fhal be appointed and there to confulte what is to be donne foi ile bettei
Foitificaion and Stienght of ile faide Ifle and to piele theiin wⁱⁱ Effich

Itoi

Item he ſhall alſo trevſe every yeare or oftener for the better trarnge of them raule the Centons w.ᵗʰ the able men in there Cetony before him to muſter and ſhall ſe tl e ſame effectually done both for the Furniture of Armor and Weapon and there vetter Exercyſe.

Item he ſhall cauſe the Statut's for Tymber Wood and Coppices be forthw.ᵗʰ put in Execucon w.ᵗʰin the Iſle and that he cauſe Enquiries by Inqueſts to be made of the Defavlts thereof and he ſhall forthw.ᵗʰ phibit that nether Timbre Wood nor Cole ſhol be carȳed out of the Iſle to any place.

Item he ſhall phibit and in her Ma.ᵗˢ name ſtraightly Chardge that no Fre-lovlder ſhall lett or ſett any Ferme or Copprehould Duble to the Hinderaunce of the Iffracōn and Mannor of the ſaid Iſle.

Item her Ma.ᵗⁱ is pleaſed that no manor of pſon ſhal be called to any Aſſiſe or Seſſions out of the Iſle, but only for Matter conſiẽinge the Inhitavnts of the Iſle or the Lands of the Iſle for which purpoſe the ſaide Capp.ⁿᵉ ſhall have a Warrant Dormant remaininge w.ᵗʰ him teſtiſing the ſame from tyme to tyme to the Sherif of the Shire of Southampton.

Item the ſaid Capp.ⁿᵉ ſhall ſe that every Pʃon or Vicar having any Benefice w.ᵗʰin the Iſle ſhall kepe Reſidence thereuppon and yf they do not he ſhall thereof pticularly advertyſe her Ma.ᵗˢ Privy Counſell ſo as order may be geven to redreſſe the ſame

Item he ſhall alſo cauſe the Statute for reedyſienge of Fermes Tenẽnts and Cop-pyhoulds and maintenãce of Huſbandry and Tyllage to be put in dewe Execũcon w.ᵗʰ ſpede wherecas there is grounde ſufficient belonginge to any of the ſame.

Item Ler Ma.ᵗⁱ woulde have ſtraight Chardge and cõmavndmẽt geven that no man.ʳ of pʃon dwellinge w.ᵗʰout the Iſle ſhoulde have in his hands or mantñrance any Ferme voyde Ground or Tenenẽt w.ᵗʰin the Iſle But yf any Pſon will obſti-nately ſtand to the Contrary that his Name be forthw.ᵗʰ certyſied w.ᵗʰ the circu-ſtances to the Privy Counʃell.

Item Ler Ma.ᵗⁱ will that no Souldior that taketh her Ma.ᵗˢ Wages ſhould kepe or inhabite any Houſe or Tenenẽt of Huſbandry but that he ſhoulde applye the Place of her Service

Item her Ma.ᵗⁱ forbiddeth all man.ᵉ of Perſons reſidinge or that ought to re-ſyde w.ᵗʰin the Iſle to be retained eyther in Lyvery Wages or Fee to any man.ᵉ of Pſon otherwiſe the.ⁿ to ſerve his Lord or Maſt.ʳ in Colleciõn of his Rents w.ᵗʰin the ſaied Iſle to avoyde Excuſe of Abſence in tyme of Service there.

Item for the more ſtrenght of the Iſle her Ma.ᵗⁱ would have it ordered in that Iſle, that all manor of Pſons havinge Lands to the clere yearely valewe of 20 ᵗⁱ Marke ſhoulde find one Haquebutier furniſhed in tyme of Warre to remaine in the

Iſle

Ifle under the Rule of the Capp.ne duringe the tyme of Warrs And that every other Pfon having 40.s Land and fo uppward untill 20.ti Marks fhoulde be contributory to the lyke Pporcyon joininge fo many togetler as fhall amounte to the yearely valewe of 20.ti Marks and fo chardge the' all jointlye w.th one Harquebutier And for more Ctenty of this Ord.r the Capp.ne fhall w.th Confereice of the Freeholders of the Ifle make perfecte Boke hereof And fo Accorde uppo the Nomb.r to be founde.

Item her Ma.tie would that no Shepe fhoulde be fedd uppon the Wofte Grounds w.thin the Ifle but the fame fhould be employed only w.th greete Cottel for maintenance of Tillage.

Item it fhall be prohibited that no man that keepeth a Towne Houfe fhall kepe and occupy Hufbandry.

Item the Capp.ne fhall ufe all convenient meanes that the Mcchaunts Artyficers and Craftfmen fhall onlye lyve uppon there Handye Crafts and not intermedle w.th Hufbandye.

Finally Her Ma.tie willeth and comaundeth the faide Capp.ne to employ all the endever to the Poeplinge of the Ifle and to put the fame in Warlyke Array on fpecyally for the Encreafe of Haquebufry and whenfoever he fhall finde him fealf to to lacke auctoryty to pfecute any good purpofe in that behaulf he fhall fignify the fame to her Ma.tie or her Pryvye Councell for her Councell for her Ayde Further that all Fyfhermen dwellinge w.thin o.r faide Ifle fhall have Libty to carye and fell all kinds of Fyfhe taken bye them whether theye lyfte.

Item that the Hufbondmen and others dwellinge w.thin o.r faide Ifle fhall hve libtie uppon the Licence of o.r Capp.ne there to tranfporte and fell where they lyfte any Graine growen w.thin the Ifle when the Price of a Q̃rter of Wheate fhal be in the Marketts there under 13s 4d.——And the Q̃rter of Moult under the Price of 10s.

The ordinary Chardgs now appointed to continue in the Caftells and Forts w.thin the Ifle.

	£.	s.	d.
At the Caftell of Carefbrooke 2 Armorers, one at 8.d the day the other at 6d —On Harquebutemaker at 8d the day—One Boyer — On Fletcher — On Carpenter —One Wheelewright at 6d. the daye a pece—p. ann'.	69	19	2

	£.	s.	d.
At *Sandham Baye* a Porter at 8d. the day—3 Gonners at 6d. a pece the daye—At the *Weft Cowe* a Porter at 8d. the daye and 3 Gonners at 6d a daye a pece—At *Yearmouth Caftell* a Porter at 8d. the daye and 3 Gonners at 6d. the day a pece—At *Sherpnode* and *Worfley's Towne*, a Porter at 8d. the day and 3 Gonners a' 6d. ye day—p. Ann'.	158	3	2
The Raunger of the Forreft p. Ann'm.	6	13	4
The two ridinge Fofters p. Annum	—	100	—
The Steward of the Knighton Courte—p. Ann'	—	26	8
The Forren Baylelf of the Ifle p. Ann'	4	—	—
The Reve of Nighton—p. Ann'	—	10	—
Yearly allowance to the Reve of Nighton for Rent there decayed p. Annm.	—	21	10 ob.
A Perpetuitie to the Vicar of the Caftell of Carefbroke p. Ann'	6	13	4
Payed to the Erle of Southampton for the Pafture of certeine Beafts going in a grownde called Lyme	—	40	—
To the Pfon of Whippingham for the Tythes of Cleybroke—per Annm.	—	5	—
To the Archdeacon of Winton for the Pourac̄on and Synidolls of Goddfhill and Carefbroke	—	24	10 ob.
Allowance for certain Pencons	23	15	8
Allowaunce for a certeine Porcōn of Tythe appointed to the Vicar of Carefbroke	3	—	—
Allowaunce to the Fermor of the Pryorye of Carefbroke for making ye defence againft ye Foreft. p. Annm.	—	16	—
Allowaunce evrye thirde yeare 10s. paied unto the Biffopp of Winton for his triannual Vifitac̄on p. Ann.	—	3	4
To the Reve of the Manor of Afpe per Annm.	—	20	—

The Total Yearely Ordinary Chardge of the faide Ifle. } Five hundred threfcore & Seven Pounds—In wch Some is comprehended the Some of CCIIII.^{XX} l.^h VIII.^s IV.^d Payable for Fees and Wages expreffed in the Patent.

N° XL.

N° XL.

The prefent Military Eftablifhment of the Ifle of Wight. 21 Geo. III.
A. D. 1781.

		Per Diem.			For 365 Days.		
		£.	s.	d.	£.	s.	d.
Governor		1	7	4¼	500	—	—
Lieut. Governor		1	—	—	365	—	—
Sandown Fort.	Captain	—	2	6	45	12	6
	Twelve Warders each 8d.	—	8	—	146	—	—
	One Mafter Gunner	—	2	—	36	10	—
	Three other Gunners each 12d.	—	3	—	54	15	—
Yarmouth Caftle.	Captain	—	10	—	182	10	—
	One Mafter Gunner	—	2	—	36	10	—
	Five other Gunners each 12d.	—	5	—	91	5	—
Carifbrook Caftle	Captain	—	10	—	182	10	—
	One Mafter Gunner	—	2	—	36	10	—
	Three other Gunners each 12d	—	3	—	54	15	—
Cowes Caftle.	Captain	—	10	—	182	10	—
	One Mafter Gunner	—	2	—	36	10	—
	Five other Gunners each 12d.	—	3	—	91	5	—
	£.	5	11	10¾	2042	2	6

Nº XLI.

A Lift of the Members returned to Parliament by the Three Boroughs in the Ifle of Wight, from the Time of their fending Reprefentatives, to the prefent Time, including the General Election in Sptember 1780.

23 Edw I	John de Cofkeville returned to reprefent the Ifland*.		
	Newport	*Newtown.*	*Yarmouth*
27 Eliz. 1585	Sir Arthur Boucher, Knt Edmund Carey, Efq.	William Mewes, Efq. Robert Ridge, Efq.	Anthony Gorges, Efq William Stubbs, Efq.
28 Eliz. 1586.	Richard Sutton, Efq. Richard Hardy, Efq.	Richard Hewifh, Efq Robert Dillington, Efq	Thomas Weft, Efq. John Duncombe, Efq.
31 Eliz. 1588.	Richard Sutton, Efq. Richard Hardy, Efq.	Richard Hewifh, Efq. Richard Sutton, Gent.	Daniel Hill, Efq. John Howe, Efq.
35 Eliz. 1592	William Cotton, Efq. Richard Hewifh, Efq.	John Dudley, Efq Richard Brown, Efq.	Robert Dillington, Efq. John Moffe, Efq.
39 Eliz 1597.	William Cotton, Efq Richard James, Efq.	Thomas Story, Efq. Thomas Crumpton, Efq.	Benedict Barnham, Efq. John Shaw, Efq.
43 Eliz. 1601.	Thomas Crumpton, Efq Richard James, Efq	Robert Wioth, Efq. Robert Cotton, Efq.	William Cotton, Efq. Stephen Theobald, Efq.
1 Jac 1603.	Richard James, Efq. John Afhdale, Efq	Sir John Stanhope, Knt William Mewes, Efq	Thomas Cheke, Efq. Arthur Bromfield, Efq.
12 Jac. 1614.	Sir Richard Worfley, Bart Richard James, Efq.	Sir Tho. Barrington, Bart John Ferrone, Efq	Arthur Bromfield, Efq. Thomas Wriothefley, Efq.
18 Jac. 1620.	Sir Richard Worfley, Bart Sir Richard Uvedall, Knt	Sir Tho Barrington, Bart John Ferrone, Efq	Arthur Bromfield, Efq. Thomas Wriothefley, Efq.
21 Jac 1623	Philip Fleming, Efq Chriftopher Brock, Efq *Sir John Danvers, Knt. in the room of C Brook, Efq who made his election for the city of York.*	Sir Tho Barrington, Bart Sir Gilbert Gerrard, Bart *George Gerrard, Efq in the room of Sir Gilbert, who made his election for the county of Middlefex*	Thomas Wriothefley, Efq. William Beefton, Efq
Car I 1625	Sir Nathaniel Rich, Knt Philip Fleming, Efq.	Sir Tho Barrington, Bart Thomas Mallet, Efq	John Oglander, Efq. John Cheke, Efq
2 Car I 1625	Sir Chrift Yelverton, Kt Philip Fleming, Efq	Sir Tho Barrington, Bart Thomas Mallet, Efq	Sir Edward Conway, Kt. John Oglander, Efq.
3 Car I 1628	Sir Chrift Yelverton, Kt Philip Fleming, Efq	Sir Tho. Barrington, Bart Robert Barrington, Efq	Sir Edward Dennis, Knt. Sir John Oglander, Knt
15 Car. I. 1640	Lucius Ld Vifc Falkland† Sir Henry Worfley, Bart	Nicholas Welton, Efq John Mewes, Efq	Philip Lord Lifle, Will. Oglander, Efq John Berkley Efq. }
16 Car I 1640	Lucius Lord Vifc Falkland Sir Henry Worfley, Bart Will Stephens, Efq elected on Lord Falkland's vacating in 1645.	Sir John Mewes, Kt Nicholas Welton, Efq Sir John Barrington, Bart and John Bulkley, Efq were voted in by the Houfe of Commons, in the room of Sir John Mewes and Mr Wefton	Philip Lord Lifle Sir John Leigh, Kt.

* The De Cofkevilles were a confiderable family in the ifland, in the reign of Henry III.
† The celebrated Lord Falkland.

	Newport.	Newtown.	Yarmouth.
A. D. 1654.	Colonel William Sydenham*, and John Lisle †, Esq returned to represent ...		
A. D. 1656.	Col William Sydenham, and Thomas Bowerman, Esq returned to represent ...		
A. D. 1658.	Thomas Bowerman, Esq	Thomas Lawrence, Esq	John Sadler, Esq
	Robert Dillington, Esq	John Maynard, Esq	Richard Lucy Esq.
12 Car II 1661	Robert Dillington, Esq	Sir John Barrington, Bart	Sir John Leigh, Knt.
	William Oglander Esq	Sir Henry Worsley Bart	Richard Lucy, Esq
13 Car. II. 1661	William Glascock, Esq	Sir John Barrington, Bart	Richard Lucy, Esq
	William Oglander, Esq	Sir Henry Worsley, But	John Smith, Esq
	Sir Robert Dillington, Bart in the room of Sir William Oglander, Bart deceased in 1670	Sir Robert Worsley, Bart in the room of Sir Henry deceased, 1666.	
29 Car II 1678	Sir Robert Holmes, Knt	Sir John Holmes, Knt	Sir Richard Mason, Knt
	Sir Robert Dillington, Bart	John Churchill ‡, Esq	Richard Lucy, Esq
31 Car II. 1681	Sir Robert Dillington, Bart.	Hon Daniel Finch	Sir Thomas Lyttleton
	Sir Robert Holmes, Knt	Sir John Holmes, Knt	Lemuel Kingdon, Esq
1 Jac II 1685.	Sir Robert Holmes, Knt.	William Blathwaite, Esq	Thomas Wyndham, Esq
	Sir William Stephens, Kt	Thomas Done, Esq	William Hewer, Esq
1689 The Convention Parliament	Sir Robert Dillington, Bart Sir William Stephens, Knt Edward Dillington, Esq on the death of Sir Robert.		
1 Will & Mary 1689	Sir Robert Holmes, Knt.	Richard Earl of Ranelagh.	Richard Norton, Esq
	Sir William Stephens, Kt	Thomas Done, Esq	Henry Slingsby, Esq
2 Will & Mary 1690	Sir William Stephens, Kt	Richard Earl of Ranelagh	Sir John Trevor, Knt
	Richard Leveston, Esq	Thomas Done, Esq	Sir Chs Duncomb, Kt. Henry Holmes, Esq on Sir John Trevor's ...
7 William III 1695	John Lord Cutts	James Worsley, Esq	Anthony Morgan, Esq
	Sir Robert Cotton, Bart	Thomas Done, Esq	Henry Holmes, Esq
	Sir Henry Dutton, Knt in the room of Lord Cutts, who made his election for Cambridgeshire.		
10 William III 1698	John Lord Cutts	James Worsley, Esq	Anthony Morgan, Esq.
	Sir Robert Cotton, Bart	Thomas Hopton, Esq	Henry Holmes, Esq.
12 William III 1699.	John Lord Cutts	James Worsley, Esq	Anthony Morgan, Esq
	Sir Robert Cotton, Bart	Thomas Hopson, Esq	Henry Holmes, Esq.
	Henry Greenhill, Esq in the room of Lord Cutts, who made his election for Cambridgeshire.		
13 William III 1701.	John Lord Cutts	Thomas Hopson, Esq	Anthony Morgan, Esq.
	Samuel Sheppard, Esq.	Joseph Dudley, Esq	Henry Holmes, Esq
	Henry Greenhill, Esq. in the room of Lord Cutts, who made his election for Cambridgeshire.		

* Col William Sydenham was governor of the Isle of Wight, a great friend of Oliver Cromwell, who made him one of his lords of parliament, a commissioner of the treasury, and one of the committee of safety

† Mr Lisle was likewise a friend of Cromwell's, and a commissioner of the great seal

‡ John Churchill, Esq was afterwards the great Duke of Marlborough

	Newport	Newtown.	Yarmouth
1 Anne 1702.	John Lord Cutts William Stephens, Esq James Stanhope, Esq. in the room of Lord Cutts, who made his election for Cambridgeshire	John Leigh, Esq Thomas Hopson, Esq.	Anthony Morgan, Esq Henry Holmes, Esq.
4 Ann, 1705.	John Lord Cutts. William Stephens, Esq Sir Tristram Dillington, Bart in the room of Lord Cutts deceased	James Worsley, Esq. Henry Worsley, Esq	Anthony Morgan, Esq. Henry Holmes, Esq.
7 Anne, 1708	Sir Trist Dillington, Bart William Stephens, Esq	James Worsley, Esq Henry Worsley, Esq.	Anthony Morgan, Esq. Henry Holmes, Esq.
9 Anne, 1710	Lt Gen. J Richm Webb William Stephens, Esq General William Seymour, in the room of Lt. Gen Webb.	James Worsley, Esq. Henry Worsley, Esq.	Sir Gilbert Dorben, Bart. Henry Holmes, Esq
12 Anne, 1713.	Lieut General Webb. William Stephens, Esq	James Worsley, Esq. Henry Worsley Esq	Sir Gilbert Dolben, Bart. Henry Holmes, Esq.
1 Geo. I. 1715	Anthony Morgan, Esq William Stephens, Esq James Stanhope, Esq. in the room of Anthony Morgan, Esq. and again Sir Tristram Dillington, on Mr Stanhope's * being made a peer.	Sir Robert Worsley, Bart James Worsley, Esq.	Sir Robert Raymond, Bart. Henry Holmes, Esq. Sir Theodore Janssen Bart. and Anthony Morgan, Esq were declared by the House of Commons duly elected in the room of Sir Robert Raymond and Mr Holmes
7 Geo I 1722	Charles Cadogan, Esq Charles Whitworth, Esq Sir William Willis, Bart in the room of Mr Cadogan, created a peer.	Charles Worsley, Esq William Stephens, Esq	Anthony Morgan, Esq. Colonel Thomas Stanwix.
1 Geo. II 1727	George Huxley, Esq William Fortescue, Esq	James Worsley, Esq Henry Holmes, Esq Sir John Barrington, Bart an Colonel's Ar Poulet, Esq were upon petition ... duly elected April 29, 1729, in the room of Sir John Barrington and Mr Holmes	Maurice Morgan, Esq Paul Burrard, Esq.
8 Geo. II 1734	George Huxley, Esq William Fortescue, Esq	James Worsley, Esq. Thomas Holmes, Esq	Anthony Chute, Esq. Paul Burrard, Esq
15 Geo II 1741	Anthony Chute, Esq Moncur Cope, Esq	Sir John Barrington, Bart Maj Gen Henry Holmes	Lt Gen Maurice Bocland. Thomas Gibson, Esq.
21 Geo. II 1747	Anthony Chute, Esq Moncur Cope, Esq ...	Sir John Barrington, Bart. Lt Gen Maurice Bocland	Thomas Holmes, Esq Lt Gen Henry Holmes.

* He afterwards was Secretary of State, and was words created Earl of Harrington.

	Newport.	Newtown.	Yarmouth.
28 *Geo. II.* 1754.	Tho. Lee Dummer, Efq. Raph Jennifon, Efq.	Sir John Barrington, Bart. Thomas Powell, Efq.	Thomas Holmes, Efq Lt Gen. Henry Holmes.
2 *Geo. III.* 1761.	W. Rawlinfon Earle, Efq Tho. Lee Dummer, Efq. *Thomas Dummer, Efq. on Mr. Dummer's death.*	Sir John Barrington, Bart Harcourt Powell, Efq.	Thomas Holmes, Efq Lt Gen Henry Holmes. *Jeremiah Dyfon, Efq. on the death of Gen Holmes, and John Eames, Efq. in 1764, on Lord Holmes death, lately created an Irifh Peer.*
9 *Geo III.* 1768	Hans Sloane, Efq. John Eames, Efq *Honourable John St. John in the room of John Eames, Efq. 1773.*	Sir John Barrington, Bart. Harcourt Powell, Efq	Jervoife Clarke, Efq William Stroude, Efq *Hon George Lane Parker, Thomas Dummer, Efq. voted in on petition in 1769.*
14 *Geo. III.* 1774.	Sir Richard Worfley, Bart. Hans Sloane, Efq. Sir Richard Worfley vacated on accepting one of the Clerkfhips of the Green Cloth, in Dec 1777, and re-elected the fame month, and vacated again Dec. 1, 1779, on being appointed Comptroller of the Houfehold, ftood a poll for the county on the death of Sir Simeon Stuart, but not fucceeding, was re-elected Feb 1ft, 1780.	Sir John Barrington, Bart. Harcourt Powell, Efq. *Charles Ambler, Efq. in the room of Mr. Powell, who vacated in March 1775. Edward Meux Worfley, Efq in the room of Sir John Barrington, Bart. who vacated in Dec. 1775.*	Edw Meux, Worfley, Efq. Jervoife Clarke, Efq. *James Worfley, Efq in the room of Edward Meux Worfley, Efq who vacated in Feb 1775. Robert King jun ll, Efq Dec 1779, in the room of Jervoife Clarke Jervoife, Efq elected for the county, having vacated his feat Nov. 26, 1779, by accepting the place of a Militia Regiment.*
20 *Geo. III.* 1780.	Rt Hon Sir R. Worfley, Bt The Hon. John St. John.	Edw Meux Worfley, Efq John Barrington, Efq.	Edward Morant, Efq Edward Rufhworth, Efq.

N° XLII.

Summonitio Regis ad convocandum Clerum ad Parliamentum, 23 Edw. I. *

REX venerabili in Christo patri R. eadem gratia Cantuariensi Archiepiscopo, totius Angliæ Primati, salutem. Sicut lex justissima provida circumspectione saciorum principum stabilita hortatur et statuit, ut quod omnes tangit ab omnibus approbetur; sic et innuit evidenter ut communibus periculis per remedia provisa communiter obvietur, sane satis nostris, & jam est ut credimus per universa mundi climata divulgatum, qualiter Rex Franciæ de terra nostra Vasconiæ nos fraudulenter et cautulose decepit eam nobis nequiter detinendo. Nunc vero prædictis fraude et nequitia non contentus ad expugnationem regni nostri classe maxima & bellatorum copiosa multitudine congregatis, cum quibus regnum nostrum & regni ejusdem incolas hostiliter jam invasit; linguam Anglicanam, si conceptæ iniquitatis proposito detestabili potestas correspondeat (quod Deus avertat) omnino de terra delere proponit. Quia igitur prævisa jacula minus cædunt, et res vestra maxime sicut cæterorum regni ejusdem concivium agitur in hac parte; vobis mandamus in fide et dilectione, quibus nobis tenemini, firmiter injungentes quod die Dominica proxime post festum sancti Martini in hyeme proxime futurum apud Westminster personaliter intersitis. Præmunientes priorem et capitulum ecclesiæ vestræ, archidiaconum totumq. clerum vestræ diocescos, facientes quod iidem prior et archidiaconus in propriis personis suis, et dictum capitulum per unum, idemq. clerus per duos procuratores idoneos, plenam et sufficientem potestatem ab ipsis capitulo et clero habentes, una vobiscum intersint modis omnibus, tunc ibidem ad tractandum, ordinandum, et faciendum, nobiscum, et cum cæteris prælatis et proceribus et aliis incolis regni nostri, qualiter hujusmodi periculis et excogitatis malitiis obviandum. Teste Rege apud Wengeham tricesimo die Septembris.

* *Edward the First (wishing to recover Gascony, which had been seized by the King of France) summoned the Clergy, as well as the Citizens and Burgesses to the Parliament call'd upon that occasion, as appears by the above writ.*

N° XLIII.

Nᵒ XLIII.

The Copy of the Deed of Conveyance of Hunny Hill, to the Corporation of Newport, 1 Henry V.

SCIANT præfentes et futuri qd. nos Agnes qui fui uxor Johannis Attelode et Johes. Erlefman fenior dedimus conceffimus et hac pnti. charta nra. confirmav. Willmo. Farfye & Willmo. Gandere ballivis de novo burgo de Newporte Johanni Compton Johanni Langftoke Willmo Paxhulle Richardo Shide et oibus. alijs burgenf. ejufdem burgi omnes terras et pafturas quas hamus fup. Honiehulle in borial. pte curfus aque voc. Lukkeley et in occiden. pte. foffat. priorat. fce Cruc. voc. Monken Woodich : habend. et tenend. omnes terras et paftur. prtas. cum ptin. fuis prefatis Willmo. Farfye Willmo. Gandere Johanni Compton Johanni Langftoke Willmo. Paxhulle Rico. Snide et oibus. alijs burgenf. burgi præd. et heredibus fuis imppm. de capital. dnis feodi illar. p. fervic. inde debit. et de jure confuet. Reddend. inde annuatim nobis et heredibus nris. vigint denar. ad feft. Pafche et fce. Michis. arch. p. equales porcones. pro oibus. al. fervic. exactionibus five demand. Et nos vero predic Agnes et Johes Erlefman et heredes nre. oes. prdtas. teri. et paftur. cum fuis ptin. prefatis Willmo. Farfye Willmo. Gandere Johanni Compton Johanni Langftoke Willmo. Paxhulle Rico. Shide et oibus alijs burgenfibus predic. burgi et heredibus fuis contra oes. gentes wariantizabim. acquietabim. et imppm. defendem. In cujus rei teftimon huic prefenti charte nre. figilla nra. appofuim. Hijs teftibus Willmo. Bremefkete Willmo. Ringborne Thome Brereding Johanne Hakett Johanne Heyno et alijs. Dat. apud Newporte pred. qrto. die menfis Octobris anno regni regis Henrici Quinti primo.

The original deed is in a fmall black box in the town Cheft, at Newport.

APPENDIX.

Nº XLIV.

A Copy of the Rate made March 17th, 1653, for the Maintenance of the Minister of Newport.

WHEREAS this Towne and Burrough is become very populous, confisting of 2500 foules and upwards, and the Church or Chappell thereof is not endowed w.th any Means or Maintenance for the Subfiftance or livelyhood of any Minifter, or Minifters, to preach the Word of God, or officiate therein as a Minifter, or Minifters; By Meanes whereof all Godly Minifters are utterly difcouraged to take the care and buithen of the faid Place and People upon themfelves, to the great Damage and eternall hazard of the Soules of the poore Inhabitants of this fame Towne. The w.ch the Mayor and chief Burgeffes of this Burrough are willing, as much as in them lyeth, to remove, redreffe, and for the future p'fent, it being a Duty incumbent on all Magiftrates, and therefore have thought fitt to conftitute, ordeyne, and appoint, and do hereby, at this p'fent affembly conftitute, ordeyne, and appoint, That for, and towards the Maintenance of fuch Minifter, or Minifters, as are, or fhall be thought fit and appointed to officiate in the aforefaid Church, or Chappell, a Rate, Tax, or Affeffm.t. not exceeding the Some of One Shilling and Six Pence upon every Pound, for one whole Yeare, be made on all the Lands and Tents lying w.thin the fame Burrough, and alfo on all the Rents and perfonall Eftate, and Eftates, of all the Inhabitants, refiding w.thin the aforefaid Burrough, with refpect to their beft Abilities in that Behalfe, by the Mayor, and the Chiefe Burgeffes of the fame Burrough, or the Major Part of them, together w.th Eight, Six, or four of the able Inhabitants refideing wi.thing ye fame Burrough. And that thofe for the fame purpofe fhall be from Time to Time elected, named, and chofen by the faid Mayor, and Chief Burgeffes for the time being, for that Purpofe.

From the Court Book, page 76.

Nº XLV.

N⁰ XLV.

A Copy of the Articles of Agreement between Lord Cutts, Governor of the Isle of Wight, and Sir Robert Worsley, Bart. James Worsley, Esq. and the other principal Gentlemen of the said Island, respecting the Rights, Privileges, &c. of the several Corporations. Signed at West. 17th. of March, 1697.

ARTICLES made and agreed on between the Right Honourable John Lord Cutts, His Majesty's Governor of the Isle of Wight, &c. and Sir Robert Worsley Barronett, James Worsley, Esq. Anthony Morgan, Esq. Henry Holmes, Esq. in behalf of themselves and all other Gentlemen of the said Island, who shall afterwards sign the same.

That there shall be, from the day of the date hereof, a reall, sincere, mutuall, and lasting Friendship between the Governour and Gentlemen of the said Isle, as also between their Dependants, Friends, and Servants, to all Intents and Purposes.

That all Quarrels, Lawsuits, Animositys, and the like, relating to Corporations and Elections, that have at any time happen'd between them, their Dependants and Servants, shall, ipso facto, cease, and be absolutely forgotten, as if they had never been.

That Sir Robert Worsley, his Friends, and the Partys, who have signed these Articles, doe ingage to assist any Person recommended by the Governor to be chosen Members to serve for the Corporation of Newport, in the said Island, for the ensuing Parliament.

That the Governour shall, before the first of May next ensuing, (by himself or lawfull Deputy) call a Hall at Newtown, examine Witnesses concerning the Ancient Method of Chosing Members to serve in Parliament for that Corporation, and Effectually restore the said Corporation, and all who have a Just pretence to be Members of it, to their Ancient Rights of Burgage-Tenure; Provided always that the said Governour be first put in possession of a qualifying Burgage-Tenure, Sufficient to enable him to be a Member and Elector of the said Corporation. He paying for the same.

That the Election of Members to serve in Parliament for the several Corporations in the said island shall be managed by all who shall at any Time hereafter stand for the same, and by such as recommend or appear for them, with all Calmnefs and Good Nature, and no Animofitys or harfh proceedings be encouraged or practiz'd on Either fide.

That when any Perfons ftand for Parliament Men, at any Time in the faid Ifle of Wight, who are not of the faid Ifland, the Governours Recommendations fhall be preferr'd againft fuch Perfons not being of the Ifland, before any other Recommendation whatfoever.

That all due refpect fhall be had upon all Occafions, and by all perfons to His Majefty's Commiffion, vefted in the Governour, and to every thing thereunto belonging.

C U T T S.

Signed at Weftminfter, this 17th. of March, 1697-8, in the prefence of

J. SMITH.
CHA. SRUBSHAW.

N° XLVI.

An Agreement between the Bayliffs of Newport and the Clothiers of Shipton-Mallet, A. D. 1578.

𝕿𝕳𝕰 Sixth Daye of Julye, in the xxi Yeare of the Reyne of our Sovereyne Ladye Quene Elizabethe Anno Dm. 1578, It is orderd and concluded betweene the Bayliffes of this Towne of Newport, and Richard Biffe of Cofham, Edward Moffe of Cofham, Richard Goodall of faid Cofham, Edwᵈ. Shoude of Shepton Mallet, and Henry Cabell of Mcber, Clothyers, as well for themfelves as for all other Clothyers of the County of Somerfet, as will hereunto affent for and concerning the Petit Cuftomes of the Wolles by them, or any of them, bought within this Ifle, by the Mediation and award of Sʳ. Edward Horfey, Knight, Captayne of this Ifle, and in the prefence of diverfe Gentlemen of the faid Ifle then prefent, as followeth,

In Primis, the faid Clothyers, or Wolmen, and every of them, granteth, and are contented to fatisfy and paye to the Bayliffes of this Town of Newport, for the Time being, and their fucceffors, for, and in Confideration of the Petit Cuftomes of all Wooles, by them, or any of them, hereafter to be bought within this Ifle, in Manner and Form following, that is to faye, for every Lode of Woole conteyning two

Sacks

Sacks, and a Rider, ij vj^d. that is to fay, xii^d. for every Sacke, and vi^d. for the Ryder.

Item, if any of them fhall hereafter happen to carry in One Lode lefs than two Sacks and a Ryder, as aforefaid, then they are contented to pay xii^d. for the Sacke.

Item, It is agreed that the faid Clothyers, and every of them, fhall receive of the Hands of the Bailiffes, for the time being their Cockatts for the tranfporting their Sacks of Woll.

Item, the faid Bayliffes granteth, and are contented for themfelves, or there Officers or Steward, to make to every of the faid Clothyers, demanding the fame, there Cockatt indented, receiving only for the Fees thereof iii^d. and farder, that every of the faid Clothyers fhall pay but for one Cockatt, notwithftanding he fhall at feveral Times in one Yeare receive feveral Cockatts of the Bayliffes or there Officers.

In Confideration of the faid Sums of Money, to be paid by the faid Clothyers, and every of them, in manner and forme aforefaid concluded, and by the faid S^r. Edward moderated and limited, the faid Bayliffes are contented, from henceforth, not to demand or receive the Petite Cuftomes for Wooles according to their cuftomary of

the Tode, nor to vex nor trouble any of them therefore.

In Witnefs whereof the faid Sir Edward, as the Baylives and Clothyers above named, have hereunto fubfcribed their Names.

N° XLVII.

Litera Epifc. Winton. de vi Armata apud Goddfhull.

EXCELLENTISSIMO Principi Edwardo, &c. Frater Henricus Divina Permiffione Winton. Ecclefiæ Minifter, falutem in Eo per quem Reges regnant et Principes dominantur. Quia quidam vi laicali tetenent armati in Ecclefia de Goddfhill noftre diocēs. quo minus officium noftrum exequi libere valeamus; voftre majeftati regie humiliter fupplicamus, quatenus vie veftro de Suth' fi placet precipiatis ut eandem vim prorfus amoveat ab Ecclefie memorata et ulterius contra dictos armatos exequatur, quod officio fuo incumbit in hac parte; et Celfitudinem veftrum regiam confervet Altiffimus, ad regimen regni et populi

vobis

vobis fubjecti ad tempora profpera et longæva. Dat. apud Marevell viij. kl. Apr. A. D. 1307, conf. me. 3º.

Alia Litera Epifc. Winton. ad Regem.

Adam, &c. excellentiffimo Principi Dño. Edwardo regi Anglie, &c. fal. Excellentie veftre regie tenore prefentiam intimamus, qd. quidam maledictionis filii, fue falutis immemores, et in fui interritum jugiter laborantes, Ecclefiam de Goddfhull Infule Vecte, ab olim Divinis obfequiis confecratam, nuper cum vario armorum genere violenter ingredientes, ipfam Ecclefiam vi armata, obftructis oftiis contra facios canones, &c. per non modica tempora occupare et incaftellare aufu facrilego temere piefumferint; ipfamq. adhuc poteftate laicali detinent, occupatam Divini minifterij cultum nofq. quo minus noftrum paftorale officium inibi exercere valeamus dampnabiliter impediendo. Quocirca celfitudini veftre attentius fupplicamus quatenus dictam poteftatem laicalem a dicta Ecclefia amoveri precipias, &c, A. D. 1340.

Ex Regif. Adam de Orlton, epi. Winton. p. 88.

Nº XLVIII.

A curious Grant to the Monks at Carifbrook, by Richard Triftram, of himfelf, and all his Lands at Afton, which he fwears to at the Holy Altar of the Priory.

CARTA Richerij Triftram de Semetipfo cum Terris fuis Sciant Preientes et Futuri Quod Ego Richerius Triftram de Affeton Dedi Deo et Sctæ Mariæ de Carefbrock Meipfum cum Omnibus Catallis meis Ad Servitium Et Obediendum juxta Rationabilem Difpofitionem Prioris ejufdem Loci Et Totam Terram meam cum pertinentijs in Affeton quam Robertus de Affeton dedit mihi pro fervitio meo In Perpetuam Eleemofynam Et hæc Obtuli et Feci et Juravi ad Tenendum Super Altare Sanctæ Mariæ de Carefbroc pro falute Animæ meæ et Predecefforum et Succefforum meorum.

Nº XLIX.

The Rents and Profitts of all such Lands as were appointed by
Richard Worsley, Esq. deceased, unto George Worsley, his
Son, from the Feast of St. Mychell th'Archangell, 1565,
unto the Feast of St. Mychell then next ensuing, A 1566, as
followeth.

		£.	s.	d.
Rents lib. pip̃is, lib. commĩis.	Impm̃is for the Manor. of Norwhitch	13	18	—
	Itē for the Manor. Chidhm̃ Hackett	11	—	8
	Itē for the Tenement at Christchurche	—	40	—
	Itē for certeine Lands in Stenburve in the Isle of Wight	5	1	8
	Itē for a Tenement in Bordwood in the said Isle	—	5	—
	Itē for a parcell of Land cauled Spiceis	—	—	20

Sm̃   30.li   13.s   lib̃. pip̃is et
lib̃. cĩmmĩis

Rents, Pencon's and Tythes apperteyninge to the Pnorye of Caresbroke.	Impm̃is for certeyne Tenem̃ets in Caresbrooke	6	6	7
	Itē for certeyne Tenem̃ets in Newporte	3	19	10
	Itē for certeine Tenem̃ets in Godshill	12	—	16
	Itē for certeine Tenem̃ets in Freshwater	4	9	—
	Itē for certeine Tenem̃ets in Chale	—	14	8
	Itē for certeine other Rivillets to the said Pryore apperteyninge	5	7	—
	Itē for certeine Pencons thereto belonging	13	3	8
	Itē for a Percell of Demeines with a Mille lattlye Letten out bye a Coppy	—	54	—
	Itē for the Tythe of the same Mille	—	3	4
	Itē for certeyne other Tythes to the Priorye belonginge as apperethe uppō the Rent Roll	104	12	9
	Itē for the Free Suters apperteyninge to the said Pnoryc	—	29	—
	Itē for the Tythe of the White of certeine Kyne	3	3	4

Sm.   158.li   4s.   6d.

Profits growinge upon the Demeines of the Pnorye wth. certeine Tythes allwaies gathered by the Baylieffe	Impm̃is for 39 Qr̃teis of Maulte at 13s. 4d. the Qr̃ter sold	26	—	—
	Itē for 6 Qr̃ters & 6 Bushells of Wheat solde at 20s. the Qr̃ter	6	15	—
	Itē for 234 Lambs sould at	28	10	4
	Itē for 8 Steers, & 2 Heyfers sold	15	—	—

q   Itē

	£.	s.	d.
Itē for 32 Todd of Woule ſould at 23s. 6d. the Todd	37	12	—
Itē 34ʰ. qrr. Lambes Toe & Locks	—	11	4
Itē for 16 Waite of Butter ſould at 16 the Mayle	—	21	4
Itē for 6 Sheepe Fells	—	3	6
Itē for odde Tythes of Lambs	—	—	5
Itē for Tythes at Nunwell	—	9	2
Itē for 13 Caulfs	—	57	—

Sm. 119ˡⁱ. —s. 1d.

Whereof allowed

Chardges.

	£.	s.	d.
Impm̄is for the Steward's Fee	—	26	8
Itē for the Receyvo.ʳˢ Fee	—	53	4
Itē for theire Chardgs in Rydinge for the kepinge of the Courts	—	12	—
Itē for one whole Yeares Rent of the Priory	105	6	2
Itē for the Bayleiffs Wags and for other neceſſary Chardges	12	19	10½

Sm.———122£. 18s. 1d.

Sm.
{
of the Receypts of the ſaid Rents of Lands. } 30.ʰ 13s.lib. pipis et com̄in.

of the Receypts of Rents & other Profitts of the Pryorye } 277ʰ· 4s. 7d.
}
307 17 7

Wherof

Sm̄ for the Allowance 122 18 1

Sō

Remaynethe de Claro CIIII. IV. XIX. VI.
xx li s d

APPENDIX.

N° L.

Carta Engelgerij de Bohun de Hafeleia.

QUONIAM vita mortalium in hoc mundo admodum brevi inter-
cluditui fpatio, et anteceffoies noftri corporijs indumentis exuti veriffi-
mis hoc approbant indicijs, oportet nos eoium adhuc fupeiftites ulti-
mam refolutionis in clementiam cum omni cautela providere, et quili-
ter in divinæ majeftatis præfentia veniam confequamui utiliter pietrac-
taie fanctorum etenim patrum auctoritate docemur, quod hæc activa
mortalitatis vita ad contemplativam celfitudinem fit quoddam affentio-
nis adminiculum, et ideo bona tranfitoria nobis divinæ laigitatis dono
conceduntur ut æterna veieq. monentia Deo reddente viciffitudirē per
caiitatis officium mercemur. Quapropter ego Engelgerius de Bohun in
noticia omnium Chrifti fidelium tam prefentium quam futuroium Do
in eleemofinam Deo et ecclefiæ fcte. Maiie de Quadiaiia et monachis Deo ibidem feivientibus pro falute animæ meæ et paientum
meorum, terram meam de Hafeleia quam in infula de Wicl a progenitoribus meis jure heieditaiio poffideo, do inquam eindem teriam
libeiam et quietam piedictæ ecclefiæ perpetuo poffidendam ficut ego
libeiius poffedi. Sciant etiam prefentes et abfentis quia ab abbate
prediti loci quinquaginta marcas aigenti pio donatione accepi ut fi
quis hanc donationem violaie volveiit jvre emitio aefendıtur in ju-
dicio. Qui vero hanc donationum violaie piefumfeiit æteina maledictione puniatur. Ego Engelgeiius hanc donationem hoc figno con-
fiimo.

N. B. This deed, which is to be found among Dodfwoith's MSS.
in the Afhmolean Library, Oxford, is alfo fealed with the feals of
Algar bifhop of Conftance, Hugh abb. Ceiafij Letri abb. of Montf-
burgh, Theodore abb. of St. Lard. Serlo abb. of Savegney, W. de
Bofeville, Bigot, et alioium.

No LI.

Nᵒ LI.

Carta Fundationis et Confirmat. Richardi Comitis Exoniæ.

QUONIAM vita mortalium, &c. Quapropter ego Richardus
comes Exon. comitis Baldwini filius, concedo et confirmo eleemofinam
quam pater meus, concedente Henrico venerabili Angl. rege, dedit
Deo et fcte. Virgini et Dño Galfrido abbati de Savinaceo in Infula de
Wict terram fc. ad edificandum cænobium manerium fc. Arreton ficut
in fuo dominio habebat, et teiiam de Sieca de Boccumba et duo mo-
lendinia fc. de Chriftechuich et Holehurft, &c. Et quinque folidatas
teiiæ juxta molend. de Holehuift, &c. Et Suein manfuram quam ipfe
tenet, &c. Et terram Anfketilli camerarij de Louecumbe, teiiam Hu-
Lei i, teiiam di *Tidlingham*. Et concedo et confirmo donum Hugonis
de Magnaville de teiia de *Louecumbe* quam ecclef. &c. contulit; et donum Hugonis de Vernun de teiia *Shaldeflete*, et capellam fcti. Nicholai,
caftello de Carefbioc edificatam, quam pater meus dedit piedict. ecclef.
et omnia &c quam capellam &c. dederunt pro anima patris mei prefat.
ecclefie Quarrare Hugo Vernun et Guarinus de Haila et Brienus de Infula et Gautiedus Jordani filius   quietam et folutam ab omni
exactione. Et concedo et confirmo molendinium de *Shaldeflete* quod Gau-
fiidus Joidani filius eidem ecclefiæ dedit, et donationem totius decimæ
falis omnium falinarum Lemintoniæ quam pater meus eidem ecclef dedit &c. et donum Roberti de Witvilla &c etiam donum Pagani Tienchard qui unam falinam dedit in Hoidella &c. et donum duæ Hadewitz
de Chielle &c. et donum Hugonis Anglici de i viig. teir. in Cumpton
&c et donum quod Simeon Hugonis de Magnavilla fil dedit &c fc.
ecclef. de Hardinftoniæ Confirmo etiam tei. Hugonis fratris Joidani
in *Sosewella* quam Hugo dedit &c. confenfu Gaufridi filij Joidani. Et
concedo donum teiiæ Forwode quam Hubertus de Valle piedict. ecclef.
dedit et donum de *Efhelderimb* &c. et ex dono Hadewific foioris meæ
un. virgat. teiiæ in Pideltona et domos unum ten. Reina'd. alteium
Biiftun in caftello de Caiefbioc Et concedo etiam abbatiæ quam &c.
omnes eleemofinas quas omnes barones mei predictæ ecclef. dederint five
in teriis five in aliis beneficijs liberas &c. Item hominibus in eleemofi-
iam piedicta ecclefia manentibus concedo, &c ut ad nullum hundredum eant nifi ad hundiedum latioxim Et fi contigerit eos cadeie in
aliquod foiisfactum jufitia inde fit mea et emendatio et catellum fit
     abb.

abb. &c. eandem etiam libertatem. Concedo terre Hafeleie quam Engel. de Bohun predictæ ecclef contulit quam ut eleemofinam patris mei et meam conceffi. Qui vero hanc donationem violare prefumferi æterna maledictione puniatur. Ego Ricardus Exoniæ comes Baldwini comitis filius hanc donationem hoc figno + confirmo. Teftibus hijs Henrico de Am. Willô de Moreville, Gaufrido de Infula, Willô filio Stur. Willô filio Radulfi, Oliverio Avenal, Roberto de Curci, Roberto Trenchard, Simone Godfhull, Willô filio Urri, et alus.

Monaf. Ang.

N° LII.

Carta Henric. Normanorum Ducis, Filij. Imperatricis. Temp. Steph.

HENRICUS ducis Normann. et comitis Andegaviæ filius, archiepif. epifc. comitibus baronibus vicecom. jufticiar. et omnibus fidelibus fal. Sciatis me dedifle et conceffifle Deo et fcte. Mariæ de *Quadrar a* in infula de With in perpetuam eleemofinam *Loccvellum* ad faciendum ibidem capitalem abbatiam p fâl. et incolum. dni Gaufridi Normanniæ ducis et com. Andegaviæ nec non p. fal. duæ imperatratricis matris meæ et mea et p. flatu regni Anglorum et p. animabus Henrici regis avi mei et M. reginæ omniumq. predeceffoium meorum defunctorum. Et ideo volo et firmiter precipio quod prememoratæ abbatiæ monachi predictum locum habeant libere et quiete et honorifice et plenarie cum omnibus illis libertat. et confuetud. quas dña. imperatrix mater mea et ego dedimus et conceffimus Drogoni dñæ matris meæ camerario, ficut nos donum illud eidem Drogoni carus noftris quas prædicti monachi habent teftamur et confirmamus Teftibus Roberto decano Sarefberiæ, Magiftro Matheo, Greg. Day, Humf. de Bohun, Huberto de Vallibus, et al.

Monaf. Angl.

N° LIII.

Carta Confirmationis Hen. II. Regis.

HEN. rex Angliæ Dux Normanniæ & Aquitaniæ & comes Andegavis archiepifcopis, &c. falutem. Sciatis me conceffifli & in perpetuam eleemofinam confirmafle Deo et fanctæ Mariæ de Quadraria & monachis

ibidem

ibidem Deo ſervientibus, omnes terras et tenuras quæ eis in eleemoſinam rationabiliter date ſunt & quas habuerunt, ex dono Baldwini comitis ejuſdem eccleſiæ fundatoris & filij ejuſdem Ricardi comitis terram ad edificandum cænobium manerium, ſcilicet Arretone, ſicut in ſuo dominio habebat, terram de Sueta in Boucumbe, molendinum de Chriſteſchierche, molendinum de Holeherſt cum mollis ſuis cum terra & pratis eiſdem molendinis pertinentibus cum operatione hominum eorundem maneriorum, ad excluſagium tenendum et reficiendum, ligna in boſco ſuo ad opus eorundem molendinorum, terram quam Toſti de Holeherſt tenuit, ſcilicet quinque ſolidatas juxta molendinum de Holeherſt cum Briſtinus qui eam coluit & Swten. et manſuram quam tenut juxta molendinum Chriſtechierche, terram Anſketilli camerarii, terram Huberti, terram de Tidelingeham, ex dono Hugonis de Magnavilla terram de Lowecumbe, ex dono Hugonis de Vernon terram Eſceldfloet. Ex dono comitis Baldwini & filii ejus Ricardi comitis & Hugonis Vernon & Garini de Halla & Brieni de Inſula & Gaufridi filii Jordani, capellam ſancti Nicholai de Caſtello Carefbroc cum pertinentis ſuis in decimis & terris & oblationibus & omnibus rebus. Ex dono Gaufridi filii Jordani molendinum de Eſceloſloet; ex dono comitis Baldwini et filii ejus comitis Ricardi decimam omnium ſalinarum de Limentona; ex dono Roberti de Witvilla & filii ejus Hugonis decimam omnium ſalinarum ſuarum, ex dono Pagani Trenchart unam ſalinam in Hordella; ex dono Hadewiſæ de Chale unum molendinum cum terra eidem molendino pertinente; ex dono Oddonis Anglici unam virgatam terræ in manerio de Comptona quam Robertus Lovel tenuit; ex dono Simonis filii Hugonis de Magnavilla eccleſiam de Haidindona, ex dono Hugonis filii Jordani terram in Sorewella, ex dono Huberti de Vals terram de Forewode, terram de Schaldecumbe cum pertinentiis ſuis, terram de Hampſtede quam Rogerus Pynchon tenuit in villa Carefbroc, duas manſuras quarum unum tenuit Reinaldus Laxman et alteram Briſtwine; ex dono Engelgeru de Bohun terram de Haſeleia; ex dono Baldwini de Poitieia terram de Trundſtapula; ex dono Cecelia & filii ejus Willielmi unam virgatam terræ de Huveſtane; ex dono Henrici de Tracy & Oleveri filii ejus & Arnulphi Anglici terram de Farcweia, ex dono matris meæ imperatricis duas caretas equorum in Nova Foreſta de boſco juxta Suthantone ſingulis annis ad Paſchæ et ad feſtum ſancti Michaelis de mortuo boſco. Quare volo &c. T. Cantaur. archiepiſcopo &c. apud Wirtoniam.

Monaſ. Ang.

APPENDIX,

No LIV.

Carta Galfridi de Infula, de Molendino de Schaldflete.   Hen. II.

IN nomine Individuæ Trinitatis notum fit cunctis, quod ego Galfridus de Infula filiis Jordani concéffi abbati &c. fancte Marie de Quarraria molendinum et Schaldflete cum tota fua mulcta, quod molendinum mater et dña Havifia pio anima patris mei antea donaverunt, viventi fc. domino meo comite Baldwino, et hoc ipfum carta fua confirmante.   Tefte Guarino de Aula, Roberto Trenchard, Willo. de Storewell, R. de Parco, G. de Clavill.

No LV.

Carta atteftat. divifi Richardi Comitis Devon.   Hen .II.

NOTUM fit omnibus fidelibus tam futuris quam prefentibus, quod Julianus prior de Chrifti Ecclefia et duo canonici fui fc. Radulfus filius Theobaldi et Radulfus parvus fuerunt ad divifum comitis Ricardi, et audierunt quod ipfe comes pro falute animæ fuæ divifit et dedit Deo et abbatiæ fanctæ Mariæ de Quarraria viginti folidatas terræ bonæ in manerio fuo de Wroxala, prefentibus etiam et hæc audientibus, Ricardo priore de Plimptona, Henrico de Riverijs, et Willo. de Vernon, patribus ipfius comitis, et Hawdewifia de Riverijs forore ejus.

No LVI.

Carta Henrici de Clavill.

HENRICUS de Clavill æternum in Dominio falutem.   Noveritis pro falute animæ meæ et antecefforum, me dediffe fanctæ Mariæ de Quarrara xi *acre* terræ in Wippingham, quæ jacent in parte auftrali de Mareflint.   Tefte Gaufrido de Infula, Jordano fratri ejus, Thoma de Aula, Rogero filio ejus, Hugono de Clavill, Robtō. de Oglander, Rogero Mobray, Rogero de Norreys.

N. B. Clavill's coat is a Key.

No LVII.

Nᵒ LVII.

Carta Roberti de Giros.

ROBERTUS de Giros conceſſit abbati ſanctæ Mariæ de Quar-
ıera unam marcam argenti annuatim, quam debent mihi p. terra de
Wella. Teſte Alano de la Mara, Wautero de Inſula, Gaufrido filio
ejus, et Hugone de Giros.

The ſeal, thrıce Lyoncelles on a chief.

N. B. The ſeven precedıng deeds, were found in the collection of
Sıı William Pole, Bart. com. Devon.

Nᵒ LVIII.

Carta Galfridi de Inſula. Temp. Hen. II.

GALFRIDUS de Inſula fıl. &c. Scıatis quod pıo ſalute animæ
&c. et p. anima Hawıſiæ uxoris &c. conceſſi terras &c. abbatı de Quaır.
&c. Teſte Willō. de Inſula, filio noſtro et herede, Waltero de Inſula,
Rich. de Langford, Johanne de Wyvill, Rogero de Aula, Petro Ac-
kard, Will. Maitell, Hug. de Chekhull, Hen. filio Roberti, Hen. Cla-
ʋel.

Carta altera ejuſdem Galfrıdi.

GALFRIDUS filıus Walter de Inſula fıl. &c. Noverıtis me pro ſal
animæ meæ et Hawıſiæ uxoris meæ et omnium anteceſſ. &c. conceſſiſſe
abbati de Quarr terras &c. Teſte Hugone prıore de Kaıeſbroc, Rich. prioıe
de Apuıdurcombe, Tho. de Aula, Jordano de Inſula, Tho. de Quercy,
Waltero de Greınvıl, tunc conſtabulıo caſtrı de Kareſbroc, Gilbeıto
de la Maıe, Rog. de Moubray.

Nᵒ LIX.

Carta Hugonis de Wıtvılla de teı in Sueia. Temp. Hen. II.

NOTUM ſit omnıbus pıopıſ. hominıbus tam futuris quam præſen-
tibus quod ego Guarınus de Aula fui præſens & hoc audıens quod Hugo
de Wıtvılla dedit Deo & abbatiæ ſantæ Maıiæ de Quaıara in perpetuam eleemoſynam totam teıram quam habebat in Sueıa, cuɪn hominibus

bus & molendino & omnibus alijs ejus pertinentiis liberam et quietam ab omnibus terrenis servitiis donis et auxiliis; quoad servitium regis & comitis & omne aliud servitium quod super terram illam evenerit, ipse et hæredes sui de suo dominio debent facere, et hanc eleemosinam monachis prædictæ abbatiæ ex toto debent quietare. Hoc affidavit Hugo de manu sua, concedente Matilda sponsa sua & Willelmo Roberto & Will elmo filiis suis, Jordano etiam & Willelmo fratribus suis, & Willelmo Maschel nepote ipsius. Teste Gaufrido de Insula, Willelmo filio Stui, Willelmo filio Pagani, Roberto de Parco, Willelmo de Sorewill, Jordano forestario, Willelmo Flameng, Ada de Compton, Roberto de Celerton, et multis aliis.

N° LX.

Carta attest. et confirmat. Tho. Arch. Cant. de terra de Whitefield.

T. DEI gratia Cantuariensis archiepiscopus Angliæ Primas & Apostolicæ sedis legatus universis ecclesiæ Dei fidelibus salutem. Noverit universitas vestra quoniam Hugo de Witvilla ante nostram præsentiam veniens, donationem quam fecerat ecclesiæ sanctæ Mariæ de Quarraria in insula de Wict, de terra quæ dicitur Whitefield, quam eidem ecclesiæ & monachis ejusdem loci donavit, & per cartam suam confirmavit, fide in manibus nostris præstita corroboravit a se & heredibus suis perpetuo pro viribus observandum ab omni terreno servitio liberam præter orationum suffragia: Nos igitur ejus audita devotione et fidei, suæ cautione de collato eis beneficio firmando suscepta auctoritate fungimur eis prædictam terram confirmamus & præsentis scripti nostri testimonio donum corroboratum perpetuo eis habendum & quiete possidendum statuimus; prohibentes sub anathemate nequis de cætero in terram illam vel bona eorum manum violentam extendat, nec eis injuriam faciat. Valete.

N. B. An ancient memorandum is annexed to this charter wherein it is said, that Hugh de Witvilla, A. D. 1158, granted the manor of Whitfield to the monks of Quarrera in frankalmoigne, and that St. Thomas, archbishop of Canterbury, among others there named, confirmed the grant.

A P P E N D I X.

Nº LXI.

Inter Petitiones Parliamenti, de Ann 7. Edw. III.

A noſtre ſeignr. le Roy & a ſon conſeil môſtre. ſon leige Morgne abbe de Quarrera de l'iſle de Wight.

Que comme il eit ſuive devers noſtre dit ſeignr. le Roy par petition en parlement de reavoir le mannoir de Whitfield en la dit iſle dont les predeceſſeurs de dit abbe furent paiſiblement ſeiſez, et leur ſeiſine long temps continuerent, tanque un Johan de Wyvil les diſſeiſi et puis celle diſſeiſine le dit mannoir devint en les mains des progenitors et j'a en les mains noſtre ſeignr. le Roy, comme eſt contenuz en la petition. Le dit abbe de ceo p agard le parlement devant ſie Jeoffry le Scroop et ſes compagnons mande deſtie tie et ſur la verite termine. On l'avant dit abbe par enqueſte des chevaiers et autres plus vaillants de pais devant le dit ſie Jeoffry et ſes compagnons de ceo priſe et ſa petition avant dite en touts points averre. et toutes les places le Roy eſcerchez par brief on certifie que rien n'eſt trouve pour le Roy et les juſtices ne voilent ſur le verdict jugement rendre ſanze comandement noſtre ſeignr. le Roy. Dont le dit abbe prie par Dieu et en deſcharge des almes des anceſtres a noſtre ſeigni. le Roy, qui ont le dit mannoir iſſint detenutz que le dit noſtre ſeignr le Roy voille de ſa tres bone et droituriele ſeignorie com'ander bref a ſes juſtices de ſon banc, devans queux la petition avant dite pend, qu'ils aillent a judgement rendre ſur le verdit, &c.

(Dorſo.) Soit mande par bief de chancellerie a monſ. Jeoffiy le Scroop qu'il face venir le record et proceſs touchent cet beſoigne devant conſeil de Roy en chancellerie, et illeoque viens et examine.

Nº LXII.

Certificatio Hawdewiſæ de Ryveriys ad Pontificem de Donatione Eccleſiæ de Fleet, dioceſ. Sarum.

REVERENDISSIMO patri & domino Dei gratia ſummo pontifici, humilis ancilla ſua Hadewiſa de Riveriis filia comitis Baldewini ſalutem. Cognitum ſit vobis atque certiſſimum me aſſenſu & bene placito bonæ memoriæ Jocelini hinc Sareſburienſis epiſcopi dediſſe & carta mea confirmaſſe Deo et monachis ſanctæ Mariæ de Quarraria, eccleſiam

manerit

maneiii mei de Floeta cum omnibus pertinentiis suis, in puram & perpetuam eleemosinam ab omni seculari servitio penitus emancipatam;
salvo jure matris Saresbiriensis ecclesiæ. Hanc autem ecclesiam multo
jam tempore transacto prædictis monachis me dedisse et eandem ecclesiam eisdem monachis supradictum Saresbiriensem episcopum sua carta
confirmasse, pro certo scitote monachi vero de Munteburgo, qui modo
ipsam tenere videntur ecclesiam post donationem nostram monachis de
Quarraria factum per fratrem meum Henricum de Riveriis, meam de
ipsa ecclesia cartam injuste adepti sunt. Quo circa preces vobis suppli-
ces offero quatenus sæpedictos monachos Quarrariæ in possessionē ecclesiæ quam eisdem pro salute animæ meæ contuli sicut jus æquitatis exi-
git induci faciatis.

N° LXIII.

Carta Confirmationis Walteri Motte.

SCIANT omnes tam præsentes quam futuri quod ego Walterus
Motte pro salute animæ meæ & omnium antecessorum meorum dedi &
concessi & præsenti carta confirmavi Deo et beatæ Mariæ de Quarraria
et monachis ibidem Deo servientibus, totam illam terram quam Aliz.
amita mea prædictis monachis moriens testamento divisit. Scilicet,
duodecim acras rusticanas quæ incipiunt a fossata quod est inter terram
meam & terram prioris de Christi Ecclesia & pertingunt usque ad fossa-
tum quod est ad orientam & inde versus aquilonem usque ad lacum
qui est inter me & Simonem de la Brigga, ad meridiem vero ter-
minantur in parvo fossata quod est in cacumine montis. Hanc terram prædicta Aliz amita mea, quæ post patrem meum fuit hæres pa-
trimonii mei, dedit prædictis monachis de Quarraria, coram me &
Juliano presbitero et Thoma Malet viro suo, ab omni servitio liberam et
solutam & quietam, sicut puram eleemosinam in perpetuum possiden
dam. His testibus Waltero Camerario, Pagano Urii, Simone de
Blakeland, et aliis multis.

N° LXIV.

Carta Walteri de Infula. Temp. Hen. III.

SCIANT præfentes et futuri quod ego Walterus de Infula, affenfu & voluntate Galfridi filii & hæredis mei, dedi et conceffi Deo et beatæ Mariæ de Quarraria & monachis ibidem Deo fervientibus terram cultibilem lateris montis fancti Bonifacii qui eft verfus Luvecumbam ufque ad divifam quæ facta fuit communi confilio abbatis & noftri. Ita quod nullus a modo prædictam divifam in aliquo violare vel frangere præfumat, et ne aliquis hæredum meorum erga præfatos monachos calumpniam vel moleftiam de prædicta terra movere poffit, hanc donationem meam præfentis cartæ munimine & figilli mei atteftatione confirmare curavi. Hiis teftibus Willelmo filio Stur, & Willelmo filio ejus, Willelmo Avenel, & Olivero filio ejus, et multis aliis videntibus & audientibus.

N°. LXV.

Carta Comitis Willielmi de Teir. de Welee, (or Weilow.) Temp. Hen. III.

UNIVERSIS Sanctæ matris ecclefiæ fidelibus tam præfentibus quam futuris Willielmus de Vernon Comes Devoniæ & filius Comitis Baldewini falutem. Cognitum fit vobis atque certiffimum quod ego pro falute regis Henrici & omnium antecefforum fuorum & fuccefforum pro falute animæ meæ & patris mei comitis Baldewini & matris meæ Adeliciæ comitiffæ & fratris mei comitis Ricardi & uxoris meæ Mabiliæ comitiffæ & omnium antecefforum & parentum meorum dedi et conceffi Deo & beatæ Mariæ de Quarrara & monachis ibidem Deo fervientibus, ducentas acras terræ in manerio meo de Walega Scil. terram de &c. Hanc autem totam terram præfatis monachis dedi in puram & perpetuam eleemofinam cum omnibus pertinentiis fuis, pratis acquis & pafturis, tenendam de me & hæredibus meis liberam & quietam & abfolutam ab omni terreno fervicio donis & auxiliis & confuetudinibus & exactionibus univerfis quæ ad me vel hæredes meos pertinerent. Et ut hæc donatio mea rata & inconcuffa permaneat eam præfentis cartæ munimine & figilli mei impreffione confirmavi. Hiis teftibus Mabilia comitiffa, Willelmo filio Stur, & Willelmo filio ejus, Ro-

gero de Aula, & Thoma filio ejus, Waltero de Infula, tunc temporis
ballivo infulæ, & Paulino clerico, qui duo ex parte comitis monachos
de prædicta terra faifaverunt; Roberto filio Brien. Willielmo Avenel,
Roberto de Sorewelle, Henrico Trenchard, et multis aliis.

Monaft Angl.

Nº LXVI.

Carta Willi de Vernun Comitis Devon.

SCIANT omnes &c. quod ego Willielmus de Vernon com D.
pro falute animæ meæ & patris mei. comitis Baldewini & matris meæ
& omñ. anteceff. meorum, dedi & conceffi Deo & beatæ Mariæ de
Quarraria & monachis ibidem Deo fervientibus uram parvam infulam
quæ eft ante pifcatoriam meam de Chrifti Ecclefia, et unam parvulam
infulam quæ eft fubtus præfatam pifcatoriam, et novum mefuagium
juxta molendinum eorum, quod olim fuit vicus communis. Hanc
vera donationem prædictis monachis in puram & perpetuam eleemofinam
liberam ab omni fervitio in perpetuum poffidendam prefenti carta confirmavi. His teftibus Willielo. filio Stui, Wilhelmo Avenel, Roberto
filio Brien Roberto Pincerno, Paulino clerico comitis, Symore de
Diva, Willielmo & Waltero filiis Pagani, Wilhelmo filio Walteri,
cementario, Wilhelmo Purchez, Wimundo, et multis aliis

Monaf. Angl

Nº LXVII.

Carta Alwarie de Newton, vel Niton. Temp. Hen. III

ALWARIE de Newtona et uxor mea, confenfu dni. noftri Richi.
de Leftre conceffim abbiti &c. de Quarreia totam terram quam h bui
fub falafia de Newetona * &c. Tefte Galfrido de Infula, Jordano
et Waltero filiis Gilberti Clavill, Roberto filio Haroldi, Willielmo de
Infula, Wilo. Walleiand, Rog. de Bofco, Hug. Cofkevill, & Rolto.
Clavill.

* Unde. CiT

Nº LXVIII.

APPENDIX.

Nº LXVIII.

Ceſſio ſeu Confirmatio doni Adeliz. et Walteri Motte ad Abbatem et Conventum de Quarr.

HÆC eſt finalis concordia facta inter Henricum abbatem & conventum Quarrariæ ex una parte, et Thomam de Niweham * & Sabinam uxorem ejus ex alia, de duodecim acris terræ cum pertinentiis in Neweham quas dictus abbas petierat ab eis per breve domini Regis de recto. Quas acras Aliz. Mote monachis Quarrariæ quondam teſtamento delegavit, & Walterus Mote qui ei in hæredite ſucceſſit, per cartam ſuam eis confirmavit. Videlicet, quod dictus abbas pro ſe & conventu ſuo & ſucceſſoribus ſuis remiſit & quietum clamavit prædictis Thoma & Sabina & hæredibus ipſorum in perpetuum totum jus & clamium quod habuit in prædictis duodecim acris cum pertinentijs in Niweham. Et pro hac remiſſione quieta clamancia & concordia prænominati, Thomas & Sabina conceſſerunt pro ſe & hæredibus ſuis quod ipſi & uterque eorum poſt deceſſum alterius et hæredes ipſorum ſolvent annuatim abbatiæ S. Mariæ de Quarraria duodecim denarios ad feſtum S. Michaelis. Et ſi forte ipſi Thomas & Sabina aut alter eorum poſt deceſſum alterius aut hæredes ipſorum dictos, duodecim denarios annuos ad terminum ſtatutum aliquando (quod abſit) non ſolverint, conceſſerunt pro ſe & hæredibus ſuis ex aſſenſu capitalis domini ſui Thomæ de Aula qui ſimiliter conceſſit pro ſe & hæredibus ſuis dictis abbati & conventui & ſucceſſoribus eorum quod liceat eis namium capere in feode de Niveham quicunque illud tenuerit quouſque de ſolutione prædicta eis fuerit ſatisfactum & illud namium ducere ad grangiam ſuam de Luvecumbe, ſive maluerit ad Haſclegam. Hanc autem conventionem & concordiam fideliter & abſque dolo obſervandam affidaverunt ſæpedicti Thomas & Sabina & inſuper ſigilla ſua uni parti præſentis cyrography appoſuerunt, et abbas alteri. Actum apud Quarrarium anno incarnationis Dominicæ milleſimo ducenteſimo viceſimo octavo, quarto die poſt feſtum ſancti Marci evangeliſtæ His teſtibus, Galfrido de Inſula, Thoma de Aula, Waltero de Parco, & Thoma filio ejus, Simone de Davintre, Rogero Mobray, magiſtro Philippo, Waltero de Blakelond, Ricardo Flandrenſi, Willelmo Malet, & multis alijs.

* Forte, Newnham.

Nº LXIX.

N° LXIX.

Carta Excambij de Comblei et Blacland.

UNIVERSIS fanctæ matris ecclefiæ fidelibus p. abbas & conventus ecclefiæ S. Mariæ de Quararia falutem & pacem. Sciatis quod Symon filius Huberti reddidit nobis & in manu mifit & omnino quietam clamavit totam terram quam pater fuus habuit in Combelia, & fuper facro fanctus reliquias juravit quod nunquam amplius per fe neq. per alium nobis inde calumpniam faciet et querelam; fed fidelitatem ecclefiæ noftræ in omnibus pio poffe fuo tenebit et cuftodiet. Nos vero in excambio totius ejufdem terræ dedimus & conceffimus ipfi Symoni & fuo hæredi terram de Blacalandei illam fcilicet quam Ediicus Sculfus Oiduicus & Ricardus tenuerunt; duodecim tamen nummatas quas Orduicus tenuit inter viam & ductum aquæ ufq. ad x. annos debemus tenere fingulis annis reddentes ei xii. denarios ad feftum fancti Michaelis. Hæc igitur dedimus ci foluta & quieta ab omnibus fervitiis de quibus abbatia fe poterit defendere. Ad fummonitionem tamen monachorum debet pio negotiis abbatiæ intra infulam ubi juffus fuerit ne, et ficut liber homo, abbati fervire. De hoc autem fcudo nobis homagium fecit. & ficut prædictum eft per hoc excambium totam terram quæ fuerat patris fui abjuravit & penitus folutam & quietam nobis dimifit & conceffit & a fe & a fuis pro poffe fuo guarantizare conftituit. Tefte Gaufrido de Infula, Jordano de Cofkevilla, & Hugoni frater ejus, & multis aliis literatis & laicis.

N° LXX.

Compofitio per Albm. de Lyra pro Decimis Terrarum, &c. de Quari. Temp. Steph.

NOTUM fit omnibus tam præfentibus quam futuris Domnum Heldearium abbatem de Lira cum affenfu capituli fui, conceffiffi Geivafii abbati & monachis fanctæ Maria de Quadraria, decima liborum & nutrimentorum fuorum habere quietas pro xl. folidis; quos prædicta ecclefia S. Mariæ de Quadraria eidem fupradictæ ecclefiæ S. Mariæ de Lira annuatim & æternaliter in Pafchali termino folvere debet fcilicet, decimas Airetoniæ, Hafeliæ, Luvecuirbæ, Tidelinghamiæ, Schalde-

Schaldecumbæ. Teſte comite Balduino, & Ricardo filio ejus, Willelmo de Morevilla, Willelmo Carbunal, Pagano * vicecomite, Gaufrido filio Jordani, Brieno, Roberto de Witvilla, Willelmo de Goddeſhella, Gozelino & Willelmo de Niechirche.

N° LXXI.

Excambium inter Abb. de Quarr. et Rectorem de Arreton. 40 Hen. III.

AN Dni MCCLVI. ſabat proximo ante cathedram S. Petri, facta eſt hæc convencio inter fratrem Andream abbatem de Quarraria & ejuſdem loci conventum ex una parte, et Walterum Tholomei Rectorem eccleſiæ de Aireton ex altera. Videlicet, quod idem Walterus dedit & conceſſit memoratis abbati et conventui de Quararia totam terram ſpectantem ad eccleſiam ſuam de Arieton, illam ſcilicet quæ jacet permixtim intra dominicum eorundem abbatis et conventus in manerio ſuo de Aireton. habendam et tenendam ſibi & eorum ſucceſſoribus in perpetuam, excepta una acra teriæ quæ jacet juxta gardinum dicti Walteri verſus orientem. Pro qua donacione & conceſſione dederunt ipſi abbas et conventus eidem Waltero & eccleſiæ ſuæ de Aireton tot acras teriæ in dicto manerio ſuo de Arreton quot ipſi abbas & conventus ab eodem Waltero ſecundum menſuram perticæ receperunt quæ videlicet terra jacet juxta teriam quæ fuit aliquando Willielmi Stuke, ſcilicet ab occidente chemini quod ducit de Arieton uſq. ad Horingford. Idem præterea Walterus dedit eiſdem abbati & conventui totam terram quam habuit ſpectantem ad eccleſiam ſuam de Arieton, quæ videlicet jacet ſub Berdune in manerio de Cumbele, pro qua teira ipſi abbas & conventus dederunt eidem Waltero & eccleſiæ de Aireton medietatem tantæ teriæ juxta dictam aciam jacentem juxta gardinum ejuſdem Walteri quantam ipſi abbas & conventus de eodem ſub Berdon receperunt, ſecundum menſuram perticæ. Et idem Walterus ammovebit ædificia conſtructa in duobus meſſuagiis ſitis in prenominata terra quam recepit de eiſdem abbate & conventu, & ſumptibus propriis eriget ea ubi abbas voluerit in manerio de Aireton. Et ſi ipſa ædificia amovere noluerit faciet propriis ſumptibus nova æque valencia et ea eriget ubi abbas volu-

* Trenchard

erit

erit in manerio de Aireton. Idem etiam Walterus pro dicta ecclesia
sua de Aireton remisit & quietam clamavit eisdem abbati & conventui
totum clamium quod posuit & ejus quod habuit vel habere potuit ad
comunam pasturæ quam petiit ab eisdem in manerio de Aireton. Hæc
autem convencio de consensu & voluntate domini Wintoniensis electi
roboratur & confirmatur qui super præscripta commutacione diligentem
fieri fecit inquisitionem per decanum Insulæ Vectæ & quosdam eccle-
siarum Rectores & Vicarios qui eandem commutacionem testantur ecclesiæ de Arreton esse necessariam. In cujus rei testimonium tam abbas
de Quarraria quam idem Walterus presenti scripto in modum cirograph.
inter eos confecto mutuo apposuerunt sigilla sua. His testibus dominis Rogero de Wynceftre, Willelmo de Cobeham, Willelmo de Engle-
feld, justiciariis itinerantibus tunc temporis apud Suthampton dominis
Willelmo de Insula, Waltero de Insula, Rad. de Gorges, Adam. de
Cumpton, et aliis.

N° LXXII.

Carta abbatis de Quarr. Terrarum ad Priorem et Conv̄ de Christ-
church pro reddit. ex Man̄. de Ningewood et Milroid. 17 Edw.
II.

HÆC indentura testatur quod frater Walterus abbas de Quareria &
ejusdem loci conventus dederunt & concesserunt ad feodi firmam nobis
fratri Edmundo priori & conventui Christi ecclesiæ de Twynham &
nostris successoribus unam messuagium terram prata et unum molendinum cum secta debita, cum omnimodis pertinenciis suis quæ habuerunt in La Thorp die confectionis præsencium. habendum & tenendum prædicta messuagium terra prata & molendinum cum secta debita
cum omnimodis pertinenciis suis nobis prædictis priori et conventui &
nostris successoribus de capitalibus dominis illius feodi, per servicia inde
debita & consueta in perpetuum. Et pro hac concessione nos prædicti
prior et conventus dedimus & concessimus prædictis abbati & conventui
& suis successoribus undecim libras Sterlingorum annui redditis percipiendas apud abbathiam de Quareria prædicta, de nobis prædictis
priore & conventu & successoribus nostris de prædictis messuagio terra
pratis & molendino, ad duos anni terminos; videlicet ad festum na-

talis Domini & ad feſtum nativitatis S. Johannis Baptiſtæ æquis porci-
onibus in perpetuum. Et etiam nos prædicti prior & conventus dedimus & conceſſimus prædictis abbati & conventui & eorum fucceſſoribus
quoddam meſſuagium in villa Chriſti Eccleſiæ cum omnimodis ſuis
pertinenciis, quod Henricus Boſſe quondam tenuit in vico qui vocatur
La Mulſtele; habendum et tenendum prædictum meſſuagium in villa
prædicta prædictis abbati & conventui & eorum fucceſſoribus de capitalibus dominis feodi illius. Et nos prædicti prior & conventus & ſuc-
ceſſores noſtri ipſum meſſuagium cum omnimodis ſuis pertinenciis prædictis abbati & conventui & eorum fucceſſoribus warrantizabimus & de
duodecim denariis Sterlingorum annui redditus prædictis capitalibus dominis debiti de prædicto meſſuagio, nec non de omni alio debito ſervi-
cio ſæculari exactione & demanda verſus eoſdem capitales dominos &
omnes mortales acquietatibus & defendemus in perpetuum · ſimul cum
una bona carucata boni fœni percipienda ad dictum meſſuagium in prædicta villa Chriſti Eccleſiæ ad cuſtos noſtros carianda ad feſtum tranſla-
tione S. Thomæ martiris annuatim, et cum duabus carucatis foragii
eodem modo ibidem annuatim ad feſtum S. Michaelis cariandis & per-
cipiendis in perpetuum Et ſi prædictum meſſuagium vel molendinum
in La Thorp in domibus vel in aliis pertinenciis ſuis in toto vel in parte
devaſtentur ſeu quocunq modo deteriorentur nihilominus nos prædicti
prior & conventus & noſtri fucceſſores ad integram ſolucionem totius
annui redditus undecim librarum fœni & foragii faciendam prædictis
abbati & conventui & eorum fucceſſoribus ut præmittitur tenemur in
perpetuum. Et ad majorem ſecuritatem ſuper hoc faciendam nos prædicti prior & conventus volumus & concedimus quod prædicti abbas &
conventus de Quareria & eorum fucceſſores recipiant annuatim loco &
terminis ſupradictis prædictas undecim Libras annui redditus de nobis
& fucceſſoribus noſtris de excitibus exeuntibus de terris et providentibus
maneriorem noſtrorum de Nyngewode & de Mulleford, quæ quidem
maneria nos prædicti prior & conventus ad hoc obligamus per præſentes
in perpetuum diſtringenda ad quorumcunq. manus ipſa maneria in poſ-
terum devenerint. Et ſi contingat quod prædictus annus redditus undecim librarum fœni & foragii prædictis abbati & conventui vel ſuis fucceſſoribus terminis ſupradictis aretro fuerint in parte vel nos prædicti
prior & conventus Chriſti Eccleſiæ ac etiam prædicti abbas & conventus de Quareria ſigilla noſtra huic indenturæ alternatim appoſuimus.
His teſtibus, dominis Radulfo de Gorges, Johanne de Inſula, Mauri-

cio Le Brun, Johanne de Langford, Petro Deverci, Johanne de Chaucumbe, militibus; Theobaldo Ruffel, Johanne de Glamorgan, Willelmo de Infula, Willelmo Peveral, Johanne de Grimftede, Waltero de Butefhorn, & aliis. Datum apud Chrifti Ecclefiam die Lunæ proxima ante feftum B. Margaretæ virginis & martiris, anno Domini MCCC vicefimo tercio, anno vero regni regis Edwardi filii regis Edwardi feptimo decimo.

N° LXXIII.

Carta Rad. Fulcher.

NOTUM fit omnibus fanctæ Matris ecclefiæ fidelibus tam futuris quam præfentibus quod ego Radulfus Fulcherius pro falute animæ meæ & anteceflorum meorum, dedi et per hanc cartam confirmavi Deo & abbatiæ S Mariæ de Quarraria in perpetuam eleemofinam quandam mafuram terræ quam habebam in Sueia de feudo Hugonis de Witvilla, illam fcilicet quam Edricus Cugget tenuit, cum omnibus ejufdem mafuræ pertinenciis liberam & quietam ab omnibus ferviciis donis & auxiliis, omnem etiam calumpniam quam ponebam in molendino de Sueia & in mafura Roberti Pelliparii monachis de Quarraria quietam ab omnino clamavi Conceffi quoque eifdem monachis tota vita mea in minifterio meo pafturam equabus & animalibus fuis quieta & abfque confuetudine contentionem autem quæ erat inter me & ipfos de noftris divifis ex toto dimifi. Ut videlicet in bona pace terram in toto, nos prædicti prior & conventus volumus & concedimus pro nobis & fucceforibus noftris quod extunc prædicti abbas & conventus & eorum fuccefores de die in diem diftringant nos & fuccefores noftros per bona mobilia in terris & tenementis prædictorum maneriorum de Nyngewode & de Mulleford inventa & etiam in prædictis mefluagiis terra pratis & molendino in La Thorp pro voluntate eorum abbatis & conventus & fucceforum fuorum abfq. ulla contradiccione noftra dominorum ballivorum feu quorumcunq. aliorum. Et quod hujufmodi diftricciones ad quemcunq. locum in comitatu Southampton voluerint ducant fugent & detineant per quofcunq. miniftros fuos donec eifdem abbati & conventui & fuis fucceforibus de prædicto annuo redditu undecim librarum foeni & foragii & de arreragiis, fi quæ fuerint plenarie fuerit fatisfactum

tum

tum una cum dampnis & expenfis ; fi quæ vel quas prædicti abbas &
conventus fecerint vel habuerint occafione prædicti annui redditus non
fo'uti, nos vero prædicti prior & conventus & fuccefſores noſtri prædictum annuum redditum undecim librarum foeni & foragii prædictis
abbati & conventui & eorum fuccefſoribus de prædictis maneriis de
Nyngwode & Mulleford mefſuagio terra pratis & molendino levendum
warrantizabimus acquietabimus & defendemus contra omnes gentes in
perpetuum. Et prædicti abbas & conventus & eorum fuccefſores nobis
prædictis priori & conventui & noſtris fuccefſoribus prædicta mefſua-
gium terram prata & molendinum cum omnimodis fuis pertinentiis
prædictis in La Thorp contra omnes mortales warrantizabunt acquieta-
bunt & defendent in perpetuum. In cujus rei teſtimonium fuam habeant apud Sueiam deficut figna foreſtæ antiquitus poſita demonſtra-
bant. Hanc igitur donationem meam de prædicta mafura cum tota
terra ad eam pertinente & cætera quæ hic dicta funt concefſerunt filii
mei Euſtachius Gaufridus & Walterus, ita fcilicet quod idem Euſtachius de manu fua dextera afſidavit quod totam iſtam actionem ex fua
parte fine fraude cuſtodiet abbas autem & monachi de Quarraria Gau-
fridum filium meum pro amore Dei & meo fufceperunt ad monachum
fecum faciendum. Teſtibus hiis G. & multis aliis.

N° LXXIV.

Carta Willelmi de Oglander.

WILLELMUS de Oglander univerfis Sanctæ Matris ecclefiæ fidelibus & omnibus hominibus fuis Francis & Anglicis ad quos præfens
fcriptum pervenerit falutem. Sciat univerfitas veſtra me concefſifſe &
dedifſe & præfenti charta confirmafſe Deo & S. Mariæ de Quarraria &
monachis ibidem Deo fervientibus, et pro falute animæ meæ & pro re-
medio animarum omnium antecefſorum & fuccefſorum meorum, in
puram & liberam ac perpetuam eleemofinam ab omni fervitio & auxilio
& exactione quietam totam terram & tenementum quod Robertus Ric
tenuit de terra mea de Penna quam Rogerus de Oglandis filius avunculi
mei habuit de me ad firmam aliquanto tempore. Sed poſtea eodem
Rogero & me convenientibus in unam & ad unam accepi præfatam terram & tenementum in manum meam, pro qua prædictus Robertus Ric

folebat

solebat reddere prænominato Rogero de Oghadei cognato meo annuatim tres solidos. Hanc itaque terram sicut prædictum est concessi & donavi præfatis monachis, habendam & tenendam in perpetuam cum omni libertate, nullo sæculari servicio mihi vel hæredibus meis inde retento. Et ne aliquis hæredum meorum aut aliquid alius huic donationi & eleemosinæ meæ contraire vel eam aliqua perturbare præsumat, sigilli mei defensione, & subscriptorum testium copia & attestatione eam corroborare atque munire & confirmare curavi; salvo tantum servitio forinseco comitis domini mei. Testibus istis Radulfo de Glamorgan, Roberto de Haula, Philippo de Glamorgan, Roberto le Bastart, cognato meo, abbate de Caretot, Willelmo de Blakepenna, homine meo, Roberto Clerico, Roberti de Haula Esturmi Sacerdote de Wippingucham, & aliis pluribus.

Nº LXXV.

Carta Willelmi de Caulburn

SCIANT præsentes & futuri quod ego Willelmus de Caulburn dedi & concessi & hac præsenti carta mea confirmavi Deo & beatæ Mariæ de Quarraria & monachis ibidem Deo servientibus totam partem meam aquæ de Maresfleth cum fundo ejus, et etiam totam partem meam aquæ in Medene usque ad Schyepewasse cum fundo ejus, habendas & tenendas de me & hæredibus meis sive assignatis meis ipsis monachis et successoribus suis sive assignatis eorum, libere quieta & pacifice ad quoscunque usus dictas aquas convertere voluerint, sive ad molendinum construendum sive ad piscariam ibidem faciendam sive ad utrumq. reddendo inde annuatim mihi & hæredibus sive assignatis meis unum sterlingum ad festum sanctæ Michaelis pro omni servicio & exactione vel demanda. Concessi etiam prædictis monachis & eorum successoribus sive assignatis & omnibus ad molendinum eorum euntibus vel inde redeuntibus chiminum sufficiens ad caretas sibi invicem obviandus per terram meam a chimino quod ducit de Novo Burgo versus Wippinkeham per Bromhilldach usque ad molendinum eorum; et chiminum liberum ad piscariam suam quociens opus habuerint absque omni contradictione & impedimento mei vel hæredum meorum sive assignatorum. Concessi insuper prædictis monachis de Quarraria & eorum successoribus sive assignatis, terram sufficientem de terra mea proxima adjacenti ad stagnum molendini

conftruendum & quotiens opus fuerit reficiendum. Ego vero Willelmus de Caulburn et hæredes & affignati mei warrantizabimus prænominatis monachis & eorum fuccefforibus & affignatis dictas aquas de
Maresfleth & de Medene cum fundis ipfarum & chiminum tam ipfis
quam aliis ad molendinum ipforum euntibus five inde redeuntibus per
terram meam & etiam terram fufficientem ad ftagnum molendini conftruendum & reficiendum, & chiminum liberum ad pifcariam ficut fu-
pradictum eft, contra omnes mortales in perpetuum, pro hac autem
donatione conceffione & confirmatione mea habenda dederunt mihi fæ-
pedicti monachi undecim folidos fterlingorum in gerfumam. Ut autem hæc mea donatio conceffio & confirmatio firma & ftabilia in pofte-
rum permaneant eam præfentis cartæ meæ atteftatione & figilli appofi-
tione roboravi. His teftibus, Hugone de Chekehull, Henrico de Infula, Ric. Noreys, Mich. de Godefhull, Henrico de Clavill, Waltero
Clerico, Willelmo de la March, et multis aliis.

<hr>

Nº LXXVI.

Carta Matildis de Eftur. Edw. I.

SCIANT præfentes & futuri quod ego Matildis filia & hæres Baldwini le Eftur in ligia viduitate mea pro falute animæ meæ patris & matris meæ ac anteceflorum meorum, & pro falute animæ Walteri de Infula quondam mariti mei, dedi conceffi & hac præfenti carta mea confirmavi Deo & beatæ Mariæ de Quarraria & monachis ibidem Deo fervientibus, fex folidos fterlingorum annuatim recipiendos de me & hæredibus meis ad Pafcha apud manerium meum de Gatecumbe fcilicet
de camera mea & hæredum meorum quoufque ego Matildis vel hæredes
mei providerimus & per cartam noftram dederimus alibi eifdem monachis
fex folidatas annui redditus in certo & competenti loco recipiendas. Et
fi dictos fex folidos eifdem monachis & eorum fuccefforibus ad dictum
terminum non folverimus annuatim volo & concedo pro me & hæredibus meis quod ballivi infulæ qui pro tempore fuerint diftringant me vel
hæredes meos per namia in dicto manerio de Gatecumbe quoufque dictum redditum prænominatis monachis folverimus: et quam cito ego
Matildis vel hæredes mei providerimus & dederimus per cartam noftram
eifdem monachis folidatas certi & annui redditus præfens carta nullius
erit roboris aut valoris. Ut autem hæc mea donatio conceffio & con-
firmacio

firmacio ftabilis permaneat præfentem cartam figilli mei impreffione roboravi. His teftibus, dominis Johanne de Wyvill, Willelmo de Infula, Johanne de Infula, Rogero de Aula, Jordano de Infula, Adam de Compton, Thoma de Evercy, Adam de Reppling, tunc ballivo infulæ & multis aliis.

N° LXXVII.

Carta Ifabel. Comitiffæ Albemarlie & Devon.

SCIANT præfentes & futuri quod ego Ifabella de Fortibus comitiffa de Albemarliæ & Devoniæ ac domina infuæ in ligia viduitate mea, pro anima mea & animabus domini mei Willielmi de Fortibus comitis Albemarliæ & patris & matris meæ puerorum mecum & animabus omnibus anteceflorum & fucceflorum meorum conceffi & hic præfenti carta mea confirmavi Deo & beatæ Mariæ de Quarraria in infula Vecta, & monachis ibidem Deo fervientibus & in perpetuum fervituris totas donationes conceffiones & confirmationes in terris tenementis libertatibus & omnibus aliis ad ipfas terras tenementa & libertates pertinentibus in puram & perpetuam eleemofinam quæ vel quas anteceffores mei per cartas fuas eifdem monachis dederunt & confirmaverunt, abfque ullo retinemento mei hæredum vel affignatorum meorum in perpetuum. Concedo vero & hac præfenti carta mea confirmo pro me & hæredibus meis & affignatis in perpetuum ablata & monachis prædictis totum tenementum & manerium cum pertinentiis de Ancton & terram & tenementum de Scece quæ quondam pertinebant ad manerium eorum de Iovecumbe, & duo molendina, fcilicet de Chrifti ecclefia & de Holhurft cum multis & fectis fuis, cum terra tenemento pratis eifdem molendinis pertinentibus & opera hominum & hæredum five affignatorum de Chrifti Ecclefiæ & de Holhurft ad exclufagium dictorum molendinorum tenendum & reficiendum quociens neceffe fuerit, & ligna apta de bofco meo in Holhurft ad prædicta molendina fufficienter emendanda fuftinenda & reficienda Et totam terram & tenementum de Holhurft cum pertinentiis fuis juxta molendinum de Holhurft & decimam omnium falinarum mearum de Lementone, prout hac mea & cartæ anteceflorum meorum plenius proportant. Concedo etiam & confirmo prædictis monachis donum & confirmationem Hugonis de

Magna-

Magna villa de terra & tenementis cum pertinentiis de Lovecumbe, & molendinum de Schaldeflet juxta Wod ntone cum pertinentiis suis quod Wilhelmus Galfridi filius ipsis monachis dederat. Concedo etiam & confirmo eisdem monachis pro me & hæredibus meis & assignatis in perpetuum totam terram & tenementum cum pertinentiis de Forwode, & terram de Scandeflet cum omnibus pertinentiis, & donum terræ & tenementi cum pertinentiis de Roweberе, & donum terræ & tenementi de Sneye cum molendinis moltis & sectis suis, & donum terræ & tenementi cum pertinentiis de Hamstede, & donum terræ & tenementi de Haseleye, & donum terræ cum tenemento & pertinentiis de Yerde, & donum de Bikeberye cum pertinentiis suis. Do etiam concedo & confirmo pro me & hæredibus meis & assignatis, prædictis monachis omnes eleemosinas quæ in terris tenementis libertatibus & omnibus aliis prædictæ ecclesiæ & monachis datæ fuerunt, vel in futurum de feudo meo quocunque modo datiræ sunt vel venditiræ, & liberum habeant ingressum per totas terras meas & tenementa meas terias libertates tenementa & omnia alia ut sibi viderint expedire emendi vel ex dono recipiendi absque ullo impedimento aut contradictione mei vel hæredum seu assignatorum meorum. Do insuper & concedo & præsenti carta mea confirmo prædictis ecclesiæ & monachis in perpetuum pro me & hæredibus sive assignatis meis has libertates subscriptas habendas & tenendas in perpetuum videlicet quod nullus de hominibus dictorum monachorum nec ipsi nec tenentes ipsorum vel aliquis de feido ipsorum sectam aliquam ad curiam meam vel hundredum meum vel ad curiam sive ad hundredum hæredum meorum sive assignatorum meorum, de cætero faciant nec toltam dent nec aliquam districtionem faciant, nec dampnum vel gravamen per me vel per ballivos sive hæredum vel assignatorum meorum habeant nisi indictati vel rettati fuerint de aliqua criminali causa veluti de latrocinio homocidio & aliis quæ ultimo puniuntur supplicio. Et si contigerit gentes dictorum monachorum vel eorum tenentes aliquid forisfactum facere excluso facto criminali prædicto judicii sit mea amerciamentum emendatio cum catallis eorum, sint ipsorum monachorum in perpetuum absque ullo impedimento mei hæredum vel assignatorum meorum. Has vero omnes libertates cum terris & libertatibus præscriptis, cum donationibus & confirmationibus antecessorum meorum & eorum pertinentiis omnibus, dedi concessi & hac præsenti carta mea confirmavi pro me & hæredibus meis sive assignatis Deo & beatæ Mariæ & monachis de Quarrera habendas & tenendas in

puram

puram & perpetuam eleemofinam libere quiete bene & in pace ficut li-
berius vel melius ego vel aliqui antecefforum meorum prædicta tenementa & libertates & ad ea peitinentia habuimus & tenuimus, in terra
in mare vel in litore maris quiete ab omni exactione & omnibus auxilis
tallaquiis donis quærelis & omnibus aliis demandis &c. Hiis teftibus
dominis Th. de Aula, Th. de Evercy, Willielmo de Stui, Willielmo
de Sancto Maitino, Ricardo de Afton, Jordano de Kyngeftone, Jacobo
de Hautone, militibus, Johanne de Infula, &c.

Nº LXXVIII.

Conceffio annuæ Penfionis ad Epifcopum Winton. ab Abbate et Conv̄. de Quairara.

NOVERINT univeifi per præfentes nos Abbatem & Conventum
de Quarrera ordinis Ciftercienfis in Infula de Vecta Wyntonienfis diœcefis teneri & per hoc præfens fcriptum indentatum firmiter obligaii ie-
verendo in Chrifto patii ac domino, domino Henrico Dei gratia Wyntonienfi Epifcopo ejufque fuccefforibus ac Ecclefiæ Wyntonienfi in decem folidis Steilingorum bonæ & legalis monetæ nomine penfionis annuæ folvendis eidem Revendo patii fuccefforibufq fuis ac Ecclefiæ
Wyntonienfi prædictæ, de nobis & fuccefforibus noftris in perpetuum
ad feftum Pafchæ, ratione indempnitatis Ecclefiæ Wyntonienfis prædictæ pio Ecclefia de Arreton in Infula Vecta prædicta Wyntonienfis
diœcefis ante dictæ, nobis & Monafteiio noftro dicti Reverendi patiis
auctoritate Pontificali & ordinaria canonice unita annexa & appropiiata
& in ufus noftros proprios poft ceffionem feu deceffum Rectoiis Ecclefiæ
de Arieton prædictæ qui nunc eft, convertanda tenenda & peipetuis
temporibus poffidenda; ad quam quidem folutionem annuæ penfionis
prædictæ fideliter ut præmittitur peifolvende obligamus nos fucceffoies
noftros monafteiium noftrum prædictum ac omnia bona noftia mobilia &
immobilia ubicumque fuerint inventa per præfentes. Volumus etiam &
concedimus pro nobis & fuccefforibus noftiis, quod fi hujufmod annui
penfio aretro fuerit ad aliquem terminum in parte vel in toto, tunc
bene liceat præfato, Reverendo patri ejufque fuccefforibus fructus redditus & proventus Ecclefiæ prædictæ exiftentes vel proventuios feque-
rare ac fub tuto & arto cuftodire facere fequeftio donec fibi de dicta

t

penfione

pensione annua & de arreragiis si quæ fuerint plenarie fuerit satisfactum. In cujus rei testimonium parti hujus scripti indentati penes dictum Reverendum Patrem remanenti sigillum commune domus nostræ prædictæ apposuimus ac parti hujus scripti indentati penes nos remanenti idem Reverendus Pater Wyntoniensis sigillum suum apponi fecit in fidem & testimonium præmissiorum. Datum in Domo nostri Capitulari quoad sigillationem patris nostri vicessimo die Novembris anno Domini Millesimo quadringentesimo quinto.

N° LXXIX.

The King's Order to remove the Prior of Appuldurcombe, with the Monks, from thence to Hyde Abbey, near Salisbury, during the War with France.

REX Ven.li in Christo Epo. Wintor. Sal. Licet dilecti Nobis in Xto Priori de Appu'durcombe in Insula Vecta & duo Socij et Commonachi sui alienigenæ a Prioratu socio usque abbatiam de la Hyde in Diocesi Vestra p. vos virtute cujusdam Ordinationis nuper per nos & Consilium nostrum factæ de Religiosis Alienigensis in quibuscunque Religiosorum infra regnum nostrum prope mare situatis commorantibus ad alia loca a mari remotiora prætextu turbationis inter nos et illos de Francia motæ transferendis, nec non cujusdam mandati nostri vobis inde directi &c. Quia tamen ex certis causis jam eidem Priori pro se et dictis Socijs suis licentiam dedimus & concessimus, qd. ipsi cum sibi viderint expedire ad Civitatem nostram Sarum, quæ multo longius a mari quam dicta Abbat a de Hyde distat ibidem in quibusdam tenementis infra Clausum Canonicorum erectæ B Mariæ Sarum situatis Abbati de Montisburgo in Normannia ut Præbendai Prebendæ de Lodris in eadem Ecclef Sarum ab Antiquo pertinentibus &c.

Mon. Ang. vol. l. p. 230 Ex Rot. Alemat 13 Ed. III. m. 6. In Dorso.

N° LXXX.

N° LXXX.

A List of the principal Manors, &c. in the Isle of Wight, their ancient and present Possessors, from the Conquest to the Year 1780, extracted from ancient Deeds, Pedigrees, and Records.

The Manor of Afton.	The Crown—De Afton — Biekenford—Ringebones—Buin. Now Urry.
The Manor of Avington, or Carisbrooke	The Crown—De St. Martin—Popham—Wadham—Hervey—Leigh. Now Miller.
The Manor of Applesford.	Fitz Azor, De Infula, or Lifle — Pike Now Carter.
The Manor of Alverston.	Fitz Azor — Lifle — Awmaile — Maltravers—Stafford—Strangeways—Broad—Alcoin—Popham. Now Holmes
The Manor of Bowcombe.	The Crown—Lords of the Island—The Crown again—granted by James First to Christopher Villais, Earl of Anglesey — Knowles — Stephens. Now Blachford.
The Manor of Brook	The Crown—Mascarell—Glamorgan—Rookley —Bowerman—Gilbert. Now Bowerman.
The Manor of Brixton.	The Bishops of Winchester — The Crown — Mountacute, Earl of Salisbury—Neville, Earl of Warwick—George, Duke of Clarence—Countess of Salisbury. Now Barrington.
The Manor of Briddlesford.	FitzAzor— Lifle—Burton — Wray. Now Hearne and Tarver.
The Manor of Bonchurch.	Lifle — Dennis — Broad — Alcoin — Popham. Now Popham and Hill.
Compton.	The Crown — De Compton — Lycte, Clerk — Comber—Miller. Now Bowerman.
The Manor of Chale.	Fitz Azor — De Vernun — De Cauncellis—De Langford—Pound. Now Worfley of Appuldurcombe.
The Manor of Cheffell.	Trenchard—Dupfden—Brutenell—Trenchard—Waller. Now Worfley of Appuldurcombe.
The Manor of Chillerton.	Fitz Azor, or Lifle, from the Conqueft.

t 2

The

The Manor of Kings Freshwater.	The Crown—D'Arsie—Mary, Daughter of Ed. I.—Beauchamp—The Crown—Urry—Morgan. Now Holmes.
Forde.	De Molendiries—Beauchamp—Newnham. Now Worsley of Gatcombe.
The Manor of Gatcombe.	Fitz Stur—Lisle—Bremshot—Dudley—Packenham—Pole—Earnley—Worsley of Apuldurcombe. Now Worsley of Gatcombe.
The Manor of Kingston.	The Crown—De Kingston—Popham—Drewe—Meux. Now Worsley of Gatcombe.
The Manor of Knighton.	De Morville—De Gorges—Hackett—Gilbert—Dillington—Bocland. Now Bissett.
The Manor of Lemerston.	The Crown—De Lemerston—Tichbourn—Stanley. Now the Right Hon. Wel. Ellis, and Christ. D'Oyley, Esq.
The Manor of Motteston.	Fitz Azor—Mascarell—Glamorgan—De Langford—Chyke—Dillington—Leigh. Now the Heirs of Leigh.
The Manor of Merston.	Fitz Azor—Lisle—Chyke—Mann. Now Blachford.
The Manor of Nunwell.	De Oglanders from the Conquest.
The Manor of Niton.	The Crown—Lords of the Island—Piers Gaveston—William Earl of Salisbury—George Duke of Clarence—The Crown—Meux—Coteile. Now Lord Edgcumbe.
The Manor of Northwood.	The Crown—Lords of the Island—The Crown—Earl of Anglesey—Knowles—Stephens. Now Blachford
The Manor of Osborne.	Fitz Azor—Lisle—Chyke—Mann. Now Blachford.
The Manor of Pann	The Crown—granted by Edward VI, to Carew—Colnett—Kemp—Bromfield—Gilbert. Now Rolleston.
The Park.	Walter de la Parke—Conduit—The Crown.
The Manor of Roude.	Fitz Azor—Lisle—Pyke. Now Bonham.

The

The Manor of Swainston, or Calbourn.	The Bishops of Winchester—the Crown—Mountacute Earl of Salisbury—Neville Earl of Warwick—George Duke of Clarence—Countess of Salisbury. Now Barrington
The Manor of Shalfleet,	Fitz Azor—Trenchard—Dupsden—Brutenell—Trenchard—Waller. Now Worsley of Appuldurcombe
The Manor of St. Lawrence.	De Aula—Russell—Hacket—Leigh. Now Worsley.
The Manor of Stenbury.	De Aula—De Heyno—Beauchamp—Pound—Ratcliff Earl of Sussex. Now Worsley of Appuldurcombe.
Shide.	The Crown—De Argenton—St. Martin—Popham—Wadham. Now Smith.
East Standen.	Fitz Stur—De Evercy—Glamorgan—Urry—Brenshort—Alcorn—Smith. Now Christchurch College, Oxford.
The Manor of Shanklin.	Lisle—Dennis—Broad—Alcorn—Popham. Now Popham and Hill.
The Manor of Thorley.	The Crown—The Lords of the Island—Piers Gaveston—William Earl of Salisbury—George Duke of Clarence—Urry—Lucy. Now Holmes.
The Manor of Wroxall.	The Crown — The Lords of the Island — Piers Gaveston — William Earl of Salisbury —George Duke of Clarence — The Crown — Coteile. Now Lord Edgcumbe.
The Manor of Wootton.	Fitz Azor, or Lisle, from the Conquest.
The Manor of Wellow.	The Crown—the Lords of the Island—the Duke of Clarence — the Crown — Hopson — Cateile. Now Lord Edgcumbe.
The Manor of Willmingham and Debourn.	The Crown — the Lords of the Island — the Duke of Clarence—the Crown—Hopson—Comber. Now Miller.
The Manors of Whitwell.	Fitz Stur—Lisle—Bremshot—Pole—Newnham. Now Worsley of Appuldurcombe.
The Manor of West Court, or South Shorewell.	Lisle — Dennis — Broad — Alcorn — Popham. Now Popham and Hill.

The

The Manor of Weftover.	Fitz Stur—Lifle—Bremfhot—Pole—Eainley—Erlefman—Dillington—Urry. Now Holmes.
The Manor of Wolverton.	De Wolverton — Dingley — Hunt — Morgan—Delgarno—Serle—Goodenough. Now Clarke.
Wolverton.	De Wolverton — Dingley —Hunt—Morgan—Delgarno. Now Jolliffe.
Watchingwell.	Trenchard—Dupfden—Brutenell—Trenchard—Waller—Worfley—Goodenough. Now Barrington.
The Manors of La Wode, Middleton, and Wolverton, alias Bembridge.	Mafcarell — Glamorgan — Ruffell — Hacket—Leigh—Gilbert. Now Worfley of Appuldurcombe.
The Manor of Whitfield.	The Crown — Mary, Daughter of Edw. I —Tracey—*De Hardington* — Edw. III. Now Oglander. N. B John de Hardington granted the Reverfion, after his Life, of the Manor of Whitfield to Edw III in confideration of being made by that King Conftable of the Ifle of Wight for Life.
The Manor of Yaverland.	De Aula — Ruffell — Hacket—Hatfield—Keyneis—Richards. Now Wright.

The following Manors have been granted to Religious Houfes.

The Manor and Priory of Appuldurcombe, together with Week and Sandford	Redvers Earls of Devon—the Abbey of Mountfburg in Normandy —The Convent of the Minories without Aldgate, London—The Monaftery of Sheen—Leigh. Now Worfley.
The Manor of Aireton.	Fitz Stur—the Abbey of Quarr—Bennet—Lord Culpeper. Now Lord Fairfax.
The Manor of Apfe	The Crown — Redvers Earls of Devon — the Priory of Chriftchurch— Dillington—Leigh—Chichefter. Now Worfley of Appuldurcombe.
The Manor of Afhey.	The Monaftery of Whorwell—Worfley—Coteile. Now Lord Edgcumbe.
The Priory of Carifbrook.	The Abbey of Lyra in Normandy—the Monaftery of Sheen—Worfley—Sir Francis Walfingham—Bromfeild. Now Dummer.

The

The Manor of Cofham.	De Cofham — Godfhoufe in Southampton. Now Queen's College, Oxford.
The Manor of Godfhill	The Abbey of Lyra — The Monaftery of Sheen — Walfingham — Miller. Now Worfley of Appuldurcombe.
The Manor of Hafely, together with Combley, Quarr, and Newnham Kerne.	The Abbey of Quarr — Mills. Now Fierming.
	Ruffell — the Knights Templars — the Crown — Godfhoufe in Portfmouth. Now the College of St Mary's, Winton
Langbridge.	The Monaftery of Whorwell — Worfley — Dillington — Bocland. Now Eiflent
The Manor of Ningewood.	Redvers Earls of Devon — the Priory of Chriftchurch — the Crown — Hopfon — Comber. Now Miller
The Manor of Ride.	The Monaftery of Whorwell — Worfley — Dillington. Now Player.
The Priory of St. Crofs.	A Priory belonging to Tyrone in Normandy. Now the College of St. Mary, Winchefter
The Manor and Priory of St. Helens	A Priory belonging to an Abbey in Normandy Now College of Eton
The Manor of Shorwell, or North-Court.	The Crown — De Shorwell — the Nunnery of Wilcock — the Crown — Thomas Leigh, the Heirs of Leigh.
The Manor of Shalcombe.	Redvers Earls of Devon — the Abbey of Quarr the Priory of Chriftchurch — Henry VIII — Hopfon — Stanley. Now the Right Hon W. Ellis, and Chrift D Oyley, Efq
	N. B. Henry VIII. exchanged the Manor of Shalcombe with Hopfon for the Manor of St Mary Le Bone, which he had lately purchafed of Sir Reginald Bray.
The Manor of Uggaton.	Mafcarell — the Knights Templars — Godfhoufe in Portfmouth — the Crown — March. Now Powell and Bagfter.
The Manor of Whippingham, or Barton.	Fitz Stur — Lifle — the Oratory of Barton. Now the College of St Mary's, Winchefter

A P P E N D I X.

Nº LXXXI.

Return made by the Dean of the Isle of Wight, to Bishop Woodlock.
Ann. 1305.

Decanus Inf. Vecte   mandat.
  venerabilis patris epī. Winton. mihi direct. reverenter sum executus
in hujus

Shorewell.	Est peñs Priori de Karefbrook in xxs. annue. Peñs. Insuper abbas de Lyra percipit omnes maj. decimas de dominijs abbatiffe de Laycock, et de majoribus de diīis Rad. de Wolverton et Johīs de Olde; et decimā. molendini dīn Rad. de Wolverton Abbas et conventus de Quarr. percipiunt de dominico dīn. Johīs. de Lifle qd. habet in eadem Parochia maj. decimas. Et vicarius de Caftro percipit duas partes minut dec de dčto. donico.
Brightfton.	Confuevit ecclā ibm. adjacere ecclefie de Caulborn tanquam matrici ecclefiæ.
Carefbrook.	Ecclefia parochialis cum capellis de Newport et Northwood.
Goddefhull.	Abbas et Conventus de Lyra percipiunt decimas majores et min. de veteri dominico de la Wyke et Appuldurcombe et Willi de Heyno apud le Stenebury. Abbas et Conventus de Quarrera percipiunt omnes majores dec. de veteri dīnico Johīs de Infula apud Roude et de terris Adē. Piftoris & Walteri de Gafterne, de quibus etiam vicarius Caftri percipit ibm. omnes dec. minores. Percipit etiam abbas de Quarrera omnes dec. majores de dominico Johīs. de Infula apud le Rewe una cum medietate minutarum. Insuper Rector Capellæ Sčti Laurentij percipit dec. majores de veteri dominico de la Hawle apud le Spann.
Gatecumb.	Rector Ecclie ibm. percipit omnes dec. maj. et min. de dīnico. Baldwini de Infula apud Whitwell in Goddefhull una cum omnibus oblationibus oblatis altari beate Rodegunde Euftachius de Sčo.
Lemeifton.	Martino Cuftos Capelle de Lemeifton; et funt affignat. 3 caruce terre Cantuaræ dеč. Capelle, in qua refidere debent et refident 3 Cappellani defervientes dič. Capelle.

               Newchurch.

Newchurch.   Abbas et conventus de Lyra percipiunt omnes d̄c. maj̄ et min̄. de doico. de Wroxall et mej̄ dec̄ minerij de Apuldurcombe juxta le Stone, et maj̄. dec. de veteribus dominicis de Apſe et Holeway et Knighton.

Benſtede.   Eſt perſ. in 2s. *annuatim* faciſle ſti Swithini Weſton.

Sct. Elene.   Prio. habet Eccleſiam ſibi appropriatam.

Breiding.   Prior et convent. de Brymore habent Ecclm̄. ſibi appropriatam. Abbas et conventus de Lyra percipiunt omnes d̄c. maj. et min de vet dominicis Henrici de Oglonder in Nunwell, et de doico. Roberti Glamorgan militis de Woolverton. Abbas et Conventus de Quaricra percipiunt in d̄cta, parochia omnes dec maj et min in doico. Johis. dē Weſton in Middleton.

Alfredſton.   Capella ibidem.

Whitfield.   Capella ibm̄. et pertinent Conteariæ d̄c. Capeliæ o̅s. dec. majores de Whitfield.

Woolverton.   Capella ibri.

Shalfleet.   Abbas et conventus de Lyra percipiunt dec omni modo maj. de veteri doico. de Ningewode una cum medietate minutai ū dec. ejuldem veteris dominij cum dec. etiam omnibus maj de veteribus & donicis de Cheſtel de Shalfleete. Rector de Caulborn percipit in par. de Shaldefleet min. dec. de terris et tenementis quæ Willūs. Stur quondam miles appropriavit eidem, de quibus Rector de Shaldfleet percipit dec. majores.

Arreton.   Abbas et Convent de Quarera percipiunt in paroch. de Arreton o̅s. dec. maj et min. et ſolvit abbati et convent de Lyra noīe. annuæ penſ. xjs

Wodyton.   Capella ſcti. Edmundi in Capella de Wodyton cum Capellano eidem Capellæ ſcti Edmundi.

Briddlesford.   Capella ibem. cum d̄c. de donicō. Jo. de Inſula in Briddlesford.

Standen.   Capella ibni. percipit o̅es. dec. maj. et min d̄ doico Petri D'Evercy in la Wode in par̄. de Breiding et mediet. decimarum in Standen; et Rector de Arreton percipit alteram medietatem.

Freſhwater.   Abbas et convent. de Lyra percipiunt o̅es. maj. dec de doico. dominiorum Roberti de Affecon et Roberti Aguillon et Willi Biekebeuf militum ac etiam dec. maj. dn̄i. Glamorgan, de

u   Picke

Broke Capella.   Broke et etiam dec̄ maj. de doñico. dm̄. de Compton, peñs. matrici ecclē. de Freshwater in 7s et confiſtit folum in poffeffionibus terrarum affign. ad Cantuariam dc̄t. capellæ

Eremouth.   Ecclia. de Eremouth eſt peñs eccliæ de Shalfleet in 13s. 4d.

Thorle.   Prior et convent. Chriſti Eccliæ habent Eccliam de Thorle appropriatatam, qui peñs noīe annuat. fol. abbati et Con de Montſburg xxs. ratione dec. maj. et min. quas prior et Con. Xti. Eccliæ. percipiunt in Thorle de doñico. quondam Amicie Comitiſl. Inf. quas dec. maj. et min Abbas et Conveñt. de Montefburg antiquitus percipere confueverunt.

Chale.   Abbas et Conveñt de Lyra percip̄ medietat. oūm. dec. maj. et min et medietatem oblationum et obven̄tum dc̄tæ. Eccliæ qualitercunq̄ et Rector percipit alteram medietatem

---

No LXXXII.

Valor. Beneficiorum in Infula Vecta; ex Librio Hen, Beaufort Cardinalis.

Ecclefia	Marc	Vicaria de Shorwell non taxat.	
De Freshwater	60	Chale	30ᵐ·
Penſion	dimᵐ·	Gatecomb	25ᵐ·
Brennew	1ᵐ	Neweton, or Niton	12ᵐ·
Thorle	12ᵐ·	Peñs	5ˢ·
Peñs	xxˢ	Goddſhill	100ᵐ·
Schaldeflet	40ᵐ	Peñs	20ᵐ·
Vicaria de Schaldeflet	cˢ·	St. Hellena	30ᵐ·
Cauleborn	40ᵐ	Woodyton	12ᵐ·
Motteſton	20ᵐ·	Peñs	dimᵐ·
Brightſton	30ᵐ	Breidynge	80ᵐ·
Carefbrook cum capellis	40ᵐ	Vicaria	8ᵐ·
Vicaria de Carefbrook	16ᵐ·	Newchurch	100ᵐ·
Shorwell	40ᵐ·	Peñs	4ⁿ·
Peñs	20ˢ·		

Arreiton	50ᵐ·	De ſcᵗᵗo. Licio.
Peñs	40ˢ·	De Broke.
Vicaria de Arreiton	8ᵐ·	De Alfredeſton.
Whippingham		De Appleford.
Peñs	10ˢ·	De Beneſtede
Standen	6ᵐ· & xlᵈ·	De Yaverland.
Bonichurch	cˢ·	Scᵗi. Johis de Sentling.
Capella de Caſtro	cˢ·	Ex Regiſtro Wintoñ
Capella Scᵗi Laurentij	6ᵐ·	
Portio procuratoris de Lyra	40ₘ·	
Capellæ ſequent. excuſat. ppter.		
exillitatem.		
Capella		
De Kingſton.		

N. B. The chapels of Burton and Lemerſton are not found in this taxation; being accounted religious houſes, and therefore exempt.

Nᵒ LXXXIII.

An Inſtrument of Accord concerning the Right of Fiſhery in Brading Haven. 6 Edw. II.

LE Lundy prochein apres la feſte S. Hillaire en l'an du regni le roy Edward fitz le roy Edward, fezisme, fut eſt ceo covenant entre sire Jean de Weſton le Pere chevaler de une parte, et Peres Devercy chevaler, Johan le fits jadis sire Robert de Glamorgan d'autre part. Ceo eſt a savoir que com un play fuſt meu nagueres en la court noſtre feignr. le Roy entre l'avant dit sire Johan de Weſton demandant, & les avant dits sire Robert de Peres defendants, de ceo les avant dits sire Robert & Peres deſturberent & nettement hoſterent le dit sire Johan de Weſton de ſa pecherie entre le Giogne de la blanche faloyſe et le Groyne de St. Elene en l'iſle de Wight; de ſa Partie de avantage de chacune de mer, et de croye vendre, donner, prendre et emporter, cum afferra a la tierce partie de troys feignuries, ce eſt a ſavoir le tierce tieyt de la pecherie, ou la tierce partie de deux trois ou de' un, ſi plus ne ſoient, et la tierce partie de la moyte de chaunce de mer, ſi chaunce y ſoit pour ceo notre feignr. le Roy prendra la moyté de chaunce de mer, contre les avant dits sire Johan, Robert, et Peres, et dont sire Johan de Weſton et ſes anceſtres furent ſeiſes du temps dont il n'y a memorie. Par

conceil

councel et ordenance des communs amis entre venants, le jour et l'an avant dites, en la presence l'abbe de Quarrere, sire Johan de l'Isle, Wanter Norreys, Tebaud Rouffel, Johan Wyvile, Rich. de Hochten, Johan le Flemyng, Tho. Juel, Tho. de Cofeville, & auties, sont les avant ditz sire Johan de Weston, Peres Devercy, Johan fitz et heir, lavandit sire Robert de Glamorgan, accordees en lieux mareies, qui le ditz sire Johan de Weston   piendra   les avant ditz pef cheries, avantage de cheaunce de mer et cioye vendre

    oc ftuibance des avant ditz sire Peres et Johan le fitz Robeid de Glamoigan et de lui heirs a touz jour. En temoignance des queles choses les parties avant ditz a cestes endeutes enterchaungeablement ont mis lour seals le Lurdy et au avant ditz.

N° LXXXIV.

May 10th, 1699.

The Abstract of an Estimate of the Charge of taking in, draining, and securing of the Haven of Brading, &c.

THE damme or sea wall will be best to stand near about where the old wall stood, with some difference in the range and variation of the line thereof.

This wall will containe in length about 3400 feet, and will be cheapest and best done to consist of the nearest matter at hand, which is a strong stiffe clay, with which it is to be mingled some other proper materials. The delving, casting, filling, ramming, arming, and sufficiently defending and securing the wall, will cost about six shillings the foot running, which comes to

	£.	s.	d.
The delving... will cost about six shillings the foot running, which comes to	1020	0	0
There must be two verie substantial sluces, which will cost the sum of	900	0	0
The charge of trenises of all kinds, may amount to about	250	0	0
The charge of closing and securely shutting in of the old channel, which will be the most difficult and troublesom work of the whole undertaking, will come to the sum of	1000	0	0

L L

The proffit or recompenfe to the undertaker, whoever he may be, who fhall be found able and fuccefsfully to defign and execute the work, cannot in juftice be lefs than the fum of

1000 0 0

The total is £ 4170 0 0

HY SHER,
Surveyor.

Nº LXXXV.

Warrant to Richard Worfley, Efq. Captain of the Ifle of Wight, and al. to fearch for Queen Elizabeth's Hawks in the Ifle of Wight, which were ftolen. Dated 6th of June, 1564.

AFTER our harty Commendacõns We be enformed that certens of the Queenes Ma.ˢ Hawks have been lately ftollen in the Ifle of Wight, from the Place where they bred upon her Ma.ˢ own Ifle, and that hitherto the officers cañot learne what hath become of them. Thies be therefore to will and requyre you on the Queenes Ma.ˢ behalf that upon the fight hereof ye make diligent Enquyry and Examynacõn, both for the Hawks and for the Perfons fauties of this Stealth and prumptious Attempt, and upon fynding of the Hawks ye fhall caufe them to be delyvered to fuch of the Officers doth now repayre unto you with thies or Lres for that purpofe And touching the malefacto rs Ye fhall comyt them to Warde, fignefieng your whole Doing & Examinacõn unto us, that thereupon ye may receave furthe Direction as the Cafe fhall requyre, and if it fhall com to your knowledge that either the Pties in fault have conveyed themfelfs or the Hawks out of the Compaffe of your Authorities, Ye fhall by vertue hereof in that Cafe, addreffe your Lres to fome Gentlemen of Reputation, and Credit of the Country where fuch Conveyance is made, that the Proof of thies or Lres may be by them Accomplifhed in

fome

Forme as is before pſcribed unto yo.ᵘ for the ſaid Iſle, Whereof we pray yo.ᵘ not to faile, Thus fare yo.ᵘ hartly well. From Rychemond the 6.ᵗʰ of June, 1564.

Yo.ʳ Loving Friends,

W. NORTHT.	PEMBROKE,
R. DUDDLEY,	W. HOWARD,
C. NOYE,	W. CECILL.

To o.ʳ Loving Friends Rychard Worſley, Eſq. Capt.ⁿ of the Iſle of Wight, & al'.

Nº LXXXVI.

Grant of Lands by King Edward I. to his Daughter Mary, a Nun at Ambreſbury.

REX omnibus, &c. ſal. Sciatis qd. in recompenſationem ducentarum librarum, quas nuper pro nobis & hæred. noſtris conceſſimus chariſſ filiæ noſtræ Mariæ ſanctimoniali Fontis Ebraldi apud Ambreſbury commoranti, ſingulis annis ad ſuſtentationem cameræ ſuæ ad ſchaccarium noſtrum percipiendas, & etiam pro illis viginti dolijs vini quæ eidem filiæ noſtræ ſimiliter conceſſimus ſingulis annis, per manus vicecom. noſtri Suthampt. qui pro tempore fuerit percipienda, quamdiu ipſa filia noſtra infra regnum noſtrum Angliæ fuerit, conceſſimus ei manerium de Coſham cum pertinen. in com. Wilt in valorem quater viginti & decem et ſeptem librarum; Burgum Wilton & Bereford, cum pertinen. in eodem com. in valorem ſexaginta librarum; manerium de Porſtok cum pertin. in com. Dorſ. in valorem decem et octo librarum, manē. de Herdcot cum pertinen. in com. Som. in valorem decem et ſeptem librarum; et maneria de *Freſhwater & Whytefield* in Inſula' Vecta cum pertinen in com Suthamp. in valorem ſexaginta et decem librarum tredecem ſolidorum et quattor denariorum; habenda et tenenda eædem filiæ noſtræ ad ſuſtentationem cameræ ſuæ quamdiu vixerit et infra regnum noſtrum fuerit ſupradictum.

Rot. Pat. 30 Edw. I.

Nº LXXXVII.

APPENDIX.

Nº LXXXVII.

An Order for Arraying the Clergy of the Island, 12 Ed III. in Conquence of the King's Letter to Orleton, Bishop of Winchester.

ADAM &c. Official. Archidiacoui roftri Wirton Sal &c. Mandatum Dñi Regis recipimus in hæc verba. Edvardus Rex Gi &c. Adamo eadem Gi Epō Winton Sal. &c. Quia quamplures Homines de Partibus & Dominijs Franciæ in diverfis Galeis & Navibus Super Mare proficifcuntui regnum roftrum in partbus de Portfmouth hofiliter invadentes, as incendia deprædationes et alia facinora quamp'uiini ibidem perpetiantes, & jam Sup. Mare verfus Infulam Vectam fe tenentes intentos mala & facinora confimilia ve pejora in cadem Infun et alijs locis regni noftri inhumaniter perpetiare nifi coium Malun celerius refiænatur Ac nos volentes defenfioni et Salvationi Regii noftri providere & horum hoftilem nequitiam repellere Dño. annuente, ac adveitentes mala & pericula quæ ex hoc evenire pote ir qd homines Inf præd. tam viri Religiofi quam alij terras et poffeffiones in Infula præd. habentes & qui pro Deferfione, & Salvatione cuidem tam pro ipforum quam noftro confodo & ho ore & Sua exporere debet, fe a dicta Infula hactenus elongaruat & reti recurunt, et adhuc elongant et retirahunt. Affignavimus dilectos fideles noftros Johñn de Langford Cuftodem Caftri noftri de Careſb cook in Infula præd. Bethol. de l'Iſle & Theobald. Ruffel et corum quemlibet ad diftrengend. & alijs vijs et modis quibus poterunt Compellend. omnes et Singulos in Inf. præd. commorantes vel terras tenenes feu alias poffeſiones in eadem habentes alibi degentes qui ratione terrarem tenemeorum & poffeffionum Suaium ad Defenfionem ejufdem tenentur ad inveniend Homines ad Arma, armatos Sagittarios et alios in dicta Infula pro Defenfione illius juxta Quantitatem terrarum et poffeffion Suarum quas ibidem habent contra dictorum inimicorum Noftrorum incurfus, dum præd pericula fic imminent, & prout Temporibus progenitorum in guerraium Commotionibus fieri confuevit, ad capiend. et Seifiend. in manum veftram terras, Poffeffiones ac bona hominum prædictorum in eadem Infula, qui hos homines armatos ad arma Sagittarios et alios invenire deberent, et eos ad hoc recufarunt invenire &c. Tefte meipfo. apud Weftm 22º. April. Anno Regni Noftri 12º.

Ex Regis. Adam de Orleton Epi Winton. A. D. 1329.

Nº LXXXVIII.

APPENDIX.

Nº LXXXVIII.

Finis Levatus in *Staccario* pro Epifcopo Winton.

JOHES. Winton. epūs. redit computum de 2000*l* de fine p. habenda Carta Regis, p quam Rex conceffit et confirmavit eidem epō. et fuccefforibus fuis mſn de *Mſnes*, et omnes alias Terras et Tenementa advocationes, Abbāt Prioſāt. hofpitalium, Ecclefiarum, Vicaſiaſum; et ſocam Epiſcopi et fuburb Winton. cum pertinentijs Liberſitaſibus Liberis confuctud retorn. brevium. et aliis libertat. fuis de quibus idem epūs. feſitus fuit die conceffionis præedictæ, fcil. v. die Junij aº. 12 Regis. Et qd. idem epūs et fucceffores fui habeant liberam caccam et venationem de omnibus feris in bofcis fuis et in terris fuis inſia terias fuas, et feoda fua tam inſra libertates foreſiæ quam extra; et qd. idem epūs. et fucceffores fuis, in bofcis fuis fint quieti de vaſo et regarda affartari poffint juxta tenorem cartarum a progenitonibus ſuis confectarum. Et idem epūs. quiet clamat regi et heredibus fuis mſn de *Sſyneſton* in inſula de Wyth, cum membris et alijs pertinentijs fuis; falvis eidem epō. advocationem ecclefiæ de *Caleborſa* et cappellaſum de *Briglſtſon* et *Byſiſtede* five fuerint ecclefiæ five cappellæ.

Rot. Fin. 12 Edw. I. A. D 1284.

Nº LXXXIX.

Pro Maria moniali de Ambrefbury. 1 Edw. II.

REX omnibus &c fal. Sciatis quod cum celebris memoriæ dns. Edwardus quondam Rex Angliæ Pater nofter in recompenfationem ducentarum libiarum, quas chariffimæ forori noftræ Mariæ fancti monialſi Fontis ſbraldi apud Ambrefbury comōranti annuatim ad fuftentationem cameræ fuæ, nec non & viginti doliorum vini quæ eidem annuatim conceffeſat, affignaſſet pro fe et heredibus fuis eidem forori noftræ manerium de *Coffham* cum pertinentijs in *com. Wilts.* et Burgum de Wilton et Berefoid cum pertinent. in eodem comitatu, et manerium de *Sſuſton* in eodem com. manerium de *Poſiſtok* cum pertinen in *com. Dorfet.*

Dorset. manerium de *Herdcote* cum pertinen. in com. Minvers et maner"a de *Freshwater* & *Whitefield* in Insula Vecta cum pertin. in com. Sutht. habenda et tenenda eidem sorori nostræ quamdiu viverit et moraretur infra regnum Angliæ. At eadem sorori nostra dicta maneriorum de *Cossham* et Burgum de *Wilton* et Bereford reddent in manum nostram &c. nos loco eorundem manerij de Cossham et Burgi de *Wilton* et Bereford, concessimus eidem sorori nostræ pro nobis et heredibus nostris manerium nostrum de *Swayneston* simul cum prædict. manerijs de *Sterston, Porstok, Herdecote, Freshwater,* & *Whitefield,* ad sustentationem cameræ suæ quamdiu vixerit &c.

Rymer's Foedera, vol. iii p. 29. A D. 1307.

N° XC.

The King's Order to William Montacute, Earl of Salisbury, to put the Island in a State of Defence. A. D. 1377.

REX dilecto & fideli suo Willo de Monteacuto Comiti Sarum Sti. Quia, ut accepimus, quamplures inimici nostri qui diversas villas, in regno nostro Angliæ, Super Costeram maris, Sæpius invaserunt, & diversa incendia ibidem fecerunt, magnam multitudinem Navium, Galearum, et Bargearum, cum hominibus ad arma et armatis prædictis ad citius quo poterant applicare, et dictum regnum nostrum destruere et adnullare proponunt, nisi eorum malitiæ manu forti resistatur. Nos (volentes hujus modi damnis et Periculis, vijs et modis quibus poterimus, præcavere) vobis mandamus, firmiter injungentes, qd. vos ad terras et tenementa vestra, in Insula Vectæ, citra primam diem Aprilis proxime futuram ad ultimum personaliter divertatis, ibidem, cum hominibus vestris, et tota familia vestra, fortiori modo quo poteritis, super defensione terræ maritimæ, ibidem contra hostiles aggressus continue moraturi, vel gentes Sufficienter Armatas, pro terris et tenementis vestris in Insula predicta defendendis illic citra terminum prædictum mittatis, qui moram continuam ibidem faciant, ad resistendum fortiter Inimicis nostris supradictis Scientes pro certo, qd. si præmissa infra terminum prædictum, juxta præsens mandatum nostrum, non feceritis tunc omnia terras et Tenementa, bona et Catalla vestra in Insula præd. nomine

x districtionis

diſtrictionis in manum noſtram capi, et alios homines Sufficientes, de Exitibus terrarum et tenementorum prædictorum, ac bonis et Catallis prædictis, pro defenſione Inſulæ prædictæ invenire faciemus Teſte Rege apud Weſt non. 2°. Martij   Per ipſum Regem & Conſilium.

Conſimilia Brevia diriguntur Subſcriptis, ſub eadem Data.

Roberto de Affton		Johī de Walewain	
Theobaldo de Gorges		Johī Biemſcot	
Laurentio de Seynt Martin		Thomæ Raley	
Gilberto le Diſpenſer	*Militibus.*	Thomæ Haket	*Armigeris.*
Hugoni Camoys		Willo de Iſle de Netleſton	
Thomæ Florak		Galfrido Rokle	
Johī de Beauchamp		Ricardo Cheke	
Radulpho de Gorges		Thomæ D'Aumaile	
Thomæ de Tychebourn			
Thomæ de Langford			

De Defenſione Inſulæ Vecta.   Rvmer, tom. vii. p. 139. 51 Ed. III.

F I N I S.

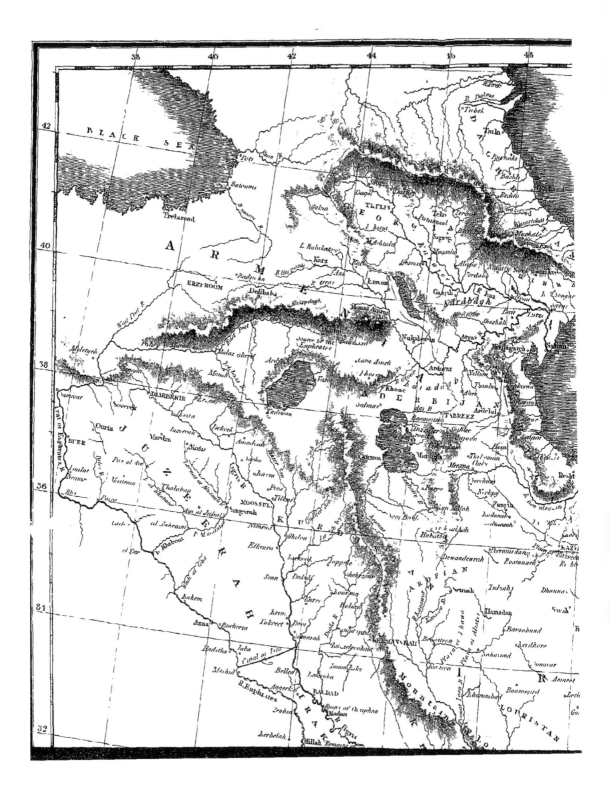

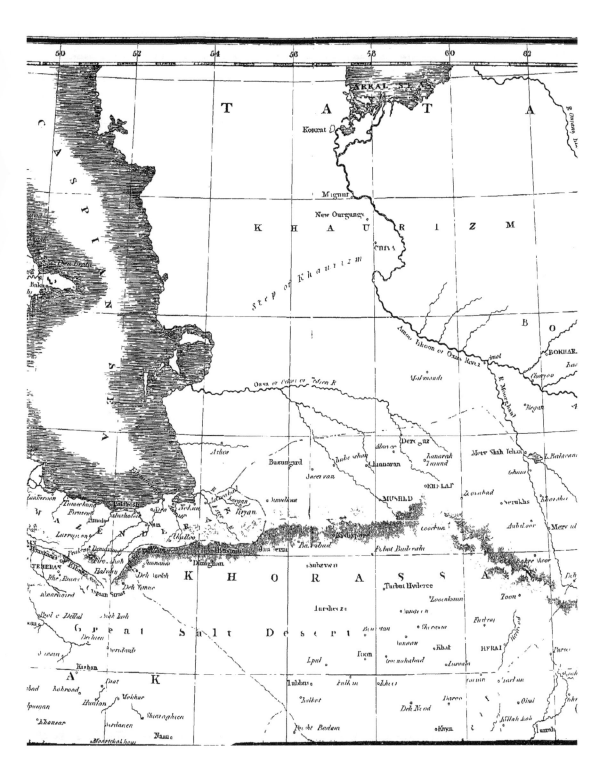

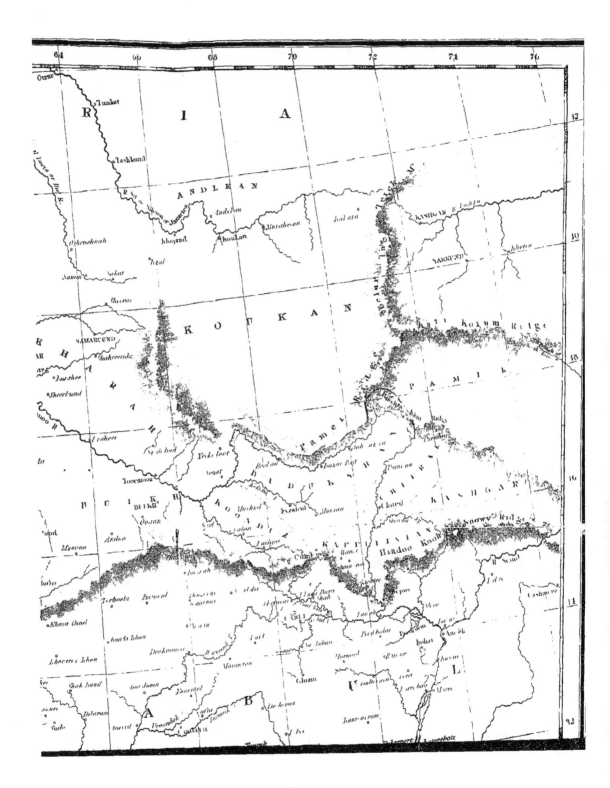

Map of PERSIA,

and

ADJACENT COUNTRIES,

FOR

Sir John Malcolm's

HISTORY OF PERSIA.

English Miles

BUSSORA

Koornah

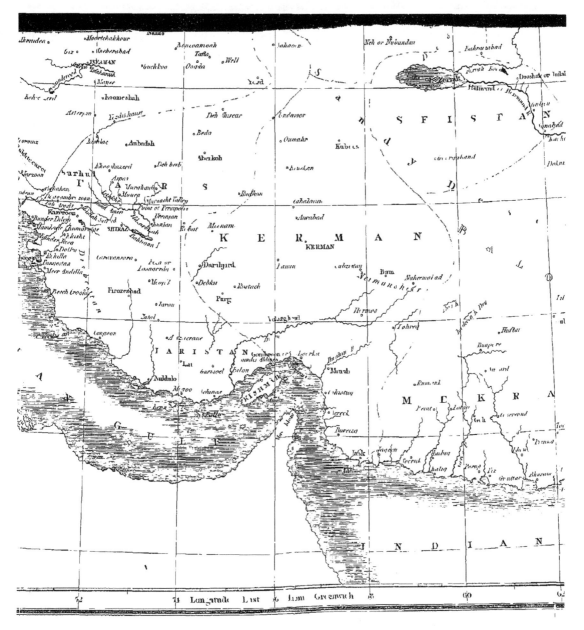

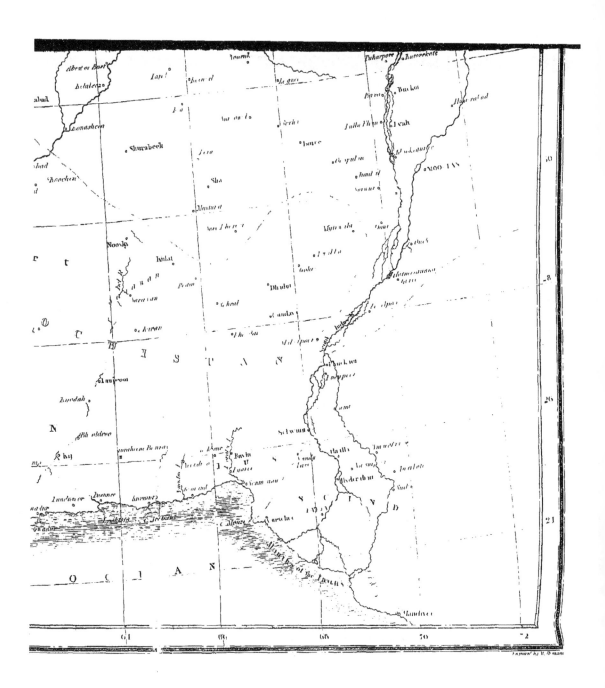

P O S T S C R I P T.

IN a work of this nature, there must be many mistakes and omissions. The Editor takes this opportunity of returning his grateful acknowledgements to those gentlemen who have assisted him in bringing this History to its present state. The Reader is desired to correct the following Errors of the Press.

P.
7 27 *for* fourel *read* fourely
58 7 *for* treafurv *read* the other
66 note * *for* fiit enth *read* fifteen,
93 24 *after* Sheriff *read* of
97 5 *after* Arm di *read* d.
134 11 *dele* only

P.
12 3 others
17 note 1 *for* XII *read* XII
101 2 others *read* thers
203 to others to John Stephens
24 3 *after* upon is to be *read*
237 others others *dele* for

No App P
I   1 Ster *read* Stan.
     4 pa *read* p 4
     5 Sher *read* Stu,
     6 Oain fe *read* Damore
        Moore *read* X bord
        pl *read* or
        XV Sol *read* X X Sol
     7 Svcymeilo *read* Swanston
        Sept *read* Senp
     8 gr *read* q^r
        pro *read* parco
V   17 Scilire d *read* cnum
X   20 Carno, *read* Ronlorne.
XI 27 Shotwe l *read* Shotwell
        Ronell *read* Ronele
        Stoner *read* Stoner.

No App P
     XII others
     XX 17 others finish propptes
            Ac promist erquires
     XXII 18 others
     XXVI 9 County
     LXXVI
     LXXIX 6
     LXXV 119 Cr

The defcription of Farlee, the pre fent text of John Sione, Efquire, in the parish of Warpsghter, has been corrected, in the table.